Female Citizens,
   Patriarchs, and the Law
in Venezuela, 1786–1904

ENGENDERING
LATIN AMERICA

Editors:

Donna J. Guy
University of Arizona

Mary Karasch
Oakland University

Asunción Lavrin
Arizona State University

Female Citizens, Patriarchs, and the Law in Venezuela, 1786–1904

ARLENE J. DÍAZ

University of Nebraska Press Lincoln and London

Publication of this volume was assisted by
The Virginia Faulkner Fund, established in
memory of Virginia Faulkner, editor-in-
chief of the University of Nebraska Press.

Library of Congress Cataloging-in-
Publication Data / Díaz, Arlene J. Female
citizens, patriarchs, and the law in Venezuela,
1786–1904 / Arlene J. Díaz. p. cm.
Includes bibliographical references and
index. ISBN 0-8032-1722-6 (cl : alk. paper) –
ISBN 0-8032-6640-5 (pa : alk. paper)
1. Women – Venezuela – History.
2. Women – Legal status, laws, etc. –
Venezuela – History.
3. Equality before the law – Venezuela –
History. I. Title. HQ1582.D52 2004
305.4'0987—DC22
2003059568

To my mother, Ghemara C. Díaz, and
in memory of my father, Rafael A. Díaz
To Luis Arnaldo González
To Marília and Claudia González-Díaz

Contents

List of Illustration and Tables   ix
Acknowledgments   xi
Introduction   1

PART 1: THE LATE COLONIAL PERIOD   21
1. A Caracas for the Mantuanos, 1700–1811   23
2. Law and Its Operation   60
3. Women and Men at the Tribunals   92

PART 2: THE EARLY REPUBLIC   105
4. A Nation for the Landowners   107
5. Equality before the Law   132
6. Ciudadanas versus Padres de Familia   150

PART 3: THE LATE NINETEENTH CENTURY   171
7. Bourgeois Caracas, 1870–1888   173
8. Women, Order, and Progress   190
9. Contesting Gender Meanings from Below   213

10. Conclusion   235
Notes   243
Bibliography   309
Index   329

Illustration and Tables

ILLUSTRATION

Bolívar con alegoría de América   114

TABLES

1. Conspiracies, Riots, and Insurrections in Eighteenth-Century
    Venezuela   32
2. Gender and Social Class of Complainants, 1786–1790   62
3. Type of Lawsuit by Social Class of Litigants, Caracas, 1786–1790   63
4. Type of Claim by Type of Court, Caracas, 1786–1790   64
5. Social Class of Litigants by Type of Court, 1786–1790   65
6. Women's Roles in Court Cases, Caracas, 1835–1840   138
7. Claimants, Caracas, 1835–1840   139
8. Type of Lawsuit by Social Class of Litigants, Caracas, 1835–1840   140
9. Percentage of Lawsuits by Type of Court, Caracas, 1786–1880   182
10. Number of Civil and Criminal Lawsuits by Year, Caracas,
    1835–1840 and 1875–1880   191
11. Social Class of Litigants in Caracas, 1786–1880   193
12. Social Class of Litigants by Type of Claim, Caracas, 1875–1880 194

Acknowledgments

Many people participated in the development of this project at different stages and levels. To them, for their solidarity as I wrote a dissertation and then transformed it into a book, I want to express my gratitude.

At the University of Minnesota, my academic adviser, Robert McCaa, was a constant source of support and encouragement then and throughout my career. I appreciate his confidence in my ability to handle large amounts of information when he challenged me to analyze a long historical period. I am grateful to Stuart B. Schwartz, now at Yale University, for his enthusiasm for my work and for his friendship. I also benefited greatly from the insightful suggestions of my dissertation committee members, Sara M. Evans, Dennis Valdés, and Kathryn Sikkink. While in Minnesota, Ricardo D. Salvatore read the first hundred pages I produced on this research, and his provocative feedback encouraged me. Since then, his friendship and scholarship have been a source of inspiration.

When I was a fellow at the American Bar Foundation in Chicago, T. J. Davis helped me to better understand the meanings of female litigants' claims in terms of the law. I appreciate his advice and friendship.

In the History Department at Indiana University, I found a very supportive and intellectually motivating community. Peter F. Guardino read and commented on various versions of this work. Jeff Gould, Michael Grossberg, Daniel James, Sarah Knott, Muriel Nazzari, Jeff Wasserstrom, and Dror Wahrman gave me important feedback on different portions or aspects of the production of this book.

In Caracas and in Chicago, I counted on Derwin Munroe's suggestions and friendship.

I also want to thank Silvia Arrom for her insightful comments on a paper based on this research that I presented at the Berkshire Conference and Patricia Seed for her generous feedback.

Asunción Lavrin and Sarah C. Chambers did a very careful reading of this manuscript and indicated ways in which I could improve it as well as ways to connect it to works on other countries.

This book also benefited from the important work done by my research assistants at different times: Angela Barrera, Cristina Alcalde, Shane Blackman, Marlene Medrano, Berta Bermúdez, and David Woken.

Without the financial support of the Ford Foundation, the Graduate School and Department of History at the University of Minnesota, the MacArthur Program, and the National Hispanic Scholarly Fund, I would not have been able to pursue this ambitious research. The American Bar Foundation in Chicago financially supported me for two years and provided the best environment one could hope for in which to write an academic work. The Department of History at Indiana University allowed me some time off from teaching duties to do the revisions to my manuscript.

Many people in Venezuela offered invaluable assistance with my research in archives and library collections. From the initial stages, Dr. Santiago-Gerardo Suárez (director), Antonio González Antías (coordinator), and the entire research staff of the Departamento de Investigaciones Históricas of the Academia Nacional de la Historia in Caracas warmly welcomed my project and were instrumental in facilitating access to the sources housed at the Academia. Dr. Ermila Troconis de Veracoechea, director of the Academia's archive, graciously granted permission to microfilm a number of court cases and periodicals to expedite my research. I also want to thank Iván Ramos of the Registro Principal del Distrito Federal and the staffs at the Biblioteca Nacional, the Archivo General de la Nación, and the Archivo Arquidiocesano de Caracas for their kind assistance.

The offices of Inter-Library Loan at the University of Minnesota and Indiana University were also pivotal in this project. They never hesitated over all of my many requests for rare books and materials, no matter how old or difficult they were to get.

Other friends and family have been very important to me throughout the production of this book. I especially recognize Eileen Walsh and Heymar I. González, who were always there in critical moments, giving support and helping me to meet my deadlines. Virginia Rivera's loving care for my daughters gave me the peace of mind and time needed for my scholarly work. I also express gratitude to the Díaz Caballero and the González Ríos families for their love and support.

My husband, Luis Arnaldo González, closely participated and encouraged me through all the years of research, data entry, analysis, teaching, and writing. I thank him for his solidarity and for graciously earning a minor in gender relations in Caracas. The arrivals of Marília and Claudia, my daughters, filled me with joy and new challenges. This book is dedicated to them and to my parents.

The publication of this research is possible, then, thanks to many people and institutions. Of course, they are not responsible for any errors contained in it.

Female Citizens,
    Patriarchs, and the Law
in Venezuela, 1786–1904

Introduction

June 6, 1794

How hard is the plight of married women! One rarely finds a husband who has the same regard toward his companion [*consorte*]. . . . The husband becomes a tyrant, the wife a slave, the home hell, and the children unfortunate witnesses of this horrible and lamentable metamorphosis. . . . Marriage, though a sacrament, always remains a pact.

Licenciado Ramón García Cádiz and Juana Feliciana Díaz

February 7, 1812

In marriage, husbands are nothing but the ones who represent the family, and women, their *compañeras* [partners], who should help them with marital obligations but are not condemned to be the husbands' slaves; nor are women of an inferior condition in the exercise of their rights; the quality of being a woman does not exclude them either from the societal order or from the guaranty to enjoy their liberty and security of their person. The law makes us all equals as citizens, and if my husband is by this right authorized to behave in a free manner, I am, by the same right, entitled to resolve my needs on my own.

doña María Antonia Pérez

November 22, 1877

Dear Friend:

I understand that my mother, Mrs. Juliana Mijares, filed a demand for betrothal on my behalf on the grounds of my state of pregnancy. I neither accept nor approve of the suit because it contradicts my feelings, because under no circumstance will I give my hand to a man who does not want to marry me, nor will I subject my name to vexing disputes. Consequently, I state to you that it is not my will to unite in marriage and that I will not marry even if the competent Court orders it, and I would like you to defend this statement subscribed by me in Court in order to stop the proceedings.

Sincerely Yours
Violante Mijares

Juana Feliciana Díaz, doña María Antonia Pérez, and Violante Mijares all went to the courts of Caracas as a last resort to solve their problems with men. Even though the language they used and their views of their conflicts changed in form with the differing times in which they lived, the three women shared a wish for a more egalitarian and dignified domestic relationship with their male partners. Juana Feliciana, like other plebeian women in the late colonial period, upheld a vision of marriage in which men and women had mutual domestic obligations. For her, marriage was more than a religious formality; it was a pact between partners. Doña María Antonia, a propertied woman, also pursued an egalitarian vision of marriage in her divorce case, but she was writing in the early republican period and her claim was expressed in the relatively new language of republican citizenship. Like other female litigants of the time, doña María Antonia expected the laws of the new republic to protect her individual liberties as well as they protected those of men. By the late nineteenth century some lower-class women like Violante were defending their freedom not to marry, even if doing so went against the government's morality campaign. For Violante, avoiding a potentially distressing relationship that was not based on mutual love was more important than following the dictates of the law.

Even though these women's voices were conditioned by changing political and economic contexts, their underlying ideas may seem timeless to us because they share liberal values of individualism and equality that still hold true today. But two centuries ago, these women were dissonant voices in the tribunals of Caracas; they were debating definitions of femininity, masculinity, and gender relations at a time when women were not supposed to contradict the government's more narrowly liberal ideas on domestic and social order. Furthermore, the actions of these and other women in the courts of Caracas demonstrated that they practiced liberal ideas in their language and/or performances. Their insistence on expressing disconformity with prescribed gendered norms at home and in the courts led to awareness among some women of the contradictions in the theory and praxis of liberal ideas as early as the late nineteenth century.

This book examines how debates over the meaning and responsibilities of gender relations transpired among ordinary people and how they related to official culture during the process of state formation in Caracas, Venezuela, between 1786 and 1904. In particular, it analyzes the interactions among competing constructions of femininity and masculinity in the government, the courts, and households during a period when liberalism became increasingly entrenched in Caracas society.

Beginning in the second half of the eighteenth century, liberalism, an ideology that supported the autonomous individual as well as such values as equality, fraternity, and liberty, gradually ingrained itself in highly stratified and multiracial Venezuela. As a thread of the Enlightenment, liberalism was expounded by thinkers such as Jean-Jacques Rousseau, François Voltaire, and Guillaume-Thomas Raynal, among others. Their writings were widely read in Venezuelan intellectual circles for their contributions to the end of the French monarchy and for their conception of a political system representative of civil society, one that would guarantee liberties, equality, and property to individuals who did not belong to the nobility. The Spanish monarchy labeled such writings subversive and banned them in the empire. Yet the ideas arrived, if clandestinely, and especially in places where the neglect of Spanish authorities had long allowed the entrance of contraband material goods and ideas. Such exchange flourished along the coast of Venezuela, whose inhabitants often interacted illegally with the French, British, and Dutch who had bases on the Caribbean and in northern South America. Writings by Rousseau and Raynal were found hidden in the hollowed beams of the roofs of creole elites' houses and were discussed at secret meetings in Caracas during the late eighteenth century. By the early nineteenth century, liberal ideas played an important role in fostering the movements for independence and the organization of the new republic.

Written in 1811, Venezuela's Constitution was the first Spanish American constitution to incorporate ideas of equality, liberty, individuality, and citizenship. These notions, however, were designed mainly for propertied men, as had been the case in the revolutions in Europe and the United States. Keenly aware of Enlightenment literature and of the revolutions in France, Haiti, and the United States, a group of elite creole leaders that included Francisco de Miranda, Simón Bolívar, and lawyers such as Juan Germán Roscio was careful not to replicate the more radical aspects of those events in Venezuela.[1] Due to the convulsions among a majority composed of blacks, poor whites, and people of mixed indigenous, white, and black origin that preceded and followed Venezuela's declaration of independence in 1811, the revolutionary leaders had to proceed carefully if they were to maintain their social position.

The lower classes were not unaware of the revolutionary happenings in the Atlantic world of the late eighteenth century, and the revolutionary leadership was mindful of that. In 1797 the plans for a major pro-independence conspiracy led by Venezuelans Manuel Gual and José María España in Caracas's adjacent port of La Guaira were found by Spanish authorities. There were many revolts during the eighteenth century, but the

Gual and España conspiracy stands out for being heavily influenced by the French Revolution and for being one of the most radical and egalitarian movement in late-eighteenth-century Spanish America. The conspirators produced and distributed, among other writings, a pamphlet on the rights of man and of citizens addressed to the people of the Americas based on the "Rights of Man and of Citizens" included in the radical French Constitution of 1793.[2] In it, the conspirators claimed an independent republic in which slavery was to be abolished and the natural equality of all inhabitants was proclaimed.

Ideas of equality found fertile soil among many common Venezuelans, most of whom were illiterate. During the eighteenth century, some were challenging the social hierarchy supported by the Spanish monarchy that ascribed to them a lower status based on their race and class. Claiming that "there was not one white Adam and another mulatto" but that whites and nonwhites were physically equals, *pardos* (light mulattos), blacks, and *zambos* (persons of Indian and black ancestry) were already displaying individualistic values.[3] During the late eighteenth century, Spanish authorities were busy persecuting and arresting immigrants and merchants suspected of spreading subversive ideas by word and paper. Some of these went so far as to celebrate French events with flares and fireworks in the capital city.[4] Yet the close supervision that Spanish authorities intended over subversive ideas did not work. The authorities as well as travelers to Caracas remarked in their documents that ideas of equality were practiced and expressed widely among common people, some of whom greeted each other using the appellation "citizen."[5]

The pamphlet on the rights of man and citizen produced by the conspirators of 1797 served as the seminal work for Venezuela's Constitution of 1811, along with the federalist ideas contained in the 1787 Constitution of the United States. The Venezuelan Constitution established that most Venezuelans were equal before the law and that "all Venezuelan inhabitants have no other title other than that of citizen." Because of the need for unity during the civil wars of independence and in order to create a sense of national inclusion for everyone, the great Libertador Simón Bolívar and other political leaders further emphasized ambiguous ideas of equality and freedom for the "people" (*el pueblo*) in their speeches. Although this abstract rhetoric of equality and promise of rights resonated well with common Venezuelans, in reality the male politicians were addressing a much smaller group of people: the propertied men who, as true citizens, could participate in elections. Bolívar skirted the egalitarian aspects of liberalism by helping to create a myth of national inclusion for every Venezuelan.[6] This myth allowed for the continued exclusion of women, racial others, and the lower classes in a republic guided by liberal principles.

In Venezuela the issue of women's rights was not part of the political discussions, nor did the Constitution grant women any specific rights. Although citizenship and equality were granted in the abstract to "all free men in Venezuela," some women felt included in the rights and privileges granted to men in the new republic. The practical definition of citizenship altogether excluded women and nonpropertied men from voting or holding office. Every free man was equal and a citizen, but only propertied men, most of whom were white, could be active citizens.

Upholding patriarchal authority was fundamental for the male builders of the new liberal republic.[7] Thus it is understandable that ruling males did not address the paradox of supporting a liberal state while maintaining the colonial social structure. The colonial antecedent is clear in the ruling elite's draft of the liberal Constitution of 1811, which provided the model for subsequent constitutions in Venezuela. The Constitution of 1811 established the continued use of Spanish legal codes such as the *Siete Partidas*, a thirteenth-century code based on canon and Roman law that supported a hierarchical society. This model was central for men; the *Siete Partidas* granted male heads of household parental rights, which allowed them to control family property and to impose their will on their wives and children by legal authority and, if necessary, by physical punishment. The Spanish colonial church and state in Venezuela dictated that, as *padres de familia* (male heads of household), upper-class men extend their authority over their dependents, including slaves and other subordinates.

This idea of upper-class male authority continued in the new republic and was justified in a political discourse that frequently used family imagery and was based on the revolutionary leader's lived experiences.[8] In Bolívar's writings, independence is presented metaphorically, as the separation from a tyrannical father who kept sons in a "sort of permanent infancy" and ignorance.[9] Furthermore, that despotic father did not allow the sons to participate in their own governance, benefited economically from the sons' efforts, and enslaved them for his own profit. These arguments were common among the Caracas aristocracy in the late eighteenth century (see chap. 1). In response, the new republic would be governed by virtuous, propertied, and learned men who would treat citizens as equals. "The American states need the care of paternal governments to heal the sores and wounds of despotism and war," wrote Bolívar in his letter of Jamaica.[10] The new government would act as the father figure, providing tutelage to those who were dependent and teaching them gradually how to live in freedom. The relationship between father and son would be based on law and equality. Yet not everyone would be qualified to enjoy the liberties provided by equality. Only those who were virtuous because of martial values demonstrated in defense of the homeland and those who were economically self-sufficient due to their profession or property – mainly padres de familia – would enjoy citizenship rights. Even though these men were united as brothers, the revolutionary leader Bolívar was referred to as the "Father of the Homeland" in the early republic, stressing the connection between father-son and republic-people.[11] In this imagery, women were invisible.

As in revolutionary France, women in Venezuela were denied suffrage and citizenship rights and were encouraged to keep their roles within the family, thus not involving themselves in politics.[12] Relationships between women and men in Venezuela were ruled primarily by a code that upheld a hierarchical society and allowed many liberties to men.[13] The radicalism of granting equality and citizenship was circumvented by continuing the upper-class male's moral authority over his dependents, slaves, and other unrelated subordinates and by treating the home as a separate sphere. While a continuation of colonial social relations is evident in the continued enforcement of the *Siete Partidas*, the use of the code allowed the prolongation of rights specifically made for heads of households as well as the continuing treatment of the family as a sphere in which a separate set of rights operated. In this sense, the Venezuelan Constitution of 1811 was in tune with the liberal revolutions in the Atlantic World.[14]

Women in Venezuela did not form clubs or committees but participated in political discussion in other ways.[15] Women related to the revolutionary elites attended and even hosted social gatherings and secret meetings where enlightened ideas and independence were discussed; some of them participated actively as messengers and spies along with their female and male servants.[16] Some lower-class women actively participated in the late-eighteenth-century revolts, and during the wars they were active in helping the troops and acting as soldiers themselves.[17] Yet contrary to their counterparts in the United States and Europe, *caraqueñas* (women of Caracas) did not seek political rights out of the revolution. Rather, they used the new political environment to claim equal protection under the law and liberties where they pertained to their relationships with men within the domestic sphere. Most of the litigants studied in this book did not express themselves as equals of men, nor did they question the institution of marriage in the late colonial period or the early republic, even though they had been challenging it unconsciously since then. Many of these women instead treated marriage or concubinage as a pact, an ongoing relationship of unequal mutuality in which men and women had certain responsibilities.[18] Extreme irresponsibility by their husbands or partners in regard to the domestic pact through such actions as physical abuse, not providing materially for the household, curtailing women's physical liberties, and mismanaging women's properties motivated these women to seek the protection that the abstract granting of citizenship afforded them through the use of the courts. Their appeals for justice at the courts were sometimes strategically expressed in a moral tone. Although male rulers viewed the home as a separate sphere, some women increasingly brought domestic matters to the attention of the state during the nineteenth century.

Even though patriarchy was reinforced in the new republic, some caraqueñas found a space in which they could assert their "rights."[19] An arena for challenge and debate over women's protection under the law within the family was opened with the disparity between liberal doctrine and legal practice in the new republic. The Constitution of 1811 abstractly granted Venezuelans the right to be citizens, while continued use of Spanish civil laws accorded women a status inferior to men's. Aware of their new relationship to the state, some women went to court to claim equal protection under the laws as citizens of Venezuela. The new liberal context created new political and legal opportunities for women and provided a language of rights for them to use. That is exactly why doña María Antonia Pérez strategically claimed her equal rights as a *ciudadana* (female citizen) in her quest to achieve autonomy from her husband to administer her properties. Yet in so doing, she challenged the patriarchal foundations of the new republic.

Venezuela's pioneering role in igniting the wars for independence in South America and in writing the first liberal constitution in Spanish America makes this country a key site for studying the gendered aspects of liberal theory and practice in the process of nation-building during the nineteenth century. Yet this work begins much earlier – in the early eighteenth century, a period marked by profound political, economic, and social transformations. The Bourbon reforms introduced throughout the Spanish Empire after 1759 were first implemented in Venezuela. The book considers the whole nineteenth century in order to see how liberal ideas became formalized and practiced by the end of that century. In Venezuela, the transition from colony to nation cannot be fully understood unless we study more than the last fifty years of the colonial period and the first fifty of the republic, as has been commonplace in Latin American historiography.

The *longue-durée* approach employed in the book allows us to carefully trace how the logic by which most Venezuelans were excluded from the polity functioned and changed from colonial to republican times and in the process of nation-building in the nineteenth century. To understand how the logic of exclusion became formalized in each period, the evolution and administration of the law must be closely followed. Here the study of ruling elites becomes a focal point, for it was they who wrote the laws and they who were most interested in the effects of those laws. Differing from other works that cover the transformation from colony to republic, this book studies the logic of exclusion from a legal standpoint and, equally important, from the perspective of the masculine struggles for domination at the state level.

In spite of the pervasive patriarchal social and political culture of Latin American societies, historians have not studied the struggles for political power from the perspective of masculinity. How men socially construct and reproduce their role of power in a given society is a question taken up in this study. In a country like Venezuela, where caudillos vying for power against military and learned men caused prolonged wars and political instability until the early twentieth century, it makes much sense to look at the institutionalized political order from a gendered perspective. The formal politics of exclusion in the liberal republic followed the masculine logic of those in power, and those in power were part of masculine struggles for domination as well. As a result of this gendered dynamic, patriarchy was increasingly reaffirmed in the state's courts even as liberalism and its ideas of equality were becoming more ingrained in nineteenth-century caraqueño society. This book traces how dominant ideas about masculinity among the ruling classes changed from a basis of aristocratic values to a basis of bourgeois principles. Only by understanding how ruling men perceived women during those two centuries can we better comprehend the laws and the practice of the tribunals.

The length of the period under study is also critical for analyzing how the perceptions of and responses to the exclusion of female litigants changed. How did women in different periods understand their relationship with other people, with the law, and with the state? How did they respond to their legal and political exclusion? Answering such questions requires an attempt to understand these women on their own terms. What may their words or actions have meant in different contexts? Why did they use certain words? Where did those words come from? To answer these questions, we need to approach the spectrum of discursive resources that were available for these women, which depended on each woman's class and racial status. Women's exclusion from the protections of citizenship was clearly based on their gender. Yet their race and their class intersected at various points of some of the litigants' lives, resulting in different understandings of their relationships with men and other women and of how the state should protect them legally. Should the state allow women to administer their property? Should the laws protect their individual liberties? Should that protection be based on property? On morals? On chastity? On motherhood? On working disciplines? By approaching this topic from the perspective of these questions, this book aims at understanding the different ways in which some women individually responded to exclusion at home and in the courts and to patriarchal domination. But the situation of these female litigants is not unique; their condition can be compared to that of other subordinate groups that suffered from a similar logic of exclusion during the period under study. By fleshing out the strategies pursued by some female litigants from Caracas, this book can illuminate how other subordinate social groups may respond to domination from above.

The claims by doña María Antonia Pérez and other litigants enhance our understanding of the gendered nature of citizenship, of the content and practice of the law, of masculinity and patriarchy, and equally important, of the ways in which people of different social backgrounds articulate their concerns and challenge a dominant culture. This work intends to analyze and link the domestic struggles aired in secular and ecclesiastical courts with the broader context of nation-building. In doing so, this research necessarily intersects with other bodies of scholarship that, while focusing on different themes, all aim at understanding the complex relationship between individuals and the state.

GENDER AND CITIZENSHIP

Many historians have studied the political dimension of the independence period in Venezuela, but few have addressed its social and gendered implications, much less the question of citizenship.[20] This is true for Latin America more generally, although there are a few exceptions. Research on the participation of women of Gran Colombia during the wars of independence has concluded that independence did not significantly change women's position in society.[21] Evelyn Cherpak argued that men and women held the same traditional attitudes concerning gender and that in Gran Colombia women had a very limited notion of their own rights.[22] Research on Mexico has presented a more complex picture of the female condition, because some women won respect, visibility, and an appreciation for their capacities through the independence struggle. After the wars, however, women went back to their traditional roles.[23] The paucity of research notwithstanding, the general notion in these earlier works is that independence from Spain did not bring major changes to the female condition in Latin America.

While these observations generally coincide with the notions that were formalized in laws, disseminated in print media, and made publicly evident, they reflect the assumption that a challenge to the status quo has to be organized, perhaps collective, but certainly manifest in the public eye. The problem with this perspective is that it fosters the impression that because women did not react in a particular way, they must have been passive members of society during a period of revolutionary change. We must consider, however, that a substantial proportion of women's everyday activities in Latin America (as in other parts of the world) unfolded not in public, mostly male-dominated areas but in unobserved places like the domestic sphere. Accordingly, we should not evaluate women's actions using a male standard. When one comes across the narratives of the Juana Felicianas, the doña María Antonias, and Violantes of Caracas, it becomes clear that women's struggles did take place but in myriad different ways.

More recently, Steve J. Stern's work on late colonial Mexico contributes to a better understanding of the way gender relations operated and connects that operation to the patriarchal nature of the polity.[24] He argues that a very important foundation of gender culture is the tension between a contingent model of gender rights and one premised on the principle of obedience. Stern found that women actively struggled for their gender rights but also assented to patriarchal principles at times, in complex ways and for practical reasons. Moving beyond the sphere of the household, Stern asserts that language that referred to authority in the political culture of Oaxaca and Morelos was based on the familial experience of power at the domestic level. At the household, community, or broader state levels, the patriarchal nature of the polity was manifest during Mexico's late colonial period.

An important addition to scholarship on the early republic is the work of Sarah C. Chambers. Her work is valuable because, through legal documents, she analyzes lower-class activities in Arequipa, Peru, during the late colonial and early republican periods. In this central area of the Spanish empire, women's confinement to their homes made their exposure to republican language and ideas more difficult, and after independence, women were still judged by their chastity and domestic behavior. In contrast, men claimed their status as citizens by making references to their virtue as hard-working members of society who could defend the new nation with arms.[25] Hence Chambers's work underscores the importance of gender in the male political culture of the early Peruvian republic.

Christine Hünefeldt's work on liberalism and gender relations in the capital city of Lima, however, reveals that women questioned the fairness of marriage and defended the value of their contributions to the family during the nineteenth century. Although women in Lima did not directly or indirectly claim equality or citizenship, Hünefeldt found that in the early nineteenth century married women took their husbands' violations of arrangements regarding the dowry as an opportunity to seek governmental intervention in private matters and to criticize their husbands' abuses. The defense of their dowries gave women a legal vocabulary with which to defend marriage as a contract with mutual obligations, much different from the situation with slaves and slaveowners. Only as the century progressed did liberal assumptions such as the protection of personal rights became more generalized by female litigants.[26]

This was not the case in Venezuela, a marginal area of the Spanish Empire in which the circulation, spread, and practice of liberal ideas was more intensive and occurred earlier than in the central areas. Trade in contraband goods and ideas with the non-Hispanic Caribbean was common in Venezuela throughout the colonial period due to its location and to Spanish neglect. Unlike Peru or Mexico, Venezuela had a radical group among the creole elites, which moved toward independence against the crown. They feared a revolution from below that would be furthered, they believed in part, by royal policies that benefited the pardo, mulatto, and black majority. In reality, however, many lower-class pardos and people of other races embraced the royalist cause in the early nineteenth century. They wanted to retaliate against creole elites' contempt for the lower classes and to gain social liberty and equality, which they believed could be better achieved under the Spanish monarchy than under a creole republic. In Venezuela, ideas of equality and liberty played out in late-eighteenth-century prerevolutionary movements and later in the civil wars for independence.

Works on gender and citizenship in other parts of the world have demonstrated the complexity of the relationship between any individual and the nation-state. As citizens, individuals become members of a political community, "which warrants the unqualified enjoyment of civil, political and social rights" and affords them a legal relationship with the state.[27] In key legal texts such as Venezuela's Constitution of 1811, the citizen is presented as an abstraction that is universal, equal, and undifferentiated in terms of gender, race, class, and sexuality. Still, in practice, the definition of a citizen is highly hierarchical, and new studies on this subject emphasize how the lived experiences of gender, race, and class relationships varied the meanings of citizenship for individuals and produced differing relationships with the state.[28]

Some scholars have argued that in analyzing the practices of citizenship, one must consider the legal aspects of the definition as well as the cultural process of "subject-making." To study issues of citizenship, then, involves analyzing how history, culture, and gender have affected the differing definitions and unequal relationships between various peoples and the state. It also requires an analysis of both the rhetoric of the law and its practice, because, as will be shown for Venezuela, analyzing the letter of the law without considering the practices of the tribunals can be misleading. Court rulings in late colonial Caracas demonstrate how, although the construction of legal subjects was formally hierarchical in Spanish laws, the courts afforded some protection to women, the poor, and nonwhites. After independence the Constitution claimed an abstract equality, but the tribunals' rulings consistently privileged the male and/or bourgeois-like citizen by the late nineteenth century.

By then Venezuelan politicians assumed that the building and modernization of the new independent nation had to be in the hands of a particular type of citizen: male, learned, and/or propertied. The consequences of this practice are evident in the ways that men and women were, in the words of Suad Joseph, "disempowered and empowered" differently.[29] This study aims at understanding the cultural process by which differing practices of citizenship for women and men were produced. What were the gendered, racial, and class bases for exclusion, and how did they form part of the emerging discourse of the Venezuelan nation? Understanding how the "citizen" is culturally and legally constructed is critical if we want to have a better grasp of the shared discursive elements and common understandings that link and separate people in their relationship with the state. In this way we can better account for less organized and more individual ways that women and men struggle to carve out their own space and define gender and citizenship in the new polity.

THE STATE, MASCULINITY, AND LAW

If the practice of citizenship privileged men, we should not assume that the state – the institutionalized political order – is a genderless institution. On the contrary, the political organization of a country such as Venezuela responds to a male logic that is reproduced in the content and administration of the law. Venezuela's process of nation-building in the nineteenth century was a volatile one: military men, landowners, and educated men struggled over state power. Once in control of the government, Venezuelan politicians consistently executed legal and administrative reforms to advance their own gender, race, and class interests. These included reforms that enhanced their own notion of masculinity over that of other male competitors, because part of the quest for legitimation and domination consists of asserting and validating one's own ideas of true masculinity.[30] This book argues that ruling males also used the laws and the practices of the courts to organize and contain the social effects of liberalism – primarily claims for equality by women, nonpropertied men, and people of mixed descent. Especially after final independence from Spain was won in 1819, new laws increasingly protected not only the right of propertied and educated men to rule over the nation but also the right of the paterfamilias to govern their homes without the intrusion of the state.

If the law and the administration of the law that govern the state are based upon a male logic, then the legal sources used for this work will reflect a similar rationale. This study reads these documents, however, with an awareness of the gendered motivations. Laws and legal reforms were partly informed by masculine struggles for domination at the state level, by male systems of representation, and by the anxieties that are apparent in men's use of language and in their behavior. This was evident, for example, in the early republic. On the one hand, legal reforms enacted by the educated oligarchy after the separation from Colombia and Ecuador in 1830 deliberately aimed at delegitimizing the power of military men who, as victorious winners of the independence war, vied for governmental power. On the other hand, during the early nineteenth century, women were seemingly absent from politicians' speeches. Yet when closer attention is paid to ruling males' rhetoric, it is clear that women are represented in the republic's imaginative life by the female allegorical figure of Liberty. In paintings and in metaphoric language, the message was that both Liberty and Woman had to be closely controlled and guided because otherwise they could lead to corruption and disorder. By being attentive to men's use of language and the ways in which they articulated their concerns in speeches, published articles, and legal sources, this book further explores the gendered nature of the Venezuelan state and how patriarchy is enforced and reproduced during the process of nation-building.

LAW AND CONTESTATION

When certain dominant ideologies such as patriarchy become accepted, taken for granted, or a "matter of widespread consensus and silent complicity," then they become hegemonic.[31] Recent scholarship is devoted to understanding the complex ways in which hegemony, the "power that 'naturalizes' a social order, an institution or even an everyday practice," is a process of constant struggle.[32] The practice of law in state institutions is one of many ways that ruling classes seek to educate people to stay within the confines of their hegemonic projects. Legal institutions are also a site of concrete struggles because they provide an arena in which dominant interests, as reflected in the law, are actively enforced, contested, and negotiated by citizens, noncitizens, and the state. This perspective helps us to think about a relationship between high and low culture that is complex, decentralized, and dynamic, not unidirectional. That is, dominant culture is not something that is necessarily created and imposed by those in power and passively assumed by the lower classes. It is instead part of a historical process in which the terms of domination are actively challenged and/or negotiated among contending parties. Consequently, before a given practice becomes hegemonic, it must first embark upon a long journey of challenge and transformation.

In Caracas, women like Juana Feliciana Díaz or doña María Antonia Pérez did not dispute the validity of the institution of marriage or patriarchy as such. Instead, they individually questioned their male partners' capacity as responsible household heads and went to court seeking to protect their bodies from abuse, to administer their property, and to defend their freedom. In short, many female litigants claimed their individual rights. Yet by directly or indirectly requesting the privileges provided by the abstract universal notion of citizenship, they were challenging the patriarchal foundations of the state. Some explicitly cited liberal republican ideas of citizenship, liberty, and equality, ultimately seeking to make the liberal project of the new nation more inclusive – a project that would give women equal protection under the law. Others resisted in less explicit ways: their words and actions showed dissatisfaction with the laws and the courts' failure to protect their individual liberties. In one way or another, women pointed out the inconsistencies of the liberal project.

This work examines the performances of domination, accommodation, and opposition within households as we can deduce them from the records of both state and ecclesiastical courts. Viewing the courts as "theaters," the book pays close attention to the language, contexts, social practices, and actions of each party as a way to understand how people sought to resist, oppose, or transform dominant legal constructions.[33] Lower-class people may selectively deploy in their everyday language the dominant class discourse that they have transformed according to their own particular realities and interests. In such a way, during the century under study some women of Caracas actively contested dominant class language about citizenship, gender, race, and class.

In similar fashion, people may choose to use certain "strategic metaphors," verbal codes, or rhetoric to negotiate or open a space in intransigent or violent situations. Women may choose to seek the protection of the law, for example, by strategically claiming their status as mothers. One pregnant litigant trying to avoid the death penalty probably used that strategic metaphor because women's reproductive capacities needed no further justification; culturally, the idea that society had to protect motherhood was unquestionable.[34] If used in a way that did not evoke potential disruption of the social order or male power, it could help women gain some receptivity for their demands. Under the legal and social conditions of women in the early republic, the use of the social function of motherhood was a logical strategy.

As the use of the metaphor of motherhood suggests, these open or hidden linguistic strategies could have contradictory results. They could help advance the cause, for instance, by exposing the inconsistencies among the new liberal legal codes, the practice of the courts, and the concrete realities of women's lives in Caracas. By using the system's institutions and values to challenge the dominant culture, however, women could ambivalently reaffirm those same institutions and be drawn, "willy-nilly, further into the dominant's points of view."[35] Some authors warn that this paradox can militate against the possibility of actual resistance and may conceal the central issues.[36] Still, it is fair to observe that such nonconfrontational strategies provided colonial and republican women a secure way to speak up and to seek changes in a public space that was closed to them.[37]

METHODOLOGICAL CONSIDERATIONS

To delve into the lives of ordinary people, this study relies predominantly on court records, or *expedientes*. They provide a valuable glimpse into how Venezuelans perceived their relationship with the new state. Litigation involving daily life offers a wealth of information that historians of Latin America have explored to analyze gender relations.[38] To capture as many cases as possible involving the social interaction of lower-class women, the sample includes lawsuits in which women were victims, perpetrators, plaintiffs, or defendants in various matters. It leaves aside cases dealing with debt, inheritance, and property because such cases often referred to the upper classes, and the objective was to examine, as much as possible, the experience of lower-class women and their resistance.[39] To have a thorough picture of the problems faced by ordinary men and women, the sample includes data that were not delimited to one particular type of claim (i.e., sexual crimes, wills, marriage oppositions) but that encompassed a wide range of suits dealing with conflicts of daily life.[40] Many of the cases deal with adultery, sexual offenses, family support, parental power, divorce, manumission letters, women's requests for power to administer property, abuse, breach of promise, slander, bodily injury, theft, murder, flights of wives, and robbery.

Although compiled by civil and ecclesiastical authorities, these sources shed light on the values, beliefs, and understandings of ordinary people. The court records contain statements and testimonies by persons of both sexes and every social condition, including slaves. Individual data on name, race, legitimacy, birthplace, residence, marital status, occupation, and age helped to broadly identify the social backgrounds of plaintiffs, defendants, and witnesses. What is particularly useful about these lawsuits is that they provide the full report of investigations, often with extensive, unrehearsed testimonies from people whose voices are rarely discerned in the historical record. Moreover, these sources include the full written record of the pleadings, briefs, judgments, and any other data submitted to the court as evidence, including more intimate items such as letters, poems, and pictures. In other words, the record of each individual suit conveys a wealth of information about controversy.

Nonetheless, these sources have limitations. For one, the authorship of documents is occasionally uncertain. Sometimes a lay individual narrated the contents of documents, perhaps with the aid of a scribe, but in other instances lawyers composed the documents. The written evidence included in the expedientes helped in corroborating the authorship of some letters but not all of them. Another issue is that of representativeness. Litigants form only a fraction of the population, and the question exists as to whether they can account for the experience of most caraqueños. Still, even with such limitations, the richness of these lawsuits allows some reasonable generalizations about gender relations, their relationship with high culture, and their transformations throughout the nineteenth century.

Other primary sources such as newspaper and magazine articles, speeches, legal codes, and treatises on law were used to enrich and cross-examine the discussion provided in the lawsuits. The racial status of litigants was not consistently mentioned in the legal documents after 1811; therefore, race cannot be systematically addressed throughout the republican period. Finally, this research deals mainly with heterosexual relations, because cases on homosexual relations were unfortunately too scant to allow any meaningful conclusions.

Selective sampling was the key to managing this voluminous material and gaining chronological breadth without sacrificing substantive depth. The sample includes documents from Caracas at three important moments in Venezuelan history: 1786–90, 1835–40, and 1875–80. Altogether, the sample collects, catalogs, and analyzes 578 cases in which women participated as litigants during the sampled years. The samples cover the period from the foundation of the Real Audiencia (High Court of Appeals) of Caracas in 1786 through the inception of liberal and positivist regimes in Venezuela during the Guzmán Blanco regime, which ended in 1888. The *longue-durée* approach of this investigation allowed an evaluation of the impact of liberal thinking in Caracas society and an analysis of how it was transformed from colonial to republican times.

ORGANIZATION OF THE BOOK

Divided into three parts, the book covers the late colonial period (1786–1811), the early republic (1830–40), and the late nineteenth century (1870–88). Each part includes a preliminary chapter that examines masculine struggles for hegemony at the government level that informed the legal and administrative reforms of each period. A second chapter in each part analyzes laws affecting the relations between the sexes and the practice of the courts. Each part concludes with an analysis of how women understood gender relations as seen in the personal narratives contained in their claims. Each part shows how women's understandings of gender and the laws challenged contemporary gender norms. The chronological endpoint of the work is 1904, when a new generation of positivists approved a full divorce law and, subsequently, reforms in the legislation affecting Venezuelan families.

Chapter 1 provides a panoramic view of the social, political, and economic history of the colony from 1700 to 1810. It examines how the exterior signs of honor and status of the creole aristocracy of Caracas (known as the *mantuanos*) became the dominant referent used to measure and discriminate among people. The privileged status of the creole elite was constantly defended from other competitors – namely Spaniards and the lower classes – who questioned the aristocrats' exclusive claims to honor. Yet by the end of the eighteenth century, the long-held political and economic autonomy of creole aristocrats over colonial matters had gradually declined. The loss of political privileges by these aristocrats engendered grievances against a Spanish crown that they increasingly accused of interfering with every aspect of their daily lives.

This assertion is further validated when the letter and practice of colonial law in Caracas are analyzed in chapter 2. In Spanish legal codes, sexual and domestic behaviors were highly regulated for women but not for men. Still, in practice, judges afforded women some protection and held men accountable for their actions. Elite male heads of household resented women's (and slaves') legal actions and court sentences, seeing them as additional encroachments by the Spanish crown on their domestic prerogatives.

Chapter 3 examines the language and discourse used mainly by the lower classes in lawsuits and analyzes their attitudes toward marriage and the hierarchical social system based on race and honor. The discussion shows how some caraqueños were somewhat uncomfortable over the prescribed social norms. Yet at the same time, common people ambiguously used the aristocrats' institutions and idiom of honor to assert their own version of personal virtue by attaching other meanings to them. The chapter shows how late-eighteenth-century tribunals ultimately served as an arena in which the lower classes could debate, contest, and transform dominant ideas, which was another source of mantuanos' concern.

The early republican period is the subject of chapter 4. It focuses on how the nation-building program of the educated male elites and landowners was accompanied by ideas about the construction of gender. On the one hand, the ruling oligarchy of educated and propertied men used legal administrative reforms to advance their gendered agenda for power that excluded military men as well as the nonpropertied population. Women, however, were absent from political writings but not from these men's imaginations. In early republican times, when literary or iconographic images of Liberty (or other ideas personified as female) were considered, even in church publications, the message was that women had to be closely controlled; otherwise, they could cause disorder and anarchy. Even when debating the death sentence of a pregnant woman, male politicians used the issue to further their struggles for hegemonic masculinity while silencing women. Thus the process of state-building in the early republic was very much infused with a gendered agenda.

Chapter 5 traces the legal terrain of the new republic and the ways in which Venezuelan politicians sought to use the law to give legitimacy, continuity, and stability to the new nation by increasing paternal authority and by implementing vagrancy laws and the death penalty. The new liberal nation also legitimized the use of various colonial codes that supported class, racial, and gendered distinctions and that allowed the continued political exclusion of the majority of the population. After the wars of independence, the need for order and peace was made a priority, and this became clear in the severe punishments for criminal behavior.

While the male oligarchy struggled to legitimize its claim to rule and to bring stability with harsher laws, female litigants used liberal ideas of citizenship to defend their aspirations for equal protection under the laws, not to claim political rights. The subject of chapter 6 is how, with the establishment of the new republic, female litigants gained new discursive tools to defend themselves in their struggles against men. Upper-class female litigants justified their status as citizens based on their property holdings, while their lower-class counterparts primarily demonstrated such values in their behavior and defense of individual liberties. Demanding equal responsibilities with men in the household, defending themselves from abusive relationships, and asserting their right to work for salaries, lower-class women protected their individual rights. Many of the female litigants expected the laws of the new republic to protect their individual liberties just as they protected men's. In this sense, poor women embraced liberal notions of citizenship, liberty, and equality supposedly guaranteed to all Venezuelans by the Constitution of 1811. Barbara Jedler – a litigant and former slave – articulated it well: "the equality of rights all Venezuelans enjoy gives more strength to my weak forces and empowers me to not hide my face."[41] Women wanted to be treated as female citizens and, as such, to receive equal protection under the laws of the new polity. In this endeavor, they met fierce resistance from their husbands and lovers, who defended their claims as true citizens and as customary heads of households and who did not want the government to intrude into their homes.

The last part, on the late nineteenth century, opens with chapter 7 and its discussion of the ways in which President Antonio Guzmán Blanco sought to consolidate his regime and organize a modern state in Venezuela. To bring order and progress, Guzmán Blanco attempted to compromise with social sectors such as regional caudillos, merchants, and landowners, who could disturb the stability of his regime. In addition, the regime embraced positivism as well as European culture, namely French bourgeois elements. Identification with Europe provided a way to distinguish the old – primarily white and propertied – group from other competitors for power, who were mainly of military or caudillo background. The policies and cultural values of the regime were also bolstered through laws and legal reforms that contributed to the formation of a modern state. Still, the poor majority was excluded and neglected by the ruling classes. The social imagery used by the regime to promote patriotism and national belonging did not have local roots. The elites' view of progress was nurtured by racial and cultural ideas that influenced the politics of the period.

In terms of the content and practice of the law, discussed in chapter 8, the ruling male elite succeeded not only in consolidating the rule of Europeanized, educated, and propertied men but also in protecting the power of the paterfamilias from the courts. The governing elite's ideology romanticized feminine domestic power while stifling social changes that might have resulted from women seeking legal protection. Only those women who followed the elite ideal of womanhood – those who proved without reasonable doubt that they were virtuous and chaste – received favorable court rulings. Socially, politically, and juridically, Venezuelans lived in a contradiction. While liberal ideas made the prevailing gender inequality in Venezuela untenable, ruling males succeeded in strengthening patriarchy under state aegis by the end of the century.

Chapter 9 analyzes how many female litigants challenged the prevailing ideals of womanhood in their civil and criminal claims against men by the 1870s. Some women concretely addressed the contradictions between the regime's discourse and its practices. Most female litigants did so indirectly, however, by infusing the prescribed roles for women with different meanings, by appropriating those elements of government discourse that empowered them, and by rejecting those that were useless. Some of them challenged bourgeois feminine values, declined to have a marriage by judicial fiat, refused to sue their lovers for their lost honor, and did not believe that illegitimacy and loss of virginity demeaned their honor and dignity as women. Although no distinct connection between women's legal conditions and their need for organized political struggle to obtain equal rights existed by the late nineteenth century, the terrain was fertile thanks to the actions of women like Juana Feliciana Díaz, doña María Antonia Pérez, and Violante Mijares, who decided not to hide their faces in order to be included in the new republic's liberal agenda.

PART 1
The Late Colonial Period

1. A Caracas for the Mantuanos, 1700–1811

In the early years of the eighteenth century, creole elites still enjoyed social, economic, and political authority in the Province of Venezuela. The creole elites consisted of a group of whites with family lineages that had long enjoyed privileged status in the colony. As they liked to say, they were the "families that conquered and populated the province with their blood and hard work," because most of their ancestors had been in Caracas if not by the conquest, then at least since the middle of the seventeenth century.[1] Creole elites cited this *antigüedad* as the source of their authority. Although they were self-described as the "nobility of Caracas," in reality fewer than ten of roughly one hundred creole elite family heads held a title by the late eighteenth century.[2]

Because many of their ancestors were Old Christians from northern Spain, where little interaction with Moors, Muslims, or Jews occurred, these elites claimed to be true Catholics and to have pure blood. These families also benefited from extensive holdings in land and African slaves, both mainly devoted to cacao or sugar production by the late seventeenth century. The power and privilege of this class rested on the members' general ascendancy and military service, the property that passed from one generation to the next, and the process by which families carefully selected marriage partners.

These self-proclaimed "familias antiguas, nobles, limpias y honradas" saw themselves as people of "utmost distinction." As loyal vassals of the king, they had the duty of defending the social order through military service. In exchange for this and other noble services, they believed themselves worthy of honor and certain privileges.[3] For example, they were the only creoles who participated in such state institutions as the municipal council, the university, and the church. They did not pay many of the taxes demanded of the rest of the nonwhite population. They sat in special places at ceremonies and wore special costumes and jewelry proper only to people of their status.

Indeed, by the eighteenth century this group was known as the mantuanos for the distinctive *manto* (veil) that covered the faces and bodies of mantuano women in public places. Elite women's characteristic manner of dress signals the importance of control over women's bodies for mantuano honor and status. Such exterior signs of honor and status set the mantuanos apart from the common people. More importantly, the public display of the mantuanos' honor became a fundamental mechanism of social control that reaffirmed the social hierarchy and order within the colony.[4]

The mantuanos' heightened sense of honor and their belief that they possessed the only pure blood in Venezuela became the basis for a society ordered on social and racial inequality.[5] By the eighteenth century the mantuanos' idiom of honor became the dominant referent for measuring and discriminating among people. This does not imply that elites' values and worldviews became the consensual culture, however, nor does it imply that the lower classes submitted to the mantuanos' cultural forms. Instead, the culture of honor became a familiar script and a "language of argument" readily at hand for all caraqueños to use for various purposes – especially to claim their own honor in certain contexts.[6] The elites had to engage in a constant dynamic of challenge and accommodation to their power. Such challenges occurred especially when plebeians used the mantuanos' idiom of honor to assert their own notion of personal virtue (see below and chap. 3).[7]

The components of honor may appear absolute and rigid among the mantuanos, but they were not. As Ann Twinam warns and as Luis Pellicer illustrates so well for late colonial Venezuela, honor was a malleable concept because its meaning and practice varied in time, place, and context. Even among elites, the code of honor allowed "passing" for those of illegitimate birth, and it even permitted such undesirable behavior as visiting the house of a pardo if the other mantuano members sanctioned it.[8] Having or not having honor was negotiable; therefore, honor was a variable quality. It could admit tolerance in several circumstances. Honor was subject to constant scrutiny, so it could be "challenged, threatened, lost, gained, and even regained."[9]

Naturally, the mantuanos became strong defenders of the social order and of their privileged position within it. Being born into the mantuano class did not guarantee perpetual privilege, because challenges and threats constantly arose. The defense of family privileges was in the hands of their male heads, or padres de familia, because the honor code established by the mantuanos associated their class privileges with masculine honor.[10] Mantuano men had to demonstrate complete authority, which meant they would sometimes defy public manifestations of power by not following the order of a superior in rank (e.g., a top-ranked Spaniard) or by challenging certain dispositions of the king. Such men enjoyed autonomy and power through the respect and deference they received from others.[11] Having a luxurious home, a large, productive hacienda with numerous dependents and slaves, a distinctive occupation, a chaste wife, and children were indicators of an honorable mantuano man. These indicators bestowed a right to power and privilege.

The rituals of male public assertion mainly addressed potential male competitors, even though the daily validation of masculinity could occur in the presence of women.[12] Women simply did not belong to the male public world; they were men's dependents, their sexual property. This "possession" enhanced the masculine traits of the padre de familia.[13] Due to their subordinate position, women's voices are not audible in the public transcripts of the time. The actions of most women were believed to be not worth recording, because the ruling men did not consider them part of history. Indeed, in the constant competition over masculinity, one whose manhood was questioned was often categorized as feminine, weak, a dependent, or of inferior honor.

Because the patriarchal system established male authority at all levels from the state to the household, male mantuanos had to assert their manhood and defend their power constantly. This was especially true during the eighteenth century, when the basis of masculine power was threatened by equals, the lower classes, and by families.[14] Approaching the late colonial period by addressing masculine competition within the ruling classes helps us bridge the different levels of power struggles, especially in the courts and domestic spheres (see chaps. 2 and 3). Most importantly, it helps us understand how mantuano grievances transcended the political and economic spheres, which have been the main focus of the historiography on Venezuelan independence. As will be discussed in this chapter, mantuano men's traditional autonomy over political matters declined partly due to the Bourbon monarchs' economic and political reforms. This decline occurred gradually. The crown consistently took political power away from the mantuanos during the eighteenth century without affecting their social status in the colony. This was achieved by granting mantuanos a few social and political privileges in order to preserve their public honor and the colony's social hierarchy.

As independence approached, the importance of kin relationships and inheritance strategies and the idea of a noble race waned, but these cultural traits did not completely disappear, allowing other men to participate in the ruling sphere. Among the new contestants, the code of masculinity rested not solely on mantuano-aristocratic values but also on education and merit.[15] By the time the new republic was established, notions of dominant masculinity had changed according to ruling men's interpretations of the economic, political, and social necessities of the time.

THE DEFENSE OF MASCULINITY AMONG EQUALS

On one horizontal plane were those men whom the mantuanos considered to be of similar social standing, such as the peninsulars in top administrative positions. Since the sixteenth century, peninsulars and mantuanos had been able to accommodate each other's needs and aspirations. They benefited especially from the lack of a strong royal presence in the Province of Venezuela. Located in a region lacking the precious metals coveted by Spain, the territory remained a neglected fringe area of the Spanish Empire until the early eighteenth century, when cacao gained ascendancy as an export crop.

Also, few peninsulars in Venezuela had an interest in participating in municipal institutions. As a result, no significant public conflicts between mantuanos and peninsulars took place until the 1720s. An increasing royal presence in the colony eventually began to provoke major quarrels between mantuanos and recently arrived Spaniards sent by the crown to fill positions in Venezuela's administration. The *costumbres* (customs) that local inhabitants developed in the absence of a strong state gave them the liberty to disregard mandatory hierarchical protocols of the Spanish bureaucracy.[16] Later, when the crown enacted policies aimed at increasing its authority, these policies inevitably touched on local costumbre and had important political consequences.

The initial lack of interest in Venezuelan matters among both resident Spaniards and the crown facilitated the mantuanos' extensive control of the colony's administration. The mantuanos' local authority had been formalized since the founding of Caracas and its municipal council in 1567. The *cabildo*, or municipal council, was appointed by the *vecinos*, literally neighbors of the city or town, who were not just any inhabitants but free men who had property or a dignified occupation, were heads of household, or were emancipated sons. In Caracas, the original founding families and their descendents were traditionally members of the cabildo. The dominion of the mantuanos in the cabildo was sealed in the late sixteenth century when the crown started selling municipal council seats in perpetuity to the highest bidders.

Among the members of the cabildo, the two annually elected judges, or *alcaldes ordinarios*, had more authority in the locality than any official except the teniente de justicia mayor and the governor. Due to delays in the nomination of interim local governors, which in Caracas came from the Real Audiencia of Santo Domingo, the crown established that the alcaldes ordinarios would replace the governor during periods of absence. This prerogative belonged to every municipal council in the Indies; yet in Caracas a royal order of 1560 established that the alcaldes ordinarios would automatically assume the position provisionally while the new governor sailed from Spain.[17] Hence the audiencia could not nominate the pro tem governor for the Province of Venezuela.

Even in 1676 the alcaldes of Caracas were granted their request for political and military authority when, for any reason, the governor could not assume such powers. In the eighteenth century alone, the two alcaldes of Caracas assumed the governorship of the Province of Venezuela ten times between 1700 and 1730. Their terms varied from seven days to a year and a half.[18] Alcaldes ordinarios carefully awaited the opportunity to exert maximum authority in the province. Having enjoyed such power and status for more than a century, the mantuanos had difficulty accepting any change that decreased this power.

The opportunity to rule the province intermittently for more than a century was a significant privilege and benefit. As historian Robert Ferry explains, one of the main responsibilities of the governor as chief military officer (*capitán general*) was to appoint officers called *tenientes de justicia mayor*.[19] The tenientes were the primary authority figures in rural districts of the province. As such, they were the judges of first instance, responsible for capturing runaway slaves and policing contraband trade. The tenientes enjoyed an authority superior to that of the alcaldes ordinarios, so they were in charge of supervising irregularities in the cabildo. By nominating men faithful to the interim governor's interests, the mantuanos could protect their authority and exercise some control over the countryside, especially the locations of their haciendas. Cabildo members could also exert control over the prosecution of smugglers when it was convenient for them to do so, because they also monitored contraband. This system worked smoothly for the mantuanos, because the audiencia of Santo Domingo usually confirmed their nominations to the positions of teniente.[20] When the audiencia of New Granada in Santa Fé de Bogotá assumed jurisdiction over the Venezuelan province in 1717–23 and 1739–42, however, the nomination of tenientes became more difficult. Naturally the audiencia gave priority to people amenable to their own interest and control.

As a result of the cacao boom of the early eighteenth century the centralizing Bourbon monarchs paid more attention to the province. This more palpable royal authority challenged the mantuanos' considerable autonomy and isolation from the royal bureaucracy. The increasing royal presence and the accompanying arrival of new Spanish administrators threatened the mantuanos' traditional control of local decision-making. Hence, conflicts with horizontal competitors ensued in the second half of the eighteenth century as Spaniards defended their assumption of superiority over the local aristocracy.

THE DEFENSE OF HONOR AND MASCULINITY AGAINST COMPETITORS OF LOWER STATUS

At other, vertical levels were the people whom the mantuanos and the Spanish crown considered of lower social position due to their race and class. Although pardos and mulattos shared a similar background of mixed African and Hispanic descent, society differentiated between them by the late colonial period. The pardos' lighter skin meant they could consider themselves, as the community did, further from slavery than the mulattos.[21] This is one reason why the word *mulatto*, like others discussed in this chapter, carried a negative connotation. Distinctions related to skin color also explain why, in the context of a dispute, a pardo was sometimes referred to as a mulatto.[22] The mantuanos, as expected, used the terms interchangeably to describe and justify these peoples' lack of honor.

A clear example appears in a 1788 letter to the king from the cabildo members, in which the mantuanos explained why pardos and mulattos were regarded with scorn. They blamed it on their origin as descendants of slaves, most of whom were illegitimate. Because of their low origin, the letter writers explained, the government issued a number of laws that obliged these people to pay tributes, to not "live without lords," to not bear arms, and to not hold a soldier's post. Mulatta women were "forbidden to wear gold, silk, and pearls." To be seen with a pardo or mulatto could affect a mantuano claim to honor; therefore "the practice among whites [was] not to allow the people of this class in their house or to walk with them in the streets."[23]

Because pardos, mulattos, and blacks lacked legitimacy, pure blood, and privilege, the mantuanos considered this "mass of human beings" devoid of any honor. The natural order of society, as supported by religious and secular laws as well as the mantuano sense of honor, dictated that each member of the lower classes be subject to a white, elite padre de familia who watched over his or her work, enforced tribute payments, and encouraged good morals. The 1687 synod for the Venezuelan province established that "the servant or slave must look upon his lord as a superior and as a father, to honor and serve him."[24] Moreover, because these people could not lead a civilized life, the "chosen people of God," the padres de familia, had to shepherd a multicolored flock. Consequently, from the mantuano perspective, losing control over the flock would bring disorder and anarchy.[25]

Because the elites' honor and power rested on the idea that all others lacked honor, mantuanos constantly denigrated pardos, mulattos, and zambos – those of mixed Indian and black heritage.[26] They promoted a negative, stereotyped image of the "Other." Ideas that conveyed prejudice against the lower classes circulated widely and freely until no one questioned their origin or purpose – until society assumed them as "natural" and as absolute truth.

For mantuanos, the lower classes represented immorality, barbarism, laziness, and ignorance. The association between negative qualities and the races of the lower classes was so entrenched that racial categories such as zambo/a, mulatto/a, negro/a, and Indio/a were commonly used for slanderous situations. The ideological rhetoric hid the mantuanos' fears that this large group of lower classes threatened to subvert the order that ensured mantuano honor and power. There was a persistent fear of such subversion in the eighteenth century.

The mantuanos' anxiety was justified. Caracas was a racially diverse city, with pardos the predominant group. In 1792 they made up 38 percent of the city's population. Slaves composed another 21 percent. Altogether, there were twice as many slaves, free blacks, and pardos as whites, who numbered around 9,000. The Indian population, by contrast, was negligible – only 743 by 1792. In proportional terms, the inhabitants of the central valley of Caracas were mainly of African descent, and the city had more slaves than any other urban center in the province of Caracas.[27] It also had the country's largest concentration of whites (peninsulars and creoles). Moreover, from 1700 to 1750, the population jumped more than threefold, from 6,000 to 20,000, and by 1800 it had reached 30,000, making Caracas the largest city in the captaincy-general.[28] In the eyes of the mantuanos, not only were they a minority but the nonwhite majority was growing too fast.

In a corporatist society with a hierarchy based on birth, wealth, and race, whites occupied the apex of the social pyramid. This does not mean that all whites belonged to the upper rungs of society; indeed, a significant number of nonelite and poor whites lived in Caracas. Nevertheless, whites dominated government institutions and commerce.[29] Even though mantuanos ranked poor whites above people of other races, poor whites still suffered discrimination by the mantuanos.[30]

As the largest racial group in Caracas, the pardos exhibited degrees of internal differentiation. Some accumulated enough money to open artisanal shops, to enjoy distinguished professions, to purchase land, and to own slaves. If contemporary observers' accounts are reliable, however, most pardos were working-class people employed in construction and other low-paying manual trades: carpenters, masons, woodcarvers, shoemakers, locksmiths, and silversmiths, for instance. Pardo men worked as artisans and in mechanical trades, while women filled menial roles as street vendors, cooks, seamstresses, laundresses, domestics, and the like.[31] Their predicament, in short, was poverty.

To compound matters, the pardos faced a host of limitations, because legally they could not serve in public office. They also could not enter the clergy or the university.[32] Paradoxically the upper classes considered these people ignorant, yet they still worried that "subversive" foreign books might reach those pardos determined to be educated. This reason is one of several offered in 1803 for prohibiting pardo admission to the university.[33]

Toward the end of the eighteenth century, however, the colonial government took minor steps to ease some of the discrimination against non-whites. These policies allowed well-off pardos to rise in the formal social hierarchy. To this end a separate militia battalion of pardos was created in 1760.[34] Pardos also benefited from the distribution of housing plots on city land in the 1770s and 1780s. Finally, in 1795 the king allowed pardos to buy certificates giving them the privileges that upper-class whites enjoyed (see below).

If the pardos achieved some measure of improvement within the social and economic life of late colonial Caracas, it did not come without a fight. The struggle warned the mantuanos that the lower classes could achieve significant gains. Although Caracas saw few major incidents of racial violence during the eighteenth century, social unrest was common in the province as a whole. Of the nineteen riots and uprisings – including a few major foiled plots organized by slaves – fourteen happened in the province of Caracas, some near the city (see table 1). These events occurred gradually: one in the 1730s, five in the 1740s, one in the 1770s, and three in the 1790s.[35]

Of these nineteen protests, slave, mulatto, pardo, or zambo leaders organized at least seven. The insurgents protested against taxes, government monopolies, the policies of the Real Compañía Guipuzcoana de Caracas (a royally chartered commercial monopoly company), and slavery. Pardos were actively involved in these events. Thus, while the city itself was quiet, social tensions elsewhere in the restless province periodically erupted into violence. Along with such international events as the 1792 Haitian Revolution, these incidents contributed to the apprehensions of the small, white, upper class of Caracas.

One general criticism that permeates lawsuits brought by pardos, blacks, and zambos is that the mantuanos did not work. Some litigants among the lower classes expressed that the mantuanos did not deserve their social position because they earned nothing through individual labor and effort.[36] From this perspective, we see that the lower classes valued their individual traits and professions. They pursued status based on individual achievement and defended their dignity by contradicting the mantuanos' negative images of them.[37] Accordingly, male pardos, mulattos, blacks, and zambos insisted that they were physically the mantuanos' equals. A slogan heard frequently among the lower classes in 1795 was, "There was not one white Adam and another mulatto."[38] Although the mantuanos in the cabildo in the 1790s claimed that these ideas of individuality and equality came from subversive foreign contraband, they actually had been prevalent for some time.[39]

Some lower classes already understood and displayed these individualistic values before Enlightenment ideas penetrated Caracas, though historians usually associate the values with the later transition to capitalist, free-contract principles.[40] For example, Luis Pellicer analyzed a case in 1780 in a rural town in Ocumare. During a party organized by an upper-class white man to celebrate his son's baptism, a conflict erupted on the dance floor. A pardo guest wanted to dance at the same time as a "decent white lady and gentleman." The host asked the pardo to dance outside the house, with his class peers. Infuriated by this denial of equal spatial rights, the pardo confronted the host, claiming that with his sword in hand he was "as much a man as anyone else" (tan hombre como otro cualquiera).[41] For Pellicer, the timing, location, and language of this conflict suggest that in practice a *convivencia* among the races ruled, as did the lower classes' sense of physical equality with the white elites.

In their dress, actions, and gestures, the lower classes defied the social order that the mantuanos wanted to preserve. One way they challenged the aristocracy was by exhibiting models of behavior that represented elite status. People utilized behavior, dress, and language – varying their meanings according to the circumstances and context – to assert individual virtue and honor. For instance, although laws prohibited non-nobles from using certain objects and dress, complaints of the time allege that mulattas and *sambaigas* abused such laws by using embroidered veils and kneeling on mats while attending mass.[42] Freed mulattas and slaves frequently adorned themselves with golden earrings and pearls, even when the *Recopilación de leyes*

TABLE 1. Conspiracies, Riots, and Insurrections in
Eighteenth-Century Venezuela

YEAR	EVENT	CITY OR REGION	PROVINCE	PATTERN
1705	Barquisimeto Conspiracy	Barquisimeto	Caracas	Separation; elite-based
1718	Guanare Riot	Guanare	Caracas	Government monopoly; elite-based
1730–33	Andresote's Revolt	Yaracuy Valley	Caracas	Government monopoly; Guipuzcoana; slave and Indian
1733–35	Caribs' attacks on missions	Orinoco River	Guayana	Indian
1741	San Felipe Riot	San Felipe	Caracas	Government monopoly; Guipuzcoana; multiethnic
1744	El Tocuyo Riot	El Tocuyo	Caracas	Government monopoly; Guipuzcoana; multiethnic
1747	Miguel Luengo's Conspiracy	San Francisco de Yare	Caracas	Slave
1749	Slave Conspiracy	Center to East	Caracas	Slave
1749	León's Insurrection	Tuy and Aragua Valleys, and Caracas	Caracas	Government monopoly; Guipuzcoana; multi-ethnic; elite-based
1764–77	Motilone's Invasion	Maracaibo Lake Area	Maracaibo	Indian
1771–74	Guillermo's Slave Bands	Tuy Valley and Barlovento	Caracas	Slave and maroon
1781	Comuneros	Andes Region and Mérida	Maracaibo	Tax and government monopoly; multiethnic; elite-based
1781	Caquetío Indians Conspiracy	Coro	Caracas	Indian
1781–89	Revolts in the Llanos (Banditry)	Llano Region	Caracas	Indian, casta, and slave
1795	Coro Insurrection	Coro	Caracas	Slave and freed people
1795	Indian Conspiracy in Jacura	Coro	Caracas	Indian

YEAR	EVENT	CITY OR REGION	PROVINCE	PATTERN
1797	Gual and España Movement	La Guaira	Caracas	Independence; multiethnic; elite-based
1798	Cariaco Conspiracy	Cariaco	Cumaná	Slave
1799	Maracaibo Conspiracy	Maracaibo	Maracaibo	Independence; abolition; pardo

Source: Manuel Vicente Magallanes, *Luchas e insurrecciones en la Venezuela Colonial* (Caracas: Academia Nacional de la Historia, 1982).

de los Reinos de Indias and the 1687 Synod of Caracas expressly prohibited lower-class people from wearing such lavish jewelry.[43] Even though the *Bandos de buen gobierno* prohibited plebeians from using arms, they tended to ignore these ordinances because weapons – swords, knives, and fire-arms – were esteemed symbols of masculinity.[44] News that a mulatto tailor was inciting other mulattos and black artisans to dress and set their hair as whites infuriated the colonial authorities.[45] The lower-class appropriation of aspects of elite material and behavioral culture demonstrates a purposeful expression of the desire to achieve equal footing with those who claimed to be of superior rank.

These individualistic and egalitarian expressions of some plebeians appear in documents that describe lower-class men's relationships with other men, including elites. Yet men of both classes did not apply such ideas in their treatment of women, especially within private spheres. Instead, men upheld the legal powers belonging to the padres de familia, which legitimized male power to rule and administer the household's physical and material property (see chap. 2). Men could not allow the demise of this important validation of their masculinity. Evidence shows, however, that some women capitalized on individualistic ideas of personal worth to challenge the domestic patriarchal order.

This individualism resembles the enlightened, liberal ideas of the late eighteenth century and the nineteenth century. Nonetheless, in contrast to France, the plebeians were not debating political equality. Instead, they were defending their demand for equal opportunity to achieve goals beyond the current legal and social norms imposed on them. Pardos and other racial groups did not accept their treatment as people wholly lacking in dignity. Many strove for social mobility, thus defending their individual sense of honor – at home, in the streets, and in court.

This attitude among pardos compounded the concerns of white elites. It became especially acute in the late eighteenth century: "the proliferation of pardos in this Province, their proud and defiant character, and the eagerness they show to liken themselves to whites, demands a political stipulation by which Your Majesty may keep them always under some dependency and subordination to whites, as it has been up to now. Otherwise, they will become insufferable due to their arrogance, and in no time they will want to dominate those who from the beginning have been their masters."[46]

During the 1790s the creole elite grew angry at concessions granted to pardos by the crown. Particularly upsetting was the Cédula de Gracias al Sacar of 10 February 1795, whereby a pardo could purchase the title of *don* and change his racial category.[47] He would become legally qualified to exercise all the privileges of whites, including access to public office, craft guilds, the church, the university, the lawyers association, and other elite positions. This statute transcended the criterion of pure blood that had previously denied pardos access to those institutions.

All these changes were anathema to the mantuanos in the cabildo, who were determined to protect the purity of their lineage. They had fought fiercely to ban even peninsulars from municipal government.[48] In their view, it was one thing to distribute land plots on the city outskirts to the poor, many of whom were pardos. But it was quite another to admit into their inner circles people who, as cabildo members wrote in an official brief to the crown, were of "inferior" background, "descended from their own or their fathers' slaves . . . whose origin is stained by a long series of bastardies and turpitude."[49]

The 1795 cédula removed the mantuanos' ability to control who could or could not belong to their class. Hence, the creole male aristocracy could not control their vertical competitors; they had to accept defeat without a ritual fight. Naturally this loss of autonomy and power was unacceptable to the aristocracy.[50]

THE DEFENSE OF MASCULINITY IN THE PRIVATE SPHERE

As Steve Stern rightly points out, "elite codes of male honor rested on cultural displays of forcefulness, household authority and social decorum."[51] The private terrain of the household was not immune to challenges to the elite padres de familia. In fact, the eighteenth century witnessed increased concern on the part of the crown and the male elites to protect the powers of the paterfamilias. Such concerns were logical. Demographically, economically, and legally, the eighteenth century brought critical changes to the traditional patriarchy of the padres de familia.

In his genealogical reconstruction of aristocratic families in Caracas, Robert Ferry finds that the traditional patriarchy of the mantuanos had declined by the second half of the eighteenth century. Specifically, he notes that after 1744 cacao expansion had failed to keep pace with the growing number of mantuano family members, causing a decline in per capita cacao wealth. This situation in which more people were dependent on fewer cacao holdings – combined with declining prices for the bean – produced a crisis among many of the leading families, particularly if they depended on cacao as their main source of revenue. Ferry relates this crisis to the fact that after the 1720s marriages among cousins increased, which had "the distinctive function of retaining for the next generation a double portion of those things that are transferred from one generation to the next, especially wealth, but also such social attributes as status and authority." Thus one of the distinctive characteristics of the aristocracy in Caracas – the tendency of its families to intermarry – probably served as a strategy for economic and social survival in the face of an impending loss of status.[52]

Additionally, from the 1730s on mantuano household heads typically died before their sons married. According to Ferry this had an enormous effect on the generational transmission of male authority, because fathers could no longer influence their adult children. Hence "much of the authority of the father's lineage that was felt and exercised by Caracas mantuano men in the eighteenth century had to be resurrected or recreated in every generation, using the symbols and inherited wealth of the deceased fathers. In Caracas, where noble titles and entailed estates were rare, the force of personality of each new husband and father must have counted for a great deal in the establishment of his stature as padre de familia and holder of community power and prestige."[53] The economic and demographic turns of the eighteenth century impinged directly on mantuano men's ability to maintain the basic justification of their privileges. Such struggles may now appear as petty quarrels over symbols of status and power, but they make sense when we consider the mantuanos' economic situation and the dominant values of the period's aristocratic masculinity.

The mantuanos probably would have preferred to conceal the decline of their traditional patriarchy, but the increased number of lawsuits filed by their wives and dependents in the last decade of the eighteenth century brought their domestic secrets to a public forum. Ironically, these private conflicts were resolved in courts dominated by Spaniards, especially at the higher levels. Thus the Spanish state again intruded in what should have been the mantuanos' foremost sphere of unquestionable dominion: their homes. Chapter 2 discusses in detail how women and subordinates such as slaves challenged the behavior and actions of the padres de familia.

Clearly mantuano defense of masculine honor linked different spheres, among them the state, the courts, and the household. All these spheres supported mantuano society's basically patriarchal nature. Throughout the eighteenth century, the Spanish state repeatedly challenged the mantuanos, as did both the lower classes and their own subordinates, including women. Men's authority was eroding in several arenas by the early nineteenth century. Analyzing the mature colonial period through this lens allows us to characterize the ways that ruling men justified their authority in relation to the rest of the population. Moreover, this historical lens allows us to understand broadly how these masculine relationships and conflicts framed mantuano men's attitudes toward the Spanish state, themselves, the lower classes, and women. This view further shows how these ideas played out later, in the state policies of the independence period and in the early republic. In this context we may better understand the responses of plebeians and women to such manifestations of honor and power, which are analyzed in the next two chapters.

THE GROWTH OF CACAO AND THE INCREASE IN ROYAL AUTHORITY, 1700–1749

The limited freedoms enjoyed by the mantuanos for over a century declined as the province's cacao economy increasingly flourished and the crown deemed it necessary to establish better control over the territory and its people. Caracas continued expanding its cacao cultivation, a trend that began in the last three decades of the seventeenth century. Most of that expansion took place to the east of the province in the valleys along the Tuy River.[54]

The combination of increased production, access to new lands along the frontiers, and high prices proved irresistible for those who wanted to make a fortune. Some of the increasing production was legally transported to the New Spain market, yet much of the cacao was illegally distributed as contraband, especially through Curaçao.[55] Such activity was unavoidable because the expansive coasts of Tierra Firme (as Venezuela was originally known), its many ports, and its lack of strong governmental control allowed frequent communication with foreign vessels. The cacao boom along with the high prices paid in the New Spain market attracted many newcomers to the hitherto forgotten Venezuelan lands. Many of the early-eighteenth-century migrants to the Tuy frontier were Canary Islanders (known as *canarios* or *isleños*) who expected to become great cacao farmers. Africans were brought to till the land as slaves alongside the canarios, mulattos, and runaway slaves who were already in the area.

The centralizing Bourbon monarchs could no longer resist intervention because opportunities for revenue were at hand in Venezuela. The need to generate royal revenue and to establish better distribution of cacao to European markets were two of the reasons behind the creation of the Real Compañía Guipuzcoana, chartered in 1728 as a royal commercial monopoly company of Basque origin. For the Spanish crown this experiment with a commercial monopoly company in the Indies incorporated Venezuela into the imperial economy and curtailed the smuggling that took away colonial revenues.[56] But the increased Spanish presence and controls ignited animosities among local people of different classes who had organized their lives before the Spanish influx.

The presence of the monopoly company restricted the political autonomy of the mantuanos, because they no longer wielded the same share of governmental power. After 1736 the alcaldes ordinarios had no further opportunity to replace the governor and to make decisions favorable to the mantuanos. To compound matters, the first years of operation of the monopoly company coincided with the long tenure of two governors of Basque origin: don Martín de Lardizábal (1732–37) and Gabriel José de Zuloaga (1737–47). The increased presence of Spanish authority through the monopoly company, together with the tenure of the Basque governors, gave mantuanos the sense of being the victims of a plot against their traditional authority. They had good reasons to believe so.

Governor Lardizábal, a fervent supporter of the Guipuzcoana, reported to the king on the abuses of power committed by the alcaldes ordinarios in the province. Consequently a Real Cédula was issued in 1736 establishing that in the absence of the governor his civil and military lieutenants, who were Spaniards, would act as interim governors. The crown used the opportunity to bring to an end the cabildo privilege of acting as pro tem governors in Caracas.[57] From the mid–seventeenth century the crown had been aware of the abuses of the alcaldes ordinarios and the disturbances that their ambition had created in the province. The immediate reaction of the cabildo members to the loss of power is still unclear. Rumors circulated at the time, however, that the cabildo members conspired to murder Lardizábal along with the agent of the Guipuzcoana. Similar rumors of a plot against Zuloaga and the Basque company circulated in 1745.[58]

Other measures further reduced the mantuano power apparatus during this period. In 1738 the governors gained the prerogative of appointing or dismissing tenientes de justicia mayor without requesting the audiencia's approval. According to Governor Zuloaga this right was necessary to more effectively control smuggling and to avoid delays caused by distance and poor roads. For the cabildo members the appointment of tenientes foreign to their interests in the countryside opened the risky possibility of a more rigorous enforcement of laws and policing of smuggling and cacao production.[59] As avenues for marketing the product illegally became more difficult, cacao producers were forced to depend on the Guipuzcoana and its low cacao prices. With record low prices for cacao in 1749, tensions peaked as a Vizcayan employee of the Guipuzcoana arrived in the Tuy Valley and was mistakenly thought to be the replacement for the local teniente de justicia mayor. Already fed up with the policies and actions instituted by Basque "foreigners," the growers rebelled.

REBELLION AND REPRESSION, 1749–1777

The presence of the new Vizcayan official in the region created a crisis because his key mission was to halt contraband. For the isleños and other small planters, stricter control over contraband meant absolute ruin because the prohibition against transporting beans through the Tuy River and the Caribbean Sea made the business of cacao unprofitable. It was an isleño, Capt. Juan Francisco de León, who actually led the protest. He marched to Caracas along with fellow isleños, free blacks, and Indians to protest against the Guipuzcoana and the new policies. León also received the support of a number of mantuanos who gave encouragement but wanted to preserve their anonymity. What began as a protest evolved into a violent rebellion.[60]

The task of reestablishing the monopoly company (which had been temporarily suspended), punishing the rebels, and maintaining order was left to the new governor, Brig. Gen. don Felipe Ricardos (1751–57). Governor Ricardos became infamous for his heavy-handed repression of those who were involved in or who supported the rebellion. The blacks, isleños, mulattos, and Indians who followed León to Caracas were jailed, whipped, or executed, and their severed heads were displayed publicly. After running from the authorities, León surrendered and was sent in secrecy to Spain, along with his son, to be judged by the Council of the Indies in Cádiz. León's voluntary surrender negated the possibility of a public execution – a spectacle that surely would have inflamed animosities again. Instead, Ricardos ordered the destruction of León's house in the Candelaria neighborhood of

Caracas, the spreading of salt on the ruins, and the erection of a plaque denouncing León's crimes.[61]

The mantuanos did not go unpunished. Those who allegedly encouraged the insurrection – Juan Félix Blanco, Miguel Blanco Uribe, and Juan Nicolás Ponte – were arrested and deported to Spain in 1751. Luis Arias Altamirano (the only person for whom the authorities had evidence of participation in the movement), Francisco Arias, Pedro Blanco de Ponte, Francisco de Paula Toro y Istúriz (the second marqués del Toro), and Francisco Nicolás Mijares y Tovar (the third marqués de Mijares) were exiled to an undisclosed location. Other leading citizens of Caracas were kept under house arrest in their countryside haciendas. By 1753 the punishment of the mantuano participants was complete. Although they were reprimanded for their alleged participation, the punishment was not public, so their status and role in Caracas society was preserved.

The movement was repressed, but it demonstrated that people of various social ranks were opposed to the crown's policies. In addition, the León insurrection had a lasting effect in Caracas. On the one hand, it radicalized some mantuanos, who became more aggressive in defending their privileged position. On the other hand, it exposed the limits of alliances between common people and the creole elites, who initially supported León but abandoned the cause when it became more generalized and dangerous to their own social position. Blame and punishment for the rebellion fell heavily on the subalterns. After the rebellion, the elites collaborated with a reformed Guipuzcoana and maintained their status, while those who once dreamt of becoming great cacao hacendados faced the possibility of remaining laborers rather than becoming producers.[62] Perhaps their memory of the rebellion made many isleños and rural workers hesitate over joining the patriot mantuano leadership in the early years of the wars of independence.[63]

Ricardos's strong grip on Caracas allowed him to initiate several royal policies aimed at securing order and Spanish authority. To subdue any opposition from the cabildo or the mantuanos and to force them to comply with the reforms, Ricardos threatened to move the civil, secular, and commercial center from Caracas to Valencia.[64] To Ricardos, the population of Caracas had proved itself disloyal and seditious during the 1749 revolt, and they deserved punishment. He established a regular standing army in the city, persecuting and even executing anyone suspected of conspiring against the crown.

To pay for soldiers, Ricardos raised the sales tax from 2 percent to 5 percent. This tax was levied on all goods for local consumption in Caracas, including foodstuffs and other basic commodities such as mules, horses, salt, and firewood. The tax remained in place for decades. Because the tax fell on basic commodities, all caraqueños bore the impact of the increase in prices, but the lower orders felt it especially.[65]

Along with institutional reforms, Ricardos showed increased concern about "loose behavior." He enforced the order that citizens had to illuminate their windows and doorways. Ricardos expelled men – mostly canarios – who did not bring their wives to join them within three years of immigration. Unemployed people had ten days to find work; those who failed to do so were sent to Spain to work for the king. The behavior of women troubled Ricardos, so he placed unemployed women in homes where they could learn "good customs." He also prohibited women from visiting soldiers' barracks and public places at night.[66]

This concern over private behavior was echoed by Bishop Diego Antonio Diez Madroñero, who arrived in Caracas in 1756. He made behavioral changes his main aspiration. For this rigidly devout Catholic, economic prosperity, the surge in legal and clandestine commerce, the importation of African slaves, and population increases – especially of people of mixed races – all implied the spread of sin across Venezuela. Alarmed by the current state of affairs, in 1761 Diez Madroñero ordered a 1687 synod reprinted.[67] Although this ecclesiastical constitution for Caracas had appeared when the province was in its infancy and the population untamed, Diez Madroñero found it useful for encouraging proper behavior in the colony. Bishop Mariano Martí followed his predecessor's guidelines during his long tenure from 1769 to 1792.[68] People from all backgrounds in the province, therefore, encountered pressures from both state and church to reform their traditional "loose behavior," especially during the second half of the century.[69]

Both bishops put the synod into practice during pastoral visits in which they persecuted those who did not conform to a Christian way of living. This oppression included white elites, who were implicated in some of the most scandalous stories. In 1765, for example, Diez Madroñero was in charge of an extensive expediente against don Juan Vicente Bolívar, the father of the great South American liberator.[70] Don Juan Vicente was accused of concubinage and of using his power as a teniente de justicia in the town of San Mateo to force single and married women to have sexual relations with him. Bishop Martí also dealt with such cases, but unlike his predecessor, he left a diary of the sins he encountered during his *visita*. The bishops' concern about the transgressions of white elite men is demonstrated by the prominence of this segment of the population in the diary.[71] The outcomes of these scandalous cases also reaffirmed the willingness of both secular and ecclesiastical institutions to gently reprove the behavior of elite padres de familia, who were supposed to be models of honor and virtuous behavior for the rest of the population. The most scandalous cases showed mantuanos contradicting the essential tenets of the honor/shame complex that defined Venezuelan society. Fearing the consequences that lost honor might entail for privileged men, the church ordered perpetual silence and the tightest secrecy.[72] The lower classes did not get such protection, for their transgressions were met with strong, public punishment.

In the context of this loss of power, the mantuanos fiercely defended their domination of government, especially in the new institutions. In 1759, for instance, cabildo members attempted to reestablish their prestige by wearing uniforms during meetings and public ceremonies, particularly when uniformed Spanish troops guarded the city.[73] Before long, however, other mantuanos also began wearing distinguishing uniforms. In 1762 some Caracas noblemen petitioned for the creation of the Company of Noble Adventurers as part of the Bourbon policy of creating armed colonial militias.[74] This company gave the rank and status of cavalry officer to many mantuano young men. Additionally, the crown raised money in the following decades by selling military titles to the richest *hacendado* families of Caracas, who thus monopolized not only noble titles but also the most visible symbols among the military.[75]

Mantuanos already dominated the spheres of alcaldes, the municipal council, and the church; yet they also wanted to dominate the military. To this end, they resisted the nomination of Spaniards to some positions. One key example was the conflict between cabildo members and don Sebastián de Miranda, the father of the Independence leader Francisco de Miranda. In 1769 don Sebastián was named captain of the Compañía de Fusileros del Batallón de Blancos, an appointment that the members of the cabildo rejected, calling him "a mulatto, a merchant, and unworthy" for the position. After the conflict forced him to retire, the cabildo went so far as to prohibit don Sebastián from wearing his military uniform. Without delay, don Sebastián responded by proving, with documents, both his and his wife's purity of blood. Thereupon King Charles III conferred on him a document of nobility, granting him the privilege of wearing the symbols of military status.[76]

Also in 1769 a number of Spanish residents of Caracas successfully petitioned the crown to make cabildo holders observe the law known as *alternativa*. This law, already in practice in the rest of Spanish America, allowed Spaniards equal opportunity to hold political and military power. The petition resulted in a 1770 Real Cédula mandating that creoles and Spaniards should have equal opportunity in the appointment of public positions.[77] In addition, four new cabildo positions were created. These new *regidores* for life could only be Spaniards.

In 1773 the creole aristocracy struck back, requesting that Europeans seeking any municipal position provide a certificate of legal whiteness. That is, the cabildo members defied the royal hierarchy by making peninsulars go through the same membership requirements that the crown mandated for creoles. In this way cabildo members applied their own version of the alternativa law to their male Spanish competitors. As a result the crown resolved in 1776 to withdraw the alternativa requirement as long as the person was white, honest, and of good reputation. In reality, the alternativa law did not reduce the mantuanos' political power because, as Venezuelan historian Alí López Bohórquez asserts, few Spaniards living in Venezuela sought government positions. Only ten Spaniards requested the application of such a law there during the time the requirement was in place.[78] Nonetheless, the alternativa permitted the governor, and later the High Court, to revoke annual elections based on the exclusion of Spaniards and the existence of kinship ties among cabildo members. In this way the alternativa gave the Spanish state another means of reducing the authority and autonomy of the local elite.

By this time the antagonism between creoles and Spaniards, whose authority in Caracas was more visible, had become more acute. Consensus did not necessarily unite the mantuanos, however. The royal political response to local autonomy was a mixed bag of concessions, "punishments," and withdrawal of privileges. The mantuanos' attitudes in favor of or against Spaniards depended on the extent to which particular events affected their own social, political, or economic situations. With Spanish troops in the city, a need for royal help in bringing more slaves to spur production, and increased participation in the monopoly company and its price-setting for cacao, many mantuanos were forced to collaborate with royal authorities to some extent.

By the 1760s members of the elite who had been the most active against the Guipuzcoana had already died, so the defense of mantuano privilege depended on a new generation. Some mantuanos already belonged to the military, and others were already conspiring against the monarchy. By 1774 secret meetings were being held at the home of one active mantuano, Martín Jerez de Aristeguieta. His father, Miguel de Aristeguieta, had secretly given monetary contributions to the Leon rebellion, but the authorities regarded him as a loyal citizen. His son pursued rebellious activities more openly and actively. Don Martín was also one of the minds behind the cabildo's 1773 request for documents certifying the pure blood and nobility of Spaniards requesting positions in the government.[79] Along with others in the new generation of creole elites, he became actively involved in the new institutions seeking to defend elite class privileges.

NEW INSTITUTIONS AND GROWING RESENTMENT, 1777–1811

The political and economic terrain of Caracas, which had been changing in significant ways, changed further as the years of independence approached. External trade played a central role in these transformations. Recent revisionist research has stressed the positive impact of imperial trade policy on the export economy of Venezuela, particularly in the province of Caracas.[80] As the crown lost the capacity to control illegal trade directly, it resorted to lifting trade restrictions on the colonies and permitting certain commercial relations with neutral and friendly countries. A 1777 imperial decree legalizing trade with the non-Hispanic Caribbean (mainly French and Dutch colonies) spurred economic growth in the province in ensuing decades. The new regulations maintained the Spanish monopoly on cacao through the Compañía de Caracas (formerly the Guipuzcoana Company) and kept restrictions on foreign imports, but they allowed the trading of other Venezuelan goods for slaves and hard currency. These new commercial opportunities increased further due to Spain's inability to supply its colonies during periods of war. As a compromise, the regime allowed open, unrestricted trade with neutral and friendly colonies and their European metropolises during 1780–84, 1797–99, 1800–1, and 1806–10.

These liberalizing measures further stimulated Venezuelan commerce, giving Caracas an advantage over other colonial domains because it could freely trade any goods – including some cacao – with outside markets. This foreign commercial network eventually encompassed the United States as well as British and Danish possessions in the Caribbean. The development of commercial links with foreign markets also contributed to agricultural diversification in the province between 1777 and 1810. These new outlets emerged at a moment when farmers were commercially developing such new crops as indigo and coffee, the two most important commodities after cacao.[81]

To promote diversification and meet the hacendados' need for a solution to labor shortages, the government purchased more than four thousand slaves between 1784 and 1787 and then sold them on credit to planters. Despite efforts to diversify the production base in the late colonial period, cacao still constituted the economic mainstay of the province, and as late as 1809 the export of indigo, coffee, tobacco, cotton, and livestock goods increasingly supplemented cacao export earnings.[82] This trade spurred ancillary activities in Caracas, which attracted a flow of internal and some external migration to the flourishing urban center. Rural people moved to cities, as did Spanish settlers.[83]

The Bourbon reforms brought other important benefits and institutions to Venezuela.[84] In 1776, a year before the regime introduced free trade, the Royal Intendancy (Intendencia de Ejército y Real Hacienda) was established in Caracas, giving economic and fiscal unity to the whole territory. This political unity emerged from the establishment of the Captaincy-General in 1777 that divided Venezuela into six provinces: Caracas, Maracaibo, Cumaná, Margarita, Trinidad, and Guayana. Except for Trinidad, which the British gained in 1797, the Captaincy-General comprised roughly the territory of present-day Venezuela.[85] Accompanying these administrative reforms, in 1785 the government eliminated the trade monopoly of the Compañía de Caracas. In 1786 a royal decree created Caracas's Real Audiencia, or high court of justice.[86]

The last major institution created by the Bourbons in Caracas was the Real Consulado (merchant guild) established in 1793. Years later the crown also introduced parallel measures into the Venezuelan church. In 1804 it elevated the See of Caracas to the rank of archbishopric, with jurisdiction over the bishoprics of Mérida and Guayana, which had formerly been subject to the archbishops of Santa Fé and Santo Domingo.[87] These key Bourbon administrative reforms transformed the political and economic landscape of Caracas.

One new institution is critical for understanding the growing resentments and conflicts among the creole and peninsular men in power: the Real Audiencia. It had jurisdiction over all the provinces in the Captaincy-General of Venezuela.[88] Previously, all legal disputes went by appeal from Venezuela to either the audiencia of Santo Domingo or that of Santa Fé de Bogotá in Colombia. As a court of law the audiencia had jurisdiction over both civil and criminal cases and served both as an appeals court for inferior tribunals in the territory under its jurisdiction and as a court of first instance within the city limits of its location.[89] The audiencia also operated as a tribunal of first instance in criminal cases in Caracas and heard cases involving royal officials and the royal treasury. In criminal cases, as opposed to civil actions, the audiencia had the final word; the litigants could not reappeal to the Council of the Indies.

Besides aiming to expedite the administration of justice, the crown's decision to create the audiencia rested on profound political considerations – namely, to further restore imperial authority. On the one hand, the town council was controlled by the caraqueño aristocracy, which had protested both policies pursued by the Compañía de Caracas and new royal measures, such as the introduction of the Intendancy and the tobacco monopoly. On the other hand, trade in contraband with foreign powers still concerned authorities, while tensions between creoles and peninsulars continued to grow. In creating the new court, Spain tried to exert more control over local politics and the province's prosperous economy.

The audiencia also played a critical role in fostering legal training and professionalizing legal practice. In 1788 it founded a lawyers' guild (Colegio de Abogados de Caracas), which regulated the legal profession, and in 1790 it founded a law school. For several years the audiencia regent, Dr. Antonio López de Quintana, directed the law school and held its chair of public law.[90] With the audiencia, the legal profession gained impetus and prestige in the colony; it eventually changed mantuanos' ideas of aristocratic masculinity. Admission to the university was open only to legitimately "pure white" men who could pay the high cost of an education.[91] According to P. Michael McKinley, late-colonial Caracas lawyers typically had modest means; they were neither poor nor very wealthy. Although a few came from mantuano backgrounds (ten of the sixty members of the Colegio in 1802), many came from families of modest hacendados or merchants from Caracas and other regions.[92] Hence the audiencia and the Colegio de Abogados provided an avenue for men outside the Caracas aristocracy to become lawyers and thereby to participate in the colony's administration. Moreover, modern, enlightened ideas had already influenced the University of Caracas, where many lawyers studied.[93] This influence may explain the progressive arguments that some lawyers used in court to defend lower-class women. With the proclamation of independence, the participation of those with legal administrative competence became critical in the new republic's organization. Thus the legal profession played a major role in redefining dominant ideas of aristocratic masculine honor by the early years of the nineteenth century.[94]

Historians have argued that the conflict between creole elites and peninsulars within the colonial bureaucracy in the late eighteenth century fueled the independence struggle in Spanish America.[95] Feeling discriminated against in the allotment of public offices, the creole elite decided to break free of colonial rule. The audiencias took center stage in this struggle, because throughout the 1700s, but especially after 1750, the crown systematically shunned creole appointees to the high court in Spanish America. The underlying reasons for this policy were varied, but they all hinged on the belief that creole dominance in the colonial administration endangered allegiance to the metropolis. The crown's aim to ensure impartial justice also was hindered when officials were bound to local interests.[96]

Created in the heady days of the Bourbon Reforms, the audiencia of Caracas was run by peninsulars or creoles born elsewhere. Neither purchase nor merit guaranteed the mantuano lawyers entry into the few coveted positions (as regent or judges) in the tribunal. The mantuanos worked in less prominent jobs as legal clerks, *conjueces* (temporary judges), temporary *fiscales*, or attorneys for litigants. López Bohórquez reports that between 1786 and 1810 the crown appointed eleven Spanish-born and five American-born *ministros* to the audiencia of Caracas.[97] One notable exception was Francisco Espejo, a Caraqueño lawyer who, in 1806, became the acting crown attorney (*fiscal*) in the absence of the fiscal in chief. After November 1808 he became an honorary fiscal.[98] During the whole colonial era, only seven Venezuelan lawyers were appointed to audiencia positions overseas.[99] Thus the crown discriminated against native lawyers in filling high positions in Venezuela and in the colonial administration generally.

Because most lawyers were natives, metropolitan authorities worried that their local ties might translate into influence that would compromise the enforcement of justice. Likewise, the Bourbon rulers believed that appointing locals to this influential office might embolden the mantuanos, who had persistently clashed with the colonial authorities throughout the 1700s. Hence lawyers excluded from the tribunal played a decisive role in forming an anti-Spanish ideology and proclaiming independence. Some lawyers occupied prominent positions in the short-lived First Republic (1811–12); one was Francisco Espejo, the former audiencia fiscal who became president of Venezuela in 1812.[100] Another lawyer, Francisco Antonio García de Quintana, a Spaniard who resided and owned land in Caracas, was never appointed to the audiencia, despite his repeated requests for a position. Having developed strong relationships with local peoples since his arrival in 1779, García de Quintana fully supported the mantuanos' anti-Spanish opinions as a member of the cabildo.[101]

In 1769 when cabildo members requested that the crown establish an Audiencia in Caracas, they believed it would help contain the governors' prejudices against them. Yet it had the opposite result. With the Real Audiencia, the cabildo members lost more autonomy, because their decisions had to be confirmed by the audiencia, which could even appeal against them. They also lost much of the local autonomy and prerogatives they had before the 1720s, which they legitimized as costumbre. The prerogatives of power that the mantuanos enjoyed and had justified in the absence of a higher Spanish institution since the sixteenth century became meaningless with an audiencia in the city.

For instance, an important aspect of mantuanos' display of honor was their participation in ceremonies, where they held the most distinctive, privileged seats. In 1787 members of the new Real Audiencia and those of the cabildo held a ceremony at the Catedral Church. The cabildo members annoyed the audiencia ministers by using the church's special tapestry-covered seats, although the law restricted them to plain benches. The municipal council responded that this was an "old tradition" and that custom allowed its continued practice. As a result, the seats were altered. The arm rests were removed, but not the tapestry. In this way the cabildo members differentiated themselves from other prominent citizens, thereby preserving honor and distinction. The audiencia had the satisfaction that the resulting cabildo benches were very different from their own. The cabildo's loss of privilege was significant; it demonstrated that the audiencia would not tolerate such "excesses" from the mantuanos.[102]

In 1793 the members of the municipal council protested that the tenientes de justicia mayor swore their oaths at the Real Audiencia, not at the cabildo. Again cabildo members claimed that right by costumbre. As the audiencia was now in Caracas, not in Santo Domingo, it and the governor insisted on observing the letter of the law in the *Recopilación*. With this ruling, the mantuano-dominated cabildo lost not only the ceremonial submission of the tenientes to their institution but also the fees that those functionaries had to pay for the ceremony.[103]

Gradually the Spanish audiencia ministers grew more intolerant of mantuanos' complaints and pretensions of being their equals. In 1795 the audiencia imposed a fine on cabildo members who dared to censure the high court's judgments. Although the cabildo appealed to the king, he did not reverse the audiencia's order.[104] In the same year cabildo locals complained about the election of an alcalde ordinario whose brother and cousin were also cabildo members. The conflict ended with rulings contrary to the mantuanos' interests. The municipal council members appealed to the governor to solve this internal matter. The governor passed the issue to the audiencia, which dictated that in the future cabildo candidates could not have close relatives in the same institution. Again cabildo members appealed to the king, but it was to no avail. With this ruling, the crown attempted to curtail the despotic behavior of the mantuanos. Yet, as López Bohórquez observes, the practice continued throughout the colonial period.[105]

Adhering to the pattern of policies followed since the early decades of the eighteenth century, the crown simultaneously punished and granted concessions to the mantuanos. Yet it did not publicly subvert their honor. In 1793 the crown created another major institution, the merchants guild (Real Consulado), which the local aristocracy controlled. By allowing local participation the crown intended to calm animosities between peninsulars and creoles over the control of new institutions. Mantuanos of the highest status, those of antigüedad who were also the wealthiest hacendados, became members and officials of the consulado.[106] Merchants were also part of the core of consulado functionaries. Most were new immigrants to the city, less wealthy and less interested than the mantuanos in dominating the main colonial institution.[107] Some of these merchants assimilated into local society through marriage; their children tended to belong to the landed class. Moreover, many owned haciendas themselves. Hence the merchants of the consulado did not compete with the mantuanos for power; rather, they tended to add themselves to the privileged landowning class.[108]

According to the consulado statutes, a prior, two consuls, and nine counselors governed the institution. The guild was both a mercantile court and a corporation in charge of administering and supporting agriculture and trade. Its main duty, however, was justice. This tribunal was expected to resolve commercial conflicts with efficient, specialized (yet lawyer-free) rulings that were oral, quick, and free. In this regard, the tribunal performed successfully.[109] It enjoyed autonomy from other colonial institutions because it was directly responsible to the king. To handle appeals, however, the king established the royal intendente and two merchants as the appellate court.[110] The audiencia's regent also acted as a judge of *competencia*, determining whether the consulado had jurisdiction over some lawsuits.

Still, the creation of the consulado led to new conflicts with the Spanish ministers of the audiencia. For example, mercantile lawsuits were now beyond the audiencia's jurisdiction, in the hands of a mantuano-dominated institution. Audiencia ministers criticized the competence of the consulado tribunal judges, who lacked legal preparation. There were also other jurisdictional problems, because some of the consulado judges' duties overlapped with those of the governors and the intendentes. The consulado intended to extend its power over commercial matters as much as possible. The king supported many of the audiencia ministers' complaints, mandating measures that would control the jurisdiction of the consulado.[111]

The consulado made significant gains, however. The vast majority of its high-level functionaries had no legal education, except for the conde del Toro, a consulado prior who had a law degree but did not practice the profession. Nonetheless they received the treatment of *Señoría*, a title given to those of high rank and distinction. In this way, the prior and the consuls of the consulado equated themselves with the audiencia ministers, who also received such titles.[112] Also, the consulado further trained the mantuanos, who were now in charge of promoting and administering what would become the national economy about two decades later.

McKinley emphasizes the important commercial achievements that the consulado made with the help of the imposing Caracas intendentes. When Spain was at war with Great Britain during the late eighteenth century, the intendentes repeatedly enacted measures to minimize harm to the region's economy. For example, in 1780 Intendente Abalos established a precedent by opening Venezuelan ports to trade with neutral countries and their colonies in wartime. At another time, when the prices for Venezuelan goods declined sharply the intendente agreed to the cabildo's petition to remove or postpone the export tariff duties to foreign colonies. This measure allowed planters to survive a difficult period, when Britain's war against Holland threatened an important Venezuelan market, Curaçao.

When a problem arose regarding the limited number of Spanish ships allowed to enter the province, Intendente Saavedra extended the agreement of free trade with neutral nations and their colonies that was granted only during wartime. In this way the intendente mitigated the negative effects of trade restrictions on the province. During these years of increased imperial control, the crown, through its local intendente, showed more concern for provincial needs. Between 1783 and 1796 a pattern of economic policies benefited the province's economy, which ensured the acceptance of the Caracas elites.[113]

Nonetheless, the mantuanos faced more than political and economic clashes with the increased presence of imperial authority. As we have seen, several issues affected mantuano men with regard to people of equal social standing, competitors of lower status, and their wives, children, and subordinates – all of which threatened their traditional bases of economic, political, and social power as well as their honor and autonomy. This process had begun early in the century, and by the end of the century mantuanos no longer enjoyed autonomy in many aspects of the colonial administration. Worst of all, in the 1790s challenges from below increased. Most problematic for the mantuanos, the king approved new policies that gave their vertical competitors special privileges.

The uproar caused by the 1795 Cédula de Gracias al Sacar makes sense only in the broader context of Spanish justice. From that perspective, one can elucidate why the Cédula sent tremors through the political landscape of the Caracas mantuanaje. A cédula de gracias al sacar was a diploma or certificate issued directly by the crown that granted an exception to a law.[114] The name given to these royal exemptions, "gracias al sacar," conveys the idea of suspending a rule – that is, of removing it (*sacar*) from the rigid corpus juris.[115] Introduced by the Bourbons in 1773, this instrument aimed at efficiently managing the numerous administrative orders (*cédulas*), pragmatics, exemptions, licenses, grants (*mercedes*), and pardons that the king frequently granted his subjects. The Spanish government thus tried to give cohesion to the wide array of concessions it had issued over the years by creating a distinct body of rules for skirting standard practice.

The paradox of the gracias al sacar is that it embodied, in perfect legal form, a law of exceptions from the law, as Santos Rodulfo Cortés has aptly observed.[116] In creating this instrument the crown formally institutionalized a procedure for circumventing the law that lay beyond the reach of the *cortes*, or parliament. Only the king and his advisory council had the authority to decide on these matters. To obtain this exemption, interested parties had to defend their cases before the sovereign, following a strict, often costly judicial procedure.[117] Applicants had to pay a standard monetary fee. Under the Bourbons, who were always eager to augment the royal coffers, the dispensation seemed to be a revenue-generating scheme, yet in practice it was not.[118] As a result, the mantuanos could not control membership in their class; their horizontal competitors could now decide who would acquire honor and privilege previously reserved for the mantuanos.

Four diplomas of dispensation were issued: in 1773, 1795, 1801, and 1838.[119] Only the second and third were ever implemented in Spanish America and, by extension, in Venezuela.[120] The 1795 document explicitly addressed such items as the sale of the distinctive title of don and of the certificate of whiteness for pardos and *quinterones* only. Commoners in Spain could not use the title don, while in Spanish America any white man – rich or poor, creole or peninsular – could be a don. Likewise, the explicit mention of pardos in the gracias al sacar clearly demonstrates the awareness of the different racial composition of the Spanish American population. The cédula provisions for pardos also suggested the political uses of color dispensations – namely, to mitigate discontent among well-off nonwhite subjects who felt discriminated against. This distinction becomes yet more evident when we realize that the 1795 dispensations targeted select groups in colonial society: whites, pardos, and quinterones, to the exclusion of mulattos, zambos, blacks, slaves, and Indians.[121]

The dispensation of the racial status of pardos was put to the test shortly after the passage of the cédula. Reeling from the massive slave rebellion in Coro in May 1795, an apprehensive Caracas cabildo asked the crown to stay the implementation of the specific clause on pardos in the gracias al sacar.[122] This request was based on an age-old tradition that granted colonial officials (from the viceroy to local judges) the discretionary power to delay or suspend the execution of royal decrees and orders that might be prejudicial, controversial, or inconvenient to local society.[123] In this case, cabildo officials implored the king to reconsider these concessions because of the dangers they posed for social peace in Venezuela, arguing that they "exempted blacks and mulattoes from their condition and rehabilitated them so that they could otherwise fill the public offices of the commonwealth that are properly reserved for whites."[124] The cabildo had previously succeeded in getting the 1789 Black Code (Código Negro) repealed and was confident that, given recent events, the metropolitan authorities would concede on this matter as well.[125] To their dismay, however, in 1796 the crown awarded the first certificate of whiteness under the new regulations to a pardo caraqueño doctor.

Diego Mejías Bejarano was one of only three pardos in the medical profession in late-eighteenth-century Caracas.[126] Licensed in 1779 at age thirty-two, Mejías Bejarano was the beneficiary of a 1777 royal cédula that granted nonwhite practitioners of folk medicine, known as *curanderos*, authorization to practice medicine because of the paucity of physicians in the city. Upon successfully passing an examination, the candidate was certified to practice medicine but could not perform surgery and had limited powers as a paramedic. Licensees were also required to provide free assistance to the poor and the destitute. Mejías Bejarano was recertified in 1790 by the *protomedicato*, the institution regulating the medical profession.

As an aspiring and successful middle-aged professional, Diego Mejías Bejarano petitioned for and obtained a royal order in 1793 that allowed his descendants admission to the clergy and marriage into white families. On 12 July 1796 the council issued the royal order on Mejías Bejarano's behalf, but the story of Diego Mejías Bejarano did not end there.[127]

The Caracas cabildo, determined to scrap the chapter on pardos in the cédula, swayed the local Spanish authorities, both the governor and the audiencia, which had reached a Real Acuerdo, to stay the implementation of the cédula until the king reviewed it. Aware of the machinations in the cabildo, Mejías Bejarano's lawyer successfully sought to have his client's dispensation ratified by the Council of the Indies on 22 September 1797. A technicality in the new decree, however, allowed the audiencia regent to stay again the execution of the dispensation until the king and his advisors thoroughly studied the whole affair. It was not until 1801 that Mejías Bejarano finally secured the coveted dispensation by a new royal ratification.

His tribulations did not end there, however. In 1803 the University of Caracas denied admission to his son Lorenzo Mejías Bejarano, who aspired to become a cleric. The elder Mejías Bejarano embarked again in petitioning and did not spare effort until he got a favorable ruling from the Spanish authorities in 1805. To his dismay, however, just a year later the Council of the Indies reversed itself, declaring that the dispensations awarded to Diego Mejías Bejarano were not extended to his children.[128]

The mantuano elite reacted with outrage to the attitudes of the ministers of the Real Audiencia toward mulattos and applicants of the cédula. Audiencia judge Francisco Ignacio Cortines was accused by the cabildo of protecting pardos and prompting the other judges to give nonwhites favorable sentences. He was also accused of being customarily accompanied by blacks and mulattos and instilling in them a desire to disrupt the social order. In addition, the mantuanos blamed Cortines for blocking their petitions for promotion while protecting mulattos. Audiencia judges Antonio López de Quintana, Nepomuceno Pedroza, and José Bernardo Asteguieta were also accused of bias in favor of blacks and mulattos. These were some of the most critical reasons why the aristocracy wanted to remove them from the audiencia.[129]

The cabildo officials were also deeply concerned that the dispensation of race might spur a wave of interracial unions.[130] A 1776 Royal Pragmatic that banned interracial marriages motivated an intransigent cabildo in 1788 to request the annulment of these unions as a means to discourage interracial marriages. The 1776 regulations on marriage sought to eliminate unequal marriages by requiring parents to authorize the formal unions of offspring under age twenty-five, although sons and daughters had the power to sue their parents in cases of parental opposition to a marriage. The mantuano reaction to the royal dispensations (and the pragmatic, as will be discussed in the next two chapters) suggests the qualms and trepidation of a group losing control over its political and economic prerogatives as well as its authority and autonomy to decide social and domestic matters.

It is clear that by 1795 Venezuela was experiencing irreversible change. Enlightened ideas that challenged the basis of the rigid corporatist hierarchy of the Spanish state – ideas that had been circulating secretly for some time – were already established in the province. This posed additional hurdles for the mantuanos' preservation of their privileged position. According to historian Elías Pino Iturrieta, many of the reformist ideas that engendered mobilization in the late eighteenth and early nineteenth centuries came subversively to Venezuela through foreign and Spanish commercial vessels.[131] The introduction of revolutionary propaganda became a concern for the Spanish state, as demonstrated in a series of laws passed after 1750 that increasingly punished those accused of participating in the spread of modern ideas and promoting popular mobilization.[132] Trinidad was an important focus for the spread of modern ideas (such as those of the French Revolution, the Haitian Revolution, and the U.S. Constitution), as the governor of Trinidad, Sir Thomas Picton, openly encouraged Venezuelans to resist the oppressive Spanish government. Large quantities of subversive propaganda arrived in Tierra Firme from Trinidad, so much so that there were accounts of a man from Cumaná who made bags for his general retail store from paper that was given to him in Trinidad and printed with Rousseau's *Social Contract* and other revolutionary texts. European travelers to Venezuela marveled at the knowledge some citizens had about international events and at the hidden libraries with copies of Raynal and Rousseau.[133] Spanish authorities repeatedly persecuted foreigners suspected of instigating revolutionary activity. Toward that end, even French ships were forbidden from entering some of Venezuela's main ports in 1792. Public parties, oral transmission of news from abroad, subversive propaganda, and informal schools organized in barber shops helped stir up "the opinion in favor of equality," nationalist sentiments, and an appreciation for individual liberties among the different classes, especially in the capital city.[134]

The political implications of enlightened ideas came to fruition in Venezuela by 1797. The authorities in the port city of La Guaira discovered a major conspiracy that sought to establish an independent nation. Since 1794 a retired captain of the Caracas veteran militias, Manuel Gual, and the teniente de justicia mayor of the town of Macuto, José María España, had planned a new republic inspired by the revolutionary ideas of the time. Gual and España were also closely assisted by Juan Bautista Picornell, one of the leaders of the San Blas conspiracy in Spain that sought to end the Spanish monarchy and establish a republic along French lines. Picornell and three other Spanish conspirators were exiled from the peninsula and temporarily jailed in La Guaira. It was there, through soldiers guarding the jail (who were themselves discontented with the Spanish regime), that Picornell came into contact with Gual and España. The three carefully organized the conspiracy and prepared a number of documents giving instructions and explaining the theoretical bases of the movement. Soon middle sectors including pardo artisans and militiamen became interested in the idea of creating a new democratic, independent, and egalitarian republic.

The first step was to organize the escape of Spanish conspirators from the jail at La Guaira, which was achieved through collaboration with the jail keeper. Two of the conspirators, Picornell and Manuel Cortés Campomanes, were able to escape to Curaçao and then to the French colony of Guadeloupe. From there, Picornell printed revolutionary propaganda such as a pamphlet titled "Derechos del hombre y del ciudadano, con varias máximas republicanas y un discurso preliminar dirigido a los americanos," which he sent clandestinely to Venezuela. The uprising was scheduled for 16 July, but the movement was discovered five days in advance. When the governor learned of the movement, the authorities forced the door at the house of Spanish merchant and conspirator Manuel Montesinos Rico and collected the revolutionary documents that the conspirators had been preparing. These included the ordinances of the movement, which listed the bases for a new government – reason, justice, and virtue. Slavery was to be completely abolished. The "natural equality of all inhabitants of the provinces and districts" was proclaimed as well as the idea that "the greatest harmony might reign among whites, Indians, pardos and morenos, who must see each other as brothers in Christ, equal under God, seeking to get ahead of each other only in matters of virtue and merit, which are the only two real and true distinctions between men, and will be the only differences from now on among individuals in our republic."[135]

One of the revolutionaries, Manuel Cortés Campomanes, composed revolutionary songs such as the *Carmañola Americana*, *Soneto Americano*, and *Canción Americana* to be used as propaganda for illiterates. Inspired by the French *Marseillaise*, the lyrics to these songs encouraged people to unite against tyranny and to claim their rights based on equality, liberty, justice, and law. In *Soneto Americano*, the main chorus reads:

Long live our People	Viva nuestro Pueblo.
Long live Equality	Viva la Igualdad.
Law, Justice	La Ley, la justicia
And Liberty	Y la libertad.[136]

The lyrics to *Canción Americana* addressed colonial plebeians:

We will all be equal	Seremos todos iguales
And there will be no distinctions	Y no habrá otras distinciones,
Beyond talent and virtue	Que el talento y virtud
And great deeds	Y las grandes acciones[137]

To distinguish those who were with the movement, a cockade of white, blue, yellow, and red – the four colors of the new flag – was to be worn in a hat. The colors represented the four main ethnic groups of Venezuela (whites, pardos, Indians, and Blacks), the four provinces of the new republic (Caracas, Maracaibo, Cumaná, and Guayana), and the four basic rights of men (equality, liberty, property, and security).[138] Such symbols were very appealing to Gual and España's heterogeneous rank and file, which included pardos, poor whites, lower-rank militiamen, merchants, and artisans.

The persecution of conspirators began immediately. More than one hundred suspects were listed, including lawyers such as Nicolás Ascanio and Luis Peraza.[139] Some of the accused were sent to Spain, while Gual, España, and Picornell escaped from Spanish authorities through the non-Hispanic Caribbean. España secretly returned to La Guaira and hid in his house for three months but eventually was discovered and executed publicly in the central square of Caracas. His wife was sentenced to eight years of seclusion for hiding her husband from the authorities. From Trinidad, Gual communicated by letter with the future independence leader Francisco de Miranda, who lived in London at the time. A Spanish spy purportedly poisoned Gual, who died on the British island in 1800. Picornell and Cortés survived and escaped from the authorities. Those who possessed copies of the "Derechos del hombre" were similarly persecuted.

In the days after the conspiracy was discovered, the mantuanos did not hesitate to offer their haciendas and their military services in order to assure "tranquility and respect for the public authorities." The governor accepted the mantuanos' offer and created two compañías de nobles to help maintain order in the capital city. A special mass organized by the mantuanos celebrated the failed revolution. By early August the mantuanaje reaffirmed their loyalty and commitment to the king in a letter signed by sixty-two members of the caraqueño nobility, including the marqués de Toro, the condes de Tovar and San Xavier, and different members of the Jerez Aristeguieta, Tovar, Blanco Uribe, Istúriz, Bolívar, Mixares, Herrera, Berroterán, Ponte, Blanco y Liendo, Palacios y Blanco, Blanco y Mixares, Toro, and Obelmexia families.[140] Although some of these same mantuanos would become involved in the independence movement by 1808, the Gual and España conspiracy clearly embraced an ideology that was too radical for them to support at that time. Mantuanos were still struggling against the Cédula de Gracias al Sacar, and they would not support a movement that proclaimed equality among the races and attacked the bases of their economic power, including slavery.

By the first decade of the nineteenth century the wealth of the aristocracy was declining. As older generations passed away, property was divided among a growing number of heirs. If by 1800 the wealthiest group of mantuanos had net assets of two hundred to three hundred thousand pesos, their children received in the best situation a little over a hundred thousand pesos, or more commonly less than fifty thousand pesos.[141] Hence the economic and political foundation of mantuano authority was in crisis by the turn of the century. Not all mantuanos analyzed the situation, however, or decided to take the same course of action to secure their position in the new century. According to some travelers' accounts, there were ideological differences among older and younger generations of mantuanos, cleavages that would become more pronounced with the crisis of royal legitimacy created by the Napoleonic invasion of Spain in 1808. The mantuanos, at this point, were struggling for equal treatment with Spaniards in the colony. Many among the mantuanaje did not struggle for independence because, in the words of Izard, they were "afraid of certain changes [promoted by the ideas of the French Revolution] that contradicted their class interests." In this sense, the mantuanos in ruling spheres lacked a definitive plan of action; they would make decisions as events evolved rather than lead the events themselves. Consequently the political and ideological alliances of mantuanos changed as the movement for independence progressed.[142]

Among the patriots of the First Republic (1810–12), there were two major groups. The first consisted of the older generation of mantuanos, those who were great landholders and slave owners. For these men, it was questionable whether order and property could be preserved without the arbitration of King Ferdinand VII. The second group consisted of many younger mantuanos who belonged to the Sociedad Patriótica organized around 1810. From the beginning, the sociedad was mainly attended by white men with patriotic ideals, yet after the Declaration of Independence in July 1811, pardos, mulattos, and blacks were admitted to the meetings, as well as a few women.[143] This more radical group was influenced by events of the U.S. revolution as well as certain Jacobin ideas. Although the radical component of the independence movement is debatable, it is clear that the sociedad played an important role in pushing for a Declaration of Independence in 1811 through one of its leaders and a member of Congress, Francisco de Miranda.

The 1808 event known as the Conjuración de los Mantuanos was not an act against Spain. Rather, it was a pronouncement against the representatives of the deposed King Ferdinand VII who had reunited in Seville with a French-influenced junta. For more conservative members of the creole aristocracy, both the central junta and the new French-backed government in the peninsula (with its revolutionary agenda of republicanism, equality, and liberty) were threats to the privileged position of mantuanos. Recent events in nearby Haiti were all too fresh in the mantuano memory, and they feared that a similar slave-backed revolution could happen in Venezuela. Uncertainty prevailed among the city's colonial authorities. The progress made by French troops in Spain, along with the lack of communication between Spanish authorities and the colonies, created a vacuum of power that those who supported full independence could use to their advantage.[144] The mantuanos feared that such anarchy in Caracas could lead to a revolt from below. This uncertainty was what the conjuración intended to resolve.

In November 1808 the mantuanos petitioned the governor to form a local junta supporting the deposed Spanish king. Forty-five men, most of them older mantuanos, high-ranking militamen, landowners, and merchants, signed the document. Yet lawyer José Miguel Sanz criticized the document, claiming that it was not "rational and fair to give six or eight persons unlimited authority" and that "the junta should be integrated by individuals of different professions, named by their own institutions." To Sanz, wider representation from different social sectors would secure greater public acceptance by taking away the appearance that a small group was usurping power.[145]

Although the young mantuano Simón Bolívar supported independence at this point, he declined to join the movement to form a junta. According to a mantuano named Martín Tovar Ponte, Bolívar told Tovar Ponte while in Curaçao that he would not join the movement because there was no assurance that the government that would replace the Spanish would be an aristocratic one. Tovar Ponte responded by reminding Bolívar that "the Venezuelan nobility was small and poor and, as such, could not rule the country."[146] On 19 April 1811 the mantuanos resolved to establish a government in the name of Ferdinand VII, presided over by the same governor and captain general of the province. Yet, in a cabildo abierto, Governor Emparán renounced any interest in assuming such a position, thus allowing the cabildo members to form their own government in the name of the deposed king, yet independent from the council regent established in Cádiz. In the confusion created by the actions of the governor and the attendants of the meeting, other notable individuals took advantage of the situation by adding themselves to the growing junta as representatives of the people (without in fact being designated by them). Some of these "intrusive representatives, [Juan Germán] Roscio, Félix Sosa, [José Cortés de] Madariaga, Francisco José Ribas take the lead, impart orders, arrest functionaries."[147] In this fashion the young men, reunited in the patriotic junta, achieved one of their objectives. Among the first orders was, not surprisingly, to dismiss the ministers of the Real Audiencia as well as other high Spanish functionaries from their employment. Still, the new authorities during the short-lived First Republic (1810–12) tried to avoid confrontation with peninsulars while keeping an eye on Spaniards suspected of treason.[148]

Understanding European events is critical to understanding how, fifteen months after the creation of the Junta Protectora de los Derechos de Fernando VII on 19 April 1810, independence was proclaimed on 5 July 1811. To the mantuanos and merchants, a Bonaparte monarchy was apparently being consolidated in the peninsula. In addition, the Regent Council in Cádiz adopted a series of improper measures, such as the prohibition of commerce between the Spanish colonies and neutral nations during the Napoleonic occupation and a draft constitution that was far too liberal for the mantuanos. Thus, as Izard argues and the Act of Independence supports, in July 1811 the Venezuelan Congress declared its independence from the monarchy of Joseph Bonaparte and the Regent Council in Cádiz that had imposed policies rolling back many of the political and commercial gains of the last two decades of the eighteenth century. That a full-fledged independence was not the dominant purpose of the act is clear; the word *republic* does not appear in the document.[149]

It would be the internal Venezuelan (not Spaniard) opposition to independence, led by caraqueños, that would eventually result in civil war. Participation in the power spheres would be mostly denied to mantuano competitors from other races and classes. Patriotic leaders – as well as the ruling elites who were undecided at this point – would support certain modern ideas, yet a bias against the lower classes still existed.[150] There was support for democracy at a theoretical level, yet the belief that other races and classes did not belong to the ruling spheres prevailed. Rather, the ruling elites believed that the lower classes were waiting for their paternal command. Parra Pérez explains it well: "The Congress of 1811 is an assembly of republicans, but they are white republicans who, noble and literate, make laws behind closed doors that benefit themselves, believing that it would be easy to replace Spaniards in Spain in the domination of the country. The Toros, the Tovares, and even others, regarded each other as equals; men like Roscio or Sanz, without heraldry of nobility but eminent in regards to character and knowledge, were highly respected in the Revolution; but none of these men deemed it possible to call upon the grocery man at the street corner, more or less pardo, to share in the governing of the country."[151]

In short, the elites did not accept "other equality but that of their equals."[152] Surrounded by pardos who were struggling for equality both individually and as a group and by the slaves who hoped for liberty, the creole aristocracy feared the large numbers of pardos, mulattos, and blacks who could rise up in revolt. The mantuanos did not confront the Spanish authorities in order to gain wholesale independence but rather because they perceived that anarchy created by the Napoleonic invasion of Spain might bring about changes that they were unwilling to accept.

Unquestionably some mantuanos played a salient role in the events after 1808. Yet some mantuanos accepted that the local aristocracy was weak and that they could not rule a country by themselves without the help of lettered men (mainly lawyers) and other individuals who were not natives of Caracas. In addition, no plan of action, much less a plan of nation-building, enjoyed a consensus among them.[153] The only tangible consensus at this time was the need to defend the rights of Ferdinand VII and the traditional monarchy. In this context, men who had experience in the colony's administration, including merchants and lawyers (most of them white), freely participated in the deliberations. The mantuanos became aware that they must have knowledge of the law if they wanted to secure their positions and property. The Congress in 1811, for instance, may have debated the content of the Act of Independence and the Constitution, but the tasks of writing and preparing the oaths were mostly put in the hands of lawyers.[154]

These new circumstances, along with the erosion of mantuano power as aristocratic patriarchs that had been occurring for almost a century, would contribute to a redefinition of dominant ideas of masculine honor. For the new republic, it would be military and administrative services that would make a man of virtue and worth, while the aristocratic ideas of antigüedad, purity of blood, and nobility would wane as dominant characteristics of masculine honor. Property and income would remain critical but would not be so strictly tied to one racial group. The Caracas of the new republic would not be one for the mantuanos but one for the landowners.[155]

2. Law and Its Operation

Elite men perceived the activity of the courts regarding women and slaves as an additional assault on their privileged position in Caracas society. A look at how the Spanish state intruded into mantuanos' private sphere adds understanding of another important dimension of the independence period and of another critical grievance that some men had against the Spanish state.

An examination of the laws regulating family and sexual matters demonstrates how the laws attempted to control women's sexual and domestic behavior. The conduct of men was not regulated, and men had legal power over women and children within their household. Still, looking at the observance and operation of law, one can discern how, in rendering decisions, judges frequently evoked the principle of *equidad*. By relying on equidad the courts (and, by implication, the Spanish judicial system) sought justice both for the good of the community and for the parties in dispute. This ideology, together with the image of a king who was fair to his subjects, mitigated the rigidity of formal law when it was applied to a given situation. Thus, while the letter of the law gave all power to men and placed stern controls on women, in practice, the law afforded women some protection and held men accountable for their actions.

Knowing how the law operated in the late colonial period is critical for understanding how it helped preserve the belief in a patriarchal justice system that was the embodiment of the monarchy. In theory, any person was entitled to receive attention from a representative of the righteous and fair king, irrespective of her or his social background or position in the hierarchical structure. Ultimately this policy had mixed results. On the one hand, by making the courts a legitimate place to resolve disputes with men, women further consolidated the role of the state as a protector of "unprotected people." On the other hand, men and household heads viewed the judicial system's public discussion of women's claims as a threat to their age-old legal prerogatives and honor in society.

Understanding how law operated in colonial Venezuela requires us to delve a little into the legal framework that was in force at the time. Unlike the clergy, the military, and members of established corporations, most civilians relied on the secular tribunals to solve their temporal disputes and on the ecclesiastical courts for spiritual and sacramental matters. Litigation in the courts of Caracas in the late eighteenth century unfolded in a society in which law determined a person's position and role according to race, gender, and the group into which the person was born.

Indians, for instance, were considered free vassals of the king. This condition was limited, however, by the fact that Indians were regarded as minors who required judicial protection and, therefore, a legal representative (*procurador general de indios* or *defensor de indios*). In places with high concentrations of indigenous populations, such as Mexico, special Indian courts were established.[1] Indians' position was different from the condition of slaves because, by law, slaves did not have juridical personality, so they could not take part in civil lawsuits.[2] There were a few caveats. In some cases slaves could and did appear as witnesses, could sue their owners in protest against excessive abuse, and could even litigate for their freedom.[3] In a few of the slave cases in the sample, bondsmen received free representation from a *síndico procurador*, a public attorney appointed by the court to provide legal representation to free indigent and enslaved people.

Likewise, gender impinged on people's legal condition. In principle a woman had no juridical personality unless she was single or widowed; if married, she was required to have her husband's permission for legal transactions. A woman could, however, go to court without a license to sue her husband in a civil or criminal court and to defend herself from a criminal lawsuit.[4] As with the poor, slaves, and Indians, the state also provided assistance to women who could prove they lacked the means to pay for legal costs. This was referred to in the documents as *pobres de solemnidad*. The data in this study show that few women used this resource to litigate in court, perhaps because of their lack of knowledge about the law. It is also possible that the provision was used more frequently but that the court did not make a record of it for every case.

Although the set of rights governing women's participation in the courts was limited, that did not stop them from using the state's institutions (see table 2). Women themselves brought most of the cases to court. The participation of women in the courts varied according to class, however. Specifically, lower-class women tended to undertake legal initiative more often than did elite women. Most of the cases that dealt with the upper classes

TABLE 2. Gender and Social Class of Complainants, 1786–1790

COMPLAINANT	UPPER CLASS (%)	LOWER CLASS (%)	TOTAL NUMBER OF CASES
Women	19.4	80.6	67
Men	32.2	67.7	62
Men and Women	75.0	25.0	4
Authorities[a]	—	100.0	7

[a] Percentage refers to the social class of the litigant, not the official who brought the case to the court.
Source: AAC, Matrimoniales, Judiciales, 1786–95; AANH, Civiles, 1786–91.

were brought to the court jointly by men and women, probably because most of those cases were requests for a marriage license, for which the bride's presence in court was required.

That most cases from the upper classes were brought by both men and women is related to the kind of cases that were brought to the court in the years 1786–90 (see table 3). Most of the cases in which the litigants were identified as upper class – as indicated by their position in mantuano circles, their properties, the number of slaves they owned, and their occupation – had to do with marriage and requests for certificates of *calidad* (prestige in terms of race and social class), which account for twenty-seven out of twenty-nine cases. In other words, these cases deal with issues that directly affected their upper-class status and reputation. Moreover, table 3 demonstrates not only that most of the cases (66 percent) had to do with the lower classes but that lawsuits brought by members of the lower classes involved a wider range of issues, from marital matters to abuse and sexual crimes.

Analyzing the participation of the litigants by type of court (see table 4) shows that the kind of court people used depended on the nature of their claims. For example, the cases in which the type of lawsuits overlapped involved matters that required actions from both secular and ecclesiastical judicial institutions. In the case of marriage licenses, the eight cases that were solved through the ecclesiastical courts had to do with couples that were related and, therefore, required a dispensation from the church. The marriage license requests that were resolved through the secular courts were related to the requirements of the Royal Pragmatic on Marriages, a matter that was mostly under the control of the state (see chap. 3). The cases of opposition to marriage are similar. The oppositions to marriage that were brought to the attention of the civil courts were related again to the Royal Pragmatic, while those that were solved through the church involved breach of promise, a matter that was the sole responsibility of the church. The only case of breach

TABLE 3. Type of Lawsuit by Social Class of Litigants, Caracas, 1786–1790

CLASS OF LITIGANTS AND TYPE OF LAWSUIT	%	% OF TOTAL
Both parties upper class		
Abuse	3.4	
Administration of women's property	10.3	
Breach of promise	6.9	
Certificate of "Calidad"	13.8	
Divorce	13.8	
Guardianship	3.4	
Marriage license	37.9	
Opposition to marriage	10.3	
	N=29	20.7
Upper class files against lower class		
Abuse	20.0	
Guardianship	20.0	
Slave claiming freedom	20.0	
Family support	20.0	
Unlawful clandestine marriage	20.0	
	N=5	3.6
Lower class files against upper class		
Abuse	7.1	
Bodily injury/incest	7.1	
Family support	7.1	
Slave claiming freedom	78.6	
	N=14	10.0
Both parties lower class		
Abuse	1.1	
Administration of women's property	1.1	
Adultery/concubinage	3.3	
Bodily injury/incest	1.1	
Breach of promise	13.2	
Certificate of "Calidad"	1.1	
Claims dealing with property	5.5	
Divorce	4.4	
Estupro	1.1	
Family support	3.3	
Guardianship	1.1	
Marriage license	39.6	
Opposition to marriage	11.0	

TABLE 3. (*cont.*)

CLASS OF LITIGANTS AND TYPE OF LAWSUIT	%	% OF TOTAL
Parental power	2.2	
Slave claiming freedom	9.9	
Unlawful clandestine marriage	2.2	
Total	*N*=91	65.7
		N=139

Source: AAC, Matrimoniales, Judiciales, 1786–95; AANH, Civiles, 1786–91.

TABLE 4. Type of Claim by Type of Court, Caracas, 1786–1790

TYPE OF CLAIM	ECCLESIASTICAL COURT	SECULAR COURT
Abuse	—	4
Administration of women's property	—	4
Bodily injury/incest	—	2
Breach of promise	13	2
Certificate of "Calidad"	—	5
Claims on property	—	5
Concubinage, adultery	3	—
Divorce	8	—
Family support	—	5
Guardianship	1	2
Marriage license	9	35
Opposition to marriage	2	13
Parental power	—	2
Slave claiming freedom	—	21
Unlawful clandestine marriage	3	—
Total	39	100

Source: AAC, Matrimoniales, Judiciales, 1786–95; AANH, Civiles, 1786–91.

of promise that was heard in the secular courts was a woman's petition to have her delinquent fiancé arrested because he wanted to run away from his commitment to her.

In looking at the social class of the litigants (see table 5) and the type of court used to resolve their disputes, one can see that a similar pattern exists for both kinds of courts. The major difference is in the category "poor versus rich." Most of these cases involved slaves requesting their liberty, an

TABLE 5. Social Class of Litigants by Type of Court, 1786–1790

SOCIAL CLASS OF LITIGANTS	ECCLESIASTICAL COURT (%)	SECULAR COURT (%)
Both parties upper class	22.5	20.0
Rich files against poor	2.5	4.0
Poor files against rich	—	14.0
Both parties lower class	75.0	62.0
Total	N=40	N=99

Source: AAC, Matrimoniales, Judiciales, 1786–95; AANH, Civiles, 1786–91.

issue that was the responsibility of the civil courts. The similar pattern of people's participation in both courts according to their class indicates that the type of complaint determined the court in which the person would appear. This does not mean, however, that people did not petition both courts seeking justice, especially if one failed to bring an acceptable solution to the problem. In some instances, this practice helped check the actions of both courts.

WOMEN, MEN, AND LAW

In colonial Spanish America, men were the representatives of the king and the state within the family. This idea is firmly asserted in the Spanish code, the *Siete Partidas*, which further established that the adult male (the padre de familia or family head) ruled his wife and children with the support of powers given to him by law.[5] Fathers had *patria potestas* (parental power), the right that family heads exercised over the person and property of family members. Under this principle, fathers and husbands enjoyed the fruits of their family property and imposed their will by legal authority and through physical punishment, if necessary.[6] In this hierarchy, a true woman was one who had the virtue of virginity and chastity; because she was thought of as fragile, ignorant, and weak, she required a guardian for her morality. These ideas, legitimized in law, justified patriarchal supervision to protect women's physical and material properties.[7]

Asunción Lavrin has asserted that church doctrine placed more constraints on the prerogatives of men and padres de familia than the state did, but this does not mean that the church did not support a hierarchy between the sexes and within society as a whole.[8] In the religious discourse of Saint Thomas Aquinas – whose work, incidentally, summarized thirteenth-century Christian thought (at the same time that the *Siete Partidas* were being drafted) and later became the official doctrine of the church in the nine-teenth century – family structure was also hierarchical.[9] The head of the household was the man, because he had the intellectual and physical capability to protect and govern the group and, therefore, the right to give orders. The church made clear that the father could give orders not in an arbitrary fashion but for the good of his wife and children. Family heads could use harsh words and even physical punishment, if necessary. Man's power over woman was justified because of woman's original sin: "The subordination of the woman to the male is justified by the order of the creation, since God created the woman for the male and not conversely. This subordination is also in the penalty of original sin and because of the weakness of the feminine sex. Man and woman are equal in what is essential of the human person, have parity in conjugal rights and duties, but the masculine sex has preeminence for its physical and intellectual qualities. From here the woman is subordinated to the male in what relates to the domestic life."[10]

Women had to be punished for the weaknesses of the first woman, Eve, and had to be closely supervised to avoid additional offenses to God.[11] During that time there was no promise of redemption for women, as there would be a century later. Notwithstanding these views, husbands and wives did have mutual obligations within the family. Women and children were subject to the power of the family head in a civil but not servile fashion. These restraints on a man's powers gave women and children more leverage in church legislation than in the law of secular institutions.

The same principles surfaced in the province of Caracas's Constituciones Sinodales of 1687. This canonical constitution was written for the purpose of organizing church administration in the province and for reforming the customs and excesses of the population. The synod followed a similar line of reasoning as that of Aquinas but added to it a class dimension. In his analysis of the Constituciones Sinodales, Venezuelan historian Elías Pino Iturrieta argues that the church supported a hierarchical vision of family relations.[12] Accordingly the synod held that the sons of God are unequal and should be treated that way. Priests were instructed to distinguish the padres de familia from the "promiscuous mass of people." Another disposition established the qualifications and duties of a padre de familia. He was a white member of the elite, who should serve as a role model to the flock and should chastise the conduct of the working poor in his service. Moreover, the synod held that the promiscuous masses were not capable of a civilized life because they lacked intelligence; also, because many were Indians and African slaves for whom Spanish was not their native language, they had difficulty communicating. As Pino Iturrieta has aptly argued, for the colonial church, Venezuelan society had to be "benignly unequal," especially at a time when sins seemed to mushroom. For these reasons, servitude to a padre de familia was necessary to guide and instruct these people in Christian mores. This method of Christian proselytization was deemed necessary for a church that, in the late sixteenth century, was not as economically and geographically powerful as in the core areas of Spanish America. Venezuela, it must be recalled, remained a fringe area until the middle of the eighteenth century.[13]

Venezuela's ecclesiastical authorities were not exceptional in supporting a hierarchical view of the sexes and of society. In other latitudes, specifically colonial Cuba, the church claimed to have an egalitarian view of society. For ecclesiastical authorities on the Caribbean island, individual morality was more important than issues of political expediency. Therefore, if a couple that was unequal in terms of race and/or class wanted to marry and if there were "reasons of conscience," such as the honor of a woman being impaired, that favored the union, the church had the moral duty to marry them, even against the policies of the state and the will of the bride's and groom's family heads.[14] For example, the church would often marry couples who had resorted to elopement in an attempt to circumvent parental opposition to their union. Yet the laws that prohibited interracial marriages with people of African descent promoted informal unions in the form of concubinage. It is telling that, even with a church that had an "egalitarian" vision of marriage, very few interracial marriages took place, at least in parishes in or near Havana in the nineteenth century.[15]

A similar situation was found in São Paulo, Brazil, where the church, while promoting marriage, supported the idea that formal unions had to be endogamous, thus creating a space in which unequal relationships in the form of concubinage took place.[16] Studies on colonial Caracas are wanting, but a cursory survey of Bishop Mariano Martí's diary, in which he reported his opinion on more than eight hundred cases of concubinage, adultery, breach of promise, and other offenses, indicates that late colonial Venezuela resembles the situation in Brazil and Cuba.[17] Bishop Martí's own policy was to separate couples living in concubinage, especially if the parties were socially unequal, unless the couple was living in a stable relationship and had children already. Thus in a certain sense we can surmise that in Venezuela church doctrine supported the legal powers of the padre de familia and the hierarchical order of society, an idea that suited the prevailing social and political order created by the Spanish state.[18]

Although women had more leverage in the church than in civil or criminal tribunals, this did not mean that the church did not support a patriarchal and hierarchical vision of society. This is particularly clear when comparing ecclesiastical policies with those of the state in domestic and sexual matters.

The powers of the padres de familia in secular and ecclesiastical legislation and the deep-rooted idea that women's mental capacity was inferior to men's served various purposes in the context of the law. An obvious consideration was protecting women, particularly their economic condition.[19] Although Spanish law assured wives' and daughters' rights to inheritance, husbands administered their wives' property and were entitled to receive half of the income arising from it.[20] Husbands and fathers were granted the right to look after the best interests of their family and property because men were believed to be wiser and more intellectually capable than women.[21] It was implicitly believed that women were easily deceived, weak, and ignorant of the content of the law. Women's alleged lack of mental capacity was contradicted in various ways in law, as we will see.

Another reason the law insisted on women's weak morality was the value placed on chastity. The purpose of guarding female sexuality was to prevent women from giving birth to unwanted heirs, who could not only affect the family's public image but could also eventually lay claim to the family's wealth. Also, guarding female sexuality served to preserve endogamy as a way of maintaining the corporatist social order. For these reasons the legal rights of women depended on their marital status, their sexual behavior, and their reputation in the community. Often it was necessary to ascertain whether the woman in question was decent and virtuous or a *callejera*, as prostitutes and women of very low esteem were known in Caracas, to know how the law would be applied.[22] Thus an important element in any case was to convince a judge of the woman's virtuous character. The classification of female sexual behavior was especially harsh for the many poor women who had to work outside the home and who often were not under the surveillance of a man. Women who worked in the streets were likely to have their honesty instantly questioned in the courts.

Comparing women's legal situation with that of men in the late colonial period in light of the *Siete Partidas* shows that men were less constrained by the state, at least in domestic and sexual matters. Moreover, comparing provisions regarding men and women in church doctrine and in the Partidas demonstrates that the ecclesiastical institution demanded more responsibilities from men than did the state, notwithstanding the hierarchical vision of society that both shared.

For most sexual offenses, both the state and the church perceived women as the ones who provoked violent behavior in men.[23] For instance, adultery was a gender-specific offense because it was defined in civil law as an action carried out by a married woman with a man and not the other way around.[24] The law held women responsible for adultery. Thus a wife could not accuse her husband of adultery, even though ecclesiastical and secular court archives are replete with cases of men who engaged in sexual liaisons with women other than their wives.[25] A husband, on the contrary, not only could file a complaint of adultery against his wife but, if he found the lovers *in flagrante delicto*, he could kill them. It seems this custom had declined by the eighteenth century. Instead the adulterous man was sent into exile, and the married woman lost her dowry and was confined.[26]

Canon law saw adultery differently. For canonists either member of a married couple could be accused of adultery on the grounds that in both instances their conjugal fidelity was at stake.[27] Juridical divisions of secular and sacramental matters between the church and the state compromised the laws. The Sínodo Diocesano de Caracas of 1687 conceived of adultery as cases of a "mixed" civil and ecclesiastical nature because the secular institutions were in charge of administering the punishment.[28] This could create conflict between the institutions because if a man was found guilty of adultery in the ecclesiastical courts, according to the *Siete Partidas* the case was not one of adultery but of concubinage, which carried a different sentence for men: the confiscation of half of their properties. Given the disparity of civil and ecclesiastical penalties, there was room for juridical maneuver for men accused of sexual crimes.

Moreover, regarding the man, even if he was married, he could be accused of adultery in secular law only if he *knew* that his relations were with a married woman. If his accomplice was single, a married man would be accused of concubinage. In such an event he might lose half of his wealth, but this did not happen very often, at least in Venezuela, where the female lover was usually exiled to a distant locality.[29] If both male and female were single, there was no punishment because neither the *Siete Partidas* nor the *Recopilación* prohibited concubinage, as cohabitation of two single people was defined.[30] It was different for the church, however, because people who lived together without marrying were disrespectful of religion and the ecclesiastical jurisdiction in sacramental matters, so they were committing an offense against God.[31] According to the Synod of Caracas, if the concubinage was public and scandalous and if the parties persisted after being admonished, then the man would be excommunicated until he ended the relationship. Thus the letter of the law allowed the possibility of living in concubinage as long as it was concealed. The woman's punishment varied according to her social condition: if she belonged to the "ordinary peoples," she was sent into exile, but if she had some "quality," she was confined to avoid additional scandals to society.[32]

If a man was found guilty of the charge of *estupro* (defined as the deflowering of a virgin woman or a chaste widow by deceit or seduction), the defendant could have half of his wealth confiscated, be publicly lashed, or be exiled for five years.[33] In many cases, however, men were never found guilty because of lack of evidence.[34] According to both the church and the state, if the woman was not virtuous, the crime would become simple fornication, which carried no major punishment. Therefore, the official and ecclesiastical stance on female virtue minimized the implications of this sexual offense for non-virtuous women – men could abuse them because they had no honor to defend.[35] Cases of estupro were a criminal offense under the jurisdiction of the secular courts.

Often cases of estupro involved situations of breach of promise, because promises of marriage by men were a common way of deceiving women. Patricia Seed has traced how the penalties for men accused of breach of promise in Mexico changed from imprisonment and exile to the Philippines to the payment of financial compensation for the women's loss of virginity. This change in the punishment for estupro reduced men's responsibilities for their actions because they could more easily break their promises of marriage.[36]

In cases of abduction the punishment was decided according to the circumstances and rank of the people involved. This crime involved the taking away of a woman by force (*rapto*). Sentences ranged from death to property seizure. If the woman was not a virgin, a virtuous widow, or a married woman, then the sentence would be lenient and based on the judge's criteria, not on the letter of the law. This was also true if the man was accused of seducing a woman.[37] The sexual demeanor of the woman could save the aggressor, because he would not be subject to punishment if the victim was not virtuous. According to law, a woman socially labeled as "public" or callejera was a social cancer that had to be extirpated, because such a woman could always seduce a family head or son. One might expect that if a woman was labeled as callejera she would have virtually no claim against the aggressor and he would usually be set free.

For the church, the heart of the matter in a violent abduction was not so much the sexual behavior of the woman involved as that a man who took a woman by force violated the woman's free will to agree or disagree to marriage, a crucial component of a valid marriage according to the Council of Trent.[38] If the abductor set the woman free, then they could get married, if she wanted to, or he could be ordered to pay her a dowry.

In terms of offenses in the domestic sphere committed by fathers, the powers of the padres de familia were hard to challenge. Only fathers could exercise the right of parental power, and they lost this right only when they died, were exiled or imprisoned after committing a crime, or legally emancipated the child.[39] If a father cruelly punished his children and wife, the children could take him to court to gain their legal emancipation and the wife could sue him for a temporary separation of bed and board. In reality such cases were very hard to prove because no guidelines existed as to what constituted extreme physical punishment and, because most of these incidents occurred in the privacy of the home, it was quite difficult for the aggrieved to marshal reliable evidence.[40]

In secular law men had full power in the family and in the community, and their sexual conduct was not under scrutiny. The prevailing thought was that a man's promiscuity was not to be penalized as a woman's was because men did not bring – in their bodies – extraneous children to the family.[41] As Ann Twinam argues, "biological differences established divergent patterns for sexuality and for procreation, as well as distinctive cultural norms for the masculine and feminine expressions of honor." That men's "virginity" could not be proved, that they did not have to carry a baby in their bodies, and that their paternity could not be absolutely certain allowed the formation of a "biological double standard that underlies patriarchal cultural codes."[42] This may explain why the sexual conduct of married women and even young daughters was so closely controlled by law. Men need not be responsible for the children they brought into the world, because the law established that paternity could be demonstrated only by the father's recognition or by proving that he lived in concubinage with the mother of the child.[43] The popular Venezuelan saying is meaningful in this context: "the son of my daughter my grandson is, the son of my son, I do not know whether he truly is [my grandson]." Yet those who did acknowledge their natural children were obliged by law to provide support, and their children earned inheritance rights as well.

Although men could leave many unattended children in the world, the law sought to prevent women from bringing unwanted children to the family. It is a paradox that in a legal framework in which women were thought of as fragile and weak, they were held accountable for controlling the sexual passions of men, who were considered more prudent, intelligent, and physically capable than their female counterparts. It was hard for a woman, at least in the context of the law, to hold a man accountable for his actions in the family because secular laws, especially, did not control men the same way they did women. Men had the biological and legal liberty to corrupt and abuse women without having their public reputation affected; men's honor was less affected by their sexual liaisons than was the honor of their female lovers and illegitimate children. In her groundbreaking book *Marriage, Class, and Colour in Nineteenth-Century Cuba*, Verena Martínez-Alier argues that this dual male behavior was structurally necessary and served to enhance the value of virginity.[44] I share her view that virginity took on added importance as a virtue in a society where the possibility of losing female honor was extremely high. This seems to have been the case in late colonial Caracas if we rely on the first-hand account of a lower-class plaintiff who stated that protecting her virtue was "precisely the merit of a woman who preserves herself amidst the fire and the enemies who constantly besiege her."[45]

Under Spanish secular law women occupied a key social position because of their reproductive capacity and their right to inherit property equally with men. Therefore, their sexuality had to be controlled in order to maintain inheritance customs and class structure.[46] Women were thus, by law, under the constant tutelage of men – even if men were not equally virtuous. This was of utmost importance for the corporatist structure of Spanish society, because a woman's obedience and submission to the "protective powers" of the husband were necessary for the maintenance of the social order. The marital society would not continue if one were not subordinate to the other, just as there would not be order if the padre de familia and his family were not subordinate to the king.

Finally, the laws that governed gender relations in the colonial period reflected the values and rhetoric of the men who produced them. The legislation silenced women in many ways by constructing absolute moral oppositions between the padres de familia and their conception of a homogenized weak female sex that had to be feared and/or punished. In doing so the laws confirmed men's superiority over, distance from, and opposition with those whose behavior had to be supervised.[47]

LAW, ITS APPLICATION, AND THE PRINCIPLE OF EQUIDAD

As stated above, formal law controlled women more than it did men and did not grant women much protection from the abuses of the padres de familia. If the letter of the law made it so difficult for women to find justice in the colonial courts, why did so many still resort to them?

I believe that women in Caracas took men to court when they found no other source of authority to which men could be held accountable. In a number of court cases, female plaintiffs made reference to their use of the courts in lieu of their absent or dead fathers or husbands. In his study of colonial Caracas Robert Ferry found that no married woman whose husband was alive would be allowed to represent herself as an individual. Similar patterns are revealed in contemporary studies on litigation in other Latin American contexts.[48] When they lacked a strong recognized base of authority such as senior family men, people tended to see the courts as a substitute for the absent father or husband in conflict resolution.[49]

A similar situation may have existed in Caracas, especially if we consider that many women were not under the "protection" of a padre de familia. According to Kathy Waldron, in 1792 women headed 37 percent of the households of Caracas, a percentage as high as in other parts of Latin America during the same period.[50] These findings contradict the long-standing myth of the extended Latin American family and show the leading role of women, often single, in the administration of the household. Women also outnumbered men in Caracas (sixty-five men per one hundred women in 1796), while mortality rates indicate that many adults' parents and elder relatives were no longer living.[51] Indeed, in thirty-two of the forty-three cases in the sample that dealt with marriage licenses, one or both of the parties did not have parents or relatives to give their consent, due to either death or geographic separation.

Moreover, most cases were brought to the courts by women themselves (48 percent); only in a few cases (3 percent) did women go to court accompanied by a man. The lawsuits filed by these women suggest that most of them were litigating against their husbands (for divorce or administration of property) or their lovers (breach of promise) and/or their families (oppositions to marriage). Because the padres de familia were the legal figures of authority within the households and would represent their members when solving conflicts through the state institutions, it is striking to find that only a few women had male representation. This evidence points to the fact that these women were acting quite independently and that they were probably suing the closest male figure in their lives.

In addition, some degree of confidence in the justice system is apparent among these caraqueño women in their attempts to solve their conflicts through the courts and not by extralegal means. A careful look at the judicial process as it played out in Caracas presents a different picture from that established in formal law. At least in the late eighteenth century, the courts tended to embrace a concept of justice attentive to what was best for the common good.[52]

This principle is known as equidad. Briefly defined, equidad conveys fairness based on moral considerations.[53] A judge, for example, could pay more attention to his sense of duty or of conscience than to the letter of the law itself in order to render a fair decision. It was understood that there could be instances in which a rigorous application of the law would be contrary to justice.[54]

This idea of justice embedded in the Spanish concept of equidad, together with the view of a king who was both the giver of laws and the utmost guardian of justice, mitigated the rigidity of formal law when it was applied to a given situation. Thus although the letter of the law gave all the power to men and placed stern controls on women, in practice the law afforded women some protection and held men accountable for their actions.

Both the church and the state relied on the principle of equidad in the late eighteenth century. A glance at the rulings on central gender issues and on crucial matters of the time provides a good idea of how the Spanish justice system balanced its understanding of fairness in gender conflicts with the imperative duty of maintaining the patriarchal and hierarchical order.

PATRIA POTESTAS AND MEN'S POWER OVER WOMEN

Under the Partidas married women had to be faithful and obedient to their husbands to avoid bringing extraneous children into the family.[55] Women were also required to be submissive because such subordination was thought of as a necessity for conjugal life. Accordingly women had to follow their husbands wherever they established residence. Living together was required in the Partidas because a key element of marriage is procreation.[56] Thus a husband could oblige his wife to stay at his residence by withdrawing his support (alimentos) and the economic benefits of the marriage.[57] This reasoning may explain why the Partidas established men as the administrators of their wives' property as well as the sole holders of parental power over their children. Women could only become guardians (tutores) of their children and grandchildren, meaning that they would be primarily in charge of educating and raising the children, not administering the children's property.[58] A slight improvement appeared with the passage of the Cédula de Gracias al Sacar in 1795. Under its provisions any woman of means could buy a legal dispensation to become the guardian in charge of both the person and the administration of the properties (tutela y curatela) of the children.[59] These dispensations were offered only if the woman was widowed and under twenty-five years of age or if she was married a second time. The certificate was one of the most expensive dispensations granted by the king.[60]

I found four lawsuits in which women accused men of dissipating their property and the marital property as well. In one case a man purposely failed to provide support in order to punish his wife. These cases were always filed by women, usually wealthy women. Of the four claims, three were submitted by wealthy women and one was submitted by a lower-class woman. Despite the provisions of the law, the courts supported the wives' claims in all three cases in which an opinion resulted.

In one of the claims a woman petitioned the civil authorities to prevent her husband from selling or abusing her slaves, and the court ruled in her favor.[61] The other two claims in which a ruling was issued were brought by a powerful and wealthy mantuana, doña Josefa Lovera, who was married to her equal and relative, don Martín Jerez de Aristeguieta.[62] (His active participation in secret meetings and late colonial institutions was discussed in chap. 1.)

This couple's divorce case stirred much controversy at the time. The two scions of the mantuanaje married in 1763 and two decades later, in 1782, entered a bitter struggle for divorce. It was don Martín who requested from the church a perpetual divorce, accusing his wife of leading the adulterous, raucous, and scandalous life of a woman of low esteem. This included giving birth to three children by another man and escaping from their home during the night, dressed as a man, and going to parties with people of "inferior class."[63]

As a result of the divorce lawsuit, doña Josefa's *bienes parafernales* (the wealth she brought to the marriage that was not part of her dowry, which, according to the law, she could manage) were seized by order of the ecclesiastical judge, who allegedly refused to force don Martín to provide regularly for his wife's support.[64] According to doña Josefa, not only had her husband publicly admitted to having married her for her fortune – which included a splendid dowry of twenty-five thousand pesos and an annual rent of thirty thousand pesos – but he was also interested in the properties she inherited from her mother, which included a large cacao hacienda in Taguaza.[65] By order of the ecclesiastical judge (*juez provisor* and *vicario general del obispado*) Vicente Pérez, the properties were confiscated and placed under the custody of a third party, who happened to be the judge's cousin and a best friend of don Martín, the husband.[66]

The agreement was that the judge's cousin would give don Martín the earnings from the hacienda and would give doña Josefa a small quantity of money for her living expenses. But doña Josefa never received such money regularly. She accused her husband of "acting like a judge usurping public authority" for having confined her in the Hospicio de la Caridad to avoid scandals that would further affect his public reputation. After complaining to the Real Audiencia, however, she was immediately placed in the house of one of her relatives.[67]

It is revealing that the high courts, both the Audiencia in Santo Domingo and the one established in Caracas in 1787 (controlled by Spaniards), were very responsive to doña Josefa's plight, while the local ecclesiastical court – which was incidentally dominated by creoles – was more favorable to don Martín. Additionally, the lawyers who represented the mantuano husband, such as don Pedro Domingo Gil, often opposed the power of the Spaniards during the late eighteenth century. The lawyer who defended doña Josefa, Dr. Gabriel Josef Aramburu, was a supporter of the cases of pardos who applied for a gracias al sacar diploma.[68] Thus the couple's lawyers had opposite political inclinations, and their interpretation of this gender conflict followed accordingly. Those who defended doña Josefa were pro-Spanish and/or highly enlightened men, favored the gracias al sacar, and sought to protect women from men's abuses. Of course, doña Josefa's lawyers may have seen this as an opportunity to reprimand a key member of the mantuanaje. Don Martín's lawyers unconditionally defended men's physical and material power over women. In addition, don Martín tried to take justice in his own hands to avoid any further stain on his public reputation.

Even without liberty and money, doña Josefa continued fighting until she obtained various royal administrative orders to correct what had been a clear abuse of power. In 1786 she appealed to the civil courts – which she referred to as the "padre general de la provincia" (father of the province) – demanding justice and protection.[69] She demanded from the civil court an explanation of the reasons that led the ecclesiastical judge to disavow the same measures that the civil court had taken in a previous divorce case heard in 1785. In this case against Juan Josef Castro, a surgeon and resident of Caracas, the king issued a cédula ordering his release from jail and the return of his property, but only after having him sign a *caución juratoria*.[70] The ecclesiastical judge who obeyed this royal order would not yield in the case of doña Josefa. For this reason, she appealed for justice to the highest civil court in Venezuela.

The governor and captain general, don Juan Guillelmi, troubled by the way the case was handled, intervened on doña Josefa's behalf to get "equitable protection" from the tribunals, a solution of "equidad and compassion."[71] The juez provisor quickly replied to the governor's orders to follow the guidelines of the 1785 royal order. For him, the provisions in the cédula were not applicable because the two situations were totally different. Although both Juan Josef Castro and doña Josefa Lovera were adulterers, her actions were more serious because of her condition as a woman. Moreover, according to the ecclesiastical judge, the royal order about Juan Josef did not mean much because the husband was always the legitimate administrator of his wife's properties. Even further, when there was a divorce because of adultery, the husband had more reason to keep those goods, at least until the final divorce verdict was read. Doña Josefa's dowry, the judge cautioned, could also be lost to her husband if the adultery were proven. The ecclesiastical judge preferred to wait until a final determination was made by the Real Audiencia in Santo Domingo, where doña Josefa was already appealing the confiscation of her properties. Doña Josefa had to rely on the Audiencia in Santo Domingo because at that time (1786) the Audiencia of Caracas was not yet functioning.

Doña Josefa did not get a response from Santo Domingo immediately, but she received something even more powerful: a Real Cédula signed on 25 October 1786 in which the king ordered as follows: "There being no other cause for Doña Josefa Lovera's prison, she must be released from jail; she must have, under a caución juratoria, the attachment of her belongings abated, and be assured of the reliefs compatible with a good administration of Justice, limiting the procedure to the civil divorce cause, which must be executed according to law and a judgment made which will not lead to well-justified complaints, so that I order that a watchful eye be kept on the procedure so as not to permit any irregularities or actions against the Law that may harm my subjects, using the protection that you should impart in my name. . . . I The King."[72]

Faced with this forceful royal order, the ecclesiastical judge had to obey. Doña Josefa was released. Her hacienda was returned, but only after another long and arduous process, because her husband was determined to make her life miserable. Yet another royal administrative order arrived, one that reminded the church judges that they could not intrude in the temporal aspects of divorce lawsuits.[73] All the issues of properties, support, *litis expensas* (legal costs), dowry, and so on were the sole responsibility of the secular courts. As discussed in chapter 1, in the late eighteenth century the crown had to continually remind creoles of their proper place and the extent of their jurisdiction.

Doña Josefa's case might be extraordinary in the sense that her immediate family and social circle dominated the leading institutions in the province of Caracas. Notwithstanding the couple's social ascendancy, it is telling that the civil authorities and the king were concerned with providing a fair trial even when she was accused of adultery. The king considered in his cédula of 25 October 1786 the facts that don Martín had abused doña Josefa and treated her cruelly, that he regularly had *torpe comercio* (obscene, lasciv-ious communication) with female blacks and mulattas – including doña Josefa's own female slaves – and, finally, that don Martín had married her because of her dowry.[74] The case also brings to the fore a problem of juris-diction between the church and the state and is an example of a case in which the ecclesiastical judge openly supported a very hierarchical and pa-triarchal vision of gender relations.

Yet the idea of fairness was repeated in other situations. In colonial times the law determined that in child custody cases, children had to be kept by the innocent party in a divorce case.[75] Children under age three were to re-main with the mother, however. At the age of three they passed to the father if he was not the cause for separation. The final outcome of doña María del Rosario Burgos's lawsuit for support and litis expensas varied from the letter of the law.[76] She was married to a poor white artisan named don Antonio Aular. Doña María won a temporary separation of bed and board in the church court due to the frequent abuse she received from her husband. The ecclesiastical judge ruled in the mother's favor, allowing her to keep the four children under her custody, while the father had to provide support for them.

Don Antonio argued that this ruling ran against his power of patria potestas and offended his status as a padre de familia.[77] In doña María's civil lawsuit for support, however, the Real Audiencia ordered that don Antonio keep the three sons while she cared for the sixteen-year-old daughter. More-over, he had to provide support regularly. To make sure that she got her money on time, the court ordered that doña Maria's alimony would come from the rent paid by a tenant of don Antonio's. The judge would also moni-tor the education of the daughter, now under the guidance of the mother. Even though don Antonio was found guilty of abusing his wife, he kept three of the four children while his wife kept the daughter and got regular alimony payments, a luxury at the time. As can be seen, the final verdict in this case did not reflect what was established in the law. The court put into practice the principle of equidad by satisfying in some way the claims of ev-ery party and by maintaining the figure of authority in the padre de familia.

MARRIAGE

Marriage issues became prolific in the courts during the late colonial pe-riod. That is because marriage was one aspect of family life that came under direct state regulation in the late eighteenth century, in spite of its status as a sacrament administered by the church. The *Siete Partidas* had established that a valid marriage must meet four basic requirements: (1) The couple must have reached puberty, that is, the girl must be at least twelve and the boy fourteen; (2) the couple must freely consent to the union; (3) there must be no impediment that demanded the annulment of the marriage (i.e., a marriage between brother and sister); and (4) a priest and two witnesses must be present at the marriage ceremony.[78] The law also established that parents or a lawful representative must give children a license and that banns must be published in the church to make certain that there were no impediments to the marriage. These two requirements could be waived through the payment of a fee, and the failure to meet them did not invalidate a marriage.[79]

In 1776 the crown issued a law on marriages aimed at reinforcing the perceived loss of power of the padres de familia over their children's marriage choices. In Spanish America the law came into effect two years later, in 1778. One of the main stipulations of the law was that women under age twenty-three and men younger than twenty-five had to request permission from their fathers to make a promise of marriage or to contract marriage. If their father was dead, they had to seek the permission of their mother or closest elder relative. Moreover, it requested that no claims for breach of promise be admitted into the church courts if they did not include the license from the parents of the bride and groom.

This law was to be observed by all social sectors, yet in Spanish America the king specified to whom it would apply due to miscegenation. Because it would be difficult for some subjects (e.g., slaves) to have the permission of their parents, the crown established that the pragmatic would not apply to blacks and people of black ancestry with the exception of those who worked in the military. The decree did encourage all subjects, however, to request permission of their parents or elders when getting married. Sons or daughters who did not comply with this requirement could lose some rights, including the right to inheritance.[80]

Drafters of the pragmatic were fully aware that Europeans, including Spaniards who were passing through or living temporarily in the colonies, would have difficulty requesting such licenses. People in such circumstances, whether native or foreign, as well those with no living relatives, had to request a license from the district judge or, in the case of Caracas, from the audiencia. This is the reason why a third of the claims (34 percent) in the late colonial sample had to do with marriage licenses.

Most of these cases (thirty-five out of forty-three) were heard in the Real Audiencia of Caracas or that of Santo Domingo. Of these civil cases, thirteen were license requests necessary because the groom's parents lived overseas and sixteen occurred because the bride, the groom, or both were orphans and had no one who could provide a license. The remaining seven cases were varied, including pardos requesting marital licenses (five cases) and other special requests.[81] These cases were usually brief, and the marriage license was usually approved after at least one family member agreed to the union.[82] All twenty-nine petitions for which decisions were reached in the civil courts were approved, and six cases were inconclusive or incomplete.

Seven requests for marriage licenses that were taken to the ecclesiastical court involved people marrying relatives, and the only other request was for the second marriage of a slave widower. As in the civil courts, marriage licenses in these situations were usually approved (seven of the eight cases).[83] It is worth noting that in four of these cases, slave owners requested that the church sanction the marriages of their slaves. These slaves were marrying related slaves of the same owner, and in all the petitions, the owners declared that if the slaves were not allowed to marry "they would offend God because they live within reach of each other."[84] Masters further argued that the slaves could not be sold to someone else because it could be detrimental to them. This type of license was contrary to the same dictates of the church, yet the ecclesiastical court approved all of them.

In 1786 Bishop Mariano Martí dispatched an order mandating that slave owners could not oppose the marriage of their slaves, whether from the same or a different master or hacienda. Martí believed that if slaves voluntarily wanted to marry and the couple was able to have marital life after fulfilling their duties, the masters could not prevent such unions. If slaves lived on haciendas that were too far apart, then the master who "needs less the slave" should sell the slave bride or groom to the other master or to someone in the neighborhood, so that the slave couple could be closer together. In a letter to Bishop Juan Antonio de la Vírgen María Viana in 1795, the priest from Tacarigua attested that those guidelines were not followed at all and asked for "a serious measure that would end such old grown evil." The priest himself had been preaching about the subject in his Sunday masses and suggested that the bishop order that priests be able to marry the slaves without requesting the masters' permission.[85] Indeed, the bishop responded to this request with a new order to the governor's lieutenants in rural districts (*tenientes*) to help slaves in such situations. The actions of the bishop were based on the rulings of the Sínodo of Caracas and the royal cédulas of 17 June 1698 and 31 May 1789 on slave marriages.[86] These actions may well have annoyed many slave owners, who could lose control over their property.

More controversial for both the state and the church were the cases of breach of promise and opposition to marriage. However difficult rulings may have been for the courts, they were issued for the vast majority of the cases in the late colonial sample. This is contrary to what this study found for similar disputes in the late-nineteenth-century sample (see chap. 8).

Of the fourteen cases of breach of promise during the late eighteenth century, most reached a ruling (ten cases) and involved lower-class women (twelve cases). In the cases in which the outcome favored the plaintiff (three cases), the church determined that the male defendant had to either marry or pay a dowry to the female. When defendants were successful (three cases), it was either because there was not enough evidence for conviction or the claim prescribed or the defendant was acquitted but had to pay court costs. Four cases were settled and four cases did not have a ruling, probably because the accused men ran away.

Breach of promise lawsuits must have been difficult for the courts because they questioned the sexual and moral conduct of men. In theory these cases implicated the parents of the couple because, by law, the parents had to tell whether they had consented to the marriage, and usually these liaisons occurred out of the sight of the parents. Indeed, most of the cases included the parental license as requested by law. One woman lost her case because, after more than five years, she was unable to produce the licenses of both her and the defendant's parents.[87] Yet even when the parents did not consent to the marriage of their children, it did not have an effect on some of the church's decisions. What is very telling is that the courts were, in some instances, more concerned with the plight of these poor women – even in cases in which the women were not virgins – than with restoring parental authority, as the pragmatic originally intended.

A lawsuit filed by María Tomasa Churión offers a clear example. On 14 November 1791 María Tomasa, a parda born to a single mother, went to court to denounce her neighbor, Joseph Matías Bolcán, a pardo born to married parents, for having seduced her under a promise of marriage.[88] Although María Tomasa's mother gave her permission to marry, Joseph Matías's father did not because he did not want his son to marry a "mulata." María Tomasa remarked that the two had started to "know each other in a carnal way" in June of 1791 and that they had been together ten times. The ecclesiastical fiscal stated in his brief that even if she was corrupt because she had not followed the dictates of the church concerning premarital relations, the truth was that in the past ten or thirteen years María Tomasa had worked hard and lived virtuously, secluded in her home.[89] For these reasons the fiscal was of the opinion that she deserved to be protected by justice (*derecho*).[90] The ecclesiastical judge agreed and ordered that within thirty days Joseph Matías should marry María Tomasa according to the requirements of the Catholic church or endow her with two hundred pesos. This opinion was based on the fact that Joseph Matías had made public his crime, and it was fair for him to compensate María Tomasa for the "damage" he had caused her (i.e., the loss of her virginity).

As one can see from María Tomasa's case, neither her lack of virginity nor the opposition of Joseph Matías's father to the marriage reduced the merits of her claim. Of course, they were both of mixed black and white ancestry (mulatto/a or pardo/a), and as such the pragmatic did not apply to them. But this aspect of the case was not even mentioned in the case briefs. The fact that the church was responsive to the plight of women, however, even if they were not virgins, is revealing and contrasts with similar situations in the late nineteenth century, as is discussed in chapter 8.

The response on the part of the church court was not unique to the case of María Tomasa. In the cases of breach of promise of María Josefa Arias and María de los Santos Márquez, which were similar to that of María Tomasa, the church followed the same rule.[91]

There were situations, however, in which the sexual conduct of women was decisive. In one example, María del Carmen Blanco took her boyfriend to court for seduction and breach of promise. The fiscal declared that the plaintiff did not prove her claims that Pedro Ignacio Barguilla had asked for her hand in marriage. Moreover, Pedro Ignacio brought credible evidence – testimony from six witnesses – of María del Carmen's licentious behavior. She had sexual relationships with different men even when she was with Pedro Ignacio. Thus the fiscal believed that even if there had been a promise of marriage, the contract lost its effect after María del Carmen committed "lascivious acts with so many men."[92] The fiscal suggested that the judge acquit Pedro Ignacio of the charge of breach of promise but suggested that a punishment be given to both parties due to the scandalously free sexual behavior to which they had both confessed. Finally, the judge acquitted Pedro Ignacio of the charges yet made him pay the legal costs and reprimanded both of them, "so that in the future they live in fear of God: living without communication with each other and if they relapse into the same lascivious behavior, a harsher punishment will be issued."[93] Although the court found the sexual conduct of the woman reprehensible, it punished the defendant as well for his sexual behavior. He had to pay the costs of justice.[94] Moreover, the court admonished both of them for the good of the community.

Cases of opposition to marriage provide further evidence not only of the legal system's sense of justice but also of how the state handled disputes involving children's marriage choices, parental power, and civil laws. Of the fourteen lawsuits of this kind that were heard in the secular courts, ten favored the plaintiffs, meaning that parental opposition to the son's or daughter's intended wedding was deemed "irrational" according to the letter of the law.[95] Because there was no substantial racial disparity between them, the bride and groom could marry even if their parents did not approve. Only in one case did the state favor the parents.[96] In this case, the woman was a white foundling, born from an adulterous relationship between parents of recognized whiteness. She wanted to marry a mulatto boyfriend, but her stepmother raised objections to her marriage.[97] The other cases were either settled (one lawsuit) or were inconclusive or incomplete (two instances).

As these broad decision patterns suggest, children's marriage choices and compliance with state laws seemed to have been more important than parental permission for the weddings. Hence, in practice, there was little state support for the paterfamilias. The perceived decline or erosion in the power of the padre de familias was seen as a menace to state order because marriages between elite whites and nonwhites might collapse the honor/class hierarchy that ordered colonial society. Thus instead of returning that power of decision to the paterfamilias, as one would expect, it was the Spanish state that would ultimately make the decisions for the father. This was made clear in a circular that the colonial authorities included along with the pragmática, which stated that:

1. Unequal marriages among the upper classes were more dangerous for the state; thus, in marriage license requests among elites, the authorities should give attention not to the parents' permission but to the equality of the couple.

2. For the lower classes, because their marriages did not cause any risk to the state, permission would be granted even when they were not equal, if the parents approved the marriage.[98]

In the context of the struggles between male mantuanos and peninsulars, here is yet another law that helped Spaniards maintain their power of decision and hegemony over mantuano men in colonial Venezuela. This may well be what made Simón Bolívar claim in 1815 that the Spanish government kept its creole sons in a situation of "permanent infancy" because the state did not allow them the power to make their own decisions, not even some concerning their private homes.[99]

Divorce lawsuits provide a good example of how arduous it was to prove charges of abuse and adultery against husbands. This did not mean, however, that men were not held personally responsible for their actions in marriage. Of the eight cases of divorce found between 1786 and 1795, only one was granted a perpetual divorce. This was the case between Martín Jerez de Aristeguieta and Josefa Lovera, discussed below. In another claim, the church granted a temporary separation of bed and board on the ground of abuse by the husband. In the rest of the cases, all of which were brought by women claiming abuse, adultery, or impotence on the part of their husbands, divorce was not approved. In two instances the couples reconciled, in one the husband was acquitted, and the rest of the lawsuits were incomplete or inconclusive.

The outcome in the divorce case between don Martín Jerez and doña Josefa Lovera, locked in a bitter and controversial dispute about the administration of the wife's properties, offers an understanding of how the church put into practice the principle of equidad in such complex disputes. This couple belonged to the most important mantuano families of Caracas – which, according to the Sínodo, must set the example for the rest of the society.[100] They had so much influence in the church, the cabildo, and the courts of Caracas that they, and especially don Martín, were able to use it to their advantage throughout their lives. Thus the case had broader implications than a single private conflict. Soon the divorce case became a political issue in which the authorities came face to face with a vexing dilemma: how to penalize don Martín's abuse of power – within and outside of his home – and the adulterous life he and his wife had carried on while not publicly undermining don Martín's authority as an elite paterfamilia. Overall, the court had to set a visible example for the good of society.

Nine long years after the lawsuit was filed, the court issued its first ruling. It awarded a perpetual divorce *coadthorum et mutuam havitationem* and ordered that doña Josefa be transferred to a house of recognized decency in the town of Santa Lucía, where she could live secluded.[101] Don Martín was aggrieved by the ruling of the ecclesiastical court, whose judge – Dr. don Vicente Pérez – was his friend. He wanted to see his wife confined to the Hospice of La Caridad, an institution that served as a jail for prostitutes and lower-class women, although it had previously served as a shelter for white, upper-class women.[102] Above all, don Martín wanted to have his honor (public reputation) reestablished by the seclusion of his adulterous and pregnant wife in a jail for lower-class women.[103] His own many adulteries, which were proven in the courts by doña Josefa, were, in his opinion, not as serious as those committed by a married woman like Josefa.

The ecclesiastical court's judgment was sent on appeal to the archbishop in Santo Domingo. On 14 August 1793 the perpetual divorce sentence was confirmed with some changes. First, doña Josefa was not to be exiled to such a faraway town, where it would be difficult to monitor her behavior. Instead, she could live in the house of a respectable relative in town. Second, the court found that don Martín had committed many excesses. Indeed, the tribunal blamed him for the marital problems: "His consort's lewdness and debauchery may well have started in Don Martín's neglect of the home and his legitimate wife."[104] For this reason the ecclesiastical court determined, finally, that don Martín should spend one month doing spiritual exercises and making a general confession in the Franciscan Convent of Caracas and then confess every month for a period of one year. Moreover, he had to contribute four pesos every month as charity to the Hospital de la Caridad.[105]

In the end, doña Josefa was allowed to live in her own house accompanied by a decent and chaste woman, her slaves, and her spurious children. This outcome was far from don Martín's wishes. He claimed that her house was so big that it was difficult to keep track of her and that she comfortably walked day and night in the streets accompanied by her adulterous children, with much scandal.[106] In this case the powerful padre de familia, don Martín, did not get the full sanction or authorization he expected from the courts, or even the king, to punish his wife as he pleased and as was written in law.

Although the higher ecclesiastical authorities gave an opinion that punished both husband and wife and that may seem fair, in the eleven long and tormenting years of this lawsuit, many injustices were done.[107] For example, the ecclesiastical judge knowingly left doña Josefa without money, and he even accepted a bribe from his friend don Martín. In addition, the powerful mantuano was not punished in either the ecclesiastical or the secular court for his abuses of power, such as intruding violently into the house of doña Josefa's mother. Finally, don Martín also instilled terror in lawyers who helped doña Josefa.[108]

The ecclesiastical courts took advantage of opportunities to make men accountable for their actions in their relationships with women. In other divorce cases this pattern can also be observed. Doña Francisca Rosalía Hernández accused her husband, don Juan Truxillo, a second-generation Canary Islander and overseer of a hacienda, of adultery and abuse. After a bitter written and verbal dispute they reached a settlement, and the judge took the opportunity to reprimand both of them: "The husband is advised to reconcile with his wife immediately, to treat her with the fondness and love that is common between spouses, to comply with the laws and obligations of matrimony, and to provide her with all that is necessary for her subsistence and the decency of a woman of her means; and she is requested to respect her husband, and to fulfill her duties, contributing each one to extricate their marriage from whatever may cause dissension and complaints."[109]

In addition, the judge made clear how the possibility of divorce not only offended God but would also affect their children and the community. For these reasons, he said, every couple should avoid these kinds of disputes. This idea was also repeated in other lawsuits in which the male defendant was acquitted. In one case a wife was unable to prove her husband's unfaithfulness with trustworthy witnesses. Hence the judge ordered her to reunite with her husband and warned him to treat his wife with equidad, "signing a caución juratoria to make certain that he would obey this order." Moreover, the suspected lover was warned not to intrude in the lives of married people, and they all were encouraged to live in fear of God.[110]

Some men of Caracas understood these rulings from both the secular and ecclesiastical courts differently. For them, the court decisions became a direct challenge to their legal powers. Indeed, there is evidence that men were annoyed by the perceived favoritism of the Spanish state and church toward women in their conflicts with men. In the words of the legal representative of one disgruntled husband, "The tribunals are no stage for whims and caprice, nor the sacred canons a pretext for married women to break the subordination owed to their husbands and deviate from the rectitude and fidelity they promised [to their husbands] at marriage."[111] He urged the judge to reject lawsuits against husbands because they served only as a facade for women's "free behavior." Interestingly, this lawyer was a creole and a patriot in 1810, suggesting that some elites were irritated with the opinions of the courts, which lessened their full authority as patriarchs.

This kind of petition is parallel to those made by slave owners, whether female or male. Because a slave who took a master to court, either seeking liberty or accusing the owner of abuse, could be depositado while the case was being heard, the owners complained that such lawsuits by slaves were only an excuse to be unsubmissive and to advance their mean intentions. Moreover, owners claimed that slave lawsuits harmed them financially because they did not receive the slaves' salaries while the court held custody.[112] Other slave owners went even further, complaining that they had to bring food to their slaves when they were depositados in the jail and claiming that the slaves had to keep working while the resolution of the case was pending. In one of these cases the slave's prosecutor agreed to return the slave if the owner agreed to spare punishment and to give the slave two hours each day to take care of her lawsuit.[113]

Given the complaints of husbands and slave owners about participation in the courts by women and slaves – people who were legally subordinated to men – one wonders whether there were significant differences between rulings in cases of enslaved humans who were considered chattel property and cases, for example, of spousal abuse or estupro. Did the principle of equidad also challenge the powers of the padres de familia with regard to slave "property"?

SLAVES LITIGATING AGAINST THEIR OWNERS

The sample for the late colonial period included twenty-one cases in which slaves sued their masters for their freedom. Of these, in seven cases the court ruled in favor of the slaves, in two cases the masters won, one was settled with a compromise, and eleven cases were inconclusive or incomplete. In addition, in six of those incomplete cases either the slave claimed that the master asked an excessive price for her or his liberty or the slave's freedom was entangled with the complicated inheritance partition of the owner.

Although a slave's suit might meet with mixed results in the courts, there were instances in which the civil court put the principle of equidad into practice. One example is the case filed by Juana Bautista Páez, the parda slave of don Josef Quintero. In 1788 she went to court claiming that she had given her master 250 pesos for her liberty. Her master left for the Canary Islands, and his cousin, in charge of don Josef's property, was reluctant to free her and refused to produce a document certifying her liberty.[114] The slave produced witnesses to the transaction, but even under oath, don Josef's cousin denied the existence of such a document. On 5 December 1788 the court threatened to put don Josef's relatives in jail because they probably were not telling the truth. Eleven days later the master's relatives suddenly "found" a note that read, "I received two hundred fifty silver pesos from my slave Juana for her liberty and I am providing this as an assurance of this transaction."[115] In this case it seems that the court went out of its way to seek justice and to confront the master's family with its reluctance to acknowledge a slave's freedom.

Rita Antonia Díaz had a similar experience. According to Rita Antonia, her owner, doña María Antonia Díaz, was asking an excessive amount for her liberty. Rita Antonia was forty-five years old, almost deaf, and had syphilis. Her owner was asking for the salaries that Rita Antonia had earned in the past nine years (a half real daily). Rita Antonia believed that this was unfair. She had been working with her owner all that time, and she had even supported herself and her daughters with the money she had earned. She asked the judge to assess her value as a slave and to be placed in depósito in the house of the notary public of the church because the jail would be hazardous to her health. In the end Rita Antonia was appraised at fifty pesos, and her owner gave her a letter granting her liberty.[116]

Even when the slaves lost their disputes the court tried to provide some protection. For example, Inés María took her owner to court, accusing him of having promised her liberty in exchange for sexual favors. She claimed that children had been born out of the relationship. Inés María was unable to prove her claims, however, and the court acquitted her owner. In order to spare her any punishment from the resentful owner, the court gave Inés María eight days to look for a new owner; otherwise, she had to return to the house of her present owner.[117] In the case of two slaves of doña Josefa Lovera who were involved in a divorce lawsuit as witnesses for don Martín Jerez de Aristeguieta, the court cautioned doña Josefa not to offend the slave who would remain on her side.[118] The other slave was allowed to find a person willing to buy her.[119]

Probably because they occasionally found some protection in the courts, slaves held the institution in high regard. One slave referred to the court as being "fair to the *infelices* [unprotected, helpless people] against the powerful."[120]

SEXUAL CRIMES

Decisions in cases involving sexual crimes show that the courts generally followed the guidelines provided by law, especially if the evidence presented was convincing.[121] Although the number of sexual crimes collected for this sample is too small to draw any definitive conclusions, the cases point to the possibility that the application of the law was difficult for women when compared to sentences in civil trials.

The main problem in obtaining justice related to sexual crimes was presenting credible evidence about actions that were usually committed in private and under much secrecy.[122] In the only case of estupro in this sample, the accused was set free because of lack of evidence. In another case studied by Venezuelan historian Juan Carlos Reyes, the defendant was found guilty.[123] In this lawsuit, the prosecution demanded a punishment of two hundred lashes and six years of prison in Maracaibo, but the final sentence did not include the physical punishment. It was also established that the victim, a six- to seven-year-old girl, could marry the aggressor if she wished to do so after he got out of jail.[124]

It is not clear whether women totally lacked protection from the courts in these situations. For example, in 1789 Leonardo Ponte went to court to complain that his daughter was reluctant to obey him. The daughter claimed that on two different occasions she had gone to other, lower courts to denounce her father for trying to sexually abuse her. Although the father never brought evidence to back up his claim about his daughter's "scandalous life," the court decided that to achieve peace within the family the daughter should be brought to court "to be instructed of the obligations and the respect she must profess to her father and in his presence display the most vivid proof of submission and obedience."[125] The daughter was to be placed in the house of a respectable woman who would watch her behavior, while at the same time she would have some protection in case of potential abuse by her father.

In one case of incest, the father ran away from justice while the daughter bore the brunt of the law. She was sentenced to five years of imprisonment in the Hospital de la Caridad, which also served as a jail for women. After completing her term in jail, she had to enter the house of a respectable white person to work as a domestic and to learn good manners.[126] Only further research can determine whether this sort of sentence served as a punishment or helped to protect women involved in sexual crimes.[127]

WOMEN, EQUIDAD, AND THE EROSION OF MEN'S LEGAL POWERS

The Spanish concept of justice embodied in the principle of equidad did offer some protection to women in colonial Caracas, and at the same time it tried to discipline and instill morality in both genders. Both the ecclesiastical and the secular courts, through different measures, intended to control and punish the behavior of some men. In addition to being punished by sentences, men were also sometimes chastised through lawsuits. For example, a fairly common practice in colonial Caracas was to incarcerate men or women after a complaint was filed, especially if the plaintiff so requested. No evidence was needed to send someone to jail, yet to obtain freedom the person had to provide evidence of the falsity of the claims.[128] The samples included eighteen instances (eight ecclesiastical and ten secular cases, out of a total of twenty-six) in which men were put in jail immediately after women made petitions to the tribunals, especially in cases of breach of promise, divorce, and abuse. This recourse provided some protection to women, in that they would not be abused and men would be confronted with their abuses of power by the authorities, forced to respond to the women's claims, and most importantly, forced to abide by the court decision.

These assurances are exemplified in the breach of promise case between doña María Manuela Roxas and don Luis Ruiz Rivera.[129] In June 1790 doña María, a white, upper-class woman, filed a suit against her lover, claiming that he had seduced her with his love letters and promises of marriage. She requested that he be placed in the royal jail because she was afraid that he would flee his responsibility. Don Luis did not spend more than three weeks in jail. As soon as the ecclesiastical court acquiesced to his request to marry doña María, don Luis indeed fled.

In another instance, Juan Fernando Flores, a poor, free pardo, was imprisoned after his parda girlfriend, Juana María Aponte, accused him of breach of promise before the ecclesiastical court.[130] Juan Fernando was not only sent to jail on 23 November 1787, but his meager belongings were also seized. Almost a year later, on 18 October 1788, the defendant asked to be set free because Juana María was pregnant by another man, and she had even dropped the claim. The court acquitted Juan Fernando of the charges but made him pay the court costs. The judge found evidence that proved that he did seduce Juana María under a promise of marriage and then avoided the wedding. Juan Fernando complained that he had to spend money to prove that he was not the father of Juana María's child – he even sold his cape to pay for the investigation – and that the lawsuit left his pockets empty. As these cases demonstrate, by making the court issue detention orders against their seducers, women found a weapon to challenge men's power in Venezuelan society. Some women did abuse this resource, however. María del Carmen Blanco, after losing her case against Pedro Ignacio Barguilla for breach of promise, delayed in returning the records to the tribunal in order to prevent Pedro's release from jail.[131] Some men, especially those from the mantuanaje, were never brought to jail after the order was issued. Don Martín Jerez de Aristeguieta, the aforementioned wealthy and powerful mantuano, never served his jail sentence for abusing a white girl.[132] In another case, a man had an arrest order because his wife accused him of incestuous concubinage in a divorce lawsuit, but he took refuge at the home of the powerful marqués del Toro, where he indeed avoided going to jail.[133]

For men, of course, being in jail was a disgrace, because they could not earn their living, they had to find someone to bring them food (apparently meals were not provided for inmates), and for many it was a public taint to their masculine honor.[134] Moreover, jails were not very sanitary.[135] Many padres de familia resented these actions of the Spanish colonial courts. These cases may have contributed to antagonism toward a Spanish crown that was systematically attempting to diminish the powers of creoles in the local administration and, more intimately, in their own homes through the protection provided to women, children, and slaves in the courts. From this point of view, the Spanish administration of justice was seen as an institution that eroded the power of men in a sphere in which the padres de familia were legally entitled to have full control. Not only were the mantuanos already a racial minority in the late eighteenth century, but the government was intruding on and undermining their powers politically, economically, and domestically. The court cases proceeded publicly, clearly affecting mantuanos' masculine honor in the eyes of their vertical and horizontal male competitors. Indeed, most of the complaints against the state's perceived favoritism for women's causes came from people who belonged to the upper strata of society. Here was another arena where men, especially mantuanos kept from top administrative positions, criticized and contested Spanish rule.

Rulings that sent men to jail immediately upon female complaints, that made men sign public documents certifying that they would not abuse women or slaves, and that gave harsh sentences to men in some instances may have helped to mitigate the rigidity of patriarchal laws for women. Therefore, some women may have seen some degree of protection in the colonial courts, while many men saw this "protection" as a menace to their powers in the family and even to their property (slaves). In the tribunals women found a legitimate arena in which to challenge the abuses of patriarchal authority in their private lives. More importantly, when the courts did enact concrete measures that relieved women from male abuses of power, the state publicly contradicted the legal powers of those men, while for women the courts became true patriarchs that protected them from abuses of power. For these reasons, women increasingly used the tribunals to solve their conflicts with men.

The way in which the courts operated made some female litigants and other subordinate sectors (such as slaves) support the Spanish government even when the state maintained certain inequalities that affected them directly. Still, the fact that there was a formal avenue to voice grievances against the padres de familia, and one that usually rendered positive results for women and slaves, undoubtedly kept, in the eyes of these people, the criticism against these patriarchs legitimate and alive.

3. Women and Men at the Tribunals

In the case against Matías Bolcán for promise of marriage, the plaintiff's lawyer made painstakingly clear the hardworking nature and seclusion of his parda client in the first paragraph of the lawsuit.[1] His strategy, it seems, was to position María Tomasa Churión and her good behavior appropriately on paper within the expectations of the corporatist society.

Even though the state and church supported a hierarchical society, this did not prevent close contact among the sexes, races, and classes of Caracas. At the level of the household, many people often slept in the same room, including slaves and the free.[2] In his diary of the pastoral visit to the province of Venezuela between 1771 and 1784, Bishop Mariano Martí advised his parishioners to prevent members of the opposite sex from sharing the same bed and room, which was quite difficult in the overcrowded housing conditions of late-eighteenth-century Caracas.[3] The cramped conditions in which people lived made the ideal of female isolation or separation from males difficult to accomplish. Separation of the races was equally improbable.

María Tomasa accused her neighbor, Matías Bolcán, of seduction, meaning that he induced her to engage in sexual intercourse. He followed her when she ran errands in town. Many of the seducers and lovers in the court records lived on the same block as their victims and frequented their houses.[4] In another case, doña Francisca Hernández denounced her husband's affair with a female slave whom she had found in bed with her husband. The female slave continued with the relationship and even bragged to the other slaves of enjoying the "privileges of housewife" when her master's wife was away in *depósito*.[5] In another suit, don Juan Matías Ramos took his slave Inés María to the festivities in the city to avoid her complaints if he did not do so. It was known in the same case that Inés had gone to a dance (*fandango*) when her master was absent from the house.[6] These cases show the fluid nature of the male-female relationship and the power that some women had individually.

While the dominant culture called for the seclusion of women, the stories from these court cases suggest not only that relationships were fluid but that poor women conducted their daily lives with much autonomy. This might be due to the fact that poor women, even slaves, had to work for their daily sustenance and thus did not depend on men as the sole breadwinners.[7]

However autonomous and bold these women might be, their poverty probably discouraged more of them from resorting to litigation because, as Juana María Muñoz observed, her "extreme poverty didn't permit her the luxury of being in the tribunals for she depends on her own labor for a living."[8] The poor had to seek their food daily. Thus going to court took an economic toll on the poor, even though the law provided free legal assistance to indigent people.[9] Still, this did not prevent poor women from filing many of the court claims (46 percent of the 139 cases for the late colonial sample).

The problems described in the lawsuits present more proactive and autonomous women than one would have expected. This is also evident in their attitudes toward marriage and the whole corporatist idea of status – the main focus of this chapter. In this period marriage became a contested terrain. Although people regarded formal unions highly, they were discouraged from marriage by the complex bureaucratic requirements. As a result, marriage became a social institution that everybody admired but few people could attain. Nevertheless, in the process of marrying, women and men used concepts derived from the system itself to reaffirm their individuality, modify the dominant culture, and/or turn against this culture to contest some of its biased presumptions about women and plebeians in general. By individually creating a culture of opposition, women and the lower classes not only confronted the dominant culture on their own ground but also ambiguously incorporated themselves into that culture's worldview. Herein lies another arena in which mantuanos' privileged social position was challenged daily by the lower-class litigants of Caracas.

THE VALUE OF MARRIAGE FOR WOMEN

The individuality demonstrated by women during the late colonial period did not mean that they did not seek to fulfill ideal roles as wives and mothers. The eloquent words of María Tomasa Churión aptly convey this idea: "This [marriage,] the most powerful invitation a woman can get, led me to pay more attention to him."[10] In most if not all seduction and breach of promise cases, women had sexual intercourse with their partners because they understood that a promise of future marriage had been made. Even stable, informal unions were established in the hope of a formal marriage. For instance, María de los Santos Márquez of Guanare, a city in western Venezuela, asked her witnesses to testify whether it was true that her partner, "using the pretext of marriage has lived with her in illicit union for eight to nine years and that she stayed on because of the hope of marrying Díaz given his certain promises of wedding her."[11] Another woman, Juana María Muñoz, decided to grant her lover the "greatest submission" and to wait to get married until he completed his training as a mason.[12]

The social merit of marriage was especially important among women, as Robert McCaa shows for the case of Parral in northern Mexico during the second half of the eighteenth century. Through an analysis of marriage patterns, McCaa convincingly argues that marriage was the main factor that defined women's social standing, whereas for men, marriage was not as important as their occupational standing. What this analysis of a colonial northern Mexican town demonstrates is that women had to depend on men, not only in law but also in practice, for gaining status and for improving their economic condition.[13] Only when a woman was formally attached to a man did she gain social and moral standing; alone, she was nobody.

Marital bonds provided plebeian women with a contract "linking people to the moral economy of society." Even if they were freed slaves and members of the castas, "Christian marriage attached every station of people to rights meant to be universal."[14] Receiving the sacrament of marriage allowed women to assert their inclusion in that moral order and to claim rights from it.

Marriage gained much more value in the context of a society in which illegitimacy and concubinage abounded. Although no work on this particular issue exists for Venezuela, documents from the period indicate that informal unions were common. Bishop Martí's diary attests to the widespread existence of concubinage in the country. Martí took note of the moral scandals people confided to him. Kathleen Waldron quantified all the denunciations reported by Martí and concluded that more than 80 percent of the cases involved premarital sex, adultery, fornication, and concubinage. The latter two offenses dominated. In addition, many references to concubinage mentioned interracial relationships. Waldron reports that 58 percent of the three hundred cases of fornication and concubinage involved a white man and a woman of Indian, mestizo (offspring of a white and an Indian), pardo, or black background, a trend that suggests to her that "interracial marriages were discouraged in the light of social prejudice and widespread concubinage."[15]

The lower classes seemed to view not only virginity but also their relationships differently from the upper classes. Available evidence in the province suggests that a woman might be willing to exchange her virginity, the one thing that determined her and her family's honor in society, for a promise of marriage. Men were aware of the benefits of making a promise of future marriage in exchange for enjoying women's sexual favors. This is neatly exposed in a 1788 seduction case in which all the defendant's witnesses asserted that it was fairly common for men to seduce women "by promising favors or help not with the intention of marriage but rather with the goal of using her body, which is what people do around here."[16] The defendant claimed that men customarily aspired to marry only women who were virtuous and, therefore, faithful.[17] This defendant's argument points again to the double standard that surrounded the female condition in late colonial Venezuela.

When accused in court, men usually tried to discredit women by trying to prove that they behaved as *callejeras*, "exposed all day and night to all kinds of misfortunes and vices."[18] Men also typically argued that another person – usually another man – seeking revenge motivated the woman to file a lawsuit. This tactic sought to shift the focus of attention away from men's behavior and toward that of women.[19] Here men also implied that women lacked the intelligence and will to articulate a complaint against them in court. This was another common argument posed by men, as revealed in the expressive words of a defendant: "Doña Josefa's thinking is the result of female brain disease. Those ideas belong to her sex, produced by a way of thinking typical of her weak condition."[20] Another popular strategy among men was to flee when they were certain that they had no chance of winning the lawsuit. This was a common last resort in cases of seduction and breach of promise because in the last instance, male defendants did not want to get married, at least not to the plaintiff.[21]

Probably because it was common for men to escape from these situations in Venezuela, as we saw in the preceding chapter, women usually asked the tribunals to jail the accused men while the indictment was being investigated. For a woman, an unfulfilled marriage promise was a major problem because it allowed her reputation to be questioned publicly. Some women tried to corner men by discussing in advance the usual male argumentation and reasoning. María Tomasa Churión again provides a vivid example in her complaint against Matías Bolcán for breach of promise and seduction.[22] Her lawyer's brief evaluates four arguments commonly made by men. First, it points out that Matías tried to get off the hook by claiming that he had not made any promise of future marriage and that María Tomasa was not a virgin. In an effort to debunk Matías's excuse, María Tomasa and her lawyer countered, "If [she] was not a virgin, why did he not reprimand [her] on the spot?" Second, the brief dismissed the popular religious image of women as devils, the ones who seduce men.[23] Instead, they reminded the court that the devil was a male who deceived a female by offering advantages so that she surrendered to his wishes. Third, the brief mentions that Matías believed that María Tomasa, because of her condition as a woman, would not have the courage to file a suit against him. Usually men did not believe that women would hurt male honor by questioning their private behavior in public.[24] Finally, Matías was asked what attractions he had as a man to make María Tomasa so desperate to marry him that she would even bring a case against him. He was a "mulatto," like her, both were poor, and she was not so unattractive as to be unable to find someone who would like her. María Tomasa won her case, but by the time she obtained a favorable ruling Matías had fled, allegedly with the help of his father.

MARRIAGE AS A CONTRACT AND AS A SACRAMENT

Formal marriage did not always resolve the plight of women because even in marriage some men were not willing to be responsible partners. This is most evident in divorce cases, in which wives often complained that husbands were abusive, unfaithful, and neglectful of the family's material needs. Many women had a particular vision of proper gender relationships, one in which women and men had mutual domestic obligations. Ignacia Azcarate, a poor white woman, claimed in court that "a woman is given to a man in marriage to become his partner [compañera], not to suffer vexation, oppression, and violence from ill-tempered men who, abusing their power and physical strength, forget their main obligations as husbands, as Christians, and as citizens."[25] In the same vein, Juana Feliciana Díaz wrote to the court: "How hard is the plight of married women! One rarely finds a husband who has the same regard toward his companion [consorte]. . . . The husband becomes a tyrant, the wife a slave, the home hell, and the children are unfortunate witnesses to this horrible and lamentable metamorphosis."[26]

Both in the late colonial and in the early republican periods, images of marriage as slavery and of wives treated like slaves appeared constantly in the records. As dependents of the padres de familia, women and slaves shared the language and actions of such dependency. Because men had control over the persons and property of their families, sometimes men had the mistaken belief that women were sexual property and were obliged to serve men. Both women and slaves were also *depositados* when they accused their masters and husbands in court.[27] Again, the case of Ignacia Azcarate serves as a good example. Her husband came home with empty promises "to have a slave, to serve and look after him and his children, enduring the yoke of his ill-temper."[28]

In these and other cases, women referred to their marriage as a contract, a pact among equals or *compañeros* (partners).[29] In the eloquent words of Juana Feliciana Díaz, "marriage though a sacrament always remains a pact."[30] It is under this belief that they claimed rights in court and complained about the abuses and lack of responsibility of the men in the relationship. In so doing, these women challenged the normative hierarchy of power.

Men had a different idea. The information available in the court records indicates that men conceived of marriage as a sacrament, an unbreakable bond in which the relationship of power between husband and wife was inherently unequal. One husband defended himself by arguing that "my legitimate wife may have believed that the marriage bond, vested with the respectable condition of the sacrament, was a toy or a matter of little importance."[31] Husbands seemed to perceive wives' view of marriage as an attempt to appropriate *patria potestas*, and thus they wanted to make sure, every time, that "in the family, no one else governs but them."[32]

The interplay between the sexes in Caracas provides a good example of the many ways in which gender relations became a relationship of power intrinsically related to the power and organization of the patriarchal state. The case of colonial Venezuela also illustrates how men adapted to prescriptive roles, while many women accepted their assigned roles but gave them another meaning. Women, in their inferior social and legal position, contested male power both in the household and in the courts, seeking a more egalitarian relationship in which both men and women met their mutual obligations to the family. The husbands' main concern was to keep their position of command over the household.

THE ROYAL PRAGMATIC ON MARRIAGES, 1778

The observations of the French traveler François Depons in 1803 may have been an echo of an enraged public opinion against the results of what he called the "viciousness of the Spanish laws." Depons shared the male viewpoint that husbands, as well as the family, were hurt by the "blind protection that the Spanish laws afforded women." No one was more unfortunate than a Spanish man who had a jealous wife, according to Depons, because women could easily go to the civil or ecclesiastical authorities and request that their husband be imprisoned for a groundless complaint. "She is credited upon her bare word," he added. Moreover, Spanish laws that gave fathers too little control over their children's choices were troubling the family institution. Instead of supporting the father's decisions, the law allowed a child to sue his or her parents if they opposed a marriage.[33] In summary, Depons blamed Spanish legislation for what he understood as fathers' declining powers over their families.

This traveler was commenting on his understanding of the unfulfilled aim of the Royal Pragmatic on Marriages that was extended to the Spanish American colonies in 1778. This law sought to end the frequent "abuses" committed by children who married without parental consent, thus preserving the authority of the padres de familia "as it ought to be." According to the text of the pragmatic, these offenses were a detriment to the padres de familia, who were the guardians of order in families, and certainly to the good order of the state. As Twinam argues, the law "empowered fathers to become gate keepers, for they could judge if a questionable daughter- or son-in-law had passed sufficiently to be admitted into the family. If the answer was no, they could rely on the state to support them."[34] The law established that children under twenty-five years of age needed their parents' permission to marry. Parents could prohibit a son's or daughter's marriage if there was "a fair and *rational* reason to prevent a marriage such as if the marriage constituted an offense to the state or the family." The rationality of parents' dissent was related to the degree of social inequality between the partners in terms of racial disparity.[35] The law also obliged the courts to reject breach of promise lawsuits if the parents had not granted permission to marry.

This law applied only to whites and Indians of every social class, and inequality was implied in terms of interracial marriage with blacks or people of black descent. Parents of African descent had no recourse under this law, unless the father was in the military. In practical terms the slaves, free blacks, and pardos who comprised the majority in Caracas of – 66 percent of the total population in 1802 – were not covered by the law.[36] Yet there are cases in which pardos filed lawsuits against parents who opposed a marriage. In most of these cases the court allowed the children to marry, ruling that the objection was not rational because the issue was not one of race, as stipulated in the law, but rather a parental wish to impede a marriage based on other considerations.

What Depons criticized, however, was the article in the pragmatic that allowed children to file a lawsuit against their parents if the parental opposition to the marriage was deemed irrational.[37] As with his reproach about wives' complaints in the courts, Depons was right in the sense that the lawsuits challenging the power of the family heads were becoming quite numerous. In the late colonial sample claims that directly challenged the patriarch's power constituted 48 percent of the 103 cases dealing specifically with family affairs.[38] More important is the fact that children were usually very successful in the courts, although in reality the number of cases dealing specifically with parental opposition to marriage as such was not large. Judgments favored children in ten of the fourteen such cases in the civil courts. Only once did the court determine that parental opposition was rational. In that instance, the bride, a white foundling of elite parents of "recognized purity of blood," wanted to marry her "mulatto" boyfriend.[39] Compare this to the case concerning a white elite couple in which the groom's father opposed the marriage on the ground that his son did not have the means to sustain a family. The court granted the license anyway.[40] Venezuelan colonial authorities gave more importance to the racial equality of the couple than to parental permission among the elites, as was discussed in the preceding chapter.

The act of complying with the legal rituals surrounding marriage – that is, of seeking licenses, presenting them to the court, and seeking witnesses if needed for the publication of banns – provided an opportunity to make public the honor of a family. Here honor was understood as the public regard of a family, including their race, behavior, purity of blood, and ability to meet social expectations according to their rank in society.[41] For example, the woman who raised Ana Josefa, a foundling who was allegedly the daughter of white parents of known reputation and whiteness, opposed her marriage but could not provide much information about her background because doing so could threaten the good reputation of her parents.[42] It is clear throughout the sample that going to court had enormous implications for the standing of both parties. As the father of a male defendant argued, "I ponder the insolence of this woman who showed up at the tribunal, allowing the public to know her misdoings."[43]

Litigation in court was an open invitation to publicly expose the racial background and reputation of the parties. This might explain why Don Juan José Mora, a prestigious member of the aristocracy, requested a special *certificado de estimación y calidad* (certificate of public reputation and race) from the king. Don Juan José sought to protect his reputation and that of his family after the court upheld an impediment (which was not mentioned in the certificate) to his prestigious marriage to the widow of don Miguel Aristeguieta, doña Josefa María Blanco y Herrera (don Martín Jerez de Aristeguieta's stepmother). He asked the court to clear his name from any "insult, injury or offense resulting from the impediment, whether due to mistake or to the evil minds of the people who knew about the proposed marriage and spread it around the country."[44]

Frequently a former concubine of a groom impeded his marriage by claiming that he had first promised to marry her. Usually these women already had children from the relationship and learned about the groom's intentions to marry another woman from the publication of banns.[45] This happened to José Juan Artiaga and María Florencia Mendoza, who decided to marry in a distant parish to avoid any obstacle to their marriage. José Juan had earlier promised to marry Antonia Vargas and had had three children with her. Both José Juan and María Florencia were imprisoned, accused of clandestine marriage for marrying in the wrong parish.[46] In another case, Norberta Quijano delayed for two years the marriage that her former boyfriend was to celebrate with María Valeriana while the ecclesiastical court investigated his previous betrothal to Norberta. José Vicente Cordero had a similar problem, but his case took six years to resolve.[47]

The process of getting married could also involve considerable expense. The court often asked the plaintiffs to prove that they had no relatives who could give permission for the marriage. The process of gathering such evidence was so laborious that a person would not have time to earn his or her daily living while trying to comply with the court's request.[48]

People also sought ways to circumvent the laws. In some situations the party requesting a license would lie about the existence or, more commonly, the absence of parents or relatives. This was the situation of don Antonio del Castillo, a nonelite white, whose brother opposed his marriage to María Josefa Navarro, a parda. Don Antonio moved far away from his brother and did not mention to the courts that he had a brother who could give permission for his marriage. At the same time María Josefa's father took her to the rural parish of Santa Lucía to effect the marriage with less hassle. In another case, María Nicolasa Tovar and Vernardino Cueva filed two different license requests at the courts: one in which they claimed that his sister had no rational basis for opposing his marriage since both of them were pardos, and another in which Bernardino claimed that he had no relatives who would give him a license.[49] Others tried to deceive the authorities by bribing impostors to pose as parents or relatives who approved the marriage.[50]

Finally, some resorted to unlawful clandestine marriages to avoid major impediments to their union. Couples would sometimes tell a priest that they had taken each other as wife and husband, but there would be no ceremony and no license. If there were at least two witnesses to the declaration, the marriage was valid according to the Council of Trent. The authorities harshly prosecuted this type of offense, however, because it was becoming increasingly popular in the late eighteenth century and thus posed a threat to the Royal Pragmatic on Marriages.[51]

Most of the obstacles to formalizing a union in the late colonial period were the result of the Royal Pragmatic, which required that children provide a license from their parents. Evidence from court cases suggests that it was difficult to present such evidence, whether the parents were alive or dead.[52] Also, the pragmatic had another important implication: people had to demonstrate their *calidad*, the term used in the documents to refer to both racial and social status, so that the applicability of the law to their situation might be evaluated. In a hierarchical society in which people who looked more white were better regarded than dark-skinned people and blacks, race was a very sensitive issue.

Establishing a person's true racial identity proved difficult in the face of widespread miscegenation. In some cases the scribes and even some witnesses could not agree on a single race to assign to the bride.[53] In light of this reality, some people, especially elites, requested a certificate of purity of blood from the authorities.[54] The white father of one groom presented witnesses to prove that it was well known that he was "white, with no taint of Moorish, mulatto or Jewish blood nor of being newly converted to the Catholic Apostolic and Roman Faith."[55] The plaintiff, who was a Spanish-born elite, opposed his son's marriage to a "mulata" by arguing that his son was a "pure white."

Members of the white elite were not the only ones to make such claims. Pardos and mestizos defended the status of their race by claiming that the color of their skin was lighter than others', by showing that their military status gave them a better reputation, or, more importantly in the context of Caracas, that their families had no links with slavery. As Verena Martínez-Alier found in Cuba, caraqueños were also reinterpreting the elites' concept of purity of blood. Some pardos and blacks created their own sense of lineage by arguing that they did not have slave blood and by stressing any military linkage that would give them more prestige than other nonwhites.[56] This served as another way of contesting an elite ideology that viewed poor nonwhites as socially worthless. By applying this elite concept to their own reality, some poor pardos and mestizos found a way of asserting their individual rights, honor, and integrity in the corporatist society, thus diminishing in a way the social distance between the elites and the nonwhite poor. Thus, while they modified and opposed the elites' concept of purity of blood without direct confrontation, they accommodated themselves as individuals to the elites' values.

The case of María Josepha Graterón, an alleged mestiza, and Ramón Ortíz, a pardo, provides a good example of the use of the concept of purity of blood among plebeians of mixed race. The natural mother of María Josepha opposed their marriage, claiming racial disparity, and asked her witnesses to indicate whether it was true that "she and her daughter were pure mestizos, with no trace of black or mulatto race."[57] In another case, the defendant in a seduction case claimed that the female plaintiff had "the sad color of black" in her, while he was a pardo born from a legitimate marriage and son of an official from the pardo militia of Caracas.[58] To make reference to a military position was important for pardos because the pragmatic excluded people of African ancestry except for men in the military. In this the law implied that pardo soldiers in the military had a reputation to defend, unlike the rest of the pardo population.[59]

Defending a person's race, honor, and reputation presupposed that the qualities of the contending party had to be downgraded. In such situations people also defended themselves in the courts. Specifically, people fought back when the derogatory word *mulatto* was used to refer to them. This word comes from the Spanish word *mulo* (mule) and denotes a comparison between the hybrid nature of the mulatto and that of a mule.[60] People preferred the use of *pardo*, which means "of a neutral color" and is more dignified than *mulatto*. The issue of the usage of *mulatto* to refer to people of African ancestry became so delicate that in 1777 a royal decree ordered the word be replaced with *pardo* in every document pertaining to the Pardo Battalion.[61]

The French traveler François Depons was rather happy to include in a footnote to his diary that a new Spanish law would put an end to children's abuses of the male family head. Depons was referring to the pragmatic sanction of April 1803, which established that males under twenty-five years of age and females under twenty-three could not marry without the consent of their parents, who now did not have to give reasons for their refusal. The law was addressed to those members of the white elite who intended to marry persons of black ancestry, even if they were of age.[62] The law also prohibited all claims of betrothal that were not registered with an official notary.[63] By doing this, the Spanish crown expected to curb children's challenges to family heads in cases of breach of betrothal and opposition to marriage. Fathers were expected to have more leverage over children.[64]

Multiple factors made formal marriage difficult in the late colonial period.[65] Despite these difficulties, the lower classes had a high regard for marriage and searched for ways to fulfil their wish to marry. Yet the hassle of getting married may have discouraged many from formalizing a union, especially if they were involved in an interracial relationship.

In the process of seeking to marry, however, the lower classes defended their individuality and honor in court. Although the law was ambiguous about the need for parental permission among blacks and pardos, these people also went to court to contest parental authority and to defend the dignity of their person and their race. Plebeians' skin color did not define their social and personal worth, contrary to the elites' ideas of purity of blood. The plebeians' public recognition of reputation and character, their calidad, was at the base of their concept of honor. This is understandable; only by proving his or her reliability could a person maintain the network of credit and aid so necessary for survival among people of limited means.[66] They defended their individual right to possess honor through different strategies at home, in the streets, and in the courts.[67] In this way they publicly validated their personal honorability and modified the concepts derived from the system itself.

As María Teresa Rengifo, a parda, stated, "a person's calidad depends not only on his or her lineage but on other circumstances that must be taken into consideration."[68] The lower classes were contesting the biased presumptions of the dominant culture by proposing another perspective on social stratification – one in which a person's publicly recognized individual qualities were more important than lineage.

PART 2
The Early Republic

4. A Nation for the Landowners

In 1819, having attained independence from Spain, the former Captaincy-General of Venezuela, the Viceroyalty of Santa Fé de Bogotá, and the Audiencia of Quito formed the Republic of Colombia (referred to by historians as the Gran Colombia). The great Bolivarian dream of unity was short-lived and ended abruptly in 1830 with the dissolution of the political entity into three independent states: Colombia, Ecuador, and Venezuela. By then a general consensus existed among the Venezuelan landowning, merchant, and lettered male elites about the need to promote social peace, to reactivate the devastated economy, and most importantly, to protect individual property, including their private homes.

This nation-building program, based on the promotion of agriculture that directly benefited ruling elites as a class, was accompanied by exclusionary ideas based on class, race, and gender. Women were publicly invisible in the new masculine republic, yet they were not completely absent. An exploration of some gender representations characteristic of the early nineteenth century will show how women, allegedly because of their sinful female bodies and propensity to passion and because of men's anxious response to public female mobilization, were relegated to a domestic, private space and were silenced from politics. Beginning with Bolívar's writings and his iconographic representation of the new nation, this discussion first considers how the Libertador cleverly articulated a discourse of unity based on the political aspirations of the majority while maintaining the exclusionary practices of the elites and validating prevailing ideas on gender, which outlived him.

There is continuity in Bolívar's ideas after 1830. Yet the larger political discourse was recurrently devoted to the contest between the ruling educated and propertied male oligarchy and the military men who claimed state power. The civilian men had to legitimize their claims to power and eliminate demands made by military competitors. The oligarchy achieved such goals by curtailing the power of institutions such as the church, which supported their main competitors for power, and by accusing their competitors of being too violent and educationally unprepared to rule the nation.[1] Using legal administrative reforms and law, the ruling elites defended a project for hegemonic masculinity that excluded most men of arms as well as the non-propertied population.

Although women were not part of political discussions, the debate over the death sentence given to a pregnant woman in 1836 opened a unique opportunity for women to enter public discussions as subjects and as participants. Even when the space for public discussion was centered on a female figure, the content of the arguments was not about women but about a critique of the republic of landowners by elite men who opposed the regime. The debate over the death sentence of that woman, Vicenta Ochoa, demonstrates how, in the practice of politics, women were ultimately silenced and excluded from public discussions by the ruling elite men. It also demonstrates the strategies pursued by some women who, in a political environment that did not welcome women's opinions, publicly demanded the execution be stopped.

THE LEGACY OF THE LIBERTADOR

During his career as leader of the wars for independence and as president of the Gran Colombia, Bolívar developed the ideas that underlaid a double discourse of national identity: one that included every Venezuelan, and another in which only a few propertied and learned men exercised the privileges of citizenship. Bolívar clearly understood the political need to provide an image of collective unity and a sense of inclusion in the polity for common Venezuelans (or rather, Colombians).

From 1815, in his Letter of Jamaica, and again in his key Discurso de Angostura of 1819, Bolívar stated that Spanish America had no usable past from which it could develop a nation.[2] Its people "hardly preserve a vestige of what was in other times, and . . . are neither Indians nor Europeans, but a sort of middle species between the legitimate owners of this land and the Spanish usurpers."[3] The difference between Spanish American reality and conditions in the Old World made him question the local population's capacity for civilization. Instead of civilization as such, he believed it was *pasiones* (passions) that dominated the continent. Bolívar used *pasiones* in a negative sense to refer to destructive violence, vengeance, hatred, and greed that were not conducive to national unity. The word *pasiones* had a racial connotation for Bolívar in the sense that he identified "violent passions" and turmoil primarily with mulattos and blacks.[4] He concluded pessimistically in his Angostura address that deciphering the nature of the Spanish American race was as difficult as conciliating the different political aspirations of its people. For this reason, he insisted that "we are in need of equality so that we can recast, so to speak, into one, the species of man, political opinions, and public customs. . . . Unity, Unity, Unity, should be our banner. The blood of our citizens is different; let us mix it so that we can unite them."[5] This idea of unity and of acting with a collective identity different from that of other people was developed and strengthened in the course of the independence wars.

In Bolívar's Angostura speech of 1819, he maintained that although nature had made men unequal, laws could correct such differences so that through education and work men could achieve an artificial social and political equality. Clearly influenced by the ideas of Jean-Jacques Rousseau, Bolívar believed that a strong government could form citizens out of the common people and consequently create a nation.[6] Because liberty and democracy could be guaranteed only through their practice by virtuous citizens, Bolívar envisioned the republic educating children and men and instilling in them "the public spirit, good customs, and republican morality."[7]

These ideas were the foundation of his support for a strong centralist government for Gran Colombia. In order to have a society that enhanced civil liberties, property, and political stability, he advocated a state that included a hereditary senate and vice presidency and a president who could choose his successor from among the most virtuous citizens. Moreover, he divided the citizenry into two parts: one of passive, nonpropertied individuals and another of active, propertied, and learned citizens. By allowing only virtuous men to rule the nation, Bolívar created what has been characterized as a democracy-aristocracy in which only a few had actual citizenship rights.[8] This exclusionary meaning of *pueblo* became institutionalized once the state and the polity were organized.[9] This way of conceiving of the "people" reflected how an egalitarian rhetoric so widespread in Venezuela in fact concealed and denied formal equality in practice. While politicians talked about equality and freedom for the pueblo – a term intended to include every inhabitant – in reality this discourse of equality was specifically addressed to a much smaller percentage of the population. The pueblo to which the male politicians referred was the citizens, that is, the select group of propertied men who participated in elections.[10]

Bolívar was able to combine linguistically the inclusive and egalitarian rhetoric of wartime with the exclusionary precepts and practices of the ruling classes. The Great Liberator skirted the radical aspects of liberal ideology by creating an illusion of national inclusion for everyone, while in practice the ruling of the polity remained the exclusive domain of a few male, propertied citizens. "Men, and not principles, are the ones who form governments. . . . virtuous men, patriotic men, learned men constitute a Republic!" Bolívar energetically stated in Angostura.[11] Thus, when politicians during and after Bolívar's administration used images of national belonging, they ambiguously intertwined ideas of collective unity with exclusionary understandings.[12] As anthropologist Julie Skurski aptly explains, "Given the great disparities between the two meanings [of *pueblo*], and the institutionalized gap between liberal doctrine and political practice, the concept became a central site for the establishment of hierarchical and exclusionary premises and practices within an abstract rhetoric of equality and an inclusionary promise of rights, as well as for the ongoing contestation of exclusionary practices."[13]

Bolívar's ideas also contributed to furthering a highly masculine concept of personal power and of the state in the early republic.[14] Bolívar propagated a history of independent Venezuela that began with the deeds of the virtuous fathers of the homeland whose heroic sacrifices made independence a reality.[15] The gift of liberty that these extraordinary military men gave to Venezuelans had to be kept in the collective memory, and their achievements were to be completed by virtuous and learned men. Thus Bolívar requested of the Congress in Angostura that the nation reward these professional soldiers materially and assure their place in history. The leaders of the independence wars, and especially Bolívar, became celebrated for their "selfless actions and ability to lead the pueblo," through which "they established the nation as the locus of the collectivity's bonds to the sacred [heroic legacy], and only through the pueblo's continuing devotion to their patriotic mandate [could] the promise of collective redemption be achieved."[16]

As Skurski points out, the dissemination of this "patriotic religion" around the "Founding Fathers" has been part of the consolidation of the Venezuelan state; the observance of the emblems of nationhood, such as the anthem, flag, and pantheon of national heroes, has since become a major concern of the governments in Venezuela. The cult of the Founding Fathers sought to reassert the relationship between the people and the nation in which popular rebellion was praised while giving "alliance to state authority."[17] Bolívar became the center of this cult – especially after the Guzmán Blanco government in 1870 – because the worship of his figure by the people as an allegory of liberation and redemption provided the unity necessary to achieve progress and to create a modern nation. While providing a means for unity, the cult of Bolívar and the Founding Fathers has served to silence the actions of common Venezuelans. It is only those great men who had state authority who are the true providers of liberty and democracy in Venezuela. Thus, while building a sense of allegiance, of a common struggle, this construct has helped to conceal power struggles between elites and noncitizens.[18]

It is not surprising that Bolívar and other politicians chose to preserve the figure of authority in the fathers in the new nation. In his speech at Angostura and in his Letter of Jamaica, Bolívar referred to the Spanish monarchs as the ones to blame for keeping the colonies in a state of permanent infancy, without knowledge and reason. Using family imagery as a metaphor, Bolívar supported the emancipation of Spanish America from a tyrannical father who never allowed his children to make their own decisions and was only interested in enslaving them for his own economic benefit. The government of the new republic, composed of virtuous and learned men, would act as an enlightened father, providing for the moral education of its passive citizens.[19] The paternal role of the state in this regard was clear among educated people: they would teach those who were dependent how to live in freedom, because not everyone was qualified to enjoy the liberties that equality granted. As the newspaper *Semanario de Caracas* expressed in 1810, the government should protect "those who do not own a possession, those who subsist from a daily wage, those who live from the favors of others and depend on others."[20] These were the people whose pasiones had to be civilized, especially the rural poor, many of whom were blacks and mulattos.

Only those men who were virtuous because they had participated in defending the fatherland with arms and were economically self-sufficient due to their profession and properties could qualify to enjoy the liberties and rights of the new republic. In other words, the true padres de familia, the male elite heads of household as in colonial times, many of whom were white, would enjoy citizenship rights. Consequently, in the early republic the colonial notion of masculine power persisted in dictating that economically independent people should rule over dependents and the weak. The continued use of the *Siete Partidas* prolonged the rights and privileges of the padres de familia over their dependents in the new republic. It also allowed the family to be treated as the private property of the padre de familia, sheltered and protected by a different set of rights in which these men held the authority and the state should not intervene. As one male litigant put it, "public authority commences only where the husband's authority does not reach."[21]

Although it is true that Bolívar's discourse was highly gendered in favor of men, it merely reflects how much he was a man of his times. Women hardly appear in the political writings of these decades, even when they were publicly active during the wars of independence. Evelyn Cherpak and Ermila Troconis de Veracoechea have documented female participation in important preindependence revolts such as the 1795 slave rebellion in Coro and the Gual-España conspiracy of 1797. In the latter case the wife of the principal leader, Manuel Gual, hid him from the authorities, participated in a slave insurrection, and distributed propaganda throughout Caracas with the aid of a parda friend.[22] In the independence wars, poor women called *troperas* – soldiers' wives, friends, or lovers – followed both patriot and rebel troops into the countryside, preparing food, assisting wounded soldiers, and even taking up arms when needed. Others stayed in the city to defend urban dwellers. Such was the case of Juana Ramírez, who organized a group of women to defend the town of Maturín.[23]

If women's actions were highly visible, why did men not include them in their political writings? As in France or the United States, ruling men of the early Venezuelan republic did not consider this half of the dependent and "weak" population part of public history. Still, women were not completely absent from the intellectuals' sphere of imagination; women occupied a different place. According to Rebecca Earle, who studied Colombia between 1810 and 1830, men were anxious about women's increased mobilization during the wars and, in response, encouraged them to participate within the confines of their homes.[24] Men insisted on representing women as passive victims of rather than active participants in the wars. They also portrayed themselves appreciating symbolic feminine support as a way to promote this representation (i.e., women donating their jewels to the patriotic cause) and/or to not accept publicly the contributions that women such as the troperas rendered to the independence cause. In independence writings women generally were seen as innocent victims whose domesticity had been threatened by the violent wars and now had to be reestablished by a caring, paternal republic.[25]

This idea of "woman as passive victim" merged well with the symbol of liberty as a feminine figure that was so central in the narratives of the independence and postindependence periods. When represented in art, liberty was conceived by the Venezuelans as it was by the French – an ideal woman who held the promise of freedom and sublime virtue.[26] As Joan B. Landes has asserted, the female figure of liberty is profoundly ironic when it comes to represent a "polity that sanctioned a limited domestic role for women."[27] As she goes on to explain, however, women were included in this allegory not because men truly believed that women were free but because of the improbability that women could practice such concepts. In the case of the Gran Colombia, Indian women or young women still under the authority of their father or the state were sometimes chosen to represent the republic.[28] This representation of women as passive and symbolic patriots conferred on them an ornamental role among the nation's symbols but not a participatory one in its politics.

In early republican iconography Bolívar, the Father of the Nation, is shown embracing "liberty" in a protective posture (fig. 1). While the woman in the painting resembles the French female allegory of liberty in both her pose and her clothing, she also represents the nation as an indigenous female surrounded by local American fruits and flora.[29] Because they shared a common land of birth, creole independence leaders claimed to be heirs of the "rebellious spirit" and "natural desire for freedom" of the natives who resisted colonization. The leaders of the new republic mentioned these qualities of the indigenous peoples at the same time that they stressed that indigenous people's tendencies toward anarchy had to be guided and controlled.[30] While the painting makes a connection to the American past to give authenticity to the new nation, it is clear that the artist, Pedro José Figueroa, is making a native interpretation of Revolutionary France's iconic symbols. Yet in France the female figure of liberty always stood alone and was usually surrounded by abstract emblems of authority to represent the "virtues so desired by the new order: the transcendence of localism, superstition, and particularity in the name of a more disciplined and universalistic worship. Liberty was an abstract quality based on reason. She belonged to no group, to no particular place."[31]

In Figueroa's painting Bolívar and the indigenous female shared a common land of birth, and that union represents the new nation; the native female figure is "protected," however, by the virtuous creole Father of the Fatherland, Bolívar. In this image, the dual discourse of equality and hierarchy is reproduced again.[32] That female allegory of liberty and nation represented those who needed to learn how to live in a civilized nation and to become virtuous citizens. The fathers of the homeland, as virtuous and learned men of reason, would teach noncitizens how to live in liberty.

Bolívar believed that granting the population an absolute liberty that did not take into account their collective well-being and individual rights could lead only to disorder and anarchy. To properly cultivate and enjoy it, liberty had to be conditioned and controlled.[33] This image of a liberty that had to be policed paralleled ideas about women in this period. Women could also be a source of pasiones – the "female savage of uncontrollable desires, voluptuous and lawless" that corrupted both men and civilization.[34] Here the

Pedro José Figueroa (ca. 1770–1838), *Bolívar con alegoría de América*, 1819. 125 cm × 97 cm. Casa Museo Quinta de Bolívar, Bogotá, Colombia. Reprinted with permission.

influence of Rousseau on the one hand and of the church on the other converged in Venezuela. For Rousseau the relationship between the sexes could be a starting point of solidarity that could lead to civilization as well as a cause for disorder. Acknowledging sexual differences, the French philosopher stated that women had a greater sexual capacity than men did; thus lascivious women could sexually manipulate and control men. Women's sexual power, if uncontrolled, could corrupt modern society and overturn the ordained relations of power between the sexes.[35] For these reasons men should have a "monopoly of political power" and be "the custodians of a domestic regime where their authority was dependent on the consensual restraint of more sexually potent women." In contrast, as has been discussed in the case of France, the idea of the "separate spheres" helped to conceal men's sexual weakness and their claims to power in society.[36] This likely became another reason politicians agreed that the state had no right to interfere in the private domestic sphere in early republican Venezuela.

The church in Venezuela treated women in a similar manner, complementing dominant opinions about the need to keep women confined to the domestic sphere. Differing little from the colonial ecclesiastical discourse on lust and chastity, nineteenth-century religious publications dwelled on the consequences of women's sinful bodies and devilish behavior. Not only did women's sexual desire drive men to stupidity and loss of common sense (as in the story of Adam and Eve), but such sin robbed men of their youth and health. Equally important, it also led to the loss of property. In sum, women were the "ruin of the Christian people" and the "home of lust and administrator of the demons," and their powers could make men lose their dominant role in society.[37] If uncontrolled, women were to be feared.

Women supposedly lacked intelligence, so they had to be enclosed in their homes, away from the exterior world, and to be obedient to the guidance provided by men.[38] In Bolívar's virtuous republic, women had a role in helping the nation by educating republican citizens within their homes. Motherhood offered an important opportunity for women to demonstrate their patriotism.[39] Their symbolic citizenship was to be exercised within the confines of their homes. Publications such as the *Crónica Eclesiástica de Venezuela* served the didactic purpose of instilling good domestic values in literate women while inculcating fear about French revolutionary ideas such as divorce.[40] Indeed, teaching desirable domestic behaviors was even more pressing in a country where a majority did not formally marry and where at least one-third of the families lacked an elite or lower-class padre de familia. Following the civil wars of independence, which mobilized different races and both sexes for over a decade, it became imperative to create an order that would re-emphasize female domesticity and the male role of protecting the nation and the home.

A man who served the nation was thought by Bolívar to be a man of "virtue."[41] Some scholars have argued that this Rousseauian influence denied women the possibility of becoming true citizens because their actions were to be confined to the home and not extended into the military or public sphere.[42] While this is true, one must consider other ways in which people daily resisted such exclusion. As will be discussed in chapter 6, the egalitarian rhetoric and the ambiguous discourse of citizenship provided caraqueño women with a philosophical foundation and language of rights to be used in their conflicts with men. Thus the same process that excluded women from the public sphere contained within it the seeds of its own contradiction.

FROM MILITARY MEN TO A REPUBLIC OF LANDOWNERS

During the early republic conflicts ensued between military leaders, who gained ascendancy during the independence wars, and civilians, many of whom were lawyers. Gen. José Antonio Páez, a military hero, expressed doubts about the intentions of the lawyers because he believed they invented laws aimed at reducing the power of military men.[43] A bold llanero chieftain, General Páez played a decisive role in rallying the plainsmen behind the patriot cause. He soon became a leading political figure as well as one of the wealthiest hacendados in all of Venezuela, with vast holdings of cattle and agricultural estates. Páez's wealth reportedly originated from speculation in government lands.[44] At the end of his life he became a cultured man, very well versed in literature and music. Páez's reconciliation with lettered civilians occurred only when they accepted and submitted to his ruling power. On the other hand, lettered men understood that to maintain order and stability and to promote the economy, they needed someone who could be both a political and a military leader.[45] The events of 1826 in Valencia, which precipitated the disintegration of Gran Colombia, united the lettered civilians and some members of the military in a common cause. The Valencia rebels supported the leadership of Páez, who had just been dismissed from his position as comandante general of Venezuela by the government in Bogotá. The notable citizens – including educated, landowning, and military elites – reunited in Valencia and used the occasion to demand separation from Colombia. Other municipalities quickly joined the separatist movement in Venezuela, while politicians in Ecuador discussed their sovereignty and Colombia battled against the opposition to the government.

As opposition grew, in 1828 Bolívar decided to establish a dictatorship to prevent the disintegration of Gran Colombia. Not surprisingly, this act earned increased hostility to the Libertador's rule. In an 1829 convention in Valencia that reunited "vecinos, padres de familia, merchants and agriculturalists," Bolívar was accused of imposing on Venezuela a centralist government that was contrary to the Constitution of 1811.[46] The convention also declared a desire to separate from Colombia, and this idea quickly gained support in Caracas. Bolívar's authority was consequently denied, and he was prohibited from entering Venezuela. In March 1830 Bolívar resigned from the Colombian presidency, and he died in December, far from his native Caracas.

After separation from Colombia in 1830, Venezuelan president Páez united with landowners, slaveholders, merchants, and learned and notable citizens to address the devastated economy and to build a new Venezuela. As in other parts of Spanish America, the struggle for independence in Venezuela dragged on for years. Between 1811, when independence from Spain was formally proclaimed, and 1821, when Spanish forces capitulated, patriot and royalist factions fought fiercely for control over Caracas, which remained the most important stronghold of pro-Spanish forces throughout the period. In the war-torn city, calamity piled upon calamity. In 1812 an earthquake destroyed as much as 90 percent of the urban center and took the lives of as many as ten thousand people. To compound matters, agriculture and commerce suffered greatly as looting and destruction, the flight of laborers and slaves, the collapse of internal and external trade, declining revenue, and inflation all led to a social and economic crisis of catastrophic dimensions.

After 1821 the capital city underwent a gradual recovery of sorts. A census taken in Caracas in 1826 showed that with a population hovering around thirty thousand the city was almost as large as it had been before the outbreak of war.[47] The greater degree of political stability allowed internal trade to resume and with it urban demand for produce and other goods from the countryside. Foreign travelers to the city in the 1820s attested to the widespread availability of fresh produce and manufactured goods in the local markets.[48] Still, bad roads, currency depreciation, and a negative trade balance all hindered swift economic recovery.

Such conditions in Venezuela called for the immediate action of men who were directly involved with the economy as owners of land and slaves and as commercial proprietors as well as those who simply possessed the knowledge of how to improve conditions. At least this is what these educated economic elites – Pino Iturrieta called them notables – believed, especially when comparing themselves with the past leadership.[49] The military groups that played a leading role in the wars of independence were incapable of completely severing their ties with the colonial regime. Instead, the notables claimed that military officers who now claimed to be "democratic" were in reality proponents of a "military feudalism." The militaries supported liberal and federalist ideas along with privileges and special advantages for themselves and the church without having a specific plan of nation-building.[50] For these reasons the ruling oligarchy of the 1830s linked this group of military men – many of whom were great property holders and had the support of some liberal civilians – with a further continuation of the independence wars.[51] This led the notables to censure and fear the men of the military because they could instigate violence and hinder economic and political development. Equally important, the notables believed that members of the military had little to contribute toward solving the republic's economic problems. As in the late colonial period, military aristocrats were seen as "parasites" and "enemies of prosperity" because they were accustomed to living from inherited wealth or rent payments, not from their own work.[52]

In 1829, when separation from Colombia was imminent, Páez invited to his home a group of prominent landowners, merchants, and lettered men to discuss the problems of the republic and possible solutions. This group of distinguished men founded the Sociedad Económica de Amigos del País to improve and encourage agriculture, commerce, education, the arts, and employment throughout the population.[53] Despite his military background and prowess, Páez chose the cadres that would run the country from among the educated and financial elites. In building a civilian bureaucracy, he tried both to isolate pro-Bolivarian factions and to neutralize fellow caudillos who vied for power. Páez held the office of the president from 1830 to 1834 and again from 1839 to 1842. Even when he was out of office, evidence of his undisputed supremacy can be seen in instances when he intervened to restore order and crush the opposition in times of trouble.[54]

Between 1830 and 1847 a high degree of consensus was reached regarding both the economy and the political situation. In particular, the oligarchy agreed to follow the dictates of liberalism and to consolidate a government that respected individual rights, especially the right to own private property.[55] With this in mind, a number of measures designed to revitalize business and agriculture in a free-market framework were implemented.

Achievement of the economic plans depended on strict adherence to the Constitution of 1830, which seemed to have overwhelming support among the notables. The Constitution was drafted to suit their interests, which they believed were those of every Venezuelan.[56] For the notables, the imperative of the Constitution was to distance Venezuelans from the Spanish past and from obscurantism by substituting free-market competition for the heavy god-fatherhood of the state (*padrinaje estatal*). By promoting agriculture through the introduction of new laws – such as the controversial creditor law of 10 April 1834 that provided liberty for contracts and easy credit transactions between planters and creditors – and through the importation of machinery and improvements in science and technology, the country could join the civilized nations that were illuminated by reason.[57] In order to achieve economic progress through free competition, freedom of the press was deemed as necessary as the foundation of civil liberties.[58]

MALE COMPETITION AND THE CASE OF VICENTA OCHOA

In 1830 and 1831 the Páez government faced two military revolts, both of which were put down quickly. The relative peace lasted until 8 July 1835, when another coup took place against elected president José María Vargas – a physician, a scientist, and the first director of the Sociedad Económica. By 20 August 1835 Vargas was back in the presidency with the military and political support of Páez. Members of the military and landowners who participated in the "revolución de las reformas," as the revolt is known, sought major reforms from the government such as the abolition of the free contract law of April 1834, which had led to the increasing ruin of a number of landowners. Among its leaders were Gen. Santiago Mariño (a candidate for the presidency in 1834 and an independence hero), Pedro Briceño Méndez (independence general and lawyer), and Francisco Rodríguez del Toro (the last marquis of Toro).

With the coup against President Vargas, the military intended to proclaim a federalist republic, recuperate the privileges that they as well as the church had lost with the Constitution of 1830, and criticize those who had censured them.[59] While the military was not successful in this bid for power, it planted a seed of doubt among the regime's followers. For example, it called attention to the contradictions of a regime that, in the name of moderation and of fostering a collective well-being, was dramatically increasing the wealth of the oligarchy in power.[60] As stated in a 1836 reformist manifesto, "The *godos* ["goths," a disparaging term for the ruling elites], who have become arbiters of Venezuela's destiny, give and take away employments, protect and give self-pride to their supporters, squander the funds of the state, dispose of our property, hurt our children, [and] insult the fair sex."[61] Members of the military further claimed that most of the regime leaders were former royalists (thus the military faction called them godos, as Spaniards were called during the colonial period) and that they did not know how to rule a nation, because most of them became politicians after independence was already achieved.[62] As Gen. Briceño Méndez stated in 1830, the process of guiding the nation should be in the hands of those who *"derramaron su sangre"* (spilled their blood) in the struggle for independence.[63] While the oligarchy legitimized their power based on their property and enlightened education, the opposition cited their military leadership and sacrifice in the war for independence as evidence of their ability and right to rule the nation.

After 1835 there is evidence of increasing opposition to the policies of the oligarchy, especially to the April 1834 law. Although the April 1834 law allowed an increase of private capital to improve agriculture, it eventually became dreadful for landowners. The new law allowed lenders to impose interest rates that they deemed appropriate, and with the judicial support of the government they could compel landowners to meet their obligations. There were no limits on the amount of property that could be seized due to lack of payment, and even worse for the landowners, the property could be sold at any price offered during the public auction.[64] The effects of this law on the landowning elite prompted a break within the ruling elites and the formation of an opposition party by the last years of the 1830s.

Another major policy opposed by Páez's critics was that on cruel punishment. This policy, also known as the *ley de azotes* of 1836, allowed the physical punishment of those who attacked private property. For example, someone accused of theft would be publicly displayed for four hours with a sign announcing his or her crimes, after which the person would receive two sessions of one hundred lashes each.[65] The law was criticized because it was cruel, it caused deep wounds and bloodshed, and furthermore, it contradicted the desire indicated in the Constitution of 1830 to curb death sentences.[66] These oppositional ideas circulated well in the capital city.

The 1830s witnessed the most prolific political debate in the history of Caracas, especially through newspapers, pamphlets, and flyers.[67] The press was very free, and the presses of Valentín Espinal, A. Damirón, and Tomás Antero assured the rapid and thorough circulation of publications in the city.[68] One important debate at the time of the reforms was the death sentence of a mother-to-be, Vicenta Ochoa, seemingly a nonblack who was accused of murdering a female slave. (For more details, see a discussion of this case in chap. 6.) Two flyers signed by "the Constitutional Friends of Humanity" were distributed in the streets of Caracas pleading for the commutation of the death sentence.[69] These flyers, as well as transcripts of her death sentence and letters sent to the president of the nation, provide an opportunity for analyzing the arguments made by male critics of the regime, including their ideas on women and masculine values. In other words, the case of Vicenta Ochoa allows the rare analysis of the links among gender, social order, and the state for the decade under study.

The debate over Vicenta Ochoa's death sentence occurred during a moment of increased public debate over executions. After the 1835 coup against President Vargas, he supported the imposition of severe punishment for the conspirators. Moreover, many congressmen advocated the execution of the reformist conspirators, because this would eliminate opposition to their economic policies. Although Páez, as the chief of the armed forces, favored pardoning the conspirators, Congress did not. This stance of the government in favor of cruel punishment provoked a heated debate that circulated in printed as well as verbal form in 1836.[70] Although the debate against the death penalty continued until it was abolished in 1849, opponents of that government policy likely used the execution of Vicenta Ochoa to further their claims. The arguments used by these men suggested that the authors of the flyers, and even the priests who wrote to the president, were part of a growing opposition to certain policies of the regime.

Demonstrating the high value that elites placed on enlightened knowledge, the male authors of these documents went to great lengths to expound their vast constitutional wisdom in defense of Vicenta Ochoa.[71] As in the 1811 and 1819 versions, the revised Constitution of 1830 symbolized the recently acquired and much heralded liberties upon which the establishment of a civilized humanity was predicated. Hence their defense was imperative. The documents claimed, for example, that Ochoa's execution violated the individual rights guaranteed by the Constitution of 1830 because the events leading up to her judgment did not follow due process. According to article 117, number 21, pardons in death sentence cases were to be decided by the executive in consultation with the cabinet (Consejo de Gobierno). In this case, however, the decision to continue with the execution was made solely by the vice president of the Republic, who was acting as the executive at the time.[72]

According to one flyer, if the execution order continued it would further violate the Constitution because articles 186 and 187 mandated that no government official could execute orders that were against the Constitution or its formalities. It was made painstakingly clear that the "constitution refers to every official without exception."[73] It was also repeated throughout that, although past governments had approved of death sentences, article 206 of the Constitution of 1830 sought to curb death sentences as much as possible.

As if the constitutional discussion were not enough, the flyers also recalled centuries-old laws coming from the *Siete Partidas* and the *Recopilación de Castilla*, which were still in operation in Venezuela. Citing these, the flyers raised doubts about Ochoa's guilt, especially because there were no witnesses and because some thought that the medical examination of the victim was inconclusive. Thus in this case, the death sentence should not have been given because there was no certainty that Ochoa was the killer.

In addition, it was argued that Ochoa had been acting in self-defense in her own house, and according to the old codes and the new Constitution (art. 191), "no one may impunitively intrude [into] the home of a citizen, nor insult him while on the premises, nor provoke him in his castle [castillo] of repose and security."[74] As with the ardent defense of private property made by ruling elites since independence, the flyer asked the government to respect the family and their home as a private domain. In Argentina male immigrants made a similar argument when defending an allegedly pregnant murderer, Clorinda Sarracán, from the death penalty in 1856. According to Ricardo D. Salvatore: "The liberal state . . . ought to respect families in the same way it respected private property. To violate the bodies of women was an inadmissible intrusion of the state in the male private domain."[75] State officials extended their powers too far into the domestic sphere when they sentenced a pregnant woman to death. Yet it is telling that during this period the family and home were understood to be the private domain of male, not female, authority. The argument did not note this contradiction nor did it mention the rights of Ochoa's husband, who incidentally was not an active citizen. Were these men defending Vicenta Ochoa because they believed that she was entitled to be treated equally as a woman under the Constitution, or were they defending themselves from the presence of the state in the private sphere that they ruled?

Vicenta Ochoa's case was considered during a period in which a new constitution was ratified, strategies for economic revitalization were implemented, and the use of the death penalty came under question. To create a new Venezuela, social peace and the protection of the individual and property were imperative. Harsh criminal laws such as the ley de azotes were enacted, in addition to others established by Bolívar (see chap. 5). As a consequence, those accused of a criminal offense, whether male or female, would suffer harsher punishments in the early republic.

In the new republic criminal acts such as murder were vigorously prosecuted as a way to curtail the excesses witnessed during the wars of independence. To attain peace and order, the tribunals used both Spanish and early republican laws to support their decisions, although it seems that in the colonial period sentences such as the death penalty were not prevalent. The severe sentencing pattern of the early republic did not discriminate in terms of gender, and indeed, women's crimes were treated as seriously as men's, as will be discussed in chapter 5. This was reminiscent of the wars of independence, when women's actions became more visible and hence were deemed as dangerous as or more so than those of men, especially when considering the contemporary religious and political ideology surrounding women.[76]

The argument consistently made about the privileged status of the female sex raises doubts as to whether the men who produced the flyers were thinking about women in equal legal terms. Although the Constitution embodied ideas of equal rights for "the people," these writers did not refer to women's equality before the law but consistently alluded to centuries-old Spanish concepts of female privilege based on women's supposed inherent weakness of body and mind. Although the flyers in support of Vicenta Ochoa were printed on the press of a liberal critic of the regime, Tomás Lander, their arguments were consistent with the defense raised by clergy in their letter to the president. The flyers argued repeatedly that the female sex had a distinct set of privileges and that "the laws of all times have viewed men in a different manner in the application and execution of punishment, even when in regard to equal crimes." Thus, although the Constitution of 1830 had been "modernized" to guarantee civil liberties to "the people," the antiquated expectation that the application of these laws would vary between the sexes was still very much alive. These arguments also supported the idea that the family belongs to a different legal jurisdiction where the state should not intervene.

To further the claim that Ochoa had a privileged status based on her sex, she was described as a "madre de familia" – defined by the jurist Joaquín Escriche as a woman who lives virtuously in the home, even if she does not have children – and not a female head of household, as one would be led to believe. Head of household status was reserved for the padre de familia, who governed and ruled the home.[77] Indeed, the future leader of the liberal opposition, Tomás Lander, wrote in 1835 that the most significant role for someone in Venezuela was that of "hacendado, citizen and padre de familia."[78] The term madre de familia was used to argue that Ochoa was going to bring up a new citizen and servant of the republic, so her life was worth saving for the benefit of the new nation. In the late colonial period female litigants used motherhood as a defense strategy in court, but it was not until the early nineteenth century that the argument of motherhood as a social function was widely used. In Ochoa's case, it was claimed that she was a faithful wife "whose example in matrimony is very useful to society," evoking the pedagogical function of the female figure in bringing up citizens and in serving as an example of domestic virtue. The same idea was repeated in a progressive legal journal, El Foro, in 1857: "The fatherland must be interested in having fit and educated mothers who know how to guide the infancy of its citizens."[79] Ochoa belonged to the fair sex and was a valuable figure in the family; hence her life had to be preserved.

Given Ochoa's gender, what in the government's view should have resulted in a spectacle of death to instill fear among violent and "uncivilized" people actually had the opposite effect on the population. Rather than inspiring better conduct in society through fear, the prospect of an execution touched on the sensibilities of caraqueños who interpreted it as an act of inhumanity on the part of the government. It was stated in the flyers that it was "of no use to the order of society, because society only feels pity, and does not remember the crime, nor the law, but rather those that suffer from a lack of humanity." The execution of a woman would make people forget the crime that was being punished, especially in a city that "has no memory of a punishment of this sort" under the circumstances of Ochoa's case.[80] All the writings agreed that her execution would inspire compassion among caraqueños while generating a feeling of horror against the government. Such an action would trigger among the population only collective memories of the violent wars.

Along those lines, the propaganda and a letter written by priests emphasized how Ochoa's death would besmirch the good character of the executive. This was a major concern if Venezuela was to enter into modernity. Because the agenda of the government was to distance itself from what its members thought was a backward and barbaric Spanish government, a public spectacle such as the execution of an expectant mother would not be appropriate if Venezuela was to claim membership among the "civilized" nations. One must recall that the massacres and bloody acts attributed to the Spaniard Boves (among others) during the wars of independence and the killings of patriots by the Spanish authorities were still fresh in the collective memory, although the patriots had exhibited similar behavior. More importantly, the high degree of political stability enjoyed in the 1830s provided impetus for not regressing into the past.[81] When, after much consternation, he enacted a decree of immunity for the conspirators of July 1835, Páez showed how the fear of another civil war outweighed the probability of repercussions and harsh criticism from members of the cabinet: "The decision to dictate this decree was based on the clamor of my feelings and horror at the disasters of civil war and not on the desire to conserve my popularity, to increase the affection of my fellow citizens, and fortify the influence of my services."[82]

The male arguments demonstrate that publicly supporting Vicenta Ochoa was not an act on behalf of a woman per se but was used as an excuse to further the political and personal concerns of the notable male citizenry, opponents of the regime or not. As Romano de Sant'Anna has aptly argued in the case of Brazil, "the representation of the world as that of their own world is a masculine discourse about women; they describe it from their own point of view, which they confuse with the whole truth."[83] The way in which the rhetoric of equality and citizenship developed by the ruling males was articulated in daily practice had the result, deliberate or not, of excluding women's voices or women's issues as well as those of other noncitizens from public discussions. This closed male conversation among those who felt responsible for ruling the rest of the people revalidated dominant ideas about women. Men used the case of Vicenta Ochoa to further a political and masculine claim against a regime that they believed intended to revert to barbarism and violent passion by condemning a pregnant woman to death.[84] Opponents of the regime sought to contradict the ruling oligarchs who affirmed a superior civil masculinity, prided themselves on being the protectors of individual property, and claimed to be bringing progress and modernity to Venezuela. Yet these men were not necessarily acting on behalf of the female sex per se, nor did they publicly acknowledge in their writings that they were persuaded by the individual and collective actions of women who mobilized to save the life of Vicenta Ochoa. These men's sensibilities may have been touched by these women's pleas, but, as in the wars of independence, they would not publicly validate the effects that women's activism had on politics.

FEMALE STRATEGIES

The first participant to employ what might be called a female strategy within a very limited space for public debate was Vicenta Ochoa herself. On 21 July 1835, thirteen days after the military revolt that briefly ousted President Vargas, she wrote to the insurgent government seeking clemency from the executive. It is not clear whether Ochoa herself wrote the letter, but it is intriguing to observe that she or whoever wrote the letter (the handwriting did not match her signature) strengthened the arguments made by her lawyers. Ochoa took the opportunity of the coup to call for reforms in the administration of justice and to plead for clemency:

The reforms that Caracas proclaimed as necessary to different branches and above all to the administration of justice are the same ones that have moved me to address your Excellency with the hope that dignifying us by receiving my solicitation . . . will bestow all the honor that is owed to one of the most grandiose eras of Venezuela. The constitution that ruled the old system and that has provisionally remained in use . . . concedes the president of the state the authority to grant favors like the one that I implore today of your Excellency who, while simultaneously occupying one of the highest positions, is interested above all in my favor, in an event as dignified as it is necessary.[85]

Ochoa, or her scribe, did not hesitate to praise the personality of the new executive at every available opportunity, appealing to the "grandeur of your soul," to the revolutionary moment as "one of the most grandiose eras of Venezuela," and to the sensibilities "of your Excellency the first example of kindness in this era of triumphs . . . the hero of the greatest magnitude" in order to adulate the masculinity and political agenda of the executive.[86] Moreover, she thought that her case might possibly serve as benevolent propaganda in favor of the new regime. Indeed, the letter suggests that public opinion was on her side and that the "popular clamor" would hinder any attempt on her life. To further assert the veracity of her claims, she argued that the Superior Court had moved to Puerto Cabello to escape the opposition to their death sentence ruling. It was likely, however, that the court members were hiding from the turmoil created by the coup.

In her letter Ochoa not only insisted upon her absolute innocence but also expressed indignation that while her criminal charges were going through the tedious legal process the "true killer" (Corporal Bastardo) was at large. As such, the letter suggests that Ochoa had been the victim of a system that still privileged the military, even though such privileges had been formally abolished by the Constitution of 1830. With this insinuation, Ochoa or the writer attempted to call attention to the need for changes in the reigning administration of justice. These arguments might not have sat well with the revolutionary government because that group sought – as part of the reforms they wanted to implement – to reestablish military privileges.[87] That the argument appears inappropriate under the circumstances could be because the coup was highly heterogeneous in its rank and file and in its agenda. Hence the goals of the reformists might not have been manifest to the general public initially.

Before ending the letter Ochoa informed the reader about the child to whom she gave birth while in prison and whom she was breast-feeding at the time, emphasizing the latter to express the extent of her bodily commitment to her maternal and patriotic duties.

Her strategy and arguments failed, however. By 20 August 1835 Vargas was back in the presidency, and Ochoa's letter was filed with a note: "As this request is not addressed to the government it appears to be a random plea."[88] She addressed her grievances and requests to the wrong people, and so her letter was simply filed away.

By the time the court denied her appeal and the executive ratified her execution on 17 May 1836, there was little she could do. Eight days later she was taken to the chapel in preparation for the execution, as was customary in these cases, and it was there, after many tormenting hours, that she communicated to the authorities that she was expecting her second child. Doctors were sent immediately to examine her, and Ochoa told them that she had stopped menstruating three months before and that her belly and breasts were enlarged. Doctors recommended that the execution be postponed for two additional months to confirm her pregnancy. Despite the doctors' recommendation, the judge by law had to continue with the plans for execution until he received orders to the contrary from the executive or the high court.

To expedite the orders the lower-court judge wrote immediately to his superiors to suggest that Ochoa's execution be postponed until her pregnancy was confirmed. To make them aware of the growing public support for the commutation of her sentence, copies of the printed flyers that were being circulated in Caracas were attached to the letter.

The prompt attention that Ochoa received from both the courts and the public after announcing her pregnancy point to the receptivity that motherhood engendered in the cultural milieu of Caracas. It was as if there was an implicit understanding that women's reproductive capacities were conceived as a "private property" that society had to protect. Indeed, the pregnancy plea became the most effective strategy to evade execution, at least temporarily. In Roman law infants could not be harmed if their mothers were going to be executed, and according to the reigning laws in Venezuela, even if the pregnancy was used as a strategy to postpone a death sentence, the execution had to be put off.[89] Ochoa may have used her pregnancy to manipulate judges and public opinion in order to postpone her execution. The attention that she was unable to obtain through the courts and written petitions to the executive was quickly obtained by her ability to bear children.

Indeed, the city seems to have been mobilized somewhat by the news of the death sentence of a pregnant woman. Printed flyers were distributed and letters were signed and sent to the president of the republic soon after the pregnancy announcement was made. Women used this opening in public opinion to seek understanding within their limited space of action and to give their unsolicited opinion on the need to abolish capital punishment. In their letters they incorporated language and images that emphasized their irreproachable modesty and their strict adherence to cultural and social norms regarding female domesticity and motherhood. The desired outcome was to foster an unquestionable consensus around the plight of a mother.

Ana Salias, owner of the murdered slave, wrote to the executive: "I must unite my voice with those of the majority of the habitants of this city who desire the commutation of the death penalty."[90] She asked the acting president to give life to Ochoa, even if the tribunals sentenced her to death. There was a possibility that Ana Salias wrote the letter herself, as her signature resembles that of the handwriting in the document. She stated that there were many serious and powerful reasons for pardoning Ochoa, the most persuasive being that she was pregnant. Furthermore, Salias claimed that Ochoa's suffering while in the chapel had nearly propelled her into a state of dementia. All the suffering of this unfortunate mother became nothing more than "an object of compassion for the sensible caraqueños." Salias's letter ultimately alluded to the constitutional right that permitted the executive to pardon individuals who were sentenced to death (art. 117, item 21). Finally, Salias did not argue for the innocence of the murderer of her slave but requested an alternative punishment compatible with her sex, state, and circumstances. As with all the writings by women and men in this case, this letter does not indicate any deliberation over the conflict between the constitutional dictum of equality before the law and the call for continued protection based on gender. That seemed to be taken for granted. Yet one is left wondering whether some women were demanding protection that they felt society owed to motherhood as a way of claiming or obtaining the equal protection of the law that was not practiced nor granted in the tribunals otherwise.

On 24 May 1836, in a letter signed by twenty-seven married mothers, the madres de Caracas also requested the commutation of Ochoa's sentence.[91] Contrary to the other letters, this one began by qualifying motherhood as a respectable title that touches "sensible souls." It was because of that noteworthy title that these mothers were encouraged to write to the president of the republic, the person in charge of guarding the "codes of our sacred rights." They appealed to his "heart of a tender father and loving husband" to engage his attention to this case. Following that preamble the writers stated how anomalous it was in Venezuela to apply a death sentence to the "weak sex." Anomalous because, in Caracan society, proper and delicate treatment of the female sex was considered a noble and humanitarian attribute. By commuting the death sentence of a mother, "Your Excellency will add to the glory of your illustrious name by your virtues, the surname of HUMANE and PHILANTHROPIC, always desired by just men."[92] Thus in the latter instance, saving a weak mother from death is what would bestow greatness upon him and his name.

While on the one hand it was motherhood that united them and gave them the power to write to him as president and make a request, the women were also making a personal appeal to his honor as a man when they emphatically stated that he would earn important qualifiers by pardoning Ochoa. The adulation of the president seemed to have been an approach that helped them to avoid the impression of a possible confrontation with male power, while simultaneously making him more receptive to their claims.

To these petitions was added that of the nuns from the cloistered convent of Concepción, the Carmelitas and Dominicans who wrote directly to the vice president requesting that Ochoa be spared from execution.[93] Discovering that a woman had been sentenced to death by the tribunals of justice caused them great anguish, and knowing that the government cabinet had the power to forgive her, they requested such commutation "so that in Caracas an execution so horrible as that of a poor woman is not seen, and so that the Republic conserves a mother and a good wife." The nuns stressed motherhood as a social function in a religious interpretation. They relied on the scriptures that call for forgiveness as more important than punishment. "It is always more glorious to forgive than to punish." Yet pardoning a woman, a member of the weak sex whose brain does not account fully to her actions, is even more glorious. Although they acknowledged the importance of a madre de familia to society, they nonetheless requested the forgiveness of a woman who by means of her sex did not inspire the fear that her mistakes would be repeated: "What is lost in pardoning one who because of her sex does not inspire the fear that she repeat her errors? A great deal would be lost by punishing a married mother who could be so useful to society." The nuns combined the argument of women's inherent weakness and their pivotal role in society but added to it a religious tone of forgiveness. As in the other letters, the nuns did not forget to praise the executive as well: "That she not die, Sir, that this unfortunate woman not die. This is what we hope from your Excellency's generosity."[94]

Whether these women perceived their actions as a conscious political statement is not completely clear, especially when their arguments are examined in contrast with those of litigants from the late nineteenth century (1875–80) who explicitly saw motherhood as a generator of rights. However, their boldness and courage to claim a collective plight in the context of their ambiguous political and legal situation is important. That they sought ways in which to make a claim and to seek the attention of ruling men points to how women – and people in general – found ways to maneuver within a limited margin of action while covertly challenging the subordination that was expected of them. That these women used motherhood as their argumentative avenue or "strategic metaphor" is understandable, since their reproductive capacities needed no further justification; culturally the idea that society had to protect motherhood was unquestionable.[95] If that image was used in a way that did not evoke the idea of disruption of the social order or male power, it could help women obtain some receptivity to and support for their demands. While the use of the social function of motherhood in the feminist movements of the early twentieth century has been interpreted as conservative because it reaffirmed women's domestic roles – which is a legitimate argument – Ochoa's case in the early nineteenth century helps us understand the logic of that strategy.[96]

In the end Vicenta Ochoa's sentence was commuted from death to exile to the island of Margarita for six years. Since no prison existed on the island at that time, it was expected that she would live there in relative freedom. The courts did not wait to confirm whether she was pregnant before they made their decision, which reaffirms that society and the law respected motherhood deeply. Ochoa's case may not have been decisive in convincing the government of the need to abolish the death penalty, but it served to invigorate the debate that led to the gradual decline in the use of the death penalty for murder cases after 1849. In addition, it may have been an important step toward the use of motherhood to claim legal and political rights by the late nineteenth century.

No one, however, remembered María de la Cruz, the strangled slave. A samba slave woman, María de la Cruz was also considered a woman with a bold and peevish character. In the minds of the ruling classes, this characterization may have been uncomfortably reminiscent of the violent passions and unsubmissiveness of the wars of independence, characteristics they did not want associated with their Venezuela. It is ironic, however, that while it was Ochoa's pasiones that had provoked her to kill, it was her image as a mother, useful to society, and possibly her light skin that ultimately saved her. Vicenta Ochoa may have been dead many times according to the law, politics, and the exclusionary language of the ruling classes, but it was motherhood – and perhaps her race – that kept her alive in the end.

5. Equality before the Law

A long the lines of the gendered discourse and interaction among the ruling elites, the legal environment of the new republic framed women's lives within the domestic sphere. This recipe for elite patriarchal order also dictated that labor be controlled and disciplined and private property protected through harsher punishments. While the immediate rulings by republican courts did not contradict the desires of the padres de familia, they were not completely encouraging for men either: the use of colonial legislation in the early republic carried on the continued intrusion of the courts into men's private sanctuary and created an opportunity for some women to challenge patriarchal privileges in times of equality and citizenship.

LAW AND THE NEW REPUBLIC

With the birth of the new republic, profound changes were sought. The Constitution of 1811 abstractly established that "all free men in Venezuela" were equal before the law. No one would have a title or privilege other than that of being a citizen of the nation.[1] This meant that the law would not recognize any special privileges, ranging among those of birth, purity of blood, nobility, or corporate status like that enjoyed by the Indians. By the same token the law revoked all ancient laws that "imposed a civil degradation upon a portion of the free population of Venezuela known as pardos" and made them equal to everyone else.[2] This legal language of equality and citizenship was highly inclusive. It is not surprising, then, to read the observation by an English traveler to Caracas in the 1830s that "a general degree of freedom . . . now exists among the races." He added that "negroes and mulattoes [have] the privilege of greeting any person, whatever his rank or situation in life, with the familiar appellation of citizen."[3]

Although the early republican government officially followed liberal ideas, the Spanish legal tradition was maintained. The law of 13 May 1825 established that the hierarchy of laws of the new republic would be as follows: (1) laws decreed by the legislative power; (2) pragmatics and other laws and orders such as cédulas, órdenes, decretos, and ordenanzas from the Spanish government that were approved by the law of 18 March 1808 and observed in the republic's territory; (3) the laws of the *Recopilación de Indias*; (4) the laws of the *Nueva Recopilación de Castilla*; and (5) the *Siete Partidas*. It was also established that all laws that directly or indirectly contradicted the Constitution or the laws of the legislature would have no effect.[4] As shown in chapter 2, the force of colonial laws legitimately continued the patriarchal authority of male household heads in the early republic. It also allowed that class, race, and gender distinctions formed the primary basis for determining people's rights in courts. The use of colonial legislation gave continuity as well as legitimacy to Venezuelan judicial institutions.

While most Spanish laws affecting women were still in use, the principle of equidad that had protected women from the rigidity of Spanish patriarchal laws disappeared in the early republic. The certainty of the laws as enacted by the republic's legislature was preferred in the new nation over the legal uncertainty created by judges' discretionary powers allowed by the principle of equidad. We should remember how the rulings by colonial judges were deemed an arbitrary and authoritarian maneuver of the Spanish crown to intrude in men's private domains (as shown in chap. 2).[5] The disappearance of equidad did not completely silence men's criticism about the court's excessive interference in domestic affairs, however. Women still received some protection from the republican courts.

The integration of liberal ideas into the juridical system, particularly the rights that applied to ordinary citizens, would have to wait until the drafting of the Civil Code of 1873. The situation was similar throughout Spanish America. Thus for the next six decades, prior to the enactment of a civil code that lauded the autonomous individual, the state and citizens had to deal with the contradiction between some women's claims of inclusion in the abstract definition of citizenship as ciudadanas (female citizens) and the inferior status accorded them by Spanish civil law. Yet only some men could legitimately participate as "active" citizens due to their age, status as married men, properties, income, and profession or even on account of their wives' properties. The vast majority of Venezuelans, including women, could not participate in political election as candidates or as voters, however, nor could they legitimately claim the protections that citizenship provided to its active members.[6] Civil liberties, equality, the use, enjoyment, and protection of a person's property, individual security, and the fair and honest exercise of such rights were guarantees made since the Constitution of 1811 to the citizens.[7] The rhetoric of equality concealed who were the true recipients of such protections: propertied male padres de familia.

New laws dealing with marriage reinforced the late-colonial trend of curtailing legal actions that challenged fathers' authority over their children. Such was the case with the law of 7 April 1826 that limited sons' and daughters' legal challenges to parental authority by prohibiting them from filing lawsuits against their parents when the latter opposed their marriage.[8] The 1826 law also lowered the age of majority, after which parental permission was not required, from twenty-five to twenty-one for males and from twenty-three to eighteen for females. This law ruled, however, that all women and men over those ages had to request the permission of their parents, but they could marry freely after postponing the marriage for three months if parents still objected. Younger children could not marry without parental approval, and in cases of disobedience, the parents could disinherit the children or ask the authorities to put the defiant children in jail for six months. Finally, the law echoed the colonial 1803 pragmatic, stating that the court would consider only those claims of betrothal that were formalized in a legal or notarized document.[9]

The law of 7 April 1826 increased parental authority by limiting the powers of children in the courts while at the same time augmenting the autonomy of children on marriage choices by allowing them to marry at younger ages without parental permission. In practice these laws cancelled each other; children could marry at an earlier age – even without parental approval – and parents could not be sued.[10] According to the law, these actions were intended to promote marriage, to stop offenses to public morality, and to foster an increase in the population by stopping the opposition that impeded marriages. Indeed, the government passed another law that made the marriage ritual free of charge.[11] Besides a three-year prohibition against marrying Spaniards initiated in 1828, freedom of marriage existed for everyone, and the only legal obstacles to marriage included insanity, prolonged absence in a foreign country, forced exile, and imprisonment.[12] Parents were the only party capable of restricting a marriage, but only if the bride and groom were under age.

Other legislation, such as vagrancy laws, directly affected lower-class women and men. Vagrancy laws were intended to provide more laborers for a healing agricultural economy as well as to bring a considerable portion of the population under the control of elite heads of household, as in colonial times. One of the most consistent concerns of the elites in the postindependence period was that unreliable wage earners were affecting production. In

1827 Gran Colombia's president Simón Bolívar lamented the moral corruption and lack of good work habits among the population. He suggested imposing "on the *jornaleros* [wage earners] a system of constant and rational dependency" under which they would be subject to the "guidance" of the police authorities and the hacendados. Bolívar believed that this would help to discipline the work and family habits of jornaleros. Jornaleros would have to become regular workers because they would have to meet new family needs.[13] Bolívar's belief in a paternal state is seen here in practice, as the dependent population would be supervised by property owners – most which, incidentally, were active citizens and padres de familia – and the authorities.

Laws were passed to discipline the labor force and to enforce the dependence of the lower classes (mainly slaves, free blacks, and pardos) on the hacendados. The Ordenanzas de Policía defined a wage earner or a servant as a person of either sex who worked for a period of time as a field laborer or a domestic. This included even those who had a small piece of cultivated land, cattle, or employment that generated less than one hundred pesos annually or those who had only a small piece of property that generated less than fifty pesos annually after payment of taxes. The majority of the population fell into these categories. Women were directly mentioned in the law: "Women who work lands in the countryside or who live in shacks, huts, or houses having no known honest occupation to subsist will be destined to work in the fields or in the house of an honest town resident for the salary or wage provided by a government agent or the person assigned in charge of the women."[14] Women without male protectors were included under this legislation. Orphans or children younger than fourteen years of age without tutors were treated as servants without pay for a period of eighteen months.[15] As in nineteenth-century Argentina, in Venezuela the idea of controlling the lower classes "seemed to depend largely on questions of class, public order, and labor needs."[16] It also reaffirmed the patriarchal foundations of the new liberal state, as the padres de familia would theoretically control the lower classes and also a labor force.

To further impose order and protections to private property, Bolívar decreed the death penalty for anyone who disturbed the "public order, peace, and tranquility."[17] All civil and military courts would follow this mandate. Another law, that of 3 May 1826, also instituted the death penalty for those accused of theft and robbery. By means of the Decree of 12 January 1824, the death penalty was extended to corrupt government functionaries.[18] Finally, Bolívar also established by decree (24 November 1824) the need to expedite the judicial procedure in criminal cases as well as for those accused of stealing money from the public treasury. To these laws the Páez regime added the ley de azotes of 1836, which physically punished those who attacked private property. As a consequence, and as is discussed below, those accused of a criminal offense, whether male or female, would suffer harsher punishments in the new republic.

LITIGATION IN THE EARLY REPUBLIC

Confusion was inevitable with the many laws that were in effect in the new republic. The courts ruled using a combination of codes such as the Spanish *Siete Partidas* and the *Novísima Recopilación*, the decrees enacted by Bolívar, and the new constitutions. Many cases made reference to the confusing body of laws and jurisdictions.[19]

In spite of this, the judicial system was able to function. The need to provide cohesiveness to the state and to consolidate its legitimacy helped support a working judicial apparatus. Legal institutions maintained Spanish juridical traditions, establishing continuity in the system even in periods of social and political crisis. In this context, and when considering the variety of people who relied on the tribunals for solving conflicts, the generally positive balance that the tribunals had is truly remarkable.[20]

Historian David Bushnell reports a "general increase in judicial business" in Gran Colombia between 1819 and 1827, partly because some cases that had been heard elsewhere before independence were now being decided in local courts. He also suggests that the new climate of liberty made more people willing to defend their natural rights through judicial institutions.[21] The economic havoc and social dislocations created by the civil wars of independence further increased criminal offenses in the early decades of the nineteenth century. This situation was not unique to Gran Colombia. Sarah Chambers found that in Arequipa, Peru, the number of trials began to rise in the last decades of Spanish rule; especially after independence, the number of violent crimes accelerated.[22]

In Caracas court claims dramatically increased and became more diverse after 1790. During the first four years of the colonial sample (1786–89), property-related problems among the elites were the norm, while in 1790 marriage and personal conflicts became more common. Court claims increased twofold in 1790 when compared to the claims of the previous four years, and most of those claims were filed by the lower classes. This 1790 trend continued in the 1835–40 sample, as lower-class people visited the courts more frequently to defend their individual rights in cases dealing with personal conflicts.

In the early republican sample (1835–40), cases of *injurias*, or contumely, were the single most common type of case tried, amounting to 11.3 percent of the 240 cases. Lawsuits involving violence were also important in this sample; cases of bodily harm (*aporreos*), violent estupro, abduction, bodily injuries (*heridas*), murder, and physical abuse accounted for 22.2 percent of the 240 cases. These cases could have resulted from conflicts arising from the precarious economic and political conditions of postindependence Caracas. With the new legal and political environment, people were encouraged to defend their property, individual honor, and natural rights as formulated in the Constitution of 1811. The period's new discourse of egalitarianism and liberty was reflected in the conflicts and the language used by litigants (see chap. 6).

The extent of female participation in court as litigants belies the entrenched belief that women as a group were passive. Table 6 shows the roles women played in court. Although 19.2 percent of women were victims, one wonders whether this indicates that women were submissive, as is generally believed. The attitudes and actions of the caraqueñas in this study contrast sharply with the demeanor of women in late colonial Buenos Aires studied by Susan Socolow.[23] The fact that in 43 percent of the cases women acted as plaintiffs in both the late colonial period and the early republic is rather astonishing considering the dominant idea that women were passive and did not belong in such a male-dominated world as the tribunals.[24] Indeed, a complaint brought by a woman was considered an offense to the male defendant's honor and could lead to acts of revenge.

An example of this type of reprisal is the case of a wealthy adulterous husband who threatened to leave all his goods to his illegitimate children. A more common form of vengeance among husbands was to stop the support that they were required to pay, as they had done in the colonial period. In another case, a man hit a nonelite young woman on the street. Some women hesitated to go to court, fearing that they might come across their husbands in the streets. In one case a woman asked a neighbor to escort her to the place where the official stationary for juridical use was sold for fear of her husband's punishment if he found out that she was suing or accusing him in court.[25] Men had a very defensive attitude when it came to lawsuits brought against them by their wives or partners.

To further illustrate the initiative of these women, table 7 shows how the cases were distributed in terms of gender and the relationship between the plaintiff and the individual who submitted the complaint to court. It is worth noting that half of the claims were initiated by women themselves, whether married or single, even though the law allowed married women to go to court only to accuse husbands in criminal or civil cases, to defend themselves against a criminal charge, or to make their own will.[26] To file any

TABLE 6. Women's Roles in Court Cases, Caracas, 1835–1840

ROLE	%
Plaintiff	43.3
Defendant	8.3
Plaintiff and defendant	8.8
Victim	19.2
Aggressor	2.9
Victim and aggressor	7.5
Accomplice	0.4
Accused	1.3
Interested party	6.3
Other[a]	2.1
Total	N=240

[a]Owners of the houses where crimes were committed; two cases in which there was no woman involved (sodomy and bestiality).
Source: AAC, Matrimoniales, Judiciales, 1835–40; ARPDF, Civiles, Criminales, 1835–40.

other type of complaint, a wife had to obtain a license from her husband. Women who were not under patria potestas and were twenty-five years of age or older needed no license.

Looking at the female plaintiffs alone (105 total), about 47 percent of the claims were filed against husbands, a process requiring no authorization. Thirty-one percent of female plaintiffs required no license because they claimed to be widows or single women older than twenty-five years of age. The rest of the cases, 22 percent, corresponded to women defending themselves in criminal causes, women who had a husband's authorization, or women whose authority for being in court was unknown.

Of these 105 plaintiffs, 30 percent had male representation in court in the form of a lawyer or a male relative. These findings may point to the fact that, overall, plaintiffs were aware of the rules about filing a complaint in court, because a case could be easily dismissed if the female plaintiff had no legal capacity.

A class variable was incorporated into the database to capture the social differentiation in the nature of the court cases. This variable was created taking into account four factors: property, income, number of slaves, and whether a person could vote. A list of qualified voters in Caracas for 1850 enabled a determination of voting status in a few cases.[27] Two broad categories, rich and poor, were established. The poor sector ranges from the indigent to those who lived modestly, on the rent earned from renting rooms or a small property or on the salaries brought in by one or two slaves.

TABLE 7. Claimants, Caracas, 1835–1840

CLAIMANT	%
Plaintiff—woman	36.7
Plaintiff—man	14.6
Victim—woman	9.6
Victim—man	2.5
Woman represented by man	3.8
Man represented by woman	12.9
Authorities	7.1
Neighbors	3.3
Slave representative	8.8
Unknown	0.8
Total	*N*=240

Source: AAC, Matrimoniales, Judiciales, 1786–95, 1835–40, 1875–80; AANH, Civiles, 1786–91; ARPDF, Civiles, Criminales, 1835–40, 1875–80.

When the class of litigants is considered (table 8) a clear pattern emerges. In the 15 percent of cases in which both parties were wealthy, most were related to the preservation of patrimony. Even divorce cases had material undertones because the mismanagement of the wife's property was a constant argument in all of those cases, as in the colonial sample. The small percentage of interclass litigation may suggest a limited interaction between the two classes in the courts. Most of the cases in which upper-class litigants filed against lower-class individuals dealt with problems stemming from cases of rich women well beyond their prime years having affairs with poor men, mostly young, immigrant Europeans (primarily Spaniards). On the other hand, poor people's cases against wealthy defendants were mostly related to claims made by slaves.

The cases in which both parties were poor were the most common (71.7 percent of all cases), indicating that some degree of legal recourse was available for all classes during the early republican period. Moreover, this category includes a wide range of both civil and criminal demands. Here the conflicts are not over property, as in the cases of wealthy people, but are matters of interpersonal conflict. As is discussed in chapter 6, conflicts among the poor, especially those involving women, dealt with the defense of their individual liberties such as the right to work for pay, to control their bodies, and to receive legal protection equal to that men received.

Given the context of revolt and turmoil during the independence wars, in which the popular classes were the main driving force, it is not difficult to understand why so many women brought their grievances to court. Many

TABLE 8. Type of Lawsuit by Social Class of Litigants, Caracas, 1835–1840

CLASS OF LITIGANTS AND TYPE OF LAWSUIT	%	% OF TOTAL
Both parties upper class		
Claims on marital property	8.4	
Divorce	11.1	
Grave acts of contumely	2.8	
Guardianship	11.1	
Marriage dispensation	2.8	
Opposition to marriage	16.7	
Parental power	8.3	
Petition for certificates	8.3	
Petition to remove daughter or wife from depósito	2.8	
Power to administer properties	16.7	
Family support	8.3	
Theft	2.8	
	N=36	15.0
Upper class files against lower class		
Administration of marital property	22.2	
Claim on slave property	11.1	
Divorce	33.3	
Family support	11.1	
Theft	22.2	
	N=9	3.8
Lower class files against upper class		
Abuse	17.4	
Claim on marital property	4.3	
Estupro, abduction	4.3	
Grave acts of contumely	4.3	
Inheritance	4.3	
Manumission/slave sale	43.5	
Opposition to marriage	4.3	
Paternity of natural children	4.3	
Support	13.0	
	N=23	9.6
Both parties lower class		
Abuse	2.9	
Administration/division of marital property	1.8	
Bodily harm	5.8	
Breach of promise	2.3	

TABLE 8 (*cont.*)

CLASS OF LITIGANTS AND TYPE OF LAWSUIT	%	% OF TOTAL
Cutting and wounding	7.6	
Debt	1.7	
Divorce	8.7	
Drunkenness	0.6	
Estupro/abduction	8.1	
Failure of a man to allow a woman to work for a salary	0.6	
Flight (of a wife)	0.6	
Grave acts of contumely	14.5	
Guardianship/power to raise a child	3.5	
Inheritance	1.2	
Manumission/slave sale	3.5	
Marriage license	1.7	
Murder	3.5	
Opposition to marriage	3.5	
Parental power	1.2	
Petition for certificates	3.5	
Petition to remove daughter or wife from depósito	3.5	
Poisoning	0.6	
Prostitution	0.6	
Restitution of furniture, clothes, or animals	5.8	
Sodomy and bestiality	2.9	
Family support	7.6	
Theft	1.7	
Trespassing	0.6	
Total	N=172	71.7
	N=240	

Source: AAC, *Matrimoniales, Judiciales, 1835–40*; ARPDF, *Civiles, Criminales, 1835–40*.

women were eager to shed any trace of submissiveness, even when the new republican state attempted to bring order and control to the population through the traditional representative of authority in the family – the padre de familia – and through new laws. Although this context could be considered a stimulus to legal participation, existing social and economic conditions may have combined to hinder women's access to the justice system.

Access to education was unequally distributed in Venezuelan society. The government of Páez was known for its neglect of primary instruction.[28] The upper classes had better access to education because they could pay for private teachers or schools and often for a private secretary or scribe. They also could afford legal representation. The poor were deprived of these key resources.

The elite-controlled government of early republican Caracas did very little to improve the lot of the poor majority. Yet the extant records of court cases investigated for this study point to a different performance by the court system. Despite the financial and communications problems that besieged public service, the courts did make an effort to administer justice efficiently, without discriminating against the less fortunate. This is important because, according to Luis Sanojo, a nineteenth-century jurist, litigation was very expensive, and even if the plaintiff won the case there was little chance that he or she would have any economic satisfaction due to the expense involved.[29] For that reason Venezuelan scholar Rogelio Pérez Perdomo argues that filing a lawsuit also had a social purpose, allowing the litigant to demonstrate that he or she was a person of prestige and standing.[30] In the context of a liberal republic, people went to court to defend their natural rights and social standing. This opportunity was open to everyone, including the lower classes.

The tribunals of Caracas honored petitions from the poor based on the Spanish law of the *Novísima Recopilación*, which provided that a person without money to pursue a complaint could be exempted from the costs of justice if he or she presented a "Certificate of Poverty." Some women, especially those seeking divorce, were issued such certificates on the grounds that their husbands were not providing support.[31] Also, the poor could attend lower courts headed by an *alcalde parroquial* (a local parish magistrate) for "conciliation" or a "verbal" trial. These common, low cost, and brief trials, in which the plaintiff orally filed a claim in court, aimed to resolve smaller complaints – such as debts of less than one hundred pesos, defamation of character, or marital fights – and to promote conciliation or an expedient solution among contending parties, minimizing the need for cases to go to a higher court.[32] Some of the 240 cases in the sample included *juicios de conciliación* and *juicios verbales* for the Caracas parishes.

Ultimately the fact that Caracas was, and still is, the major administrative, political, economic, and judicial center of the country may also have contributed to making the justice system more accessible for city dwellers than it was for those who lived in rural parishes. Given the new political and ideological context in which the domestic sphere was seen as the private domain of the patriarch, however, would the tribunals of the early republic be as responsive to the claims of women and the poor as those of the late colonial period? Were judges more restrained in intervening in family conflicts during the early republic?

In terms of civil lawsuits against husbands (and men in general), women were still receiving some protection from the justice system of Caracas. Yet it is clear that more judges were respecting the wishes of the patriarchs. Good examples of this trend can be found in cases that touched on patria potestas, challenging men's powers over women, children, and their property.

MEN'S POWERS

The sample included twelve cases in which women sued their husbands either to get a judicial license to administer their own properties or to prevent men from administering the women's properties. In six of these claims the decisions favored women, three of whom came from the lower class. In only one case did the ruling favor the defendant. Of the remaining five cases, one was settled out of court, another was dropped, and three were inconclusive or incomplete.

Even without the colonial application of equidad, women still regarded the courts as an institution that protected them, and the courts seemingly provided some relief while not contradicting men's authority as padres de familia. In this regard, the early republic was a period of transition. A good example is the case of Luiza Blanco and Silvestre Guereta.[33] In October 1836 Luiza wrote to the judge of a lower court (alcalde primero municipal) reminding him that the courts usually took care of women whose husbands had abandoned or abused them. In the early republic the tribunals "function as if they were their husbands."[34] Luiza had been separated from her husband for more than five years, so she requested a license to sell some of her small properties and use that money to repair her house. Luiza based her petition on the Spanish laws of Novísima Recopilación, as was customary in this period of Venezuelan history.[35] Due to her legal inability to sell her properties, even her slaves had to remain with her unwillingly. By law slaves had the liberty to change owners, but in this case they could not do so because their owner happened to be a married woman, who legally had no power to administer her own properties.[36]

In the end the tribunal, noting that Luiza's husband lived in the nearby coastal town of La Guaira, encouraged her to request the license directly from him. Silvestre, the husband, agreed to provide the license on the condition that she invest the money from the plots of land that she wanted to sell in one or more properties of equal value. It is unclear from the record whether this license allowed her to repair her home. Through her petition to the tribunals, however, she was able to get a marital license to manage her properties, while the court reaffirmed the husband's authority over the administration of her properties.

This pattern of rulings, in which the court granted women some protection while preserving the power of the padre de familia, is seen in other situations, too. For example, the tribunal explicitly gave a married woman named Marcelina Medina the license to administer only her properties, not those of her mentally ill husband, Ramón Guzmán. Instead, the court assigned a male relative as guardian for Ramón's properties.[37]

In cases in which the court denied women's petitions to administer their properties, the court respected the willingness of the husbands. This time the opinion was based on republican laws. For example, a judge argued that a law of the Code of Judicial Procedure (Código de Procedimiento Judicial) did not allow a woman to administer her properties if her husband was able to do so.[38] Although in this case the couple was litigating for divorce in the ecclesiastical courts, that circumstance did not affect the husband's right to grant such a license. Indeed, the court dismissed the wife's petition based on the legality of the husband's objection.

The courts reaffirmed the legal power of the padre de familia in the new republic without denying some justice to both women and children. Good examples of this ruling are the lawsuits dealing with support (alimentos). Probably as a result of the devastation caused by the civil wars and the high cost of foodstuffs in the city, wives' claims for support against fathers or partners were the third most common type of lawsuit in the 1835–40 sample. Lawsuits for support accounted for 8.3 percent of the 240 cases, preceded only by cases of contumely (11.3 percent) and divorce (9.2 percent). Most of the plaintiffs were lower-class women (16 of 20 cases). Nine of these 20 lawsuits involved support for natural children, and all were successful; 5 were settled, and 4 rulings favored plaintiffs. The courts consistently ruled in favor of children in cases of alimentos, especially if there was evidence that the defendant was actually the father of the children. Thus cases of alimentos became a means of formally establishing the paternity of natural children, who then would get inheritance rights.[39]

Married women and legitimate children had a more difficult time getting favorable decisions. The lawsuits filed on behalf of wives and children were denied in 4 of 11 instances, which suggests it was more difficult claiming alimentos for dependents in the early republic. When women married, they lost some ability to contest the patriarchal powers of their husbands, especially if judges were strictly applying the letter of the law. One such situation among married people was the lawsuit filed by Rosalía Mayora against her husband, Juan José Sosa.[40] Rosalía was a minor by law (under twenty-one years of age), and Juan José was much older. Although she was pregnant, Rosalía left Juan José a few months after their wedding because she thought he was extremely jealous, and she was not used to the "uncivilized" conduct of people from the countryside, as her husband was. The court made clear that under the Spanish laws of the *Nueva Recopilación* and also under the *Siete Partidas*, wives had to live wherever was determined by their husbands. Therefore Rosalía's case was dismissed; the only way she could receive support was by returning to her husband's home.[41]

Although the parental powers of fathers and husbands were reinforced in republican times, the courts consistently reminded men that they had to provide for their children, whether legitimate or born of an informal union. In the case of one married couple with a stormy divorce suit, the plaintiff, Micaela Ravelo, seemed to have found a way of making her neglectful husband pay for her sustenance and that of her children.[42] Micaela had taken some loans to support herself, but she was in arrears. The lenders sued her, but she lacked juridical person because she was a married woman and her husband administered all of her properties. She drew her husband, Juan José Espinoza, into the litigation. Her creditors then had to claim the loan directly from Micaela's husband, who argued that the claim was groundless because she had not requested his permission to obtain such loans in the first place. Moreover, she had voluntarily left him. The judge determined that a husband was obliged to support his family from his own properties. The aggrieved husband appealed, but to no avail.[43] In his final decision the judge established that "The law definitely forbids married women to enter contracts without their husbands' permission; but also it is certain that the right to obtain food and the obligation of the father to provide for the children, or the husband for his wife, are recognized as sacred in our legislation, because they emanate from the same precepts encoded in the law."[44]

Juan José's appeal backfired. Because Micaela already had a divorce case underway in the ecclesiastical courts, the civil tribunal gave greater weight to the fact that her husband was not providing than to the fact that she had voluntarily left his home and had obtained loans without his permission. This attitude of the judge was quite common during the late colonial period because, according to the *Siete Partidas*, providing support for someone, especially for women and children, was a duty that emanated from natural law and pity.[45] Clothing, food, and shelter could not be denied to anyone and especially to close relatives, including natural children.

That was precisely the case of Bacilia Ayala, a single mother who sued her son's father, Juan Bautista Abreu, for not providing alimentos.[46] In this case the tribunal ruled that because he confessed that the son was his, Juan Bautista should take the boy with him and look out for his education. Moreover, he had to pay court costs.

In terms of the parental powers of husbands and fathers, the early republican rulings marked a transition. While in the late colonial period women relied on judges' discretionary use of equidad to provide justice for them, in the early republic women did not receive such benefit: judges applied the letter of the laws without fully contradicting the powers of the patriarchs. Men would still criticize such actions by early republican judges. One infuriated husband complained that in republican times, as in the late colonial period, the court ruled in favor of women when the law was written to protect men.[47]

Marriage did become much easier in the new republic for couples over age and for those whose promise of marriage was not broken. The new 1826 provisions on breach of promise, which stipulated that only notarized promises of marriages would be considered in the courts, took a toll on the number of such cases that were brought to the early republican tribunals. The same law also did not allow men under twenty-one and women under eighteen to marry without parental permission. Indeed, of 240 total cases, only 4 cases of breach of promise and 13 cases of opposition to marriage were filed in the secular and ecclesiastical courts in the years from 1835 to 1840. These kinds of cases drastically declined compared to the colonial sample.

Contrary to the colonial sample, none of the four cases of breach of promise for the early republic had a successful outcome for the plaintiff. Only two cases were settled; one judgment went to the defendant, and one lawsuit did not have an ending because the defendant ran away. In most of the civil cases of opposition to marriage (nine out of ten lawsuits) judges ruled in favor of the children, who happened to be older than the age established by law. The parents won none of the lawsuits; indeed, there was only one case that had no ruling. Moreover, the most common reason given for opposing a child's marriage (when one was provided) was the financial inability of the groom to sustain a family. It is significant to note that purity of blood and honor were not mentioned as reasons for opposing a marriage, as was true in the late colonial period. Those aristocratic values waned in the new republic as well.

The state ruled consistently in cases of parental opposition to marriage, even when the legal dispute involved a reputable family.[48] The most important issue was to prove the ages of the bride and groom and their true will to marry. Whether the bride was pregnant or had borne children from the relationship does not seem to have affected the opinion of the judges.[49]

These patterns of rulings do not mean that the courts did not reprimand couples who lived in concubinage. For the courts, couples who cohabited were not people "of order," and their behavior demonstrated their lack of morals.[50] The tribunals admonished both sexes: men had to stop their lascivious dealings with women, and women were asked to be "better behaved."[51] Indeed, an environment of increasing intolerance for informal unions was apparent in this sample and became evident by the late nineteenth century (see chapter 8). In the context in which government intended to maintain peace after the civil wars of independence, those who did not live according to official domestic precepts may have been seen as potential agents of disorder, especially if these litigants were from lower-class backgrounds.

CRIMINALITY

Most of the people in the early republican sample who were involved in criminal lawsuits belonged to the lower classes, and some were not married.[52] More importantly, most of the cases dealing with criminal acts were brought to a conclusion, many times one that found the accused guilty of a crime. This is especially true in cases of murder; in five out of six cases, the tribunal pronounced guilty verdicts. Also, in five out of eleven cases of assault and battery the accused was found guilty. In cases of bodily harm and theft, however, sentences tended to vary – probably because many of these cases involved ordinary occurrences motivated by jealousy, contumely, and debt. In these cases the tribunals tried to promote settlement between the parties involved or dismiss the case after a fine was paid and after the victim had recovered.

In the early republic criminal acts such as murder were treated with great care, because it was thought that this was a way of curtailing the excesses promoted by the independence wars. To attain peace and order the tribunals used both Spanish and early republican laws to support their decisions, although it seems that in the colonial period the death penalty was not applied often. The severe sentencing pattern of the early republic did not discriminate in terms of gender.

In chapter 4 we saw how the case of Vicenta Ochoa gave elite men who were unhappy with the regime a chance to criticize it. Here we can examine the case as an important example of a stern sentence in the early republic.[53] Vicenta Ochoa was accused of murdering a samba female slave named María de la Cruz, who sold veils and skirts in the streets of Caracas. As narrated in a report on the case, Vicenta owed some money to María. From the records it is clear that Vicenta did not get along with the slave because María, according to Vicenta and many others, had a haughty, bold, and peevish character. Vicenta's race or ethnicity is not mentioned in the records, but it could be inferred that neither the authorities nor her defenders associated her with people of black ancestry.

On 28 October 1834 María went to Vicenta's home with her suitcase of goods to collect the money Vicenta owed. Vicenta called Corp. Manuel Bastardo (or Cabo Bastardo) to help her tie up the insolent slave. Vicenta, it seems, hit María several times and suffocated her with a piece of cloth, killing her instantly. With the corporal's help Vicenta placed the dead body in a sewer close to her house. She then gave a pair of earrings to the corporal as compensation, and during the night she sold the goods from María's luggage. Five days later the authorities found the corpse.

After much investigation, in June 1835 a sentence was pronounced in this case. Based on the Spanish laws of the *Novísima Recopilación* and the *Siete Partidas*, and on the republican law of 3 May 1826, Vicenta was sentenced to death in a public plaza of Caracas. Not only had she murdered a slave, but she had stolen from her as well. Although the sentence was appealed, it was ratified by the executive power and by the court again. On 25 May 1836 Vicenta was placed in a chapel to prepare spiritually for the execution. There she spent hours in torment and was said to have lost her mind. She told authorities that she was pregnant, and her lawyers argued the legality of applying such an inhumane sentence to a pregnant woman. As explained in chapter 4, many notables joined the mobilization, and a group of madres de familia (mothers of a family) and the cloistered nuns of Caracas wrote directly to the president requesting that Vicenta be spared from execution.[54] Vicenta's sentence was commuted from death to six years of exile on the island of Margarita.

Determining whether death sentences were common for convicted women in the late colonial period and the early republic is difficult. This was the only death sentence for a woman in the 1835–40 sample, although there was a similar case in which a male slave killed a female slave and was sentenced to death (1837).[55] Yet Vicenta's case was not the only time the death sentence was mentioned in cases involving female felons. Juliana López, a woman from Curaçao who owned a lodging house in Caracas, was accused with Guadeloupean Félix Ouvré of murdering and robbing a guest, Miguel Muñoz.[56] According to the sentence the death penalty could not be applied in this case because there were still some doubts and, "for the imposition of the death penalty, the evidence must be as true and clear as the light of the day at noon time."[57] Instead the judge sentenced them to ten years in a penitentiary. The records do not indicate where the defendants were sent, and there was no penitentiary for women in Caracas.

It is telling that in this case, which occurred a year after Vicenta Ochoa's, the punishment was harsher. All in all, women were not excluded from punishment for criminal behavior. Women received jail sentences similar to those of male convicts for crimes such as knifings and assault.[58] Both men and women received one- to three-month jail sentences for these crimes. However, a married woman was condemned to one month of voluntary work at the hospital while a female slave was placed in jail for a year, suggesting that penalties were conditioned by the accused's civil, racial, and legal status.

In this regard, the early republic was a transitional period in which both change and continuity can be observed. In lawsuits against the padres de familia, the protection that colonial courts granted to women and children did not disappear in the new republic, while the padres de familia found judges and laws that respected their legal powers over their families.

Most changes were related to the need to establish order and peace in the republic after the devastating wars of independence. Laws stipulating harsher punishments for crimes were enacted, and these did not discriminate on the basis of gender. Moreover, the government passed vagrancy laws that affected both men and women in order to impose greater control on the labor force. Thus although Venezuelans were now equal before the law and enjoyed citizenship status, early republican laws sought to impose greater control by enhancing laws and court rulings affecting the powers of the padres de familia, and by increasing states' and patriarchs' control over the lower classes. At that moment in Venezuelan history lawmakers and politicians were primarily concerned with promoting peace, protecting property, and encouraging economic growth. They sought to implement liberal policies in those spheres, not in the more intimate relationships among people of different gender, classes, or races.

6. Ciudadanas versus Padres de Familia

Although the legal framework in Venezuela maintained and re-affirmed the powers of male heads from the late colonial period through the early nineteenth century, there were limits to men's power over women during the latter period as well. Adult women had outnumbered men in the capital city of Caracas since the late eighteenth century.[1] Women from the popular classes dominated the streets as vendors and petty workers. Their households often had no adult men present.[2] Consequently many women were not under the patria potestas of any man. During and after the independence wars the people of Caracas experienced popular revolts and civil wars that transformed traditional urban society. The struggle of the pardo population for equality and upward mobility and the slaves' quest for liberty – which contributed to the widespread rumors of a "race and class war" that threatened the white elite – kept Venezuelans aware of their social condition.[3] For many other women, a sense of agency during these turbulent years gave them self-assurance and awareness of their capacity as decision-makers. By the beginning of the Republican era, after Venezuela's separation from Colombia in 1830, women in Caracas were already claiming their citizenship rights in court.

With political independence and integration into the capitalist-democratic world, new discursive possibilities were opened for Venezuelans. The female litigants in the sample were not unaware of the new discursive resources brought by liberalism. This chapter illustrates the ways in which many female litigants in Caracas embraced liberal notions of citizenship, liberty, and equality that were supposedly guaranteed to all Venezuelans by the Constitution of 1811. Yet the new ideas were expressed in different ways according to the social class of the litigant. Many of these women used the language of citizenship to defend themselves in their struggles against men and in their desire for equal protection under the law. Upper-class women justified their status as citizens based on their property holdings. Lower-class women demonstrated their liberal values by defending their individual liberties through their behavior. In their performances or in their use of liberal language, or both, they expressed their expectation that the laws of the new republic would equally protect their individual liberties as those laws protected men.

WEALTHY COUPLES IN CONTENTION OVER PROPERTY

In January 1836 Micaela Ravelo y Alcántara went to the alcalde municipal to ask that her husband be forced to let her administer the property she had inherited from her father. She had been married for many years to Juan José Espinosa and had borne him five children. Juan José had abandoned her four years earlier without providing support for her or the children. She complained that she lived in misery even though she had inherited wealth from which she could earn a livelihood. Yet her husband did not want to authorize her to use it.

Juan José argued that Micaela should resume "her duties as mother and as a submissive wife."[4] Moreover, he maintained that she had no judicial standing to pose a demand, because a wife's first judge is her husband, and he should have been asked first, before she brought the case to the attention of the authorities. Juan José closed his argument by reaffirming his patriarchal rights: "To behave in any other way is to dismiss a woman from the duties and rights of the man: it is to defraud the male of the privileges that he has from nature, from this nation's laws, and from the unchanging order of the whole universe."[5] He denied withholding support from his wife and family. Juan José claimed that Micaela's crazy and embarrassing behavior had led him to keep her at her mother's house. Micaela's mother provided everything for her and the children, but Juan José claimed that Micaela would only waste any money he gave her. Finally, he requested that Micaela be returned to her mother's house, from which she had "run away."

Micaela was surprised to learn that her husband was now claiming that she was "a runaway from his marital power and demanding rights from a consortium that he has completely forgotten and abandoned, ignoring his conjugal responsibilities."[6] She was astonished that her husband would make such a request after "he has forgotten my financial support, and consolation of the conjugal love, his contemptuous reproach, his mistreatment ... in which he subdued me for his unfair revenge and ugly ambition of disposing of my inherited fortune."[7] Micaela believed that her mother contributed to her "life imprisonment" to prevent her from receiving the inheritance. "Everything has been neglected by my mother and husband, she by abusing her maternal rights, which have no weight in a civil state of love and respect, and he by acting like a tyrant as if I were his slave."[8] She alleged that Juan José was administering her wealth through his right as a husband and not acknowledging that by law she had dominion and administration of the bienes parafernales, because she had not ceded such powers to him by law and by "the Constitution of the State [which gives her] the precious condition of citizen, owner of my rights, and assisted by my own properties."[9] Micaela consistently refused to let her husband administer her bienes parafernales: "For now, it is enough that the law is on my side, and the wisdom of the judges, which must not forget that although I am a married woman, I am not for that reason Mr. Espinosa's slave, neither have I relinquished my rights as a citizen, nor am I not the owner of my properties, nor do I not have the liberties that women of my condition have to allot or not to their husbands their properties apart from dowry goods."[10] Micaela based her argument on the new republican laws that guaranteed property to citizens: she considered herself a citizen because she owned property. Micaela insisted that she was not her husband's chattel (i.e., a slave), that she had rights as citizen, and that she had the right to administer her properties by herself. Finally, she asked that the court not require her to return to her mother's house because her mother would keep oppressing her and withholding her liberty to come to court to claim her inherited fortune.

Juan José argued that a married woman did not have the liberty to live wherever she pleased but had to live where her husband chose: "I know very well my rights, and I could use such rights to remove my wife from where she is without the need of the public authorities."[11] But his claims to rights stemmed from the colonial laws of the *Siete Partidas* and new republican laws, which allowed him to control his wife and children's person and properties.[12] He deemed it necessary to ask the court to return his wife to her mother's house because he did not want to use violence. He had seen the results: "Her defiant resistance, a reply based upon principles subversive to every social order, which begins with that of families that are the basis of society and the model of civil order."[13] In other words, Micaela's legal arguments based on liberal principles subverted the social order: she claimed to be covered by rights that were not intended for women. Juan José warned the court that scandal would be created if a woman, by demanding a divorce, were allowed to live wherever she pleased. This would result in anarchy, he insisted.

Micaela stood up to defend her claims:

If my husband considers himself innocent, if his conscience is clear, if he preserves intact his vows of love and faithfulness, if his life is a mirror of continence and virtuosities upon which his disgraced wife should look, take the first stone and throw it at me, like Jesus Christ advised. Go ahead with your divorce, accuse me of adultery, vindicate the rights of the bridal bed, if you consider they have been violated. I know how to defend myself, and then I will be obliged to make public the sad realities, sour truths, and embarrassing deeds that alone will take from me his confession, the haughty need of the defense. I will know then how to give proof of the tragic history that underlay my marriage, so that the church can declare and judge for the world if it can consent [to what happened] according to canon law. Espinosa may exhaust all his resources to fill me with shame, but take your hands off my property, which you have taken, let me defend myself at court and by law, do not disregard your duties of supporting me appropriately from what is mine, since he does not want to provide me from what is his as imposed by law. . . . Don't insult me believing I am defenseless, do not despoil me capriciously from my fortune, in order to succeed [in court] by the impotence and gagged incapacity of defense. If you have any trace of nobility when I am being persuaded in order to regain my affection and when indeed you want to take possession of my heart, when my property has been assaulted, when my fortune has been taken from me, with disrespect for my love and faith, then far from perceiving a decent motive, it is ambition and grossness which, masked with the name of husband, claims his rights to satisfy his ignoble wishes.[14]

The issue that incited Micaela to file her lawsuit was her husband's self-proclaimed authority to administer her bienes parafernales. The goods a wife brought to marriage as her own, in addition to the dowry, could be acquired, as in this case, by inheritance, but a husband was responsible for administering the bienes parafernales only if his wife had authorized him in writing to do so. As was true of dowries, the husband's heirs were requested to return the same property or its equal value after his death.[15]

Micaela's complaint went further, however. She complained of bearing all the responsibilities of her marriage. She cared for the children and provided economic support with what little she had because all her wealth was under the control of her husband. Micaela was not asking her husband to provide from his goods but only from what belonged to her. What is most important in this conflict, and in most of the conflicts I have studied, is the relationship between the economic support given by the husband or male companion and the women's submission or willingness to maintain a relationship with a man. In the words of Micaela's attorney:

If all the duties of the marriage fall back on Mrs. Ravelo; if she alone must be the faithful, the one who feeds the offspring and furnishes her peculium for this, then Mr. Espinosa has been entirely deprived of all kind of rights. Because in the social

state, duties and rights are relative, are mutually dependent on each other, and cannot exist without the reciprocal correspondence. This is the truth, and the contrary
would be a society against nature in which the weak party would carry the greater
burden; a leonine society in which the earnings would belong to only one partner,
and an execrable and accursed monstrosity, in which the sole name of the husband
had more force than reason and the order of things, and the male would take all the
possessions of life, without any kind of toil.[16]

Micaela pointed out that her own mother and husband had furtively
agreed "to practice a partition of the property and money acquired during
their marriage" for their benefit.[17] For these purposes, the civil legal framework helped to set the stage for Juan José's arguments. He implied that Micaela has not fulfilled her duties as mother and wife, and moreover, he suggested that she had committed adultery, a crime condemned for a woman.[18]
Therefore, it was his right as a padre de familia to discipline his wife. One
way he sought to control her is by putting her in depósito. But depósito
would have multiple implications. Depósito could be a place they both
agreed on, but usually a husband tried to find not only a respectable and
honorable family to take custody of his wife but one that would serve his interests. For instance, husbands consistently tried to restrict a woman's liberties, especially her ability to leave the house and enter the street. Of course,
this would delay any lawsuit started by a woman. A husband would argue,
for instance, that his wife was shaming the family by being seen in the street
and that she was meeting a lover. Men consistently asked the family to not
allow their wives to be in public spaces. As we will see, many women debated
this issue in court and even resisted such control by their husbands.

Another way husbands tried to limit their wives' actions in court was to
claim the juridical incapacity of wives. According to law, married women
were allowed to start lawsuits in court in only three instances: (1) to accuse
their husbands in criminal or civil cases, (2) to defend themselves from
criminal charges against them, or (3) to make their own will.[19] As described
earlier, if a woman were to make any other type of complaint, she needed
a license from her husband. Thus Micaela did not need a marital authorization to bring her husband to court, for as she observed, "to think otherwise, the matrimonial consortium would be a certificate of slavery for the
woman, and the word husband a despotic title meaning usurpation and
tyranny."[20]

Both men and women constantly invoked the metaphor of marriage as a
regime of slavery for women. Juan José kept using the word *fuga* (flight) to
refer to the fact that Micaela was no longer living at her mother's house. Mi-

caela's attorney clarified this issue in court, saying that *fuga* actually was a "word used to explain the bad behavior of a slave and not that of a ciudadana, a legitimate spouse who emerged from oppression to present herself to the public authorities."[21] The representation of his wife as a slave is especially meaningful because it shows that Juan José considered his wife to be his property and part of what constituted his power as a man.[22]

Even more serious from Juan José's point of view was Micaela's reliance on the "subversive" principles of the Constitution, that is, of citizenship and the equality of people before law. Juan José objected that such subversive thinking would lead to anarchy because the constitutional principles directly affected male familial control, which was the basis of civil society and of his status as citizen. Moreover, such principles defied his authority and honor as a male in society. A woman's lawsuit against a man was a challenge (*duelo*) to the man's honor and, as a consequence, many women had a hard time getting to the courts and finding shelter from a threatening husband.

Why was a man unable to control a woman or a family that was his kingdom of dominion? Why were the courts intervening in what was his manly duty? Drawing on his power of patria potestas, the male, not the state, had control over his family's persons and properties. Juan José indeed reminded the courts that their authority begins only when a husband's authority fails. The intrusion of the state then gave the public impression that he was incapable as a patriarch. As a male defendant in another case argued in court, "offenses to a husband are a very private matter, and even in an adultery crime the Tribunal cannot intervene if he does not want it to."[23] Especially in the liberal republic it was expected that the state, through the courts, would not intervene in domestic affairs. Yet, according to some men, the courts were interfering, and this stained the men's reputation as patriarchs.[24]

Micaela's case was not exceptional but instead reflects a strong pattern. The stories of María Antonia Pérez, Rosalía Canoso, and Josefa María Albelo, all of whom had some property, were analogous. The central issue in these conflicts is the relationship between the husbands' economic support and the wives' willingness to maintain the relationships. In each case the husband was administering his wife's property because he did not bring any property to the marriage.

María Antonia Pérez said she married Ramón Maucó in 1802 due to her inexperience and youth. By 1837 María Antonia had accumulated three coffee plantations, which she claimed produced seven hundred to eight hundred *quintales* of coffee, a number of other properties, and between six thousand and seven thousand pesos in cash. Her husband, Ramón, was a poor Spanish immigrant and former attorney of the Real Audiencia. María Antonia claimed he abused her dignity and honor, using vile language and wrongly accusing her of misbehavior. In 1811 she sued for divorce in the ecclesiastical court, arguing that Ramón was not providing a decent living, although he had wealth from her own properties. Ramón provided only one peso per day for the support of five people, "despite the high cost of food in the Capital."[25] After a fight between the two, Ramón stopped giving her that meager allowance. Also, he presented a claim against María Antonia to the public authorities, alleging that she was living an adulterous life. He claimed she wanted to divorce him and to be placed in La Victoria in the care of her mother, who had supported her throughout the marriage, so that she could continue her adultery.[26]

In 1830 Rosalía Canoso, a fifty-five-year-old, twice widowed woman, lodged a divorce suit against Ygnacio Hernández, a Spanish widower of Rosalía's age whom she had married in 1815. She argued that Ygnacio was an adulterer and that he had abused her. The ecclesiastical tribunal dismissed the claim because Rosalía's evidence was not conclusive. In January 1831 Rosalía sued for support, legal expenses (*litis expensas*), and the right to administer her properties because Ygnacio was allegedly mismanaging the three houses that belonged to her.[27] During the course of the case the real issue of contention became clear. Rosalía said that Ygnacio married her not because of his love for her but because he was after her properties. Indeed, she declared that the marriage was never consummated. Immediately after they got married he took advantage of an illness that she suffered, obliging her to sign a document that transferred all her properties to him. She revoked the document as soon as she recovered. In 1819, when the patriot forces triumphed, Ygnacio, a loyalist, fled to neighboring Curaçao. Feeling herself liberated from these tribulations, she "raised her hands to the heavens in thanks for the rescue from the worst servitude," as Rosalía vividly recounted in her testimony.[28] To her dismay, Ygnacio returned to Caracas after many years in exile. Anticipating new travails, she lashed out: "After many years, here comes a sworn cruel enemy of the country, who, calling me his wife, did not waste a step to gain possession of my houses."[29]

In June 1838 Josefa María Albelo married a Spanish immigrant known as Manuel Franco Moreno, a man twenty-five years younger than she was. A year later she filed for divorce on the grounds of abuse. Franco, as she referred to him, had entered her house because the Neris monks had sent him to collect a donation and to inquire whether he could work as an agent for her and Dionicia, her sister. María Josefa declared that Franco had the hidden intention "of seducing and deluding her to become his wife, not for love and affection, but rather to grab her property in his capacity as husband."[30] Franco, she said, used his Andalusian charm and cunning to seduce her. She married him even though her friends advised her not to do so. She even had to provide his wedding clothes. Immediately after they were married he began to treat her as a slave and assumed control of her sugar mill (trapiche) and lands, in order to have easy money for gambling. In June 1839 she also filed a civil complaint demanding that Franco be separated from the administration of her properties.

These four cases show the helplessness of wealthy women who were unable to administer their possessions, especially in situations in which husbands did not provide a proper livelihood. Perhaps during the wars of independence and the economic recovery after the late 1820s men of no wealth sought out women whom they could easily marry and whose property they could manage as husbands. These cases also show the experiences of immigrants, who, foreign travelers pointed out, were not easily accepted into caraqueño society.[31] These arguments make sense in light of Silvia Arrom's findings in Mexico City. According to Arrom the marriage rate for the upper classes remained low during the early republican years, possibly to avoid the dispersion of family property in difficult economic times. Many of Mexico City's unmarried higher-class women were classified as widows, a civil status that gave them the legal right to decide where to live and how to administer their properties.[32] Therefore, the cases of Micaela, María Antonia, Rosalía, and María Josefa could be a few among the sad stories of many who trusted their fortunes to husbands who were interested only in rising and thriving in caraqueño society.

There is a definite pattern of men claiming their rights as husbands and family heads, while women argued about their rights as citizens. The next step in these gender conflicts was women's requests to be placed in depósito. It was at this stage of the conflict that men tried everything possible to impede the continuation of a lawsuit. As discussed earlier, at this point the man's honor was put at risk: the investigation of the woman's allegations took place, and private family matters became public. Husbands tried to discredit their wives as much as they could to avoid this public embarrassment. Many charged their wives with adultery. Husbands also claimed that women lacked legal capacity to be in court and that, above all, their acts subverted the rule of law. In other cases, men would attempt to place their wives in depósitos as a means of controlling them. In these situations, the government offered a helping hand.

Ramón Maucó complained about the temporary deposit María Antonia Pérez had at Catalina Esteve's house. He claimed that his wife was always in the streets either alone or with that other *vieja* (old woman), who gave her too much liberty. He also insisted that she was using these liberties to get together with her *mancebo*, or lover. María Antonia convincingly responded that she was pursuing affairs related to her lawsuits against him because she had no one who could take care of them for her. Moreover, she claimed that the inability to go into the streets was irreparably prejudicing her interests. She asked that the court allow her out of the house in the company of her servant, a demand the court granted. Ramón, of course, was not happy with the decision. He asked that the person in charge of María Antonia's deposit not allow her to be in the streets and that if she violated this prohibition, she be taken to jail, "since on the contrary, [with a measure like this] the court will open a new manner to women who misbehave, because they lodge an imaginary and inadmissible divorce demand, as the present request is, ask to be deposited in any houses they choose, and from there they are on their own, walking without company and doing whatever they please, so that the depósito becomes a mere formality."[33] Men were critical of the opportunity that lawsuits brought women, which also hindered their rights as men when the state intervened.

María Antonia was enraged by the court decision not to allow her out of the house of confinement, even though a week before they had allowed her to go out with her servant. Her responses pointed to the abuses that were common to marriage and that in her view were supported by the actions of the tribunals:

I do not know how to declaim against the abuses which, until now, have supported the caprices of the husbands who have gained authority over women's lives. In essence, this is what happens in matrimony: The husband harasses and oppresses his consort and [unreadable] acts freely with her possessions, he orders his woman around and makes her obey him even for the most base and shameful of things, and the husband breaks frequently the sacred bond of fidelity, and tainted with all these defects, he goes to a court that not only justifies [his actions] but supports him to continue the destruction of his compañera. This is exactly my current situation, and this is how Maucó behaves toward me.[34]

This divorce case ended in part with a coerced agreement in 1812. Ramón, together with other men, caught María Antonia in the streets early in the evening and took her by force to Ramón's house. Ramón tried to induce her to stop the divorce case. In exchange, he would withdraw the criminal charges filed against her for adultery and would give her thirty pesos a month: twenty for support and ten that he would keep as rent for the house he claimed as his. In 1837 María Antonia went back to court to request an increase in her pension. The two slaves given to her in the 1812 transaction with Ramón were not with her anymore – one had died and the other, who worked as a shoemaker, ran away – and her mother had died, decreasing María Antonia's income and comfort. Indeed, she complained of being obliged to do servant's work, especially in the kitchen. She was reduced to living in misery when she had properties that could provide her a more decent life.

Rosalía Canoso also aspired to live in comfort and peace. For this reason she asked the court to allow her to stay with her adopted daughter (an orphan she had raised) and a married man who belonged to the influential Bigot family. For Ygnacio Hernández, her husband, this was unacceptable. He accused Felipe Bigot of sowing discord between him and Rosalía in order to control her properties. Ygnacio threatened to use his legal right as a husband to move his wife to another depósito. He definitely would not allow his wife to live as she chose ("a sus anchas"). Ygnacio believed that these "subversive ideas" came not from Rosalía but from Bigot, "especially in the current circumstances when the government cares about neither present nor past events." Ygnacio argued that what was behind all this was an anti-Spanish bias, and all he wanted was observance of the law because uprisings could occur if the people, especially women, were not obliged to obey the law.[35]

The civil court allowed Rosalía to remain in depósito with her daughter and even ordered Ygnacio to continue his support of fifty pesos per month. Infuriated by the court order, he complained: "Perhaps this is not the first time that a husband's just voice is disregarded to shelter and protect the stubborn and obstinate resistance of a woman, who with no cause, motive, or reason is determined to disobey the duty that she contracted."[36] As can be seen, Ygnacio was not willing to be humiliated by his wife's reluctance to comply with the law. Here again is a husband's criticism of the perceived lack of protection by the courts for men's patriarchal rights in their private homes.

To make this long story short, Rosalía resisted being placed in a depósito that her husband could control or to which he had physical access. At her advanced age of fifty-eight, she sardonically reminded the court that she was being treated as if she were a teenager. To prevent her transfer Rosalía pretended she had become very ill from a chocolate drink; Ygnacio offered to bring a silla de mano to transport her. When she was placed at her brother's house – a place chosen by Ygnacio – she escaped with the help of her slave. She did not want to stay with her brother because he was Ygnacio's partner and also wanted her properties. Moreover, he verbally abused her, threatened to hit her with a chair, and would not even let her see sunshine. Rosalía was thus able to avoid her husband's power for six years. Ygnacio died in May 1837 without vindicating his husbandly rights. Rosalía immediately filed a civil suit to get back the properties that were left from Ygnacio's administration. Control of these properties had passed to the children of Ygnacio's first marriage.[37]

In the case of Josefa María Albelo and Manuel Franco Moreno, Josefa María was able to convince the ecclesiastical court of Franco's mistreatment of her. The church approved a temporary "bed and board separation" for a period of five years. Franco was infuriated: "Now you tell me that I am worth nothing, but I used to be worth something when you said 'Come, lie down here, close to me.'" He fought very hard to keep the Albelo sisters' properties. Josefa María died two months after the divorce ruling in October 1839. Franco was frustrated because he had no access to Josefa María, even to her corpse: "One can see that my honor is compromised, as I appear in public as the man who is most heartless (*despersonalisado*) because I was deprived of the opportunity to express to her the generous feelings that reason and justice command to a husband."[38]

He continued to defend his rights to the property, even though Dionicia was the chief beneficiary in Josefa María's will. He objected in court to the deposit of Josefa María's properties under Dionicia's power.[39] Having lost that battle, he then claimed his share of the marital estate. By June 1840 Dionicia agreed to give him one thousand pesos, in exchange for which he was to refrain from filing any other case against her. She was seventy years old and aspired only to live peacefully off her properties.[40]

In these divorce cases among the wealthy, the issue of the administration of women's property or the relationship between property and women's autonomy in marriage was the main source of conflict. Here women used a modern discourse of liberty in their constant claim that marriage was slavery for women and in their use of the concept of equality, in the sense that they viewed marriage as a contractual partnership based on mutual obligations. To these women the position of padre de familia and husband was granted to men as a representative of the family and not as a privilege that allowed them to treat their family as slaves and properties for their own benefit. This same rationale was used by some litigants in early-nineteenth-century Lima, according to Christine Hünefeldt. The most radical claims came from women who were defending their assets, especially their dowries. Women claimed that their position was unlike that of slaves because marriage was a contract based on mutual obligation "guided by reason and justice" and this contract had to be observed even when a woman did not bring a dowry to the arrangement.[41]

These cases relate well to Richard Boyer's analysis of power relationships between men and women and of the normative ideas on marriage in colonial Mexico. He argues that marriage could be understood both as a mystical union based on love and as a contract based on reason and justice. Both definitions stress the reciprocal dynamic of marriage. He asserts that "the moral economy of marriages, then, is based on an ideal of reciprocity" and that in this relationship the one who dominates "must do so with legitimacy, on grounds other than naked power."[42] The subordinate person in a relationship tends to compare his or her concrete situation with the supposed norms that should guide the person of authority. Boyer concludes that "as long as norms and experience roughly coincide, one is unlikely to change course or to analyze experience; the awareness of a disparity between them is what spurs thought and action."[43]

It is clear from the lawsuits studied here that when one partner ignored his or her obligations, the other partner's obedience and submission were undermined. But unlike the colonial period that Boyer studied, during the early republic in Venezuela the terms of reference for the dominated individual changed. In the newly independent nation men and women were, abstractly, granted rights of citizenship. This act provided women with a powerful new argument to correct unfair relationships. Moreover, in early-nineteenth-century Caracas conflicts over property became the central issue in disputes over marriage rights among the upper classes. This is a modern rationale. The idea of marriage as a contract prevailed over arguments for marriage as a sacrament based on the bonds of love (as an expression of will) and mystical union.[44]

This does not mean that by the early nineteenth century the romantic aspects of relationships were no longer as important in an individual's choice of a partner. Wealthy female plaintiffs never said that they were obliged to marry; they did mention, however, their disillusionment with their partners after marriage.[45] Moreover, in the instances of parental objection to marriage, which constituted 5 percent of the 240 cases, one common parental argument was that the couple lacked any means of support. References to purity of blood or nobility, and even to race, were mostly absent from early-nineteenth-century oppositions to marriage. As is discussed in the next case, the reciprocal exchange of emotional and material goods that bonded married couples also occurred among people who were not married.

WEALTHY COUPLES AND LOVE RELATIONSHIPS

Conflicts in love relationships among the wealthy were not unilateral. Men were not always the villains and seducers. In the following detailed story a fifty-nine-year-old widow from a mantuana family sought the love of a considerably younger, poor man. What is significant is the role that wealth played in the process of seduction and the expectations that each person had in the exchange of spiritual and material goods. Moreover, the secrecy with which the love affair developed shows how difficult it was for honest women from prestigious families (who spent most of their time inside their homes) to develop a love relationship.[46] Needless to say, men and women of every social class found ways of participating in the love "fair."[47]

On 8 September 1836 María Antonia Bolívar notified the civil authorities that on 19 April of that year ten thousand pesos in gold had been stolen from her city home. She directly accused José Ignacio Padrón – a twenty-two-year-old lower-class comb maker (*peinetero*), clerk, and most recently, inn owner – of the theft. María Antonia presented the court with the results of her own investigation into the matter. She had sent an old samba freedwoman who had served José Ignacio's mother to inspect his bedroom, and the woman had allegedly found under José Ignacio's bed two silver busts of María Antonia's brother, the acclaimed hero of independence Simón Bolívar. The court was suspicious of the way María Antonia was managing the suit: she came to court four and a half months after the robbery, and she herself was making the accusation and providing the evidence.[48]

After the public authorities imprisoned José Ignacio and questioned him, another picture emerged. José Ignacio had been hired by María Antonia a year earlier to be her aide – that is, to be her private scribe and to assist with her businesses. He worked for only four months under a "private agreement" with her. Under this agreement he entered her house many times at every hour of the day and "passed the night at her house several times as a result of the private friendship (*correspondencia*) that [he] had with her."[49] He said that all the goods he had acquired were from his personal work and from some money that María Antonia had given to him. She gave him some livestock (about twenty cows) and about fifteen hundred pesos worth of gifts. He stated that he received gifts from María Antonia directly and through her servants. These included some jewelry, a small machete, a sword, gold and silver relics with chains, a bust of Simón Bolívar, a hair brush, five handkerchiefs, a small painting of two lovers with an inscription on the back written by María Antonia herself reading "For Padrón," a shirt, six hardbound books, two golden chains, and some buttons he was wearing on his shirt. She also gave José Ignacio as a birthday present a mule, in addition to some cows he picked up himself at the Bolívar family estate in San Mateo.

When the court questioned María Antonia's witnesses they stated that they saw him wearing a cloak near her city home. José Ignacio responded that that was because he had walked around her house many times, waiting to enter until few people were in the streets. Sometimes he waited at the English pharmacy, where he wrote notes to her and sent them to her via her slaves. He also acknowledged that he forced the window at María Antonia's house under her orders so that he would not have to enter through the hall, in an attempt to avoid being detected by the street dogs.

The story now had another tone: María Antonia seemed to be in love with José Ignacio, and she was jealous because he did not return the friendship, although she tried hard to protect him. José Ignacio submitted evidence of the personal correspondence he received from María Antonia, revealing a lover's feelings, fears, and expectations. In one of the letters María Antonia asked him not to play around with her because that would hurt her very much. Later she asked José Ignacio to make two combs for her to give to her friends and, "because I get jealous," she asked that he repair the inscription on her comb that read: "belongs to Ignacio, María Antonia Bolívar."[50]

The letters also served to set up their meetings and as their means of communication. María Antonia consistently advised him to have good sense, to be careful with his money (because he often gambled), and to take good care of his disgraced mother. The last letters reflected María Antonia's disappointment with José Ignacio. She claimed that José Ignacio was the strangest creature on earth because he did not respond to all her "sacrifices." She could not understand why he did not reciprocate her "friendship," because she believed that she had an important appeal to men: she was a mantuana, the sister of the Libertador, white, prestigious, and immensely rich, whereas he was nonwhite and poor. She had offered to protect him in every possible way, and yet "everything is worthless when God's fate is to make the man work." She suffered bitter disillusionment because José Ignacio never gave her anything.[51]

José Ignacio had many girlfriends, and María Antonia claimed that he had proposed marriage to each one. When she was informed that he had chosen one called Trinidad, she wrote immediately to let him know that Trinidad was a mulatta and that she would be willing to pay for the investigation to convince him of the fact. For María Antonia the concern over social status, purity of blood, and reputation were still very important.

It became clear to the courts that there had been no theft and that María Antonia had acted in a false and malicious way against José Ignacio. When the court returned the busts of Bolívar that she had provided as evidence, María Antonia arrogantly threw them to the floor, stating that they were worthless. The new republic did not appreciate Bolívar and her last name did not influence the court decision, as she seemed to expect. The judge reprimanded her, made her pick the busts up from the floor, and advised her to be more prudent and respectful of the authorities.[52]

What should be emphasized about this case is not the political and social implications of a court case involving the Bolívar family but the implicit understanding that lovers exchange some kind of material object as evidence of their friendship. María Antonia wanted to have the love of this young man, and she sought to attract him through her money and social position. The turning point in the story began when she noticed that José Ignacio was not attracted to her. He did what she asked him to do – visit her privately and do some favors. But there was no evidence that José Ignacio returned her friendship. Indeed, José Ignacio seemed to understand that his position in the relationship was guaranteed by the individual liberties brought by independence. He felt no need to make concessions to a person of high status; he was not interested in purity of blood.[53]

The relationship between José Ignacio and María Antonia demonstrates that friends or lovers as well as married people formed social interactions and sexual agreements in which reciprocity and the exchange of material and emotional goods were important. Servile relationships in which people were expected to passively serve a lord were no longer tenable. The idea of a contract, of an exchange among equals in an abstract sense, permeated many of the relationships between people, even though in reality the reciprocity may have been unequal. The examples are numerous. Micaela Ravelo y Alcántara's husband did not provide for her support, and she was unsubmissive; María Antonia Bolívar proved her love in material terms and expected the same from José Ignacio, her suitor. This pattern held true in gender conflicts among the poor. But the material realities and gender roles among the popular classes made these relationships appear in a different light.

LOWER-CLASS WOMEN DEFENDING THEIR INDIVIDUAL LIBERTIES

Early-nineteenth-century court records involving the poor indicate that more was at stake for poor litigants than for the upper classes. Through their claims, the lower classes defended their particular understanding of gender relationships and their "right" to defend their individual liberties.

For the poor, life in postcolonial Caracas presented many difficulties. To meet their emotional and economic needs in the overcrowded and expensive city, the poor developed extensive networks of friends and relatives. These solidarity networks must be taken into account if we are to understand the life strategies of the popular classes. The lawsuits in this study show that women worked for wages and usually held more than one job. A neighbor or housemate would help when a friend was in personal danger. These personal alliances were strong but could be broken by verbal offenses or physical abuse.

In male-female relationships women expected some type of material reciprocity from husbands or lovers. This could have either symbolic or material importance. Courting couples who were not living together could seal their relationship with a symbolic gift; through it, the man demonstrated his willingness and ability to support the woman.[54] Most of the cases in the early-nineteenth-century sample emphasized such an association.[55] What these exchanges of material and emotional goods may ultimately reflect is women's expectation that men responsibly fulfill a traditional role as household providers.

The cases of Dolores Blanco and Isabel Freites offer good examples of lovers' exchange of material goods and the importance of emotional bonds and fidelity. One night Dolores's boyfriend went to her house with a machete to demand an explanation for why she had gone to La Guaira (the adjacent port city) without his permission. She answered that he was not her father or mother and that he should not bother her because he had not given her anything to seal a bond between them. He became so infuriated with her answer that he tried to kill her.[56] Trying to prevent José Dionicio from stabbing her, even Dolores's friend Justa was injured.[57] José Dionicio claimed some power over Dolores without having fulfilled a symbolic ritual that was important to her. Dolores, in turn, seemed to understand that her relationship with José Dionicio would not be taken seriously until he gave her concrete proof of his commitment.

In a second case, Isabel Freites, a free woman from Curaçao who was a cook and street vendor, was accused of stealing some bottles of *rapé* (tobacco powder used as snuff). In court she was able to prove that the bottles were a gift from José, her slave boyfriend. Not knowing that the rapé was stolen, she took the bottles to La Guaira, where she sold the product at a reduced price. In the proceedings José confessed that he had stolen the bottles one by one to give to his beloved Isabel each time they met. (He had told Isabel that he had himself prepared the tobacco powder.)[58] For José, the rapé was a token of his commitment to Isabel. It showed that, to help his woman in times of need, his personal sacrifices knew no limit.

Although lower-class women were expected to contribute to the household economy, they aspired to have the male contribute.[59] Women and men anticipated some type of mutuality in the emotional and economic duties of their relationships. Because women understood their unequal domestic relationships with men as a consortium of mutual responsibilities, they vindicated their "right" to defend themselves from abusive relationships. Indeed, gender conflicts emerged when one party believed that his or her expectations were not met.

In the following cases, women were the providers for the household and problems arose when men abused women economically, verbally, or physically. Moreover, these women clearly knew that they could not live a secluded life if their husbands were not supporting the family.

In 1836 Cecilia Barraniz, a theater actress, filed for divorce on the grounds of abuse. In her civil suit she declared that during seven years of marriage she had supported her husband, Pedro Villalobos, but that he had not fulfilled his duties. Now her husband wanted her to abandon her profession and stop working. Cecilia demanded that the court force her husband either to sustain her or to allow her to work. In this case, Cecilia successfully defended in court her "right" to earn a wage.[60]

In another case, Agustina Arnal filed several lawsuits against her husband, alleging that he was crazy, abusive, given to drinking, and a vagrant. She was the sole provider for the family, but her husband demanded that she remain secluded at home to fulfill her duties.[61] Juana Rafaela Casares made a similar complaint against her husband. She requested a divorce, charging that her husband was interested only in her properties and in the labor of their children; the couple had had three children before they married. In addition, because she refused to give her scant jewelry to him, her husband had hit her, "converting himself into a Nero."[62]

Men also expected wifely faithfulness, especially when they were providing support. Even if they were not legally married, men insisted that women behave according to their traditional role as obedient wives. The dominant ideal of the padre de familia served as a legal basis for chastising and controlling women. As historian Steve J. Stern asserts, men also considered women sexual property.[63] On these grounds, men frequently went to court demanding that their spouses render the submissiveness they owed their husbands.[64]

Because of their strained financial situation, lower-class women were often induced to earn their own living. With this income they were able to obtain greater social and economic independence than their upper-class counterparts. Hence lower-class men felt anxious about the excessive "liberties" of their wives and lovers. In particular men objected to their mates' maintaining friendships with other people and to their seeming independence. Men expected them to behave as secluded, virtuous women. To attain this ideal, some men petitioned the tribunals to control their wives by applying the existing vagrancy laws. For instance, Pedro Pablo Herrera expressed concern about the drunkenness of his wife, Escolástica. She had been a hard-working woman but had become increasingly dependent on alcohol. Because he needed to go to the fields and the hacendados would not allow her to accompany him in a drunken condition, he asked the court to imprison her.[65]

Aware of their legal right to punish women for their behavior, some men took "correction" into their own hands. Antonio Romero's defense for hitting his lover provides a good example of contested perceptions of proper gender behavior. He had a love affair with Eulalia Sarmiento. With the intention of marrying her, he had paid for the house where she lived and had supported her. Her loose behavior and infidelities upset him, however. Antonio tried to split with Eulalia many times, but she kept asking for him and even took his clothes for laundering to force him to return to the house. One day he became irritated and jealous when he saw a man running out of her house. Antonio hit her to induce her to "reform herself" and stop such behavior.[66]

The inability to fulfill ideal gender roles because of poverty was another point of contention. The need for women to provide economic support for the household contradicted the code of proper womanhood. Many women could not remain in the house because they needed to seek sustenance by selling in the streets or at the market, by working at other people's houses, or by washing clothes in the river. Often women were "governing themselves" – as it was phrased repeatedly in the documents – and renting a room in a crowded house. They defended themselves physically in personal conflicts with neighbors or strangers, showing their independent and unsubmissive character. The violent behavior of men in these cases might be related to their inability to control women and, therefore, to save face in the community.[67]

Endorsement of norms for proper gender behavior by the popular classes could be taken as a sign of their acceptance of dominant family values, yet each gender assigned a different meaning to the other's role. The lower classes would follow gender role expectations, whether they were married or living in consensual unions, on the condition that the other acted accordingly. From these notions women derived particular ideas about their rights, and they defended those rights actively in the courts of Caracas.

Demanding equal responsibility with men in the household, defending themselves in abusive relationships, and vindicating their right to work for a salary, lower-class women were protecting their individual rights. Poor women may not have made verbal reference to the concepts of citizenship as often as the upper classes did, but their many actions in court suggest that they valued this status just as highly. The court records contain the "hidden transcript" of their defense of their natural rights in the domestic sphere.[68]

Wealthy women instead openly appealed to their rights as citizens when disputing with their husbands over questions of property. For example, María Antonia Pérez responded to the court's refusal to let her leave her house of confinement with these words:

In marriage, husbands are nothing but the ones who represent the family, and women, their compañeras [partners], who should help them with marital obligations but are not condemned to be the husbands' slaves; nor are women of an inferior condition in the exercise of their rights; the quality of being a woman does not exclude them either from the societal order or from the guaranty to enjoy their liberty and security of their person. *The law makes us all equals as citizens*, and if my husband is by this right authorized to behave in a free manner, I am, by the same right, entitled to resolve my needs on my own.[69]

María Antonia is only one among a group of upper-class women who were able to argue persuasively for their equal rights as citizens. What stood out was her idea of liberty and her belief that she had the right to seek her security and to fulfill her needs in the same free way as men, not as a slave. Her defense of her property and well-being carried along a strong criticism of her husband's behavior and legal powers and claimed her inclusion in the rights granted only to male citizens. She enjoyed the same rights as men, and therefore her person and properties should be protected by law.

As discussed earlier in this chapter, Micaela Ravelo y Alcántara defended her right to administer her property based on her constitutional rights and citizenship. In this case her husband accused her of relying on the "subversive" principles of the Constitution, that is, citizenship and the equality of people before law. He also argued that such liberal views would directly affect male familial control, which was the basis of civil society. Micaela's husband was quite conscious of the foundations and consequences of his power in society as well as the possible results of Micaela's and María Antonia's liberal claims.

It is hard to find such an articulate defense of citizenship rights among lower-class women. Unlike their counterparts in the upper rungs of society, lower-class women defended their equal rights as citizens mostly by their actions at home and in the courts. The cases in the sample did, however, include one instance in which a woman verbally expressed her expectations of being treated with equality. A freedwoman named Barbara Jedler complained about the cruel abuse her son suffered from his master and the provincial governor in 1835:

When I started to contend against a wealthy, powerful, and influential man, I a low colored woman, and he a high category man who is the owner of my son, what could I expect? What would be the result of a controversy among people of different spheres; and what would be my success if I did not count on the justice and evenhandedness of the court? This persuasion encourages me, and *the equality of rights that all Venezuelans enjoy* gives more strength to my weak forces and empowers me to not hide my face from Mr. Huizi's arguments . . . because, although I am a freed slave, it would depress my condition of respectful woman to other men and especially to social manners, but it should not be believed because of this that I am afraid of making use of my rights.[70]

Note that the act of complaining respectfully in court was not incongruent with the ideal of being an honorable woman. Such a woman was not willing to withdraw a just demand in the context of her equal rights as a citizen of Venezuela. On the contrary, she asserted that those rights encouraged her to pursue her claims.

In contrast to the upper classes, gender conflicts among the popular classes were related to the defense of individual liberties. Poor women questioned not the validity of the institution of marriage but the capacity and character of their husbands or lovers. They accused their partners of being alcoholic, lazy, or abusive and of not fulfilling the mutual rights and duties embodied in their formal or informal marriage contract. In this sense poor women were embracing notions of citizenship, liberty, and equality embedded in the Constitution of 1811 as they pertained to their unequal domestic relationship, not as a claim of political rights as in Europe. Lower-class women were already practicing liberal ideas in their daily relationships with men at the level of the household, a situation that was apparent in the court cases. They did not want to be abused, to be banned from working for a salary, or to be deprived of their liberty. They wanted compensation for their services and, by the same token, they wanted material contributions from their relationships. They wanted to be treated as ciudadanas, with equal protection under the law.

In early republican Caracas poor women pursued their quest for equality before the law through their numerous actions in court. Upper-class women spelled out their claim for citizenship more openly, while defending their property. Contrary to the widespread belief that independence did not bring significant changes for women, these cases show that women were individually seeking a transformation in their rights.[71] They met fierce resistance from their husbands or lovers, who stuck to their claims as customary padres de familia.

PART 3
The Late Nineteenth Century

7. Bourgeois Caracas, 1870–1888

In 1863 Adolph Ernst began his lessons on natural science based on positivist thinking at the Universidad Central de Venezuela, and with him the first generation of positivists was formed in Venezuela. One of Ernst's disciples, Rafael Villavicencio, quickly applied positivism to analyze his country's recent past. At an 1869 lecture at the university he stated: "Up until today, the career politicians have come from circles foreign to scientific knowledge, while wise men have maintained themselves alien to militant politics."[1] Villavicencio and his contemporaries, as well as the next generation of positivists, which included José Gil Fortoul, viewed pre-1870 politicians as men who did not value hard work but who enriched themselves through wars and bloodshed. Military chiefs had no merits other than the personal prestige they acquired during the frequent civil wars, especially because they could not perform the duties of any liberal profession or work in commerce or other industry.[2] Once in government these politicians became authoritarians and engaged in personalist politics. They repressed their opponents, and conservatives especially did not introduce anything that would benefit society because of their fear that they would produce more harm than good. Those men who ruled Venezuela, with the exception of Simón Bolívar and Dr. José María Vargas, lacked the education and the "know how" to rule a nation with a mixed-race population prone to anarchy.

Villavicencio encouraged university students to become knowledgeable and moral men because by becoming more civilized they become freer. Positivists believed that those who became industrious learned to respect others, improved their manners and social relations, and became less violent. Hard work and good morals would perfect citizens; yet only those who achieved merit in their work for the nation would be worthy of joining the pantheon of humanity. All people had an equal opportunity to elevate themselves, but that could be achieved only in proportion to each person's merits, a notion that helped support the positivists' hierarchical views of Venezuelan society.[3] Bourgeois masculine values had come to replace aristocratic and military ideas of honor for the positivists, who also had an obsession with capacity, virtue, and merit. Interestingly the individualistic value of hard work as a determinant of a person's social worth had been sponsored by the lower classes at least since the late colonial period and was appropriated by the elites a century after. Yet true merit was reserved for a select group of men, according to positivist beliefs.

No wonder Villavicencio praised the new government in 1870. It brought a long period of peace and good administration after the Federal Wars (1859–63), allowing the expansion of education, individual agency, and the national economy and thus creating "a new aristocracy: that of money and intelligence."[4] This was the Venezuela of Antonio Guzmán Blanco, leader of the liberal and federalist faction.[5] He was a man with a respectable genealogy: his father, Antonio Leocadio Guzmán, was a prominent politician who founded the Liberal Party in 1840, and his mother, Carlota Blanco Jerez de Aristeguieta, was kin to Simón Bolívar.[6] For historian John Lombardi, what made Guzmán Blanco special was his experience with both archaic and modern worlds. He grew up in the 1840s during the conservative-liberal controversies, but he was also integrated into European society.[7] Guzmán Blanco studied law at the Universidad Central de Venezuela and did his internship at the firm of Dr. Diego Bautista Urbaneja, the uncle of his future wife and a future minister in his government. Moreover, he occupied important government positions during the federalist government of Juan Crisóstomo Falcón (1863–67), such as secretary of the treasury and vice president, which gave him thorough experience with the financial sector and as a diplomat in charge of negotiating foreign loans in Europe. Guzmán Blanco portrayed himself as a man of so much power and merit that his "barbarous" military opponents could not measure up to him. Unlike other caudillos, he truly had the genealogical, racial, and educational baggage and power needed to shape Venezuelans' will.[8]

When Guzmán Blanco assumed power in 1870 he moved to pacify the country, bringing "order and progress" to Venezuela, at least according to his admirers. An important part of that goal was to promote the integration of the upper classes. Guzmán Blanco's regime followed a discourse of racial improvement or "whitening," in which it was believed that European standards of work, education, civility, and family life could be successfully implanted in Venezuela. The incorporation of Caracas's small foreign commercial elite to the local elite was sought in part because they could import European signs of civilization into Venezuela. Yet having a completely white elite was not possible. After many years of war, political power was opened to rural strongmen, many of whom were nonwhite, and their integration into the elite ranks was pivotal to the aim of order and progress.

To facilitate the integration of the heterogeneous local elites and eliminate the possibility of instability, Guzmán Blanco compromised with important social sectors. The incorporation of the commercial elite of Caracas with the government was achieved through an early presidential decree in November 1870 that created the Compañía de Crédito.[9] This board soon became a key institution and the merchant elite of Caracas leading players. The agency controlled virtually all government finances. It funded government projects and loans, handled the public debt, and devised policies to enhance fiscal stability.[10] More important to the achievement of peace was that the Compañía de Crédito formalized the means to redeem state loans held by merchants, providing wealthy merchants with a steady source of income while assuring that the government would meet its financial obligations. The aspirations of the merchants were satisfied by their economic role in the government.

To handle strongmen from the interior provinces, Guzman Blanco instituted a federalist policy in which caudillos were granted almost absolute authority over their regions. The central government agreed not to intervene unless the caudillos failed to maintain local peace. Moreover, many caudillos presided over public works for their regions, and they administered funds received from the central government.[11] With this policy Guzmán Blanco granted the autonomy that regional caudillos wanted, while at the same time he manipulated them by reducing their allocation of funds if they failed to do his bidding. By making regional caudillos dependent upon the federal government, Guzmán Blanco was also able to facilitate the centralization that social sectors such as the commercial elite desired while advocating "federalist" policies.[12] As a result, rural violence in the interior provinces was reduced.

Finally, the regime tried to alleviate, at least indirectly, the plight of landowners. Although their most pressing demand – that of having a reliable source of long-term credit at low interest rates – was not met, the government reduced some of their production costs. With considerable improvements in roads and the elimination of some export and import taxes and internal tariffs, landowners – and also merchants – were able to market their products more quickly and at lower cost.[13]

Along with the administrative reforms aimed at gaining the support of important social and economic sectors, Guzmán Blanco aimed at achieving social integration among elites in other ways. Because many of the new members of the elites' circle did not hold proof of nobility or colonial aristocratic ancestry, there was a preoccupation with the cultivation of bourgeois values and the construction of places in which elites could be educated about and display such values to the citizenry and the civilized world. The "spectacle of modernity" sponsored by the regime provided proof of Venezuelans' civilization and progress, making the nation attractive to foreign investors.

Structural changes in politics, society, and the economy were articulated through a discourse modeled after European culture admired by the ruling elites and influenced by positivist philosophy. Although positivism is not a political theory per se, it postulated that society was a developing organism that could only be understood and controlled through science.[14] National problems were to be resolved scientifically. Education, for instance, was oriented toward scientific and practical knowledge. Those who possessed this knowledge were to be the future leaders of the country, thus providing a rationale for the authoritarian character of positivist governments. It was understood that only through order and liberty could moral and material progress be achieved. This scientific shift evolved and was immersed in what Auguste Comte called the "religion of humanity."[15] Although it was a lay philosophy, positivism turned civic order into a religion. In the words of Brazilian political scientist José Murilo de Carvalho, "the saints of the new religion were the great men of humanity, rituals became civic holidays, theology was their philosophy and their politics, and the new priests were the positivists."[16] It is in this context that the ideological and cultural agenda of Guzmán Blanco should be understood.

As Carvalho has argued, in periods of social and political transformation – as in Venezuela after 1870 – the basic means of legitimating a political regime is through ideology.[17] For this purpose the manipulation of "social imagery" becomes of crucial importance. Cultural products such as symbols, myths, and ceremonies, for instance, helped the political regime to express its ideology and its rationale for organizing the power structures of the country. More importantly, by appealing ideologically through "social imagery" the government could attempt to manipulate the conduct of people in order to "shape" a new type of human being and gain popular support. The Guzmán Blanco regime was prolific in its use of imagery as a means to communicate and impose its positivist agenda on illiterate Venezuelans, as we shall see.

Venezuelan elites' identification with European culture stemmed from an effort to disassociate their country from the Spanish colonial past, which was considered tantamount to backwardness. They aspired to establish themselves as a powerful class that would benefit from the movement of progress that would create a civilized and autonomous nation.[18] In particular, France's Second Empire under Napoleon III epitomized everything that Guzmán Blanco wanted Venezuela to become: a cultured country with ties to the most modern nations, one that venerated its great historical past and especially the extraordinary qualities of its leader.

This admiration of France was not new. Since the late colonial period Venezuelan creole elites had been seduced by France's wide spectrum of cultural and political achievements.[19] Moreover, the French model provided both a style of government and a republican and nationalist discourse useful for creating a sense of national unity that was absent in Venezuela. The leadership of Napoleon III in France, for instance, provided an example of how a strongman could claim legitimacy using nationalistic rhetoric. Guzmán Blanco's leadership merged the French model and the caudillo's personalized and clientelistic politics that he knew so well.[20]

Because Guzmán Blanco lacked a popular base of support, he sought to create power by embodying state authority. In addition, Guzmán Blanco required a sure ground for legitimacy: he had no outstanding achievements that would win him the admiration of Venezuelans, he had no legitimate, established line of succession to power, and he was not a ruler who closely followed the Constitution.[21] In this context Guzmán Blanco had to compensate for his lack of legitimacy and popular support by rhetorically magnifying his personal services to the nation.

Drawing on his links with a superior and progressive culture and his extraordinary personal qualities, Guzmán Blanco presented himself as the only man capable of ruling Venezuela. During his first years in power he used his education and experience to claim that he could rescue the nation from anarchy. He exploited regional antagonisms and personal rivalries to his advantage while magnifying his accomplishments in the Federal Wars, especially his reputation as an administrator during the presidency of Juan Crisóstomo Falcón. He gained initial support from many politicians, intellectuals, caudillos, and common people who were moved by his actions and passionate rhetoric.

Once in power, Guzmán Blanco's personalism was forcefully displayed. He repressed opponents and stressed his will as the guiding government principle. He wanted to establish himself as a person who relied on "his supreme self-reliance and predominance into the nation and the masses."[22] By placing his kin and people of close alliance – such as his business partners – in government positions, Guzmán Blanco was able to maintain cohesion in his government. Only relatives and those who benefited directly from the government could handle a ruler who treated them arrogantly, insulted them with his insolent remarks, and rejected their views and opinions – especially if their ideas could not be claimed as his own. He referred to other caudillos as drunkards, beasts, and thieves (barbarians), and when they became threatening, he eliminated them through terror and cunning manipulation.

To create a sense of order and national identity, his government constructed and circulated a republican discourse based on patriotic male heroes. An ideology of patriotism, of attachment to the nation, was to be developed through the creation of monuments and ceremonies. The cult of the heroes of the fatherland was institutionalized to convey the idea of a country with a great past and with superior, godlike leaders.[23] The republic's heroic leaders constituted a public male sphere of propertied, educated men. Serving the republic was a male duty, especially for those who, like Bolívar, were full of merits, virtue, and contributions to the nation. Public festivities focusing on Bolívar as the true father of Venezuela aggressively disseminated this image throughout the country.

Consolidating this association in public memory required unveiling statues, publishing official state histories that venerated the heroes of independence, and naming buildings and government entities in Bolívar's honor. In 1874 a statue of Bolívar in a military uniform, mounted on a rearing horse was placed in the Plaza Bolívar of Caracas. Similar projects placed busts of the Liberator at the center of local plazas in interior towns. Moreover, in 1872 the government instituted the celebration of Bolívar's saint day (28 October).[24]

The confiscation of Santísima Trinidad Church contributed to the creation of the National Pantheon in 1875 to foster the cult of the heroes of Venezuelan history. What in the past had been of religious importance was now replaced by the "sacred" civil figures of the country – the independence leaders.[25] In 1876 Bolívar's remains were taken from the cathedral to the pantheon and placed in a tomb located where the altar had been. With the father of the fatherland lay other leading figures of the Liberal Party, including José Gregorio Monagas and Juan Crisóstomo Falcón. At this "sacred place" Guzmán Blanco gave a speech that he believed would instruct Venezolanos in the "religion of patriotism." Predicating this love for the fatherland would help provide a unifying narrative that appealed to every Venezuelan and blurred the social differences that threatened social order.[26] It also reinforced the patriarchal subjugation of the people to the heroic rulers whose actions were supported by the general will.

Through this cult Guzmán Blanco portrayed himself as heir to Bolivar's feats that had brought progress to the republic. His promotion of Bolívar as a founding father aimed at helping him to align himself "within a foundational genealogy of national heroes."[27] Both Bolívar and Guzmán Blanco were models of citizenship to emulate. There was a conscious attempt to shape national heroes in a way that reinforced dominant culture. The historical and patriotic achievements and virtues of these state leaders were exalted. Moreover, Guzmán Blanco promoted patriarchal values and emphasized the masculinity of national heroes, especially himself, by stressing his dominance over other caudillos. Guzmán Blanco liked to remind male competitors that their lesser masculine qualities made them subordinate to his power: "As a general in chief, I do not have rivals in America or in Europe. Those marshals do not measure up to my abilities [*no me dan por la cintura*] as the army chief."[28] He prided himself on demanding the privileges of manhood. For example, he demanded unrelenting acceptance of his ideas almost, if not surely, by force. To make himself more than a macho kind of hero, Guzmán Blanco stressed his image as a father, though a despotic one. As their "father," Guzmán Blanco ultimately engaged in the masculine task of challenging his competitors' lack of masculine power through his spectacles of self-adulation.[29]

His vast ego was apparent in the many titles that he made Congress grant him. In April 1873, for example, he unabashedly bestowed upon himself the title "The Illustrious American, Pacifier and Regenerator of Venezuela, and Supreme Director of the Revindication."[30] On that same date Congress ordered the erection of an equestrian statue in Guzmán Blanco's honor with the inscription "To the Illustrious American, Regenerator of Venezuela, General Antonio Guzmán Blanco, in National Gratitude, 1873." The Regenerator himself took charge of the organization of the festivities for the centennial of the Libertador's birthday in 1883.[31] Guzmán Blanco took the occasion to glorify himself: the event slogan was "¡Viva Bolívar! ¡Gloria a Guzmán!" and decorations were made out of their joined initials. A portable electric plant allowed the temporary illumination of the avenues surrounding the Guzmán Blanco Theatre, where the social elite commemorated the celebration.[32]

Signs of patriotism and urban culture were communicated through symbols that altered the Spanish appearance of the capital city as well. Many buildings, statues, and monuments in Caracas were modeled after those that Guzmán Blanco saw in Paris and were constructed to provide suitable spaces for his public and private official ceremonies.[33] The renovation of Caracas with a European appearance made Venezuela attractive to foreign capital, too. In addition to visually "educating" the citizenry, great monuments were intended to transform the Spanish colonial capital into Guzmán Blanco's Caracas. Various Caracas landmarks, such as the Capitol building, the Municipal Theater, the monuments honoring Simón Bolívar and Guzmán Blanco, the remodeled university building, and the Government Palace date from the 1870s and 1880s. Foreign travelers referred to Caracas as the city of the "Eternal Spring" during the late colonial period, but by the late nineteenth century it had become "a sort of one-story Paris."[34]

The admiration of French culture, especially its bourgeois elements, also enabled Venezuelan elites to differentiate themselves from the popular classes, which they regarded as unprogressive.[35] Bourgeois ideas were inaccessible to the poor majority, and in Venezuela French culture was brought out only in the closed circles of rich and educated elites. Hence the admiration of France fostered a culture of exclusion limited to specific familial and cultural norms and to particular places where the upper strata cultivated and modernized their manners and appearance. Identification with Europe was crucial for the ruling elites because Venezuela's civil wars had weakened their traditional social composition as a mainly white and propertied group. Now rural caudillos and high-ranking military men, many of whom were neither rich nor white, had entered the power circles of the ruling elite. Yet the French-inspired bourgeois culture created new social barriers, because only a few, such as members of the commercial elite, had direct access to imported signs of civilization. Given the outward orientation of the regime, the upper classes understood the need to educate and cultivate themselves so they could increasingly participate as intermediaries between the European and domestic cultures.

The cultural transformation undertaken by Guzmán Blanco was not merely the whim of an illustrious president. Almost one-third of the 297 decrees that he delivered during the years 1870–76 had to do with culture.[36] Of these, more than half pertained to education, and the remainder were evenly divided among state-church conflicts, the cult of national heroes, the establishment of a civil registry, and the promotion of publishing and the fine arts.[37] These decrees demonstrate the state's intention to undermine the cultural control that the Spanish Catholic church had enjoyed since colonial times.

The church had traditionally fostered the idea that knowledge was obtained through faith, which was the church's monopoly. Art and music, for instance, were to be developed for and inspired by religious themes. Moreover, the church controlled many of the centers of education in Venezuela. To pave the way for positivistic learning – in which reason and scientific knowledge became the only paths to truth, the control of nature, and the future – Guzmán Blanco had to destroy the primacy that the church enjoyed in cultural matters. As the tenor of his decrees suggests, he did this by promoting civic ideals through education controlled by the government, by making the state the main civil register for the population, by encouraging publications attuned to the new philosophical trend, and finally, by instituting public works that symbolized the new times.

The imperative of curbing the power of the church was not unique to Venezuela. In Latin America state control of the church became a critical issue for the successful implementation of liberal reforms that aimed at creating suitable conditions for the participation of these countries in the expanding world market economy of the second half of the nineteenth century. Therefore a conflict between Guzmán Blanco and Archbishop Silvestre Guevara y Lira that some historians have seen as a personal dispute should be understood in a broader context.[38]

In an early decree, Guzmán Blanco sent Venezuelan archbishop Guevara y Lira into exile because he refused the president's request to officiate at a "Te Deum" ceremony to thank God for the triumph of the liberals.[39] Guzmán Blanco interpreted this denial as an intrusion of the church into government matters; in his outrage he even hinted at the possibility of creating a national church separated from Rome. Other decrees that reduced the civil and ecclesiastical powers of the church followed, including the usual liberal repertoire of measures that other Latin American countries used against the Catholic church.[40] Guzmán Blanco expropriated ecclesiastical property and transferred it to the public sector through the main educational institution, the Universidad Central, and the national schools. He also extinguished and expropriated convents, seminaries, and religious communities, such as the Concepciones convent in 1874. Any remaining ecclesiastical privileges or fueros were abolished. Finally, in the early years of his presidency he established both civil marriage and civil registries, placed cemeteries in civil hands, and abolished all sources of ecclesiastical income. The state and the church reconciled only after Rome named a friendly archbishop in 1876. After all, Guzmán Blanco was not against religion itself; he merely opposed the obstacles to the implementation of his policies that the institution presented.[41] Moreover, according to the samples, by those years the proportion of lawsuits that were heard in the ecclesiastical courts had already declined, demonstrating that the state policy of curbing the power of the church over the population had been effective (see table 9).

By promoting education, the fine arts, and music, the state tried to encourage the cultivation of patriotic motifs and the influence of European romanticism and scientific theories. Let us not forget that according to posi-

TABLE 9. Percentage of Lawsuits by Type of Court, Caracas, 1786–1880

YEARS	CIVIL COURT	CRIMINAL COURT	ECCLESIASTICAL COURT	TOTAL
1786–91	69.8	2.2	28.1	N=139
1835–40	55.8	30.4	13.8	N=240
1875–80	66.8	26.1	7.0	N=199

Source: AAC, Matrimoniales, Judiciales, 1786–95, 1835–40, 1875–80; AANH, Civiles, 1786–91; ARPDF, Civiles, Criminales, 1835–40, 1875–80.

tivist ideas, every artistic expression should be didactic. Artistic expression should be so infused with useful and grandiose ideas that the public becomes educated by admiring them. For this purpose, the regime established an Institute for the Fine Arts in 1870 and a National Museum in 1874. It also set up a fellowship program to send students to Italy, Germany, and the United States.[42]

The visual "social imagery" was also transmitted through formal education. The curriculum of the Universidad Central de Venezuela (UCV) was revised according to the new liberal imperatives. In particular, positivist science, introduced to the university in 1863 by the German scholar Adolph Ernst and by Venezuelan Rafael Villavicencio, influenced a generation of leading intellectuals – including José Gil Fortoul, Pedro Manuel Arcaya, and Laureano Vallenilla Lanz.[43] Moreover, the less fortunate classes received some attention from a patriarchal government that wanted to educate, moralize, and civilize them. An educational policy was organized to placate popular animosity toward scant economic development that scarcely affected the poor.[44] For the first time in Venezuela, the government commissioned the writing of textbooks and supported the establishment of obligatory public elementary schools throughout the republic.[45] A special office was organized to promote public education, which in 1881 became the Ministry of Public Education. By 1885 the government claimed to have built 1,312 federal schools with an enrollment of 80,900 students and 645 municipal schools with an enrollment of 18,556 throughout the country.[46] However ambitious, this policy was difficult to put into practice. The shortage of teachers and the lack of adequate infrastructure undermined government efforts to establish a public education program.[47] In spite of the limited results of the program – and the censorship during the period, especially in the press – this was a time of intellectual and cultural effervescence.

As has been discussed, the cultural project was tied to the broader interest in creating the conditions for stability and progress to attract foreign investment. The government needed more leverage to reorganize the republic according to those goals, and for this reason it curtailed the ideological and civic power of the church. The regime believed that an educated society was necessary for the healthy evolution of the country, and better-educated Venezuelans would make improved and more productive citizens who could understand the need to follow the dictates of the state. The highly elitist belief that the civilizing government was fighting against a mass of nonwhite, barbarous, ignorant, and unprogressive people who could potentially thwart the modernization of Venezuela underwrote all of these policies. A cultural and moral struggle against the illiterate poor was undertaken to achieve economic progress. Whether the ruling elites really believed that the lower classes could be transformed is uncertain. Yet the government had to be careful not to overtly communicate this biased opinion about a majority that could be politically powerful. This was achieved in a somewhat consistent but concealed fashion.

An example of how the government tried to "reform" popular culture and customs was the recasting of the Venezuelan carnival. Celebrated between February and March, the festivities came to Venezuela with the Spaniards. Traditionally the carnival was celebrated by playing with water and eggs, especially among the lower classes. Early in 1869 *La Opinión Nacional*, the newspaper that became the official organ of the regime, expressed its doubt that the *pueblo juguetón* (playful people) of Caracas could ever learn. In an editorial, the newspaper criticized the way the people imitated French fashions and also expressed an "anxiety about public spectacles that recall the darkest days of Venezuelan civilization."[48] The bottom line of this and other articles was to transform both the carnival and the bullfights so that "learned nations do not doubt whether we are or not a Christian and civilized country."[49] By 1873 Guzmán Blanco ended the "barbarous" Venezuelan carnival, in which common people staged water fights, by organizing European-style carnivals with costumes and dances.[50] Moreover, a giant "Circo de Toros" was constructed to take bullfights out of the streets of the capital city.[51] The government attempted to portray these achievements as proof of its concern for the well-being of every caraqueño.

The subtleties of this bourgeois cultural project were revealed in the government immigration policy. With the influence of positivistic and evolutionary ideas that related progress to a particular race and place, Guzmán Blanco sought to whiten the local population as a means of modernizing the nation through European culture and genes. These years witnessed the proliferation of a discourse of "racial improvement" that continued through the early twentieth century.[52] Concrete efforts to impart European standards of education and family life and the establishment of religious freedom and civil marriage were closely tied to an immigration policy that facilitated the life of non-Catholic foreigners in Venezuela.[53] In 1874 a decree was enacted to establish agricultural colonies of, preferably, French, Swiss, and German workers, while discouraging Canary Islanders and immigrants from the Lesser Antilles.[54] Pro-immigration efforts did not yield the desired government goals, however. Between 1874 and 1888, 26,090 immigrants, mostly from Spain, Germany, France, and Italy, entered the country.[55] This quantity is small compared to figures for Argentina, which took in almost 700,000 immigrants between 1881 and 1890 alone, but it is comparable to that of Chile, with 28,000 immigrants during the same decade.[56] Immigration efforts fared better and received more attention than the regime's measures to improve the lives and education of the common folk.

There was an enormous gap between rhetoric and practice, and this undercut support for the regime. While grandiose events were organized and monuments erected, Guzmán Blanco did little to improve living conditions among the popular classes. Education was not widespread, and public hygiene, hospitals, and social services were mostly neglected.[57] His adverse use of power, denial of civil rights, and financial dishonesty became evident realities. Reactions to a government guided by appearances quickly ensued.

In 1876 Guzmán Blanco decided to leave for Europe while accusations of his shady deals involving government contracts got out of circulation. As soon as Gen. Francisco Linares Alcántara, Guzmán Blanco's chosen successor, was elected president, criticisms of the past president were voiced by liberals who wanted a representative government and by caudillos eager to reestablish their power in the countryside. With the death of Linares Alcántara in 1878 the regime's critics took advantage of the power vacuum to request from the Constituent Assembly the annulment of the various titles and honors given to Guzmán Blanco and the demolition of his statues. The assembly approved. His statues erected around Caracas were taken down shortly after, only to be put back again and with much pomposity when Guzmán Blanco resumed power in 1879. The president took vengeance on those who had voted in favor of the destruction of his monuments by imprisoning them and confiscating their property.

There are indications that some common people had already lost respect for the Illustrious American. In one 1878 lawsuit a lower-class plaintiff included a personal letter in which she mocked the equestrian statue of Guzmán Blanco, indicating that his horse would not satisfy the promiscuous desires of a woman of her community.[58] In 1885, when Guzmán Blanco was in Paris again, students attacked his image in a ceremony in honor of a poet critic of the regime, Antonio Delpino y Lamas. On this occasion Guzmán

Blanco was satirized as a poet and politician. In February 1889, at a public celebration for his sixtieth birthday, some people began catcalling and whistling at the spectacle of adulation of a man of questionable merit. In October of that year violent demonstrations against Guzmán Blanco took place while he was again in Paris. A group of students attacked his equestrian statue and shouted for the end of his "tyranny." Two months later a discontented populace demolished his statues and monuments around the city and sacked his house.[59] While Bolívar's monuments remained intact, Guzmán Blanco's were never rebuilt. This was the end of his period.[60]

These events theoretically made the relationship between the government and the people similar to that of sons unwilling to further tolerate a despotic father whose claims to power were false and imposed. Unlike Bolívar, whose merit as the Liberator of the fatherland was unquestionable and remained vivid in Venezuelans' memory, Guzmán Blanco's requests for adulation were based on invented traditions inspired in France, too far from the local experience. To the people Guzmán Blanco's "spectacles" lacked meaning, and he did not earn their obedience because, as a self-proclaimed father of the fatherland, he neglected them.

Although Guzmán Blanco was able to incorporate and promote a conciliatory policy toward merchants, caudillos, and even landowners, he approached the lower classes differently. The poor majority was excluded and ignored by the ruling elites. This was done subtly by using language and "social imagery" that did not have local roots and that blurred social differences to avoid provoking the mobilization of the lower classes.

The elites' view of progress was nurtured by racial and cultural ideas that influenced the politics of the period. Discriminatory practices were cleverly masked within a nationalistic discourse of liberty, equality, and progress that initially appealed to the popular classes. The policies promoted by the ruling classes were intended to motivate people to join a patriotic cause and become citizens of a new type. Contradictorily, it was not the father of the nation who held the most responsibility for the cultivation of a "new" Venezuela. While the government took care of establishing new norms in Caracas's cultural life, the family – or more exactly, women – would be assigned responsibility for the "moral regeneration" of Venezuelans. Positivist writers and lawyers, along with the church, would take on the "task of remaking the sinful female body into a virtuous republican body."[61] As they praised women for achieving this important goal, they aimed at maintaining women within the domestic sphere, silencing those interested in public life while also excluding the popular classes from political participation.

In newspaper editorials and articles, liberals and positivists portrayed Venezuela as a barbaric society, a place without the moral and material conditions needed to successfully pursue peace and progress. In a patent display of elite arrogance, *La Opinión Nacional* claimed that the majority of Venezuelans were illiterate, had no religious beliefs, no vocation, and no preparation for work, and were without appropriate customs or good economic habits.[62] On 9 January 1869 the paper also lambasted pervasive ignorance as a social evil capable of destroying any moral principle and any democratic idea, "because the heart of an ignorant man only gives impulse to violent passions, which make man act like a savage."[63] The lack of religion was the cause of all the vices that undermined a society: aversion to work, vagrancy, licentiousness, drunkenness, and insensibility to the joy provided by the domestic sphere. Ignorance did not bode well for family life either. Editorials stressed that for ignorant men the home did not exist, that they would shy away from their duties as fathers, and that, above all, they had no appreciation for familial love.

However bleak the situation was, writers for *La Opinión Nacional* were confident that public education was the solution. Central to this educational project was the renewed importance of the domestic sphere. Instilling new domestic habits was critical because, as an editorial put it, "men, although creatures of custom, could be reformed."[64] Such ideas justified the positivist political agenda, or the Moral Regeneration Plan, that made the discipline of Venezuelan people the proper work of the government, or rather, women.[65] As the newspaper claimed: "The woman is the bedrock of the family and the embryo of society, where the future of the Republic is elaborated and where the destiny of civilization is prepared."[66]

The process of moral regeneration faced substantial obstacles. From the promulgation of the first Constitution in 1811, all Venezuelans were theoretically equal before the law. Yet under codes inherited from Spanish rule, such as the *Siete Partidas*, women's legal submission to men continued. Equality under the law required redefining men's power to control the family and women. This was a major challenge that Guzmán Blanco liberals confronted when writing the civil and penal codes of 1873.[67] In writing these codes, governing elites had to balance the promise of individual autonomy with the need for state control. Their handling of the public versus private affairs of the family discloses the tensions with which reformers were grappling and the contradictions of liberalism as an ideology. The debate between patriarchy and equality consumed their energies.

Although the regime used the rhetoric of equality, it also stressed the conventional subordination of women and children to the male head of household. Liberals infused the new civil code with deeply embedded Spanish patriarchal ideas. The governing elites widely accepted that maintaining a stable society depended on this tradition. A government that sought to be effective had to preserve a hierarchical chain of command that began with the president's power and ended with the male head of household, the padre de familia.

The republic's leaders and rulers constituted a public male sphere of propertied, educated men. Serving the republic was a male duty. This conception of politics as male terrain did not overshadow or weaken a parallel discourse about the duties of women in the domestic sphere. Discourse about the republic had a male and a female foundation. Guzmán Blanco portrayed himself as the great patriarch, head of a civilized family and leader of a civilizing project, while his wife, Ana Teresa Ibarra, who gave birth to eleven children, became the model of female responsibility, teaching morals and patriotism within the family.[68] It was in the private sphere that women could put their domestic virtues to work for the nation.

Where customs were loose and domestic values scant, according to *La Opinión Nacional*, a cult of womanhood offered regeneration. The editors preached that if a mother could not conduct herself as a responsible and virtuous housewife, it was unlikely that she would successfully moderate the "passions" of her own children.[69] The government's concern was to return power within the domestic sphere to women so that – at least theoretically – women would assist with the transformation of the "uncivilized habits" of their spouses and children.

Despite the regime's anticlerical leanings, it sought the blessing of the church for the government's regeneration plan. In one of its first issues *La Opinión Nacional* reproduced a sermon by Presbítero Dr. Andrés Manuel Riera Aguinagalde explaining his philosophy of women's social role. This concept rested clearly on *marianismo*, the cult of the Virgin Mary.[70] Though church doctrine underlay his message, Riera's thinking dovetailed with the government's desired social reforms.[71]

Father Riera's sermon linked the regime's definition of womanhood with religious commitment. The connection becomes clear if one understands that humanity, the fatherland, and the family were cardinal values for positivists. Drawing on Comte, the reformers saw women as key representatives of altruism – ideal representations of humanity. Accordingly, they valued women for their fertility and as moral teachers of future citizens. Thus positivists easily adopted a trope of the feminine figure. Paramount among these feminine figures was the Virgin Mary, who became for positivism a cognate for the "Virgin Mother," the allegory of humanity.[72] Riera therefore provided a religious rationale for the importance of women in marriage and in forming families. He argued that women had to be rehabilitated from Eve, who participated in original sin. Christ's virgin mother represented "the new Eve," the rehabilitated woman. From that time onward, the Holy Spirit blessed women, but this new status as blessed persons entailed responsibilities and sacrifices.[73] The regime, with the blessings of the church, officially ended women's blame for the Fall of Man, which was a widespread justification for women's exclusion in the colonial period and the early republic. This change of emphasis from Eve to the Virgin Mary allowed women public recognition for their virtuous contributions within the family.[74]

Hence Riera emphasized the centrality of women's submission to men. Being the family's apostles, women had to inspire men and children to become religious, nonviolent, and responsible through their example. Within the family they had to be obedient and behave properly so as to encourage men to return to religion. Women had to teach their daughters to be obedient, because, Riera stated, "there is nothing more ridiculous than a man who is obedient but a woman who rules." Women were also supposed to have an angelic temperament in order to provide comfort and tranquility, especially in violent situations. Woman should be the center for prayer in the family in order to attract family members to worship and to promote tranquility.

Riera concluded his sermon with a warning: because of their crucial role in the preservation of society, he discouraged women from struggling for their rights. Women's mission in the world was not to seek power in the name of rights given by their virtues but rather to be obedient within the family, to provide tranquility, comfort, and submission to religion.[75] When they succeeded in this mission, they emulated all the virtues that the Virgin had taught women, that is, to quietly sacrifice themselves for the sake of the family. Accordingly, Marianismo in this context did not carry the connotation of a cult that praised female superiority, as has been argued by some authors; to the contrary, it stressed the importance of women as submissive, hard-working wives and mothers.[76]

These ideas recurred in other newspaper articles. Some pieces, for instance, encouraged mothers to make their sons useful citizens and respectable heads of households in order to perpetuate the patriarchal order.[77] Women had the pivotal role of contributing to the nation's progress by "transforming" men into good, disciplined workers. In this way, tranquility would reign in the republic's family, creating order and progress.

To achieve peace through the family, women's subordination to men was critical, but it was difficult to justify. When the regime drafted the first liberal civil code (1873) it had to resolve – or at least explain away – the contradictions between a republican constitution and the old monarchical codes. The government did not embrace gender equality. Any idea that lessened male family power seemed disruptive to the social order, especially when the government sought tranquility. One means of resolving the problem was to stress the increased importance of women in the family and the idea that both genders were equally significant in separate spheres.[78]

While publicly celebrating women's role in the family, the regime reinforced the patriarchal tradition in the courts. The court rulings analyzed in the next chapter demonstrate that judicial institutions governed women more rigidly in the late nineteenth century than they had during the colonial era. Hence, during the late nineteenth century a glaring contradiction emerged at the core of the liberal agenda. Liberal reforms made the prevailing gender inequality in Venezuela untenable, but they also strengthened patriarchy under state aegis.[79] Marianismo helped to ideologically justify this contradictory outcome. Since the late nineteenth century, family law has become a key aspect of Venezuelan government policy.

8. Women, Order, and Progress

Antonio Guzmán Blanco's rise to power in 1870 inaugurated the era of "order and progress" in Venezuelan politics. Stressing that a country's progress depended on attaining social and political stability, Guzmán Blanco set out to undo decades of economic havoc, political insecurity, and endemic civil strife. Historians have skillfully researched the new policies devised to boost economic growth and consolidate state power, but few scholars have highlighted the key place that women, the family, and the domestic sphere, more generally, occupied in the regime's program for the "moral regeneration" of Venezuela.[1] For the first time in the nineteenth century the Venezuelan government had a coherent political and ideological program, which emphasized notions of gender.

In the previous chapter I examined official discourse on gender and family life and illustrated the critical role that women occupied in the government's project for moral regeneration of the country. How that agenda played out in the legal reforms introduced in 1873 and how courts of justice implemented guidelines for women by enforcing the new civil and penal codes of 1873 are the guiding issues of this chapter. Before we turn to those issues, let us examine the profile of women's participation in the courts for the years 1875–80, which further show the distance between Guzmán Blanco's agenda and the realities that affected many caraqueños.

WOMEN AT THE COURTS OF GUZMÁN BLANCO

Women's litigation, as evidenced in the late-nineteenth-century sample (1875–80), further demonstrates that the promotion of bourgeois cultural values was targeted according to gender and social class. Resorting to this state institution became more markedly a resource for the popular classes, especially among women, whose presence in court was not proportional to their presence in the larger population of the nineteenth century.

TABLE 10. Number of Civil and Criminal Lawsuits by Year, Caracas, 1835–1840 and 1875–1880

YEAR	NUMBER OF LAWSUITS FILED
1835	285
1836	466
1837	497
1838	421
1839	432
1840	519
Total	2620
1875	210
1876	298
1877	274
1878	409
1879	421
1880	562
Total	2174

Source: ARPDF, Fondos Civiles and Criminales, 1835–40, 1875–80.

The increase in population was not reflected in the courts of Caracas. This is evident from table 10, which shows that in the 1835–40 sample more people used the civil and criminal courts to redress their grievances than did so in the late-nineteenth-century sample. This is particularly striking if we consider that in Caracas in 1873 the population was 24 percent larger than it had been in 1835. Why were fewer people resorting to the courts and the legal system?

The total number of lawsuits is indicative of the political environment of the times. For instance, in 1835 there was a reduction in the number of cases, probably because the revolt against President Dr. José María Vargas in Caracas distanced people from government institutions. In the sample for the last quarter of the century the same trend is observed, particularly during Guzmán Blanco's Septenio (1870–77), when he governed with an iron grip. Finally, not only were fewer cases filed but the lawsuits also were less voluminous, indicating that they were shorter in duration, in the 1875–80 sample. The 2,620 cases from which the early republican sample was extracted were contained in 738 large books, while the 2,174 cases from the late nineteenth century were bound in only 245 books. Therefore the political environment and overall judicial policies, discussed below, may account for the decline in the number and extent of the lawsuits.

A closer look into the class component of the records might also provide some clues to the decrease in court participation. Recall that the class composition of Caracas was transformed, particularly within the elites, due to the upward mobility of rural caudillos, high-ranking generals, and large merchants, most of whom were foreigners. According to Robert Lavenda the elite comprised around 4 percent of the total population by 1891. A middle class, although small, was becoming increasingly visible during the last decade of the century. Mainly composed of small merchants, civil servants, and teachers, this class represented 6 percent of the population of Caracas. Finally, the lower classes – the vast majority of the population (90 percent) – made up the workforce of Caracas. The lower class included skilled workers, small merchants, artisans who owned their workshops, midwives, cooks, less-skilled people such as craftsmen, and manual laborers such as masons, wet-nurses, seamstresses, embroiderers, limemakers, cigarette makers, matchmakers, and so on.[2]

I used Lavenda's classification to infer the social class of litigants in my sample. I maintained two broad categories – rich and poor – however, because insufficient information was available to allow a consistent identification of a third category such as a middle class. Yet a number of litigants were identified as middle class in the lawsuits, and I used this category for the individual textual analysis of the cases. As in the other samples, occupation, property, and lineage helped me to infer the categories of rich and poor.[3]

Table 11 summarizes the class component of the cases in the three samples. The 1875–80 sample shows a strikingly small number of cases coming from the elites (5 percent). When compared with the percentage from the other samples – 21 and 15 percent for the 1786–91 and 1835–40 samples, respectively – a clear trend is seen. While the lower classes increased their presence in the courts, the percentage of elite lawsuits declined.

As has been discussed in earlier chapters, elites consistently used the courts to debate issues involving family property and social reputation. The situation in the late nineteenth century was no different. As demonstrated in table 12, in which the different types of claims are divided according to the social class of the litigants, claims involving elites were very limited. On the one hand, they reflect women's lack of legal power to manage their own property, which since the late eighteenth century had been one reason that elite women turned to the courts. On the other hand, the cases of breach of promise and rapto in this sample involved elite females who did not have a

TABLE 11. Social Class of Litigants in Caracas, 1786–1880

YEARS	BOTH PARTIES UPPER CLASS	UPPER CLASS FILES AGAINST LOWER CLASS	LOWER CLASS FILES AGAINST UPPER CLASS	BOTH PARTIES LOWER CLASS	TOTAL
1786–91	20.9	3.6	10.1	65.5	N=139
1835–40	15.0	3.8	9.6	71.7	N=240
1875–80	5.0	2.5	2.5	89.9	N=199

Source: AAC, Matrimoniales, Judiciales, 1786–95, 1835–40, 1875–80; AANH, Civiles, 1786–91; ARPDF, Civiles, Criminales, 1835–40, 1875–80.

male representative.[4] In the latter cases the victims' mothers went to the tribunals, probably as a last resort, because no male representative was available to handle the conflict privately.[5] This was in contrast to lower-class conflicts in which women's defense of their bodies and their efforts to work and their request for the enforcement of men's responsibilities were the major causes of conflict. Thus the elites did not use the courts as an arbiter for their internal affairs, as the lower classes often did. If there had been some consistency in the way the upper classes had used the tribunals in the past, then one could infer the existence of external factors that were influencing their lack of court participation at this time.

It is possible that in a moment in which the composition of the elites had changed, elite membership standards might have become more rigid. Moreover, cultural values and family norms at the time, which valued women's domesticity, prudence, seclusion, and submission to men more than ever before, could have prevented the use of the courts. Indeed, a few court cases mentioned that virtuous women had a fuero, or privilege, that forbade them from stepping into a courtroom.[6] It is likely that the fear of damaging their social reputation by going to court and making public a private family issue may have dissuaded some elite members from using the tribunals. Moreover, it is clear that the courts, which had at least a century-old tradition of intense lower-class participation, were seen by the elites as unsuitable places to settle disputes about honor or reputation.

Despite the period's cultural values, women, especially from the lower classes, kept going to court to resolve their problems with men. In such cases women consistently took the initiative in approaching the courts. In the late colonial period 47.5 percent of the cases had been initiated by women, while a century later 66.3 percent were initiated by women. At the same time the percentage of men who lodged claims against women declined from 44.6 percent in 1786–91 to 26.1 percent in 1875–80.[7]

This broad description of the trends found in the late-nineteenth-

TABLE 12. Social Class of Litigants by Type of Claim, Caracas, 1875–1880

CLASS	%	% OF TOTAL
Both parties upper class		
Abduction (rapto)	10.0	
Breach of promise	30.0	
Divorce	10.0	
Family support	10.0	
Power to administer property	40.0	
	———	
	N=10	5.0
Upper class files against lower class		
Divorce	20.0	
Nullity of marriage	20.0	
Prostitution	20.0	
Theft	40.0	
	———	
	N=5	2.5
Lower class files against upper class		
Abduction (rapto)	20.0	
Breach of promise	80.0	
	———	
	N=5	2.5
Both parties lower class		
Abuse/bodily harm	6.7	
Abduction (rapto)	4.5	
Bigamy	0.6	
Bodily injury	4.5	
Breach of promise	20.1	
Damages	1.1	
Death (investigation of)	0.6	
Divorce	25.1	
Estupro	5.0	
Family support	5.0	
Grave acts of contumely	2.2	
Homicide	0.6	
License for second marriage	3.9	
Natural child recognition	5.6	
Nullity of marriage	2.8	
Oblige a wife to fulfill her duties	0.6	
Opposition to marriage	0.6	
Parental power	3.4	
Poisoning	0.6	

CLASS	%	% OF TOTAL
Power to administer property	3.9	
Prostitution	0.6	
Request for certificates	1.1	
Theft	0.6	
Violation of civil rights	0.6	
	N=179	89.9
		N=199

Source: AAC, Matrimoniales, Judiciales, 1875–80; ARPDF, Civiles, Criminales, 1875–80.

century sample further demonstrates that the promotion of European cultural values was targeted differently according to gender and social class. Not only were the vast majority of the cases in this sample filed by the working classes (92.4 percent) and initiated by women (66.3), but as will be discussed below and in chapter 9, in the lawsuits women often contradicted the dominant discourse of proper womanhood, probably because this discourse was not necessarily addressed to them. Moreover, the lower classes certainly interpreted this discourse differently. Their presence at the courts challenged the government's regeneration agenda.

DISCOURSE IN LAW AND IN PRACTICE

Women gained attention in official discourse during the late nineteenth century, but their legal rights remained basically unchanged from the colonial past.[8] In law and in practice, we see evidence of this situation in five pivotal areas of legislation directly touching women: patria potestas (or male authority over females), marriage, breach of promise, divorce, and sex crimes.

PATRIA POTESTAS AND THE POWERS OF MEN AND THE COURTS OVER WOMEN AND CHILDREN

Female submission to males was a cultural given in Venezuela, reinforced both in the new, liberal Venezuelan Civil Code of 1873 and afterward by court practices. As established in articles 173–86 of the Civil Code of 1873, a married woman had to submit to her husband, following him wherever he established residence. The courts regularly enforced this law.[9]

The age-old Spanish norm – men as heads of household, legal representatives of women, and administrators of their properties – continued in the 1873 code. In 1900 married women still had no juridical identity, unless they were pursuing a claim against their husbands or defending themselves against a criminal charge. Otherwise, they could appear in court only when licensed by their husbands. If the husband was unable or unwilling to provide a license, a woman could get a court license from a judge. When seeking a license from the court, a woman had to explain to a judge the nature of any transaction she wanted to make and get the judge's permission before going forward.[10]

The code of 1873 created modest improvements in women's legal status, but those improvements mainly affected single and widowed women.[11] First, the age below which children had to request parental permission for marriage was lowered, thereby increasing children's autonomy. In 1873 this age was lowered to twenty-one for males and eighteen for females.[12] In this way the new regulations increased individual freedom and limited parental authority, reflecting the influence of the liberal idea of the autonomous individual.

Second, under the new code widows could be guardians of their own children.[13] The law allowed a single mother who had recognized her children to be the tutor, having similar parental rights to those of married men or widows. Women who behaved virtuously and had no husband had more legal powers over their children than married women, but these laws were enforced only in limited ways.

Although the period's legal changes seemed promising on paper, the reality was completely different. Despite formal changes in the law, the parental powers of the padre de familia seemed indisputable in the Venezuelan courts. An exemplary case involved Juana Guevara and Manuel Lugo. This lower-class couple lived together between 1864 and 1871, and in 1868 Juana gave birth to a girl, whom she recognized as her natural daughter in a baptismal record. In 1872 Manuel, the girl's natural father, also recognized her in a public document. Juana defended her rights as the girl's guardian, however, because she had recognized the girl before the father did. Still, the Supreme Court did not approve her claim because she had not questioned Manuel's assertion of paternity. In article 285 the law established that the natural father is the guardian of the child he recognizes; the mother could be the guardian only if the father failed to recognize the child. Thus the court held that in the interest of the minor, the girl could not be "deprived without justified reason of the rights and advantages" that emanated from her father's spontaneous recognition.[14] By basing its decision on the child's interests, the court stressed the importance of maintaining the power of the padre de familia.

We may see these legal changes, as well as others analyzed later, as part of a new relationship between the family and the state. Jurists tried to accommodate patriarchal family morality to the liberal idea of the state's limited powers. To protect and promote family values, a judge was justified in deciding what was best for the children – a doctrine that U.S. historian Michael Grossberg refers to as "judicial patriarchy."[15] Judges often showed a bias against single mothers whose behavior was not proper and in favor of men who had recognized their natural children. Since colonial times men were not obliged by law to recognize their children, nor could their paternity be investigated.[16]

Although modest changes increased the legal liberties and powers of both single and widowed women, the state was more concerned with married women and the promotion of marriage.[17] Newly enacted laws on civil marriage and breach of promise increased the state's involvement in the private matters of courtship and marriage.

CIVIL MARRIAGE

The Civil Code of 1873 led to the complete secularization of the institution of marriage, but not without heated debate. In 1869 *La Opinión Nacional* devoted some attention to the issue, discussing letters sent by representatives of the church to the prominent lawyer Luis Sanojo, who drafted the Civil Marriage Law.[18] One of the church representatives' most compelling arguments was against the incursion of government into a matter that concerned only the church. For ecclesiastical authorities, internal matters of the family were totally separate from state power. If the government enacted the civil marriage law, it would be taking away from the family a key right. The letter writers particularly criticized the mundane way in which the state conceptualized marriage when officials qualified it as a contract. The lack of morality of such a law, they argued, could motivate the legal acceptance of polygamy and even divorce, paving the way eventually for the corruption of society. Moreover, the church representatives criticized liberals for intruding in the lives of individuals more than the Spanish regime had.[19]

For reformers like Sanojo, however, the control of family matters by the government was necessary to achieve justice, because it was critical that citizens live honestly without corrupting one another. The vital goal of achieving justice in society involved every aspect of social life that the state ought to protect, even family relations. Sanojo deemed it necessary to achieve harmony among people so that society could work toward common goals.[20] He justified state intervention in the private sphere as a necessity for creating the conditions for achieving progress.

For the writers of *La Opinión Nacional*, the goal of order and progress was critical in the debate over the Civil Marriage Law. Politicians viewed this law as an enticement to attract the immigration of non-Catholic peoples from Europe. The introduction of European and North American immigrants was thought of as a positive influence for peopling and colonizing the land, a way of getting disciplined laborers and instilling good habits in the native population. For instance, on 2 September 1873 *La Opinión Nacional* published an article quoting Domingo Faustino Sarmiento, the Argentine reformist president, suggesting that Venezuela should enact land-grant laws based on the experience of the United States, including also freedom of religion and civil marriage. The article praised the positive consequences of such laws in Argentine immigration efforts, specifically in the colonization of Chivilcoy.[21]

Civil marriage was also important for "achieving peace within families and for the reproduction of the species."[22] Examples from other countries, such as the United States, were used to prove that even in places where marriage was a simple contract families were peacefully organized and reproducing well. Eventually the debate with the church ended with the total separation of church and state in Venezuela, because Venezuelan liberals believed that the Catholic church in Spain and Rome did not allow freedom of thought at all.[23] Guzmán Blanco's government held that the church was an impediment to progress and that Catholic countries like Spain, Ireland, and Poland were good examples of the backwardness that a close relationship with Catholicism could bring.[24]

Today we might think that the Civil Marriage Law was enacted to promote formal marriages in a country where high illegitimacy rates prevailed. Indeed, Robert Lavenda estimated that during the late nineteenth century an average of 53 percent of the children in Caracas were born to single mothers.[25] I have found no evidence, however, that the prevalence of concubinage among the popular classes was a concern of the governing elites or Sanojo himself during the Guzmán Blanco period. This preoccupation was more evident by the time the divorce law was enacted in 1904, when a second generation of positivists made the regularization of family life an important part of their agenda.[26] Let us look first at how marriages were to be formalized after 1873.

The law required that all marriages be performed by the civil authorities in the City Hall (Concejo Municipal) and then, if the couple desired, by a religious leader. Civil marriage was also designed to be cheaper and simpler than religious marriage. The quantity of documents required was not reduced, however. According to the new law, the couple had to submit a form from the parish judge proving that banns had been posted at the municipal hall for the required period.[27] The couple also had to bring a certificate acknowledging that no impediment to the marriage had been found, their birth certificates, and written authorization from both the bride's and groom's parents or, if any of them were dead, their death certificates.[28] For those living far from a city hall, the process was even more complex and, in all likelihood, discouraged many couples. The effort of producing the mass of documents, which had to be written out by a scribe on official paper, and the court appearances involved in the new civil ritual made the procedure expensive and time-consuming.[29]

To see how the law operated in practice, Lavenda analyzed 2,382 civil marriages from a total of 11,000 marriages for the years 1874–1908 in Caracas. He found that few people had a civil ceremony before the religious ceremony. Indeed, Guzmán Blanco himself and his wife, Ana Teresa, set the example for "remarriage" as a way of enticing others to follow suit, but that did not happen. In 1874 less than 1 percent of the total population of Caracas was married in a civil ceremony. Lavenda concludes that, overall, civil marriage did not become popular during those years. Instead, the middle class and people interested in moving up to the middle class increasingly chose this form of marriage. Although the middle class constituted a small percentage of the population – about 6 percent of the total number of people employed in 1891 – by 1908, 75 percent of all marriages involved men of the middle class.[30] To Lavenda, this finding indicated the weight that the upper and middle classes gave to legal forms of marriage.

Accordingly, Lavenda found that 71 percent of men and 69 percent of women marrying in civil ceremonies were legitimate; most of the men were in prestigious occupations (professionals and merchants) and lived in upper-class neighborhoods such as Catedral, Santa Teresa, and Santa Rosalía. These findings show that, in Caracas at least, marriage, legitimacy, residency, and occupation were clearly related and that civil marriage during those years was valued and targeted to the upper and middle segments of society.

Another important point highlighted by Lavenda is the relatively large number of foreign-born marriage partners, especially when one considers that they constituted a small percentage of the population of the city as a whole. For instance, in 1873, 9.2 percent of the city's male population was foreign-born; these immigrant males made up 10.4 percent of the total number of males who married in that same year. By 1891 foreign-born males constituted 15 percent of Caracas's male population and accounted for nearly 25 percent of all males married in that year. Lavenda noted that this pattern was similar among females and that, in general, immigrants were more likely than Venezuelan nationals to resort to civil marriage. The significant use that immigrants made of this new resource provided by the state comes as no surprise, given the interest of the Guzmán Blanco government in promoting immigration by facilitating the family practices of non-Catholics in Venezuelan society.

Finally, there is another revealing finding from Lavenda's analysis of civil marriages in Caracas: the increasing abuse of marriage *in articulo mortis* (in danger of death) by people of means to circumvent bureaucratic paperwork. All the hassle involved in compiling the required documents, the waiting period while the banns were posted, and the long trips to city hall could be evaded by presentation of a medical certificate stating that either the bride or the groom was in imminent danger of death. This special situation allowed the waiver of all the required documentation, and the ceremony was performed in the residence of the ailing individual for a small fee to cover the transportation costs of the officials who conducted the ceremony.[31] Lavenda found that marriages *in articulo mortis* became more and more frequent. By 1908, 65 percent of marriages were of this sort; few of those who claimed to be in danger of death actually died. It is clear, then, that marriage *in articulo mortis* was used for a purpose other than that stipulated by the law. Also, those who were legitimate, contrary to what one would think, particularly abused this special condition. People from the lower classes, among whom illegitimacy and concubinage was fairly widespread, did not use the resource of "marriage in danger of death" to legitimize their children or to legalize consensual unions.

Lavenda's findings confirm the Guzmán Blanco regime's lack of interest in integrating the lower classes into their social policy. The findings also reveal the apathy of the popular classes toward measures that did not address their immediate needs. As will be discussed in chapter 9, in the late nineteenth century lower-class females continued to complain about their male partners' lack of responsibility for and abuse of their domestic "pact." In the Venezuelan legal context, in which men continued to enjoy undeniable privileges and impunity for questionable behaviors, it is logical that many women might have come to prefer the liberty that consensual unions provided, that is, the freedom to easily terminate a disagreeable relationship.[32]

Legal marriage did not appeal to the lower classes because the legal system was not attuned to the fluidity they already practiced in their relationships; nor would formal marriages have brought positive and evident changes in their social conditions. Thus, as will be discussed in chapter 9, the response of women from the subaltern classes to the government-sponsored policies of marriage contributed to the formation of alternative understandings of gender and family relations.

MATRIMONIO A PALOS, OR SHOTGUN WEDDINGS

One might mistakenly believe that the proviso on breach of promise in the Civil Code of 1873 was also meant to tackle Caracas's high illegitimacy rate.[33] The law had a limited effect on illegitimacy, however, because it applied only to a few women who proved that they met the elite's standards of femininity. In addition, it could force a marriage without the free consent of one party.

The new law tried to curb the false promises of marriage that men made to gain sexual access to women, a problem since colonial times.[34] If a man seduced a virtuous woman by promising marriage and pregnancy resulted, the judge could declare the couple officially married – even if the seducer never appeared in court. This legislation has been referred to as *matrimonio a palos*, because the court declared formal marriage without the couple's consent.[35] If a jury judged the woman both virtuous and pregnant, it could rule, *juris et de jure*, that the man indeed had seduced her with an offer of marriage. This jury, composed of elite men, had to decide whether the man was indeed the father of the child and whether the woman deserved legal protection because of her good morality.

The jurors had to be married, honorable padres de familia, with four children of different sexes. They also had to own property, manage a commercial establishment, or support themselves by a scientific profession.[36] If the defendant confessed to impregnating the woman or if the jurors decided unanimously that he had done so, they had to determine a date for celebrating the marriage. If the couple did not marry by that date, the judge could establish the marriage by legal fiat. If the woman involved was not pregnant, the man could either marry her or pay for the damage to her honor.[37] In such cases the only evidence of a promise of marriage admitted by the court was a proof that banns had appeared at the municipal hall.

The law tried to remedy an old problem by promoting marriage and perhaps legitimizing bastards, but to receive this legal protection women needed to prove their virginity prior to the relationship. This policy assumed that only those behaving in a "civilized" manner deserved this type of legal protection. Only women behaving "honestly" could be part of a legal family.

Cases of this sort occurred quite often in my sample of lawsuits for the late nineteenth century (1875–80). In those years 21.6 percent of the 199 lawsuits dealt with promises of marriage. Of the 43 cases I studied, the court issued a definite opinion only 9 times: in 6 cases the couple was married by judicial fiat and in 3 cases the male defendant won because the court did not consider the woman virtuous.[38]

In four of the six cases in which couples were married by judicial fiat, the defendants' lack of evidence was taken as further proof of their guilt. Such was the case of Merced Mota and Angel María Acosta. In court the defendant said that the plaintiff was "unquestionably virtuous" but that he had not told her he was willing to marry. Still, as evidence of his commitment, Merced presented the love letters he sent her. They promised marriage if she would please him sexually. For the jury, these letters proved that Angel María had seduced Merced and that his lack of defense showed his intent.[39] When Angel María failed to marry Merced in the ten days legally prescribed, the judge married the couple by judicial fiat.

The baker Ricardo Lezama experienced a similar situation. His failure to respond to the claim earned him a matrimonio a palo.[40] In March 1876 Zoila Antonia Mosquera's father filed a suit claiming that Ricardo kept delaying marriage to his daughter, although he had completed all the necessary paperwork. The problem was that there was opposition to the marriage. Ricardo's other girlfriend, Candelaria Manzo, also filed suit against him because he had offered to marry her, and she alleged that she was pregnant by him. Candelaria gave birth to a girl in November 1875.[41] While Candelaria's case was resolved in December 1875, Ricardo still did not marry Zoila, who also bore his child, in June 1876. In this case the jury took into account Ricardo's failure to answer the demand as well as the fact that Zoila had proven to be virtuous. They declared him the father of Zoila's son and obliged him to marry her in twenty days. After more than forty days Zoila's father complained to the court that Ricardo still had not married his daughter. The marriage quickly ensued.[42]

In the other two cases in which the defendant responded to the lawsuit and the plaintiff won her suit, there had been both a formal promise of marriage and parental permission to marry.[43] The parental permission was important because the defendants were minors in both cases. Because article 82 of the Civil Code of 1873 established that men under age twenty-one could not marry without parental consent, some defendants used this law to avoid a shotgun marriage. By arguing that they were minors without parental permission to marry, they used the legal authority of the padre de familia to confront the judges' power and highlighted a problem created by the state's intrusion into private matters.

In 1879 Juana Bautista Córdova, an educated, honest, middle-class, and pregnant woman, filed a claim against Pedro Pérez for breach of promise.[44] Several witnesses testified that Juana Bautista was virtuous, that only Pedro had often visited her parents' home, and that many also considered him her boyfriend because of his evident respect for her. Moreover, a credible witness said that Pedro had not denied responsiblity for the pregnancy and never indicated that Juana Bautista was not a virgin when they first coupled. Finally, another authoritative witness said that Pedro had asked him to find an abortion-inducing medicine. The defendant's lawyer proved that, as a minor, Pedro could not engage in any contract without parental consent. To substantiate his claim, the lawyer used an 1874 case of breach of promise in which the jury had accepted this argument. In no other case in this sample did a contending party use a verdict from another lawsuit to justify an argument.

In the 1874 case the defendant's lawyer explained the heart of the problem. He claimed that if the court disregarded article 82's prohibition of minors marrying without parental consent, "the law should discard this article, to avoid mocking parental authority."[45] The breach of promise law did not consider this potential conflict between parental and legal power, which created procedural problems. Should the state dictate the forced marriage of an underage son, ignoring parental power?

In the case of Pedro and Juana Bautista, the judge instructed the jurors to limit their opinion to the two points established legally, that is, to determine whether they believed that Pedro had fathered the child and to judge whether Juana Bautista was unquestionably honest.[46] Based on those guidelines, the jury ruled that the couple should marry in fifteen days. The defendant's attorney objected that the judge had not issued an opinion on Pedro's patria potestas and lack of parental permission to marry before the court reached a verdict. The judge then decided to disqualify himself. The court did not marry Pedro and Juana Bautista; the incomplete court document does not say whether a new judge was appointed.

Emancipated adults usually won cases by disclosing the plaintiff's immorality. This strategy freed Juan Antonio Sucre from a forced marriage. In 1879 Luisa López sued Juan Antonio because she was five months pregnant and he would not marry her. Juan Antonio responded that Luisa's immoral behavior had victimized him. He also said that Luisa's mother could not attest to her daughter's honesty when the mother was not legally married. Luisa's mother had a stable concubinage with Luisa's father. Thus, claimed the defendant, the mother exemplified immorality. Responding to these allegations, Luisa's father asked two prominent citizens to certify his and his family's admirable morality. To counteract this evidence, Juan Antonio presented Luisa's previous boyfriends and questioned them about her immoral behavior. This strategy did not succeed.[47]

Finally the jury held that "because the plaintiff declared that her illicit relationship with Juan Antonio began during the first week of the month of January 1876 and ended on 26 March 1879, and given that one of the conditions that the law demands to enable a pregnant woman to ask for a marriage [is that she be virtuous], the jury declares unanimously no [for the defendant]." The jury found Luisa's fidelity irrelevant; women were punishable if they consented to a long relationship without marriage. Love letters and pictures presented as key evidence of men's courting intentions were unimportant if women did not meet the moral double-standard legally required.

Indeed, in two of the three cases where the defendant won because the woman was "not virtuous," the couples already had stable concubinage relationships, which included children. The court considered this fact evidence against the woman's honesty, even if she behaved as a faithful, virtuous, and committed mother and companion.

This pattern of verdicts in breach of promise cases contrasts with similar legal cases that I compiled for the late colonial period (1786–90). In the late eighteenth century men were punished for delaying marriage while living in concubinage with their fiancées. Also, if a man was about to marry, his previous girlfriend had a chance, at least in church tribunals, to prove that he had proposed to her first. Thus the colonial courts' priority was to formalize unions and, to some degree, reprimand men and defend women in such circumstances.[48] From this evidence we may conclude that the Civil Code of 1873 and judicial practices at the tribunals worsened the legal situation of women in breach of promise and other cases.

Those who had alternative conceptions of gender relations and identity reacted against the unrealistic conditions imposed by this law. The law thus created a struggle over understandings and meanings of proper gender roles. The case of Candelaria Manzo and Ricardo Lezama discussed earlier exemplifies this problem. Candelaria dropped her lawsuit, saying, "Today, I am convinced that an imposed marriage with Lezama will not bring me the peace and happiness I seek, because we do not share the love and esteem that must constitute the basis of the conjugal union."[49] Candelaria contested the breach of promise law's imposition of marriage, for she demanded that the law recognize what she considered crucial: mutual love as a basis for marriage. Candelaria thus challenged the court's definition of marriage, which ignored human feelings and made marriage a formality without substance.

Candelaria settled the suit in exchange for her boyfriend's recognition of their daughter and his commitment to support the child and satisfy his parental duties.[50] This outcome seemed optimal for the lower classes. They appreciated the benefits of freedom from marriage, even if they lived at the margins of the law. This lower-class behavior becomes even more meaningful when one considers how difficult it was to get a divorce.

SEPARATION OF BED AND BOARD AND NULLITY OF MARRIAGE

When secular marriage was established by the 1873 Civil Marriage Law, the state had to create new divorce procedures.[51] But the new legal rationale for granting a divorce did not differ greatly from Spanish colonial law. As in the *Siete Partidas*, only death could truly dissolve a marriage, allowing the bereaved spouse to remarry.[52] Nonetheless, in some instances a separation of bed and board or divorce was permitted. A wife's adultery was acceptable grounds for separation or divorce, regardless of the circumstances. A husband's adultery was now acceptable as grounds for separation or divorce only if the concubine had lived in his house or "in a notorious place" and the situation had constituted an insult to the wife.[53] Voluntarily abandoning the home and extreme physical abuse were also valid grounds for divorce. These reasons were the most common ones given in filings for divorce.[54] Two other circumstances were new and rarely invoked: a divorce would be granted if the husband prostituted his wife or if he and/or his wife fostered corruption in their sons or prostituted their daughters.

The state's control of marriage, making it a contract rather than a sacrament, also meant that civil courts would handle petitions for nullity of marriage. As under colonial law, a marriage could be nullified only if the partners were minors, if they were close relatives, or if they had not freely consented to the marriage.[55] The 1873 code also included two new situations that could validate a petition for nullity: if either party was bigamous, and if the marriage ceremony failed to meet the legal requirements.[56]

How did the new legislation work in practice? The sample years show only three requests for nullity of marriage, and despite the weighty proofs and claims required, the court approved two of them. Both of the approved cases involved bigamy.[57] In the third, unapproved case, the couple claimed they had not consummated the marriage and that the bride's father had forced her to marry.[58]

In contrast to the rare petitions for nullity of marriage, all of which ended with a judgment, claims for divorce were numerous, but very few received a formal court sentence. Indeed, the late-nineteenth-century sample confirms an increase in divorce cases: 47, or 23.6 percent, out of 199 cases in this sample were divorce cases, while during the colonial and early republican periods divorce claims made up only 6 to 7 percent of civil and ecclesiastical lawsuits.[59] Surprisingly, only 5 of the 47 cases received a verdict; the court approved 2 divorces (4 percent of the divorce cases) and denied 3. In the samples for the colonial and early republican periods, a higher percentage was approved: 25 percent of all requests for 1786–90 and 32 percent for 1835–40. Modern courts, it seems, did not favor divorce.[60]

In cases of "separation of bed and board" that reached sentencing one litigant was upper class and the others (that is, forty-six cases) were from the working class. In all three cases where divorce was denied, plaintiffs and defendants were from the working class. As in the breach of promise cases, the litigants in a vast majority of cases that were settled, inconclusive, or incomplete were from the lower class (thirty-seven of forty-two). Only three litigants were upper class, and six were middle class. Again, these numbers suggest that the elites' use of the courts was minimal, while both working- and middle-class litigants often sought legal means of settling their private affairs.[61]

Why did courts approve so few divorces from 1875 to 1880? A close look at the denied verdicts may show the grounds that were persuasive to judges.

María Teresa Belsinger, who made cigars in the morning and matchboxes at night, sued her husband for abandoning his marital and paternal duties and often abusing her. Juan Bautista Acereto, the defendant, contradicted María Teresa's allegations, arguing that he was a poor baker, unable to provide for their eight children on his meager earnings. He maintained that he had always fulfilled his paternal duties. María Teresa's witnesses testified to the many times her husband had insulted her, beat her, and even threatened her with a knife. Juan Bautista testified that all María Teresa's witnesses were retaliating for his past insults to them. Most of these witnesses had lived with the Acereto family and had experienced their daily struggles. Juan Bautista's witnesses called him a well-behaved, hard-working man.

This lawsuit passed through four courts before receiving a definitive decision. The first court discounted all the plaintiff's witnesses, alleging their prejudice. Thus the court found inconclusive evidence that Juan Bautista had abandoned his family or that his verbal and physical offenses were excessive enough to grant a divorce. According to the court, the case exemplified causes that threaten a marriage, which a conscientious reconciliation should remedy – at least for the children's benefit – before the situation gained the criteria for granting a divorce.[62]

María Teresa appealed to the Superior Court of Justice, which ruled that her witnesses' testimony was valid because none considered themselves Juan Bautista's enemies. This court also found the testimonies of the defendant's witnesses invalid because they referred to a period long before the marital problems began. The court revoked the previous judgment, approving the divorce on the grounds that, due the couple's frequent arguments, their children and the public order would be affected if they continued to live together. Moreover, it was argued that María Teresa had proved her integrity and aptitude for bringing up the children.[63]

The angry Juan Bautista appealed; the Supreme Court revoked the second judgment, reiterating that abuse must be excessive to warrant divorce. Any quarrel or rash behavior would not suffice.[64] Without evidence of life-threatening injuries that made marital life impossible, the court could not grant a divorce. But the court made other points as well. This time the judge claimed that Juan Bautista had not abandoned María Teresa.

Moreover, the judge made clear that failure to support the family was not a cause for divorce. Basing the sentence on articles 174–75, the court established that a husband was obligated to satisfy his wife's needs only in proportion to his means and condition. In addition, the woman "should contribute to the subsistence of the husband when his means are insufficient."[65] This judgment affirmed equality – in order to defend the husband – while María Teresa may give the impression that she wanted protection and support, appealing to the inequality of custom and women's traditional role. Her true motive was to complain that Juan Bautista did not fulfill his marital duties, thus burdening her with all the familial responsibilities.

The Supreme Court verdict insisted that for the well-being of children and of society, ordinary quarrels should not lead to a separation. More importantly, "the duties as a husband and father, and the morale and respect that must be instilled in the children's hearts, require the undeniable duty of silencing resentments that are not established on any serious grounds, in order to avoid disputes and scandals that weaken the family ties *and undermine the respect due to the always sacred figure of the father*" (my emphasis).[66] This last part of the Supreme Court judgment clarifies why a divorce may have been so difficult to obtain. First, the need to keep families together was pivotal to children's well-being and social continuity. That is, familial peace brings an orderly state.[67] Second, the decision implied that a woman must bow to authority, avoiding confrontations that threaten the family. Most importantly, women had to have a sacred devotion to the padre de familia. Thus divorce lawsuits threatened not only the foundations of society but also the male rulers of that society. For the well-being of Venezuelan society, women must accept their burdens, just as Father Riera's sermons in *La Opinión Nacional* advocated. María Teresa would not relent, but her appeal to the country's highest court, the Corte de Casación, brought disappointment again. This court also sustained the previous three rejections.[68]

Even when a husband sued his wife for adultery, the court reasoned similarly. The verdict in the lawsuit of Luis Felipe Delgado against Teolinda Hernández stated: "[the] causes of divorce are not only private matters but are also matters of public order and interest, and consequently, the parties cannot agree to the separation of the marriage when there is no justified legal cause."[69] Again the court refused a separation because of the critical effect that a divorce would have on the private and public interests of the nation. Only familial peace would ultimately create order for the state. Building a modern nation required women's submission in the home, which was the rightful responsibility of the law to uphold. Hence the state's duty was to intrude into private life. Essentially, the judge used the verdict to impose domestic peace. Such judicial efforts succeeded in eight of the forty-seven divorce cases, although, contradictorily, the settlements did not require the couple to live together again.

Of the remaining thirty-two inconclusive or incomplete lawsuits, two were dismissed due to the plaintiffs' death. The lack of further information on the other cases could indicate an informal settlement by the parties, the courts' disinterest in pursuing these claims, or the loss of records. Clearly the courts seldom granted formal separation of bed and board. So how were the two cases in which divorces were granted unique? First, as in the breach of promise cases where the court ruled in the plaintiffs' favor, the defendants did not provide evidence.[70] Second, the evidence presented included prior lawsuits and formal complaints against the defendants and, in one case, the defendant's confession of adultery. In these cases the judge found the evidence too overwhelming to ignore.

One might think that once marriage became a contract controlled by the state and not a religious sacrament, people would have had more freedom to dissolve that marital contract. Yet a divorce law that allowed the dissolution of marriage and for remarriage did not appear until 1904.

Legislation regarding sexual crimes also affected women in this period. If the state regarded chastity as a key element of women's condition, would the penal code and the courts protect victims of rape? Would the tribunals punish men's sexual aggression against women?

Answers to these questions reflect the trends surrounding women's legal identity already discussed. Judges in the late nineteenth century had to balance their desire to punish immoral behavior with their need to avoid potential challenges to Venezuelan men's exalted status. Hence the aggressor was punished in only one of nine cases of *estupro* in the 1875–80 sample; in two cases the defendants were acquitted. In the other cases the defendants were released on bail because the plaintiffs made no formal accusation and, most importantly, presented no definitive proof of the defendants' guilt.

The Penal Code of 1873 introduced a new legal term, *violación*, or rape, to designate what had been known as *estupro con fuerza*.[71] *Estupro* still applied in cases in which no violence accompanied sexual intercourse but in which deceitful seduction had occurred. For the crime to classify as estupro the victim had to be a virgin between the ages of ten and eighteen.[72] The term "rape" applied when the crime involved physical violence against women of any age.

Estupro carried a lighter punishment than rape. The sentence for estupro was a maximum of eight months if the aggressor was a priest, public authority, tutor, teacher, or guardian and between three and twelve months for an unknown attacker.[73] Anyone guilty of rape could be jailed for two to five years, but if the suspect proved that the victim did not behave as a *mujer honesta* (a chaste woman), the sentence could be lowered to a maximum of eighteen months of imprisonment.

As in colonial times, the implicit understanding that women could incite such crimes prevailed. This assumption promoted the image of women as devils who seduced men.[74] If the court found any indication that a woman lacked chastity, then the aggressor did not need to take all blame for the crime. In these cases the court judged not a criminal act but the victim's conformity to the rules of moral behavior. In this way, each verdict sought to defend the dominant norm of conduct.

In my sample it is difficult to differentiate between estupro and rape in practice. All the crimes between 1875 and 1880 were committed against girls between the ages of three and sixteen, and the use of force and *honestidad* were issues to be proved at trial. Nevertheless, in six of the nine cases the person bringing the case to the tribunals claimed that the crime was rape, probably seeking a harsher punishment for the accused.

Indeed, proof is the most problematic aspect of sexual crimes. Judges carefully considered the girl's sexual and social behavior, as we see in the case of twelve-year-old María Paula Báez.[75] The court asked about her occupation and whether she had worked and gone out alone at night. The court also asked why she did not seek help immediately after the crime and whether she had resisted the aggressor.[76] María Paula's testimony did not help her. She was an orphan in the care of her aunt and godmother, and she ran errands and carried water day and night. The rapist, her aunt's brother, threatened to throw her out of their home if she refused intercourse.

By the time a doctor examined María Paula, almost two months after the rape, no evidence of a crime remained; she had only contracted syphilis. As in other such cases, the timing of the family's response also played a role. Judges interpreted a delayed complaint as evidence of the family's lack of concern. More importantly, the delay might make a physical exam useless if the doctor could no longer determine when the girl had lost her virginity.[77] Following extensive investigation, the court noted that no legally recognized representative had made a formal accusation, as required in article 46 of the Code of Criminal Procedure. Consequently, it freed the defendant and dismissed the case.

In the same vein, proving that the victim bled was critical for both the plaintiff and the judges.[78] Blood was proof that a girl had indeed been deflowered and that a corpus delicti existed. As a judge in another case explained, if physicians examining the victim determined that the hymen membrane was intact, then no crime had occurred, because only that rupture constitutes the loss of virginity.[79] When this happened the defendant was acquitted of all blame and charges.

As in the divorce cases discussed earlier, the court would not find in favor of the plaintiff without positive proof of an impairing injury.[80] In rape cases, if the aggressor used force but did not deflower the girl, this fact mitigated the sentence.[81] The intent to commit the crime, even if the assailant confessed, did not weigh as heavily as physical violence.[82] This practice allowed the court to commend men who controlled their "male instincts." It could also show that the legal system released men from responsibility for their acts: it was fine to abuse women, as long as the deed left no hard evidence.

Male aggressors were punished after a fashion, sometimes inconsistently and often lightly. In the late nineteenth century most men accused of estupro and causing bodily injury were released on bail (*fianza de cárcel segura*).[83] Judges granted bail on two grounds: either the injuries were minor and the victim recovered completely, or the crime's sentence was less than two years of imprisonment.[84] I surmise that an accused person who was released on bail could return to court if he or she committed another crime. If the person repeated the offense, the judge could not grant bail again.[85] Release on bail was a subtle way to "punish" the accused without imposing jail time. I have no evidence that judges issued verdicts when they released the accused on bail. Those released on bail also stayed under court surveillance through a bondsman responsible for their possible return to court.[86]

Prison time for convicted offenders varied greatly. The only convicted rapist in my sample spent two years and seven months in jail. In the other cases the offenders spent between thirteen days and a year in jail while their cases awaited hearing. For the public, this sentencing pattern may have seemed lenient.

We may conclude that the state was also complicit in preserving men's good reputation in cases of sexual crime. Hence the burden of the crime fell on women, who enjoyed no legal protection. The courts' actions in rape cases implied that women usually provoked these crimes, thereby encouraging justifications for controlling female behavior.

The official discourse cast a new role for women in a Venezuela *regenerada*. Still, the regime's legal reforms did not match the rhetoric. The 1873 code did not greatly change women's legal condition. The governing elites' ideology romanticized women's domestic power while blocking social changes that might have resulted when women sought legal protection. My findings suggest that only those women who followed the elite ideal of womanhood – those who proved without reasonable doubt to be virtuous and chaste – received favorable court rulings.

Court decisions served to punish women who did not heed the call to bourgeois domestic morality and progress. The courts made the law both a practice and a discourse. They penalized women who did not embody the state's ideal of femininity and, contradicting their liberal agenda, the state intervened in the private sphere by ruling on courtship, marriage, child custody, and divorce. Through law and the practice of the courts, the liberal state promoted sexual norms, family organization, and feminine honor. In this way the regime intended to legally recreate its program of moral regeneration. This project integrated patriarchy, the new family morality, and the promise of individuality and equality with the liberal ideal of limited state powers, the need for tranquility, and the desire to exclude the lower classes from power.

With a justice system that seldom disputed male power, why did women go to court? As discussed above, lawsuits in the late nineteenth century were fewer and less extensive than their colonial and early republican counterparts. This is intriguing because the population of Caracas was 24 percent larger in the late nineteenth century than in 1835. Thus we might infer that the courts heard only a fraction of the potential cases.

Many of the female litigants, consciously or not, challenged the prevailing ideals of womanhood. Women like María Teresa Belsinger – who pursued her divorce in four different courts – concretely addressed the contradictions between the regime's discourse and its practice. Most female litigants issued their challenges individually and less consciously, by infusing the prescribed roles for women with different meanings. As we will see in chapter 9, women appropriated those elements of government discourse that empowered them and rejected those that were useless. My sample showed that many litigants did not desire formal marriage and that, for them, living outside the boundaries of legitimacy was no less honorable than formal unions. In the late nineteenth century both public and hidden transcripts expressed this challenge to the state's discourse. Hence it is questionable whether the disciplinary efforts of the government were effective.[87]

Still, for jurists, government efforts to revitalize and pacify the country provided the opportunity to create a better defined, more secular family policy. The modern state was to be organized through a more competent sexual control of women, directly promoted by the courts' decisions and, more subtly, by the diffusion of ideal social roles and images. Sunday masses reproduced this discourse, highlighting the Virgin Mary as a model of behavior for women. The scandal of a lawsuit allowed the courts and the government to convey a public message about the benefits of assuming new roles and responsibilities.

In this way the judiciary became another institution seeking to promote discipline and appropriate social behavior. This strategy would produce precisely the virtuous republican mothers so deeply desired by people like Father Riera and Guzmán Blanco. In this sense, Guzmán Blanco could be better remembered for restoring domestic order than for his achievements in bringing peace and political order to Venezuela.

9. Contesting Gender Meanings from Below

María Teresa Belsinger's repeated appeals to the courts illustrate how women attempted to force men and the state to respond to the contradictions between the laws of Venezuela and a hegemonic project that valorized women's place in the domestic sphere. In a claim lodged by María Teresa Belsinger, she contested the Supreme Court's interpretation of article 152 of the Civil Code of 1873, which prohibited divorce. According to María Teresa, "The bases [of the decision] are not in harmony with that article, because if it is enforced according to our laws, one could claim the falsity of the belief that Christianity has regenerated women, giving them the same rights as men."[1]

Her argument demonstrates her belief that the government discourse of women's regeneration through education and sacrifice for their families reflected the new legislation's power to give women the same rights as men. Such was not the case, however. In the practice of the courts, the government tried to prevent women from asserting their rights. Even in the face of well-justified criticism, the courts of "civilized" Venezuela were not willing to risk the "order" that the country needed by providing greater legal liberties and protection for women. Obviously they were convinced that greater rights for women would put the stability of Venezuelan families at risk. Instead the courts consistently reaffirmed patriarchal authority over the lives of Venezuelan women, conveying the message that women should submit to the limitations on their gender sanctioned by custom.

Mercedes García also expressed doubts that her claim would be dealt with justly. Frustrated and hopeless, she filed a demand for divorce against her abusive husband. In her verbal response (transcribed by a court recorder) to her husband's petition that she be withdrawn from the depósito at her parents' home, Mercedes revealed her doubts as to whether she would be treated with equity. If the court granted the petition, "it will make me the victim of a wild beast, putting me in the situation – if I find myself abandoned by the authorities, which I do not believe that such a thing may happen – of resorting to the natural law that orders me to defend myself against the beasts and to look after myself."[2] Indeed, despite the danger of seeming barbarous by contemporary bourgeois standards, she would not hesitate to go outside proper gender roles and take justice into her own hands if the learned, "civilized" court did not protect her. As these two examples show, the correspondence between a civilizing discourse and the rights that governed women was open to question. Conforming to the normative gender roles did not guarantee these women equal protection under the law.

Any conclusions that might be drawn from the public transcripts about how women reacted to the regime's rhetoric and laws on gender relations, would be limited at best. Within a sample of 199 civil and criminal court cases, only Mercedes García and María Teresa Belsinger expressly addressed the contradictions between the regime's discourse and its practice in a concrete way. As research on Caribbean societies has shown, however, common people often express their values, norms, and possible reactions to gender roles promoted by the dominant classes in ways that do not necessarily conform to the strictures of "Western thought." Their expressions, therefore, may be overlooked – or silenced – in the "public transcript."[3]

This chapter attempts to tease out from lawsuits the ways in which women registered their beliefs about gender through their language and behavior and demonstrates how caraqueño beliefs about gender may have differed from the roles that were enforced by the regime. Court records provide a window through which to observe differences in gender meanings. When someone uses the courts to file a complaint, he or she acts on the understanding that there is some type of behavior that does not conform to what he or she believes to be the accepted norm. Individual normative assumptions differ from formal legal precepts, however.[4] A lawsuit helps us analyze debates about the meanings of the law and proper behavior. More importantly, it allows us to examine how, in their everyday language and actions, the lower classes deploy parts of the ruling class's discourse, transformed to suit their own particular realities and interests.

Although different models for understanding gender and identities might cut across class, race, and age, the defense of honor was a central concern among the litigants in this study. As has been made clear by other works on this topic, definitions of honor are contextual, depending on time, place, and social circumstances.[5] It is clear from the cases that, for these working-class caraqueñas, honor was not so much a function of social status and sexual conduct as a demonstration of moral rectitude in character and behavior. Honorable conduct was critical for the maintenance of the social networks that were pivotal to the daily subsistence of the popular classes. In a society that did not offer subsistence-level monetary compensation for women's labor, women could not afford the luxury of losing social esteem among the friends and relatives who helped them in times of need.

The majority of women in the late-nineteenth-century sample resisted proper gender roles in a less-organized or conscious manner than Mercedes García and María Teresa Belsinger did. Indeed, most women went to court to seek relief simply on an individual and personal level. Still, when the heterogeneous actions of individual women are analyzed as a group, it becomes clear that one result of women's litigation was to set the stage for future organized and purposeful political action as well as to legitimize alternative kinds of gender behavior and family formations.[6] For this reason, this study examines the use and meanings of language as well as the behavior that was systematically repeated in the actions of the litigants in different types of conflicts, circumstances, and gender relationships. This allowed a way to trace and account for the multiple ways in which the less-conspicuous actions of women creatively challenged dominant cultural assumptions and created a space in which women could assert the validity of their alternative models of gender relationships.

WIVES, MOTHERS, CITIZENS, AND THE IDEAL OF FEMININITY

Undoubtedly the official rhetoric praising women's importance to the household resonated with many nonelite women. They eagerly gave themselves merit by depicting themselves in accordance with the new values. One noticeable change in the late nineteenth century was the increasing number of married and widowed female claimants who used their husbands' last name. Today in Spanish America, people usually use both their father's and mother's last names, and when they marry, women take on their husband's last name preceded by the preposition *de*. For example, the official name of Antonio Guzmán Blanco's wife was Ana Teresa Ibarra Urbaneja de Guzmán Blanco. The use of the husband's last name signals a woman's married status and serves as formal indication of the familial dominion of the padre de familia over his children and spouse.

Use of the husband's last name became a general custom among elite women in this period and also among a number of women from the lower and middle classes who identified with the official culture and aspired to become part of it. In the colonial sample none of the women used their husband's last name, and in the early republic it was still a rare occurrence, but by the late nineteenth century 46 percent of married and widowed claimants did so.[7] This was an elite convention; most of these claimants came from the upper rungs of society (88 percent). Moreover, half of the middle-class women in the late nineteenth-century sample used their husband's last name. Among the lower classes, only half of the women in the sample over thirteen years of age were married or widowed and of these, only 40 percent followed the elite fashion. Thus although carrying the husband's last name after marriage was increasingly accepted, a good portion of lower-class women did not get married and a majority of those who did marry did not change their last name.

Women's identification with the official ideal of womanhood was also reflected in the lawsuits themselves. For example, some women articulated their belief in the importance of marriage for the well-being of society and the need for women's domestic sacrifices in maintaining family cohesion, ideas that were not much different from those of the colonial past. Yet other notions were new and responded to state and church discourse on gender relations. For example, many echoed the church's dogma that if women behaved as proper mothers and wives, men would have more consideration for them and would even modify their own behavior.[8] Francisca Lameda de Vázquez summarized both old and new beliefs when she wrote about her ordeal with her husband, a poor artisan:

I resolved to carefully fulfill those duties so that no pretext could be raised to break the marriage bond, expecting on the contrary to preserve it, in order to preserve the well being not only of my companion and the family but of society in general.

The fruits of my union with Mr. Vázquez were the seven children, the last born recently and whom I still breast-feed, as I have done with the others, devoting myself entirely to their well being and my companion's, of whom I expected consideration in due form at least in remuneration of those sacrifices that not all married women do for the family, especially when their companions do not reciprocate.[9]

Although government discourse emphatically insisted that women bear their ordeal without protest, women such as Francisca, who sued her husband for divorce, did not obey this tenet. Rather, Francisca understood that her enhanced position in the family and her work on their behalf entitled her to demand respect and reciprocity from her male companion, just as María Teresa Belsinger did. In accordance with church dictates she always tried to be submissive in her efforts to promote harmony within the family, but her husband, according to Francisca, did not fulfill the responsibilities he "contracted with me and with society" and, moreover, he "abused his authority as husband."[10]

Even in the late nineteenth century women sought a reciprocal relationship with men in which they were both respected and fulfilled and shared their duties and rights within the family.[11] This notion of gender roles contrasted with government and church ideas, which advocated women's submission to men, thus discouraging women from seeking their own rights. Yet there was no complementary discourse that encouraged men to be responsible to their duties. Women who went to court redefined the official discourse on women, probably to justify their participation at the tribunals. Whether this was a calculated decision by female plaintiffs is not clear. There is proof from the late colonial period, however, that women who went to court believed that marriage was a pact in which men and women had certain responsibilities. Women extracted from the official discourse on womanhood those ideas that empowered them and with which they identified. In this way they demonstrated that their behavior corresponded to those ideals and that, as a result, they were entitled to receive the protection of the law.

The invocation of rights based on women's important role as mothers was common and quite apparent.[12] For example, Juana Buerta de Pompa sued her daughter's boyfriend for abduction because he had induced her daughter to leave home with the promise of marriage. Yet for two years he had failed to keep his promise. Juana reminded the courts that, "according to the right granted to me by the Constitution and the Laws as a citizen of Venezuela, and the right and power that I have as a mother, I resort to Your authority requesting the proper punishment to the abductor."[13] Even though her daughter was living in concubinage as a single mother – a status that proved her lack of virtue and that lessened the merit of her claim in the eyes of the court – Juana invoked justice based on her own rights as a citizen and as a mother.[14]

In another case Amalia Bolívar resisted her ex-boyfriend's effort to take their daughter away from her, claiming that she had been a responsible mother while he had been an undependable father: "According to the plaintiff, one can resign rights but not duties, which is a counteractive argument because between my daughter Luisa and the two of us, I have more duties with regard to her than the plaintiff, because the law classifies him as her guardian and I as her mother. Because the plaintiff, in spite of the contract that compels him to provide for the girl, has not fulfilled his duty, it has become necessary to bind him over to pay back alimony."[15]

Amalia clearly stated that she was a mother who fulfilled her duties, unlike the girl's natural father. Although the law made him the guardian, he failed in his duties as a father because he did not provide support regularly as mandated by a court agreement. It did not matter to Amalia that she was not married and had two natural children by different fathers. To her the only relevant fact was that she was the one who had given birth and had cared for, supported, and reared the girl in question. In the context of the new, civilized Venezuela, in which a high respect for mothers was the rule, how could a court neglect the case of a responsible mother?

The court gave Bernardo custody because it believed the girl should not be under the care of a single woman who kept having children. Amalia resisted the mandates of the court, however, and hid the girl. As this example illustrates, women resorted to means outside the law when the state failed to respond to their cases using a standard that reflected and validated their realities and values. Venezuelan women's interpretation of the law could be regarded as an effort to make the ideals of the government fit women's lived experiences of premarital relations and the notion of equal and reciprocal relationships and rights.

PADRES DE FAMILIA

Although many women used domestic roles to legitimate their claim to a more egalitarian relationship with men, men remained firmly committed to their traditional position as padre de familia. Men embraced a government agenda that reaffirmed male patriarchal powers at home and in the tribunals.

Clearly men used their legal rights as a basis of power, and in many ways their claims resemble the discourse used by men in colonial times. For example, Juan Cleofe Morales, a defendant in the divorce lawsuit filed by his wife, Luisa Piñango, claimed that his wife had committed "some slight acts of insubordination to the respect and considerations that a woman has to have toward her husband, who as the head of the household enjoys *fueros* [privileges] and rights by law, demanding his wife with all urbanity that she should not leave the house without his consent."[16]

In another case Ramón Rojas refused to grant a license to his wife, Brígida Isabel Gascón, so that she could accept and administer a house and a plot of land that she inherited from her sister. Although the couple had been separated for fourteen years, Ramón did not want to "give up the cherished rights that laws grant me," and indeed, he dissuaded the tribunal from approving any measure that would hinder his rights as a husband.[17] Men like Ramón and Juan were conscious of their formal rights to power in the family.

Husbands' and fathers' legal rights accompanied a duty to punish family members. This colonial idea persisted in law and also in custom. A typical example of this belief was José Tomás Gil's courtroom confession that as chastisement he hit his wife.[18] Similarly men in the late nineteenth century alluded to their responsibility to enforce gender roles. Gregorio López, for instance, claimed that his wife should be in his home fulfilling the duties of her gender, that is, helping him earn a livelihood and taking care of the hens, which had died after she left home.[19] Such beliefs, expressed in both domestic and judicial contexts and formalized in law, helped to maintain the patriarchal values of Venezuelan society.

Male references to honor were also based in the patriarchal ideal. In the late colonial and early republican periods, honor (or public reputation based on one's conduct) was highly regarded in Caracas society. For example, a husband or father could be highly offended if his honor were threatened by his being brought to court. Women also referred to honor and also had defended the concept of honor since colonial times.[20] Integral to a family's honor was the conduct and reputation of its women, whom padres de familia had to strictly protect.[21] Fathers were offended when their daughters were deflowered or their wives insulted.[22]

These ideals persisted in the late nineteenth century. For example, Daniel Martínez went to court claiming that his honor had been offended when his *compadre* (the godfather of one of his children) seduced his daughter.[23] In another case a husband insisted that his wife's bad behavior tainted his honor.[24] Reputation remained an important aspect of social relations in Caracas.

Robert H. Lavenda and Julián Nava maintain that open displays of male bravado were common in late-nineteenth-century Caracas.[25] Men sought to demonstrate their manliness through an exaggerated attitude of independence, hypersensitivity to criticism, arrogance, and intolerance. For instance, society expected women to adhere strictly to domestic duties and fidelity but it did not expect similar behavior from men, who as padres de familia were the legal holders of familial rights.[26] It was common for men of every class to have mistresses and second families – a widespread custom even among public figures in contemporary Venezuela.[27]

In 1922 Dr. J. B. Ascanio Rodríguez gave an anthropological explanation of male behavior to medical students in a lecture intended to help them provide appropriate premarital counseling. Dr. Ascanio maintained that real men have at least two women because "women love their husbands more the more they have been loved by other ladies."[28] Men who did not follow this rule were not real men or had never had the opportunity to be men in the true sense of the word. By understanding this so-called law, Ascanio claimed, engaged women could be awakened and become the one chosen by their husbands by being good wives and partners. The latent message was that wives must learn to live without bitterness about mistresses, who had only secondary importance.

These early-twentieth-century beliefs do not substantially differ from those found in the legal records from the late nineteenth century. Women's frequent citation of men's infidelity in the lawsuits could be interpreted as evidence that men looked favorably upon having extra-marital affairs.[29] Moreover, some men accused of sexual offenses plainly admitted that they were unable to fulfill the sexual act that they intended with the women, suggesting that men's loose behavior was condoned in society.[30] In the late nineteenth century as well as in the late colonial period there is evidence that men shared these experiences with one another and thus knew about the sexual behavior of women and men in their community. These kinds of disclosures became pivotal testimony in lawsuits. Consider the statement made in the case of Juana Buerta de Pompa's daughter by a male witness who assured the court that "Tomás Ramón Hernández has been publicly saying that having sex took him much effort because the girl was a virgin."[31]

Increasingly aware that women were willing to take them to court, men were careful not to leave proof of their sexual affairs. In a lawsuit for breach of promise a witness with whom the defendant had a long and open conversation admitted: "In our conversation, he did not deny he had impregnated the girl, adding further that men always did this; he did deny that he was engaged to marry her, something she could not prove because he had been careful enough not to give her any material evidence of this. But when asked if he rejected the girl because she had had sex with another man, his answer was a plain no."[32]

As this testimony suggests, men learned the etiquette of womanizing through socialization.[33] They seemed to know not only about their rights but also about how to avoid punishment. In fact many women complained about the way in which their husbands or partners flaunted their actions with impunity.[34] Men avoided punishment by hiding, leaving town, or even bribing witnesses or court officials. From at least late colonial times all of these were popular male responses in cases of seduction and abuse, especially when there was strong evidence against them. Moreover, the court consistently supported and legitimized male power in the late nineteenth century, and this served to convey the idea that punishment would not be forthcoming.

LOVE, PASSION, AND A PROMISE OF MARRIAGE

Although men expected women to behave with great decorum, they had different rules for themselves. In the cases discussed later in this section, men insisted upon having premarital sex with their girlfriends, to whom they usually offered an often hollow promise of marriage in return. In contrast, a genuine promise of marriage was important to young women, who sought to remain virtuous. Even when involved in loving and passionate relationships, some women were reluctant to lose their virginity and questioned the feelings and true intentions of their suitors. Women wanted to be sure that their suitors would be responsible partners. The process through which relationships developed, which can been seen as a form of negotiation, often resulted in women's loss of virginity. It is possible that the fear of destroying what the woman believed was a potentially worthwhile relationship may have driven these women to please their boyfriends and diverge from what was considered proper feminine conduct. Yet it is possible that loss of virginity was not as important to these women, because many couples cohabited and there was a high rate of illegitimacy. Although a definitive answer might be difficult to find, the overall pattern may provide some clues as to which goal was more important to these women – preserving their virginity as the ideology of proper womanhood dictated or ensuring that their partners would keep their promises.

A case of breach of promise against Angel María Acosta illustrates these points.[35] Angel María affirmed in the tribunals that his pregnant girlfriend, Mercedes Mota, was unquestionably virtuous but that he never offered to salvage her honor with marriage. Yet his love letters proved the contrary.

The plaintiff, Mercedes, a legitimate daughter, brought to court three letters that she received in the course of their four-year relationship. In the main text of a letter of 12 June 1875, Angel María expressed his deep love and promised to fulfill his sacred pledge of marriage. In a note at the bottom of the letter, as if he were trying to ease her doubts about him, he repeated his promise. A year later Angel María referred to Mercedes as his fiancée (*prometida*) and made clear that the day she pleased him with "what he demanded from her" he would ask her to marry him in front of her family. He intentionally committed his vow to writing as a guarantee that he would not deceive her. He also assured her that she was the only woman to whom he had given his word and begged her to not refuse his entreaties. Angel María bartered with Mercedes, offering his formal commitment of marriage in exchange for sexual pleasure.

Mercedes seemed to be afraid of deception and Angel María's motives for emphatically expressing his eternal love and, more importantly, for promising marriage. Due to her insistence Angel María attempted to assuage her doubts. A third letter, dated three months later, is fondly addressed to his beloved "Negra" in an attempt, yet again, to persuade her to please him.[36] He promises that less than twenty-four hours after consummating their relationship, he would talk to her parents. He swears, even by the holy host, that he will not deceive her, and he ends the letter asserting that he is poor but honest.

These love letters provide a window through which we can observe not only a lover's passion but also the negotiation of a relationship. It can be inferred by reading between the lines that Angel María was responding to Mercedes's doubts about losing her virginity and whether he would honor his word. It is very likely that she was aware of unfortunate experiences suffered by young women with irresponsible suitors. A promise of marriage appealed to many women, although the legal and social conditions of the period made some women question the value of marriage, as is discussed later.

Angel María persisted in his demands for a sexual relationship. His strategy was to make it seem as formal as possible by committing his intentions to paper, swearing by the Holy Communion, and setting up a time frame in which he would honor his promise. As was already discussed in chapter 8, although Angel María testified to his unwillingness to marry Mercedes, his recognition of her virginity and virtue, his lack of defense to the charges, and his love letters earned him a marriage by judicial fiat.

In a contrasting case, Juan Antonio Sucre, a bakery employee, fell in love with Luisa López, the illegitimate daughter of a client.[37] Juan Antonio talked to Luisa every day through the window when he delivered fresh bread to her house.[38] As time passed their interest turned into love and passion, as can be detected in Juan Antonio's love letters. In these writings he promised eternal love and asked Luisa to notify him when her parents were not home so that they could have "fun" in the alley. Moreover, he requested a "proof of love" (sexual intercourse), which he urged her to accept without regret. Although he did not offer marriage to Luisa in his letters, he did ask her to pretend that he was her husband. Unfortunately the love letters were neither dated nor did they include information about when the relationship began.

Thus the lawsuit lacked information about how long the negotiation (courtship) took place. The records do show, however, that in an open confrontation in court Luisa admitted that the couple had been intimate for three years. For this reason the jury denied her claim of breach of promise.

A case of abduction (rapto) against Isidoro Jocko, a twenty-seven-year-old merchant born in the United States, illustrates another method through which a suitor might seduce the object of his desire.[39] On 18 November 1880 Wenceslao Villegas, a poor baker, went to court to present charges against Isidoro, the suitor of his niece, Manuela Villegas. She was eighteen years old and lived with her mother and uncle. Manuela and Isidoro had been dating for two years, but her mother, Hercilia Villegas, who was single, illiterate, and thirty-six years old, opposed the relationship. When Manuela and Isidoro first began dating, Hercilia reprimanded her daughter and, as a result, Isidoro came into the house with a revolver in a threatening manner to confront Manuela's mother. Isidoro sought to remove Manuela from her family's influence and offered to let Manuela live with him, promising to support her and to never leave her. Isidoro's love letters contain no mention of marriage, although Manuela testified to the contrary in court. He was insistent in his letters, however, of his desire for her to live with him, his wishes to begin a sexual relationship, and his willingness to give her time to make a decision. Manuela was hesitant to accept the offer. Isidoro suggested that she not take into account the romantic experiences of her mother because she had had relationships with older, married men. In addition, he advised Manuela not to worry because they were both young and single – probably a suggestion that living together was normal – and that if someone offended her dignity and honor due to her decision, she must not hesitate to defend herself.

Driven by his offers to support her (he was in a comfortable economic position) and live with her, she agreed to follow his plan to run away from her mother's house. Isidoro suggested that they provoke a dispute with her family as a way to get her out of the house. After the plan was executed, a friend quickly told Isidoro that an arrest order accusing him of abduction had been issued. He immediately wrote to Manuela to advise her about what she should say:

Manuela, how could I have been there since I was still in bed? Hipólito told me about the arrest warrant issued against me because you said I took you away under threat of a gun and had intercourse with you when you know we have not; this is what you must say, that we never had intercourse and that you left because of mistreatment and fear of losing your life, since I have not offered you anything and you left because you did not want more suffering. . . . I will not write more because I cannot.[40]

Isidoro was arrested and jailed a day after Manuela's uncle filed charges against him. At that time Manuela testified that it was true that they had been in love for two years but that she left her house of her own volition and Isidoro was not responsible for her honor (virginity). Seven days later Manuela changed her testimony. She admitted that she had made love with Isidoro so that he would have proof of her virginity and sentiments. She also claimed that he had offered to marry her and for this reason she had agreed to be intimate with him. Isidoro obtained and paid for a room and even a person to take care of her after she left her mother's house. Finally, Manuela asked the court to release him only if he agreed to marry her so that she could regain her honor.[41]

The records of this love story do not reveal the outcome. The case was inconclusive because a formal accusation was never submitted according to the rules established by law, and it ends in the middle of the formulation of an appeal. Although Isidoro admitted that he wrote the letters, his admission was not made under oath. Above all, according to the criminal prosecutor of the case, the proof was not sufficient.[42]

Isidoro, as well as Angel María Acosta and Juan Antonio Sucre, persuaded the object of his desire to violate accepted moral rules in exchange for assurances that marriage would follow this "proof of love." Men could make these kinds of demands on their girlfriends with relative ease because the moral behavior of men was not under the same social scrutiny as that of women. These cases demonstrate that courtship negotiations were not necessarily easy or quick and that women shared a common concern: they worried about whether they could trust the expressions of love, the marriage offers, and the intentions of their boyfriends. Finally, although the promise of marriage played an important role in the negotiations, these women were willing to risk their virginity to improve the odds of marriage because premarital relations and cohabitation were not uncommon practices. Even though formal marriage was publicly devalued, it did have some importance, at least for the 22 percent of women who sued their lovers for breach of promise.

DIGNITY AND HONOR . . . WITHOUT A HUSBAND

In the legal and social context of late-nineteenth-century Caracas, it is understandable that many women preferred to keep their relationships outside the realm of the law. If a woman married she lost her juridical individuality and came under the legal control of her husband; that is, her rights were less than those of single women and widows. Also, if the relationship became abusive it was difficult to obtain court approval for a formal separation. Only very extreme circumstances, such as severe abuse by the husband, served as justification for divorce. If the couple agreed to an informal separation the wife had to request from her husband or the court formal permission to manage property, among other things. Having illegitimate children was of less concern because illegitimacy was common among the popular classes. A legitimate child or a natural child legitimated by a public document or baptismal record could be taken away from the mother because fathers had priority in the legal guardianship of children. Because contemporary practices in the courts of Caracas did not protect women, there were few incentives for complying with the expensive and time-consuming requisites for a formal marriage. Some married women who went to court demonstrated their disenchantment with this institution. In the exasperated words of Mercedes García, "to tell the truth, I have wished many times to be dead rather than to be married."[43]

Working-class men did not seem to think very differently, because a formal marriage tied them to one woman and to familial responsibilities that many men did not want to have. Because these couples were poor and had little property, one important legal benefit given to men through marriage – the administration of property – was irrelevant. Overall, men were explicit about their preference not to marry.

A case in point is that of Leandro Orta, an illiterate caraqueño who was accused of breach of promise by the father of María Antonia Avilán, a nineteen-year-old legitimate daughter. According to a witness, Leandro made clear during a visit to the Avilán family that he was not willing to spend the money necessary to reap the benefits of a civil marriage.[44] María Antonia claimed that she was seduced to leave her parental home by his promise of marriage. Although he finally agreed to marry María Antonia "because she is most deserving of marriage given her flawless conduct toward him," he kept delaying the ceremony.[45] After more than five months María Antonia's father complained to the court that Leandro was shirking his responsibilities, and ten days later he informed the court that his daughter had disappeared from her depósito. It can be inferred from the record that Leandro dodged the marriage and ran away with María Antonia, who did not want to return to her parents' home.

Like María Antonia, many other young women decided to voluntarily leave their parental homes and engage in premarital sex without the sanction of the church or the state. On 15 October 1877 Juliana Mijares, the single mother of seventeen-year-old Violante Mijares, filed a suit against Carlos Ascanio for breach of promise.[46] Juliana claimed that her natural daughter was "brought up with all the estimation of a real young lady, in the bosom of a very meritorious family," and that Carlos took advantage of Violante's weakness and took her honor away from her.[47] Again, being a single mother did not make Juliana a less-worthy mother. Juliana stated that Violante was pregnant and that she wanted Carlos to marry her daughter.

Seven days later Carlos presented a letter he had received from Violante to the court:

Dear Friend:

I understand that my mother Mrs. Juliana Mijares filed a demand for betrothal on my behalf on the grounds of my state of pregnancy. I neither accept nor approve of the suit because it contradicts my feelings, because under no circumstance will I give my hand to a man who does not want to marry me, nor will I subject my name to vexing disputes. Consequently, I state to you that it is not my will to unite in marriage and that I will not marry even if the competent Court orders it, and I would like you to defend this statement subscribed by me in Court in order to stop the proceedings.

Sincerely Yours
Violante Mijares[48]

The following day Violante acknowledged that this letter was hers and assured the court official that she had not been coerced into writing it. Juliana dropped the claim three days later, stating that "after thinking over what my daughter wrote to Mr. Ascanio, I formally waive my claim."[49]

Whether Violante was indeed coerced by Carlos is uncertain. Her reasons for not wanting to marry, however, are revealing. First, she did not want to force a man to marry her. Violante demonstrates a sense of self-respect, which reflects her belief that a "shotgun marriage" is unacceptable. Second, she was not willing to place herself in the middle of distasteful court proceedings. In other words, her public reputation (her honor) would be tainted more by agreeing to a marriage without love than by remaining a single mother.

Above all Violante wanted to preserve her dignity. She realized that she could do this without a marriage and without a husband. Her claims are not unique. Candelaria Manzo declined to marry the father of her child because the two did not possess the love that each believed formed the basis of the marital institution.[50] The importance of female honor was persuasively expressed by María Teresa Belsinger when she complained about her husband, who "frequently treats me badly, shouts injurious words at me, but the worst is that the neighborhood where we live learns of these scandals against my person, which is extremely distressing for me because I lose the social esteem that I have to preserve at all costs, because my sex without honor is good for nothing."[51]

For these women there was no incompatibility between being single – or seeking divorce, in the case of María Teresa Belsinger – and being a virtuous woman, responsible mother, and citizen. They had a well-grounded understanding of their situation, even though this contrasted with the ideal of proper femininity. The ideal promulgated during this period not only was difficult to comply with but it also perpetuated women's subjugation and lack of freedom. To oblige men to marry without love and against their will would have created a situation in which women would lose. It could also have generated a number of embarrassing situations that could have affected the social reputation of the women involved, eroding social relations in a class dependent on the solidarity of family, friends, and neighbors for sustenance. Preserving one's integrity and esteem in the community was more important than following the dictates of a distant state. Moreover, marriage was not easy, and it did not provide any consistent benefit in terms of social mobility or legal protection. These women's responses to the ruling class's notions of womanhood reflected their sense of autonomy, freedom, individualism, and sexual equality, at least within the domestic sphere.

EMANCIPATED WOMEN

In a number of cases young women sought their independence from their parental homes and asserted their sexual autonomy. These young women emphasized that they were of age (older than twenty-one) and were living with their lovers of their own will. Again, by their actions these women defied the government's moral regeneration project.

Manuela Méndez de Navarro, a widow, filed a claim against her daughter's boyfriend, José María Olivo, for abduction, estupro, and seduction with a promise of marriage.[52] Five days later Dolores Navarro, Manuela's twenty-one-year-old daughter, refused to allow doctors to examine her (to assess whether she was a virgin) on two different occasions. During the first examination Dolores confessed that she had lost her virginity to José María, and in the second examination she affirmed, according to one of the doctors, that "neither she nor José María Olivo denied they had sexual intercourse, that she had wanted it spontaneously and without any promise, and consequently, she had not been cheated and therefore he may or may not marry her."[53] Finally Dolores sent a letter to the judge of the Court of First Instance to clarify the situation:

My conscience imposes upon me the duty of raising my voice in order to explain the facts. On the ninth of the present month, I left the house where I lived looking for my tranquility; I did this fully conscious of my rights, not swayed in any way by Mr. Olivo; and by that fact alone, my mother, advised by someone who wants to hide behind my honor, intent on avenging old slights, brought forward the accusation, and I, because of propriety and respect to society had done nothing until today; but now I want to make known that I reject my mother's representation, alleging that I am a minor; because I am legally emancipated as attested by the baptism certificate; and I request dismissal of the procedure against Olivo, because all of the charges are false, and I neither want nor have anything to request against Olivo. I request also suspension of the depósito. It is justice that I request in Caracas on 19 November 1878. Dolores Navarro.[54]

After this letter was presented to the judge Dolores's mother had to drop the lawsuit, dejected that her daughter had rejected her maternal love and her desire to vindicate Dolores's honor and that of the family.[55] This situation illustrates how contrasting views of honor and of gender roles provoked conflict between two generations of women. Also important is the way in which Dolores defended her right to emancipate herself from her immediate family and to protect her private sexual life and feelings.

Many lower-class women, driven by their social conditions and the cultural options available to them at the time, consciously defied the moral and sexual discipline that the state (and many parents) attempted to impose. Many poor women made clear their desire to have the freedom to love and engage in sexual relations without having to respond to others' criticism of their behavior.

Juliana Hurtado, a fifteen-year-old, confessed in a case of abduction against her boyfriend, Jesús María Jiménez, that during the four months before the case was filed they had had a "licit love relationship." Although Jesús María never proposed marriage, Juliana decided to live with him after a fight with her unmarried mother. She claimed that her mother kicked her out of the house, saying she could "live with whatever man she wanted." She also admitted in court that she had been intimate with another man who lived in the Barrio Trinidad before having the romance with Jesús María.[56]

Salomé Cabrera, a twenty-one-year-old orphan under the guardianship of her uncle, also decided to live with her boyfriend and to "govern herself."

In 1880 Salomé's uncle, Santos Ojeda de Monasterios, sued her boyfriend, Juan Hernández, for abducting his niece.[57] Santos explained in court that Juan had asked Salomé to marry him three months earlier but said that Juan's promise belied his dishonorable intentions when he took Salomé out of her house. Juan, a twenty-two-year-old shoemaker, explained that Salomé was unfaithful to him and because "a person who was unfaithful as a lover would be unfaithful as a wife," they both decided to break their marriage pact.[58] Salomé affirmed that she was uncertain about getting married and that "because he inspired love in her," she preferred to live with Juan voluntarily and accepted responsibility for her decision. Juan promised "to take care of her until the day she committed a wrong action," while Salomé agreed to prepare his meals. Moreover, Salomé insisted that they would live as "brother and sister" and claimed to be emancipated because she was twenty-two and her mother had died eleven years earlier.[59]

In these cases women agreed to leave their homes voluntarily, sometimes in exchange for a promise that their male partners would be well behaved (*portarse bien con ella*) or that the woman would not *pasar trabajos* – meaning either that she would not have to work (probably meaning for a salary) because he would provide for her or that he would not give her a hard time and would remain a respectful and responsible partner.[60] Marriage as a bargaining tool also appeared in some cases.[61] Moreover, this type of exchange also existed between married men and their concubines. It is mentioned in a number of cases that a concubine took care of a man's food and clothes, while in exchange the man provided for her upkeep.[62]

It is important to note, however, the temporary nature of these agreements. Frequently the couple agreed to the condition that they would be together until the woman did something "wrong." Ending a relationship was not much of a problem in an informal union. There was neither paperwork nor property to deal with. The only issue was children born of the relationship and how the father's compliance with his responsibilities would be guaranteed.

Contrary to what the state and church presumed, there is evidence that even outside the law many of these relationships were quite stable. In an analysis of civil marriages between 1878 and 1908 Robert H. Lavenda found that many parents legitimized their children at the time of their civil marriage. In these cases 68 percent of the children were older than ten years of age, suggesting that their parents had been living in an ongoing relationship for a considerable period of time. There is evidence in the ecclesiastical archives that parents living in concubinage often legitimated their children through the church after their ecclesiastical weddings. Most of these children were born in the 1850s (two in the 1840s), and most of the parents were married in the 1860s and early 1870s, which also demonstrates a pattern of stable cohabitation.[63]

Steady, long-term, informal unions are also evident in lawsuits. For example, Justo Ubisco and Juana Francisca Rodríguez had four children: two natural children that they legitimized with their marriage in 1872 and two children born afterward.[64] In another case, Carolina Hernández sued Juan Nepomuceno Alcántara for breach of promise in 1876.[65] They had been together for fourteen years and had nine children, but Juan Nepomuceno intended to marry another woman. They finally settled the case. She dropped the lawsuit in exchange for his legal recognition of the children and monthly family support. In this and other cases in which agreements were reached, it seems that what mattered most to women was to make men responsible for providing financial support for their children and not to force men to marry without love.[66]

According to Dr. Ascanio Rodríguez's lecture in 1922, lower-class women believed that marriage gave men the legal right to mistreat them. They also believed that the law did not provide women with the means to seek justice. On the contrary, consensual unions allowed women to be "true to their word and the law," because women could always leave a relationship that was no longer satisfying.[67] The late-nineteenth-century cases discussed here indeed sustain Rodríguez's opinion. He also asserted, however, that lower-class women were afraid to legitimize their children because that gave men the legal right to seek custody. Although this may well be true for the twentieth century, there was no evidence that women made such arguments in the late nineteenth century. Evidence suggests that some women believed that the fathers' recognition of natural children brought some social benefits and, more importantly, forced fathers to pay child support.[68]

Lavenda's work provides further evidence of the greater acceptance of lower-class family forms. He argues that consensual unions seemed appealing to men because they demonstrated the man's ability to attract a woman with his virility and his ability to provide for and protect a woman and her children. The freedom of action in this type of union was appealing to both sexes. Finally, Lavenda argues that even upper- and middle-class couples held less than consistent ideas of morality, with couples insisting upon formal marriage even though "if contemporary sources are correct, virtually every man kept a mistress."[69] Conversely, the lower classes, who had more freedom to end relationships, seemed to have more stable unions.

The existence of stable cohabitation can be elucidated, but how widespread the practice was is difficult to assess. The deliberate decision by some female and male litigants not to marry suggests that this form of family organization, whether long- or short-lived, was recognized as a desirable if not a legitimate practice. Women's challenges to the patriarchal power of men in the family and their defense of the freedom to control their own lives and bodies contributed to a greater appreciation of the value that informal lower-class unions had in the social, economic, and legal contexts of Venezuelan society.

WOMEN DEFEND THEIR INTEGRITY, THEIR LABOR, AND THEIR RIGHTS

Although gender roles and their implications were being performed and debated at different levels – between the state and the people, between husbands and wives, between men and women, between parents and children, and among women themselves – women consistently defended their physical and moral integrity and rights, as they had done for at least a century. By the late nineteenth century marriage was not as important a goal for some women as it had been a century before, but this did not diminish women's view that both women and men had responsibilities to perform in their unequal domestic relationship. Conflict arose among couples when the expected gender roles were not fulfilled.

As in the other samples, many women in the late-nineteenth-century sample complained about husbands' and boyfriends' lack of responsibility in fulfilling their duties.[70] Women such as María de los Santos Yanez, Rosalía Azcárate, Rafaela Arias de Llaguno, Bibiana Aponte, and Eusebia Hernández de Hijuelo took their husbands to court for abuse.[71] All of these women claimed that their husbands caused physical and moral injuries by unjustifiably battering them. Bibiana said that her husband verbally attacked her character and battered her every time he felt like it, "cruelly discrediting [her] publicly," a behavior that, in her own words, "threw away her honor and virtue."[72]

This type of problem was not unique to married couples. The inability to maintain expected gender roles because of concrete material realities also created conflict between the sexes in less formalized unions. Bernarda Hernández, a twenty-two-year-old cook, lived with her boyfriend, Pedro Pablo Araujo, for a year. Pedro became jealous when Bernarda refused to tell him where she was going when she left for work and when she offended him verbally. Pedro beat Bernarda with a pole, breaking her nose and knocking out a tooth. As this case demonstrates, some lower-class men were unwilling to accept the independence and freedom of action that resulted from women's need to work for a salary outside the home.[73]

Isabel Espejo had a similar experience. She was a single mother and lived with her boyfriend, Pedro Pablo Vera, who was a mason. A month after they ended their relationship, they continued to share a house. Pedro Pablo claimed that he fully supported Isabel, and he warned her that he did not want her in the streets by herself. Once she arrived home late at night, and he beat her. In contrast to the case of Bernarda Hernández, however, neighbors quickly came to help Isabel, and Pedro Pablo fled.[74]

These stories closely resemble those from the 1835–40 sample. The inability of the poor to fulfill expected roles or their lack of compliance with the reciprocal relationship caused conflict between the sexes. When poor men physically threatened women, neighbors and relatives intervened, thereby preventing men from exercising their traditional power over women.[75] This kind of intervention would have been more difficult if the couple was married and the man was exercising his parental powers.

Women also defended their right to work. They denounced their low salaries, arguing that they were not enough to sustain a family, and they criticized men's lack of support. María del Rosario Hernández complained in court that the way she had to support her family "with her meager women's work" did not even allow her to provide items necessary for subsistence.[76] María Teresa Belsinger also denounced how her work increased as a result of her husband's irresponsibility.[77] Mercedes Borges de Burgos filed a suit against her husband for abandonment and because he was not providing support for the family. In addition, she claimed that he chastised her, impeding her ability to earn the sustenance that he was denying her.[78] In other words, men's lack of support meant poverty for families that depended on women's low salaries and on the charity of friends and relatives.

More than twenty-five years after the abolition of slavery, women continued to use metaphors about slavery to describe their relationship with men – a characteristic of the colonial and early republican samples. Guadalupe Obregón told the courts that after nine months of marriage she realized that her husband did not see her as his life partner (*compañera de la vida*) but as a slave whom he believed he had the right to treat as he pleased.[79] In another case, Eusebia Hernández de Hijuelo claimed that after three years of marriage her husband treated her as a slave and not as a true and worthy wife. She added that neither love for their children nor appreciation for her domestic qualities had changed his nature. On the contrary, her husband acted as a hangman (*verdugo*), treating her cruelly and beating her with his hands or whatever he held in them. She offered to prove these accusations to the court.[80]

These examples demonstrate the ways in which women sought to defend their bodies and their dignity in court against the abuses of their partners and even male strangers. Other women, such as María Rodríguez Díaz, a young, married, and poor water carrier, took matters into their own hands. María was buying bread at a bakery close to the plaza of Capuchinos when a policeman touched her breasts. She quickly hit the offender, employing the piece of fabric used for carrying the water pail as a lash. The policeman, together with three other men, beat her so violently that María spent days in bed. María's husband took the complaint to court, but the case was not resolved, possibly because María had already recuperated and therefore the case could no longer be won on its obvious merits.[81]

Women went to court seeking the protection of the law from abusive relationships. Many times, however, women did not receive justice. The civilizing discourse of the Guzmán Blanco regime did not bring improved rights for women in the practices of the courts. Some women, like María Teresa Belsinger and Mercedes García, explicitly pointed out inconsistencies between government discourse and legal practices. They questioned how the rhetoric of the times disguised the sad but true realities of women's legal powers.

Women in the sample infused portions of Guzmán Blanco's moral regeneration plan with different meanings, fostering in this way a radical critique of the patriarchal foundations of caraqueño society.[82] For example, wives and mothers appealed to the importance of their proscribed gender roles in order to force men to fulfill their duties. This directly contradicted the government's wishes that mothers and wives be submissive and endure their ordeals without complaint. Furthermore, although marriage, according to the state, was a contract in which men held power in the family and women held crucial domestic responsibilities, women saw marriage as a reciprocal relationship of rights and duties between equals in the domestic sphere. Premarital sexual relationships lessened the merits of a woman according to the laws, but the preservation of virginity was not as important for many lower-class people as it had been in the past. Other women were adamant that men's abuse of power, irresponsibility, and impunity were offensive to female dignity and honor. Lower-class women may have referred to official notions of proper behavior in the lawsuits, but they clearly attached a different meaning to them, transforming honor and dignity into universal human qualities that transcended gender, race, and class divisions.

By the late nineteenth century there are indications that fewer people desired formal marriage than had done so in the late colonial period or the early republic and that living in concubinage or outside the boundaries of legitimacy was not considered less honorable than more legitimate unions.[83] No clear connection between women's legal condition and their need for organized political struggle to obtain equal rights existed in Guzmán Blanco's Venezuela. Yet the seeds may have been planted by the multiple actions of these lower-class women.

10. Conclusion

Countless lawsuits fill the stacks of our courts and *Oficina de Registro* [enrolling or registry office]. They talk about the uncured pains of Venezuelan homes; they blame the carelessness of our legislators or at least their apprehensiveness to break with traditional prejudices and to deal with the obstacles created by interests of other kind.

El Constitucional, 8 de marzo de 1904

W omen's growing participation in the courts over the course of a century rendered some concrete results. Their mounting presence at the tribunals was noticed and considered in the political debates of the early twentieth century. In 1904 a divorce law that allowed the parties to remarry was approved in Venezuela. It was among the first divorce laws in Latin America, after those of Haiti (1825), Costa Rica (1876), and Puerto Rico (1902).[1] The law was enacted at a critical intersection: patriarchy was reaffirmed in the state courts, more women were aware of the discrepancies between law and practice, and a new generation of positivists was vocal about reforms in family law.

At least since 1883 positivist intellectual José Gil Fortoul had been arguing that the reality of Venezuelan society ran against some priests' and conservative politicians' opposition to divorce. "[D]ivorce," he argued, "happens daily in front of us. . . . when love turns into hate in a couple's hearts . . . marriage is broken at its base. And even if the law yells at them that the contract is unbreakable . . . the innocent party will not go to the society's representatives because he/she knows that they will be deaf to their claim for justice and blind to an immoral situation."[2] As a result, and frequently among the popular classes, people engaged in the practice of informally dissolving their marriage by mutual agreement because of the deficiencies in Venezuelan legislation. Life, as it evolved daily, ran differently from archaic religious laws that saw divorce as a disease that would propagate if let free. To Gil Fortoul, individual interests should not be sacrificed because of the prejudice against divorce. Allowing people to completely dissolve a relationship that provokes unhappiness is sound for the morals of a society because it would curtail the high frequency of adultery and concubinage in the population. It prevented public scandals and gave people an opportunity to legitimately seek their own well-being and a new opportunity to be happy. Such were the arguments of Gil Fortoul in favor of the divorce law, which echoed the arguments some women made at the courts of Caracas for a century.

Gil Fortoul vigorously sought a divorce law along with other reforms such as the simplification of the marriage celebration as a way to correct the scandal of the high percentage of children born out of wedlock in the country as a whole (70 percent in 1908).[3] He introduced some reform projects for the 1916 code, such as a law that would allow natural children to investigate the identity of their fathers; a change in marriage laws to allow schoolteachers and other authorized individuals to celebrate civil marriages in order to further facilitate the formalization of relationships; legislation to allow wives to administer their property; and a law that would allow women to hold positions in the civil tribunals.[4] By improving the legal condition of women and broadening the possibilities for marriage celebration as well as divorce, Gil Fortoul attempted to overcome lower-class reluctance toward marriage and to advance Venezuela's conditions for progress by promoting a better-structured family life formalized through state institutions.

In Puerto Rico, where civil marriage and divorce laws were imposed by the United States in 1902 under a somewhat similar rationale, more people filed for divorce than married. In Venezuela, even before the divorce law was approved, divorce petitions – even though they were rarely granted and the law had limited provisions – were the most common court activity for the lower classes in the late nineteenth century. Why did Gil Fortoul insist on advocating marriage when, as in Puerto Rico, many among the lower classes did not want to formalize their relationships?

Eileen Findlay has argued that in Puerto Rico, U.S. colonial agents endeavored to promote a homogeneous standard of domesticity that featured heterosexual, two-parent families. This was done to encourage assimilation into U.S. family standards at the same time that colonial agents "attempted to construct absolute moral oppositions between their ideas of themselves and their conceptions of Puerto Ricans, thus confirming their superiority and distance from those whom they sought to reform."[5] This standard was used simultaneously as a way to foster exclusion and "otherness" by affirming hierarchical differences. Such discourse supported the idea that Puerto Ricans required the benevolent, masculine tutelage of the United

States for "feminine and childish" Puerto Ricans. By stressing marriage as a moral marker of identity and as a measure of someone's degree of civilization, the popular classes could be justifiably labeled as uncivilized and unqualified for self-governance. Moreover, formal marriage also established an acceptable social order that would help to achieve progress. These arguments as well as Findlay's assertion that the granting of the full divorce law allowed the state to strengthen the patriarchal family in less overt legal forms can be sustained for the Venezuelan experience.

The granting of divorce did not diminish the patriarchal powers of ruling men and the state; the form of domination simply took new forms. By promoting formal marriage and allowing second marriages for divorced people, men's power over women is legalized and kept alive. Marital domination was an important aspect of men's political rights in the nineteenth century. Legalized marriages also facilitated the enactment of government agendas within the household. Moreover, by creating absolute moral oppositions based on education, class, race, gender, and "level" of civilization, the ruling class justified its superiority and its distance from and tutelage over all "others," including women and lower-class men.

Gil Fortoul was a remarkable reformist who insisted on understanding the historical trajectory of the country so that laws were grounded in society's reality. Like other major early-twentieth-century positivists such as Pedro Manuel Arcaya and Laureano Vallenilla Lanz, he strongly believed that Venezuela's race and climate were to blame for the country's organic inferiority. To Gil Fortoul, problems of a moral nature resulted from the lack of population and "civilization," which was reflected in the patriarchal life that persisted in the countryside. The influence exerted by Venezuela's physical and organic characteristics on the country had to be "efficiently controlled by men to neutralize its harmful forces, while adapting the environment according to their necessities and aspirations."[6] Detrimental aspects of Venezuela's environment could be neutralized through better domestic hygiene, which he thought was the duty of mothers, and the immigration of robust, self-starter men, especially white European men. While he stressed the need to understand the country on its own terms, he also implicitly believed that providing scientific guidance to society was in the hands of certain educated and civilized men of the white race.[7]

While women's litigation rendered one positive result with the granting of divorce, this change in laws occurred at a time when men's patriarchal powers were reaffirmed, at least by the judicial system. It is important to observe that, while women used the institution of the state as one means of individually and sometimes unconsciously challenging patriarchal powers, their actions contributed nonetheless to revalidating government institutions and patriarchy in Venezuelan politics. The courts are controlled by a fraternity of male citizens associated with the upper echelons of the government, which helped to conceal the central issues surrounding gender relations. Divorce may have been granted, but the centuries-old subjugation of women to the patriarch was not touched in the early-twentieth-century reforms of the codes. Indeed, some of Gil Fortoul's reform projects pertaining to women's rights were partially or completely not approved for the Civil Code and the Code of Civil Proceedings of 1916. These included granting women the right to freely administer the goods obtained through their profession or aptitudes and the granting of divorce by mutual consent. Progressive legislation allowing the investigation of paternity by natural children, which was included in the Civil Code of 1916, was rolled back in the code of 1922.[8] Much anxiety reigned among many early-twentieth-century politicians when discussing or approving changes that affected the rights and traditional power structure within Venezuelan homes. As in the Southern Cone, changes in the civil codes had to be achieved without altering gender relations or undermining husbands' rights.[9]

According to Carol Pateman these anxieties over patriarchal rights are closely related to the highly masculine nature of liberal thought, because liberal political rights are also sex rights of men to exercise power over women.[10] Hence a man's political rights originate with conjugal rights. But liberals do not usually admit the connection between marital and political domination. Grasping this association is critical to understanding the forms of political exclusion and the link between power relations at the domestic and state levels in Venezuela. A good example of this is the critical continuity and connections between household patriarchal rule and politics in the definition of citizenship from the colonial to the national eras. In Spanish times the citizens, or those who could enjoy certain rights in Caracas (such as being members of the municipal council), were the white and propertied men, usually patriarchs with a prestigious genealogy that bestowed honor and social reputation. In the constitutions of 1811, 1819, and 1830 active citizens were the men who were "married or older than 21 years of age" and possessed a certain level of propertied or professional qualifications. It is interesting to note that in 1811 and 1819 a man could theoretically loose his citizenship if he did not live with his wife.[11] While there are continuities with colonial rule, the political charter of the first half of the nineteenth century made a clear connection between citizenship rights and the possession of patriarchal powers as padres de familia.

The popular classes' egalitarian claims during the Federal Wars (1859–63) probably motivated a change in suffrage qualifications.[12] In the Constitution of 1864 the only citizenship and suffrage requirement was to be eighteen years of age. Restrictions based on gender were mentioned only for eligibility – only Venezuelan males over twenty-one years of age could aspire to hold government positions.[13] This deceiving law on suffrage continued in the constitutions of 1874 and 1891.[14] In 1893 the voting age was raised to twenty-one, and in 1901 the suffrage law was clearly expressed as being for Venezuelan males older than twenty-one.[15] While the link with patriarchal rights was not mentioned, women could theoretically vote and be citizens but the civil codes and codes of civil proceedings curtailed their political participation and reaffirmed their continuous subjugation to the padres de familia through the use of republican codes based on the Spanish *Siete Partidas*, as Gil Fortoul observed. In one of his speeches defending women's rights, Gil Fortoul made the point that because the Constitution refers to citizens, which includes both men and women, they abstractly have equal civil rights except for those included in the civil codes that made women subordinate to men. The code of civil proceedings, for example, emphatically denies women from working in civil courts. About those who interpreted the Constitution in a restricted way, Gil Fortoul stated: "they do this according to their system of maintaining women in a perpetual inferiority, and they continue to copy without reflection the codes of foreign legislations that do not relate to our special organization as a republican-democratic organization."[16]

Moreover, electoral control was overseen by a committee that ensured that voters were those men who could "rationally exercise" the vote because they were not subordinated to any person.[17] This select group accounted for no more than 10 percent of the population. The understanding that women did not vote seems to have been quite clear, as a nineteenth-century jurist commented that no woman was known to actually have gone to polling places to exercise her vote.[18] Finally, as is demonstrated in chapter 8, judges' sentences played an active role in reaffirming patriarchal powers when the codes and Constitution seemingly improved the legal condition of women. Hence judges' role in preserving men's power became stronger as the state reformed family laws. The process of nation-building, then, privileged a certain group of men as the only ones who enjoyed certain rights based on their sex, their role as patriarchs, and their status as property owners. They were considered "individuals" in the full sense and thus enjoyed civil freedoms.

Women's omission from the central definition of citizenship has given social and legal expression to the logic of that exclusion. Women were perceived as domestic subjects legally subjugated to their husbands or fathers. Since colonial times married and non-emancipated women did not have the judicial capacity to negotiate contracts or administer properties, could go to court only when the padre de familia committed abuses or crimes that affected the household, and could not hold public office. Seen in this light, the process of nation-building has been highly gendered and defensive of the maintenance of the patriarchal connection between the state and the household as it affirmed the construction of women's subjectivity as subordinates of men.

With the Constitution of 1811's abstract grant of citizenship to all "free men" with the requirement that "all Venezuelan inhabitants have no titles other than that of citizen," an opportunity for debating inclusion was opened. More than claiming equality from men, women were motivated by unfulfilled responsibilities in the marriage or concubinage pact to seek at the courts of Caracas the protections that civil liberties granted male citizens. Some women made such claims under the belief, deliberate or not, that those rights held by men should equally pertain to them. At other times women requested such protections based on their sex or their status as mothers. Both strategies helped them, by the late nineteenth century, to gain a better awareness of the contradiction between liberal law and practice.[19]

Within this limited margin of action, women resorted to a myriad of open and less evident strategies to defend themselves while pointing to the inconsistencies of the liberal agenda. If all Venezuelans were equal citizens, why were equal civil protections not applied to women when men violated the conjugal pact? That some caraqueñas, many of whom were illiterate, insisted on searching for justice from an institution that reinforced patriarchal relations is a testimony to their agency in seeking changes in their relationships with men and with the law. Change, at least some, took a long time to come. It demanded the articulation of different strategies that helped women to effectively communicate the contradictions between liberal theory and praxis.

Women's experiences in the courts show that they used different rationales and strategies than men and that, even though the language of their demands may have changed, the basic foundation of their claims did not. That men had legal and social privileges but were not equally "supervised" and responsible in their domestic duties was a common thread in the narratives of most of the litigants studied in this work. These female litigants were delegitimizing the superior legal position of men by demonstrating that, since their male partners did not fulfill their duties, they should not be entitled to receive the protections that citizenship granted only to men. Morally they had not earned that right; legally they had not fulfilled their duties. Moreover, women voiced the contradiction between law and practice: in the early republic in their autonomous inclusion as ciudadanas and in the contradictions posed by the continued use of hierarchical colonial laws; in the late nineteenth century in the paradox between the laws and discourse that praised women and improved their rights and the practices at the courts. Some other women challenged their subjugation by not following the dictates of the patriarchs in their lives. Finally, some female litigants disregarded the dominant, bourgeois family model, expressing the honorability of forming relationships and families outside the reach of the law. While living in consensual unions was not new, by the late nineteenth century some female litigants openly defended the practice at the courts. Ultimately this became very challenging behavior from women, because it prevented men from holding legal power over women's bodies and property. At the same time it was attractive for both men and women who valued freedom in their relationships. In this context it is no wonder that Gil Fortoul wanted to encourage marriage.

The discursive resources women chose to articulate their disconformity with prescribed gender norms at home and at the courts depended on the ways in which race and class intersected at some points in their lives. For an upper-class woman in the early republic it made sense to claim citizenship based on property ownership because she wanted the right to administer the property and also because formal citizenship was based on property or income. For a woman who lacked property, transmitting conflicts with men that violated her civil liberties to the early republican courts was a common recourse to claim what only citizens could legally have. Although references to race were infrequent in the nineteenth-century lawsuits, it was mentioned by people who were black, to defend themselves from social prejudice and/or to reaffirm their hopes of protection under the law in a nation guided by liberty and equality.

While there were some feminist organizations during the Juan Vicente Gómez period (1908–36), as evidenced by the existence of feminist opinion journals such as *Nos-Otras*, it was after his dictatorship that woman's organizations and activism became well established.[20] Actually those activists of the post-Gómez period were actively involved in the campaign for women's suffrage, which was won in 1947. Even though political rights were granted to women, exclusionary practices continued based on the "natural facts of sexual difference."[21] The idea that politics is a place for men continued to inform political discourse. In present-day Venezuela few women hold positions of leadership in politics; even as active citizens, women are still struggling to enjoy full political participation in democratic Venezuela.

Elisabeth J. Friedman has found that in post-1936 Venezuela women mobilized politically under authoritarian rule but, once democracy arrived, they disbanded.[22] She argues that "the institutionalization of politics (understood as the 'active participation in the decision-making levels of formal political structures or conscious demands for inclusion in public life') during the transition impedes the forms of organization that women developed under the previous regimes and their subsequent incorporation into democracy."[23] During the course of Venezuela's democratic transitions in 1945–48 and 1958–74 certain labor and peasant sectors were allowed to incorporate, but that has not been the case with women. Friedman demonstrates how certain forms of institutionalization in the transition to democratic rule served to marginalize women. For example, highly centralized parties limited who would be allowed to be a decision-maker in their organization, thereby excluding or limiting women from positions of leadership.

Women's political roles cannot be understood without understanding the profoundly masculine character of political practice and the ways this gendered practice has taken place in Venezuela's past. This is critical because if democracy is to represent all of its citizens, political opportunities as well as gender relations upon which they are built must undergo transition. During the nineteenth century the power structure underlying gender relations reaffirmed patriarchal powers while excluding women and the poor, and one wonders if significant changes occurred in the twentieth century. Yet, as discussed above, some politicians restricted reforms in family laws that would have helped to transform gender relations in early-twentieth-century Venezuela.[24] Hence the idea that changes in gender relations at the domestic level must be sought along with changes in the rhetoric and institutionalization of politics. Understanding how patriarchy operates institutionally, how masculine power is reproduced in homes and at the state level, and how exclusion is practiced is an important step in seeking new strategies so that women will not have their faces hidden but will have their voices heard and taken into account.

Notes

See the bibliography for full names of archives, which are cited with abbreviations throughout the notes.

INTRODUCTION

The epigraphs are taken from "Divorcio—Juana Feliciana Diaz con Juan Domingo Moreno," AAC, Matrimoniales, 1794, leg. 120, fol. 8–8r; "Divorcio que prepara doña María Antonia Pérez a su legítimo marido don Ramón Maucó," AAC, Matrimoniales, 1811, leg. 187, fol. 46r–7r; and "Violante Mijares contra Carlos Ascanio, por esponsales," ARPDF, Civiles, 1877, Letra M, exp. 15. Unless otherwise noted, all translations are my own.

1. See Pagden, *Spanish Imperialism*, 141; and Castro Leiva, "Ironies of the Spanish-American Revolutions."
2. The main author of the writing seems to have been Juan Picornell, a Spanish Jacobin sent from Spain to prison in Panama. Waiting to be transported to Panama, Picornell was placed in the jail of La Guaira, from which he helped to organize the revolt and from which he later escaped. See Grases, *Derechos del hombre*, 123–49; Grases, *Pensamiento político*, xxiii. See also chap. 1; and Grases, *Libros y libertad*.
3. This is further discussed in chap. 1. The quote comes from "Autoridades coloniales."
4. Pino Iturrieta, *Mentalidad venezolana*, 28–31.
5. See chaps. 1 and 5.
6. Skurski, "'Leader' and the 'People,'" 15–19.
7. See Landes, *Women and the Public Sphere*, 202–6; Pateman, *Sexual Contract*, 78–80; and Felstiner, "Family Metaphors."
8. See Felstiner, "Family Metaphors"; Felstiner, "Kinship Politics"; and Earle, "Rape."
9. For the U.S. case see Fliegelman, *Prodigals and Pilgrims*.

10. Bolívar, *Political Thought*, 38.

11. Hunt, *Family Romance*, 71. See also chap. 4.

12. According to Belaunde, Miranda supported woman suffrage "at least in matters that concerned women such as marriage, divorce and education." Yet Bolívar made clear in a letter to his sister that he opposed women's participation in politics. See Belaunde, *Bolívar*, 77; and Chambers, "Gender."

13. For the case of the United States, see Zagarri, " Rights of Man and Women"; and Kerber, *No Constitutional Right*.

14. I thank Sarah C. Chambers for bringing the importance of this connection to my attention. See Landes, *Women and the Public Sphere*.

15. For a discussion on how women in revolutionary France asserted their place in society and their rights when citizenship rights were not extended to them, see Godineau, *Women of Paris*; Gutwirth, "Citoyens, Citoyennes," 17–28; and Hufton, *Women and the Limits of Citizenship*. For the United States, see Kerber, *Women of the Republic*.

16. See Cherpak, "Women and the Independence of Gran Colombia," 81, 114–15.

17. Cherpak, "Women and the Independence of Gran Colombia," 89–98, 112–15, 122–47; Troconis de Veracoechea, *Indias*, 132–52; and Gil Fortoul, *Historia constitucional* 1:355–58.

18. I am borrowing this definition from Stern, *Secret History*, 86–87. My evidence from Caracas (see chap. 2), however, shows that women did not necessarily understand marriage as a "virtually indissoluble pact," as Stern writes. That view was more in tune with males' ideas about marriage, which some referred to as "a sacrament."

19. See Desan, "War"; and Desan, "Religious Riots and Ritual."

20. Two exceptions are works that deal with citizenship in Gran Colombia—Pino Iturrieta, *Fueros*; and Alfonso Múnera, *El fracaso de la nación*. Interpretative works on Venezuelan independence include: Parra Pérez, *Historia*; Brading, *Classical Republicanism*; Parra Pérez, *Mariño*; Pino Iturrieta, *Mentalidad venezolana*; Vallenilla Lanz and Harwich Vallenilla, *Cesarismo democrático*; and Izard, *Miedo a la revolución*.

21. After attaining independence from Spain, the former Captaincy-General of Venezuela, the Viceroyalty of Santa Fé de Bogotá, and the Audiencia of Quito formed the Republic of Colombia, more commonly referred to by historians as "Gran Colombia." The great Bolivarian dream of unity was short-lived and ended abruptly in 1830 with the dissolution of the political entity into three independent states: Colombia, Ecuador, and Venezuela.

22. Cherpak, "Participation of Women," 230. Other works about women in the independence period in Venezuela include: Perdomo Escalona, *Heroínas y már-*

tires; Troconis de Veracoechea, *Indias*; Troconis de Verachoechea, *Gobernadoras*; and García Maldonado, ed., *La mujer*. See also Clemente Travieso, *Mujeres*.

23. Arrom, *Women of Mexico City*, 14–52.

24. Stern, *Secret History*.

25. Chambers studied the gendered dimension of the transition from colony to republic in Arequipa, Peru. Her findings are based on an examination of newspapers and mainly on criminal cases. See Chambers, *From Subjects to Citizens*, 190–215.

26. Hünefeldt, *Liberalism in the Bedroom*.

27. Stolcke, "'Nature' of Nationality," 61.

28. Joseph, "Gendering Citizenship," 3–4.

29. Joseph, "Gendering Citizenship," 4.

30. Liddle, "State, Masculinities and Law."

31. Comaroff and Comaroff, *Of Revelation and Revolution*, 1:27.

32. Lazarus-Black and Hirsch, eds., *Contested States*, 7.

33. Judith Butler's performative theory of gender has been useful in accounting for the myriad ways in which people can perform their gender roles without corresponding to the prescriptive binary gender norms. She argues that by paying attention to repeated "subversive bodily acts" we can arrive at a closer definition of how people may have understood gender and challenged prescriptive norms. For Butler, gender identities are the dramatic effect of our performances. The result of these subversive acts is what she calls "gender trouble," because the acts tend to denaturalize the dominant categories of gender. See Butler, *Gender Trouble*, 128–41.

34. See Lavrin, *Women, Feminism, and Social Change*, 5.

35. Burton, *Afro-Creole*, 8.

36. Díaz Quiñones, *Arte de bregar*, 82–87.

37. Recent scholarship stresses the ways in which the lower classes resist domination from above. See Scott, *Domination*. Additionally, Juan Flores analyzes the ways in which Latinos in the United States have used the language of the dominant culture (i.e., English) to wage their cultural politics. Flores characterizes this practice as a "social movement." See his perceptive book *Divided Borders*, 203. Jeffrey L. Gould also finds that Nicaraguan peasants borrowed symbols and language from the dominant classes and changed the meanings according to their worldviews. In this way, the rural poor creatively constructed their own counterhegemonic culture. See Gould, *To Lead as Equals*, 6–7. Other examples include Burton, *Afro Creole*; Guardino, *Peasants*; Viotti da Costa, *Crowns of Glory*; and Salvatore, Aguirre, and Joseph, eds., *Crime and Punishment*.

38. See Findlay, *Imposing Decency*; Twinam, *Public Lives*; Hünefeldt, *Liberalism in*

the Bedroom; Boyer, *Lives of the Bigamists*; Stern, *Secret History*; and Martínez-Alier, *Marriage, Class, and Colour*. See also Behar, "Sexual Witchcraft"; Boyer, "Women, 'La Mala Vida'"; and Gutiérrez, *When Jesus Came*. Brazilian historians have used lawsuit documents as sources for social history for some time, with impressive results. See Correa, *Morte em família*; Fausto, *Crime e cotidiano*; Chalhoub, *Trabalho*; Esteves, *Meninas perdidas*; Esteves and Caufield, "Fifty Years of Virginity"; Caufield, *In Defense of Honor*; and Soihet, *Condição feminina*.

39. I included a few cases categorized in the archives as dealing with inheritance or debts because they were part of larger conflicts involving women, and two cases of sodomy and bestiality for comparative purposes.

40. Most research on gender and the family has been based on an analysis of only one kind of claim. See, for example, Stern, *Secret History* (sexual violence); Chalhoub, *Trabalho* (criminal records); Esteves, *Meninas perdidas* (sexual offenses); Nazzari, *Disappearance* (inheritance records); and Caufield, *In Defense of Honor* (sexual crimes).

41. "Barbara Jedler quejándose contra el gobernador de la Provincia por el cruel castigo que ha hecho dar a su hijo Antonio Madriz, esclavo del Sr. Juan Pablo Huizi, por indicios de estar comprendido en una revolución que tramara," ARPDF, Civiles, 1835, Letra J, exp. 22, fol. 11r.

1. A CARACAS FOR THE MANTUANOS, 1700–1811

1. Quoted in "Informe que el Ayuntamiento de Caracas hace al Rey de España referente a la Real Cédula de 10 de febrero de 1795," in Rodulfo Cortés, *Régimen*, 2:99.

2. In 1650 the creole elites who controlled the municipal council claimed that the positions in that institution belonged to "aquellos que sus padres y abuelos derramaron su sangre y gastaron sus haciendas en conquistar, pacificar, poblar y sustentar esta ciudad y provincia" (Ladera de Díez, *Contribución al estudio*, 39). See also Ferry, *Colonial Elite*, 10; Pellicer, *Vivencia*, 36; and *Diccionario de historia de Venezuela*, s.v. "Mantuanos."

3. See Pellicer, *Vivencia*, 29.

4. Pellicer, *Vivencia*, 94, 100, 107.

5. Twinam, *Public Lives*, 30–33; Pino Iturrieta, *Contra lujuria*, 124–28.

6. I am borrowing here the term "language of argument" as used by Stern in *Secret History*, 386 n.25, and Putnam, "Sex and Standing," 23. David W. Sabean used the term originally in *Power in the Blood*. Judith Butler's performative theory of gender has been useful for analyzing the myriad ways in which people can,

through imitation and gradual command of public, cultural gestures, contradict the dominant categories of gender. I am using it here in a broader cultural sense. See Butler, *Gender Trouble*, 128–41.

7. See Putnam, "Sex and Standing," 23, 31; and Stern, *Secret History*, 386–87 n.25.

8. See Twinam, *Public Lives*; Pellicer, *Vivencia*; and Pino Iturrieta, *Contra lujuria*, 124.

9. Twinam, *Public Lives*, 33.

10. Stern, *Secret History*, 161–62.

11. The characteristics of masculinity and their manifestation of power as described by Ramírez and Casper are very similar to the attitudes of the mantuanos found in the lawsuits and other documents of the eighteenth century. Ramírez and Casper, *What It Means to Be a Man*, 77–78.

12. Ramírez and Casper, *What It Means to Be a Man*, 64.

13. Stern, *Secret History*, 14, 78.

14. Stern, *Secret History*, 161–62.

15. Nye, *Masculinity*, 15–30.

16. See, for example, Pino Iturrieta, *Contra lujuria*, 84.

17. The right of alcaldes ordinarios to become pro tem governors was originally granted by royal cédula to the Venezuelan town of Coro in 1560. This privilege was reaffirmed for Caracas in 1676, with the condition that the alcaldes pay the king a three-thousand-peso fee. In 1723 the right of the alcaldes was guaranteed yet again. Ferry, *Colonial Elite*, 197; López Bohórquez, *Ministros*, 77.

18. Sucre, *Gobernadores*.

19. In Venezuela, as elsewhere in the Americas, the governor also served as captain-general of the province of Caracas. Whereas the governor had civil authority, the captain-general had military powers; the official who held both titles, therefore, possessed extensive powers in political, judicial, and military affairs. See Haring, *Spanish Empire*, 138–39. Depons, *Viaje*, 2:181–87, also provides a concise commentary on the powers of the captain-general and the governor.

20. Ferry, *Colonial Elite*, 116–17; López Bohórquez, *Ministros*, 79; Morón, *Historia*, 4:195–226.

21. *Pardo* is an admittedly vague term. On the eve of the independence struggle in Venezuela, *pardo* stood for the descendants of any interracial unions, not African and Hispanic unions specifically. Throughout the colonial period, *pardo* and *mulatto* were used interchangeably to refer to the progeny of black and white parents. Pardos themselves reportedly preferred this term to such derogatory ones as *castas* (caste) and *mulatto* (see chap. 3). However, as explained in a letter from the Batallón de Pardos of Caracas to the governor, a pardo was one who was closer to whites in appearance and genealogy than a mulatto (see Ro-

dulfo Cortés, *Régimen*, 2:20). For informative descriptions of this terminology, see Rodulfo Cortés, *Régimen*, 1:88–89; *Diccionario de historia*, s.v. "pardos"; and Rout, *African Experience*, xiv–xv.

22. See, for example, "Don Nicolás Gonzáles de Palma contra Gerónima Olivares sobre desocupar una casa," AANH, Civiles, 1788, Letra G, exp. 12; and "Autos entre María Encarnación Arrechedera sobre su libertad," AANH, Civiles, 1789, Letra A, exp. 8.

23. "Representación del cabildo de Caracas al Rey Suplicando se digne denegarse a la solicitud de los pardos y mandar se mantengan estos en la misma clase que hasta ahora por los perjuicios que ocasionaria en caso contrario," Caracas, 13 de octubre de 1788, in Rodulfo Cortés, *Régimen*, 2:33.

24. Pino Iturrieta, *Contra lujuria*, 31. See chap. 2 for a further discussion of this synod. The mantuanos expressed these ideas as well. See Pellicer, *Vivencia*, 37–38. In *Manhood in Early Modern England*, Elizabeth Foyster argues that in practice, patriarchy does not mean that all men are created equal; instead, there are "subordinate masculinities." In Venezuela, this idea was clearly fostered by both church and state.

25. Pellicer, *Vivencia*, 25–39.

26. This sort of denegration was a fundamental attitude of the honor/shame system. See Stern, *Secret History*, 14, 161–64; Pellicer, *Vivencia*, 47; Twinam, "Negotiation of Honor," 94. Important works on honor in Latin America during the colonial period include: Gutiérrez, *When Jesus Came*; Martinez-Alier, *Marriage, Class, and Colour*; Seed, *To Love, Honor, and Obey*; and Johnson and Lipsett-Rivera, eds., *Faces of Honor*.

27. Waldron, in "Social History," draws these conclusions from Lombardi, *People and Places*.

28. Internal migration from surrounding areas and natural growth seem to account for much of the city's population growth in the eighteenth century, according to Waldron, "Social History," 8, 22, 62.

29. Waldron, "Social History," 64–67, 72, 99–100.

30. Pellicer, *Vivencia*, 37–38.

31. Depons, *Viaje*, 2:233; Waldron, "Social History," 78, 99–100, 196; Izard, *Miedo a la revolución*, 129; and Lucena, *Vísperas*, 43.

32. Waldron, "Social History," 74–75, 78.

33. Pellicer, *Vivencia*, 33–35.

34. The Spanish state had relied on local militias to defend its territories, but the Bourbons instituted the pardo militias as part of military reforms following the 1760s. Rodulfo Cortés, "Milicias de pardos," 30; King, "Case of José Ponciano de Ayarza," 640–67; Rout, *African Experience*, 150–51.

35. The mid–eighteenth-century's lack of riots and uprisings points to the effec-

tiveness of the controls established by the repressive regime of Governor Ricardos, who ruled Caracas with an iron hand for six years (1751–57) following the 1749 León insurrection. It would take slaves another twenty years to mount resistance again in the form of raids and attacks. A multi-ethnic rebellion did not take shape until the *comuneros* (community) of Mérida rose up in 1781, demanding an end to bad government. An extension of the Socorro rebellion in New Granada, the comuneros' rebellion demanded the repeal of a tax increase and the abolition of a recently created tobacco monopoly. The most complete study of the insurrection is Muñoz Oráa, *Comuneros*. Informative assessments are compiled in *Comuneros de Mérida*.

36. See, for example, "Josefa Febles contra José Manuel Palacios por injurias de palabras," ARPDF, Civiles, 1839, Letra F, exp. 5, fol. 3–3v; "Maria Teresa Rengifo, parda libre, fue pretendida con palabra de casamiento y fue deshonrada por Sebastián Agudelo, mulato libre," AANH, Civiles, 1786, Letra R, núm. 1, exp. 12, fol. 12r. In 1756 a black freed slave of the carabalí nation, claiming that her husband was a lazy man, said that he "se había metido a caballero." Pino Iturrieta and Lange, coords., *Quimeras*, 245.

37. Putnam poses a similar argument in "Sex and Standing."

38. "Autoridades coloniales," 68. See also Chambers, *From Subjects to Citizens*, 172; Lipsett-Rivera, "Slap in the Face"; and Boyer, "Honor".

39. See Pellicer, *Vivencia*, 111; Viqueira Albán, *Propriety and Permissiveness*, 215. Although research on popular culture in Venezuela during the seventeenth and early eighteenth centuries is lacking, the lawsuits analyzed for this book suggest such practices among the lower classes. See chaps. 3 and 6.

40. Cf. Hünefeldt, *Liberalism in the Bedroom*, 9–10.

41. Pellicer, *Vivencia*, 73–74.

42. Pellicer, *Vivencia*, 94–97. I did not find a definition for *sambaiga* or *sambaigo* for Venezuela, yet in late-colonial Mexico a sambaigo usually had predominantly Indian blood (50–80 percent) mixed with black (1.5–34 percent) and white (12–23 percent). See Stephens, *Dictionary*, s.v. "sambaigo."

43. See Torres Pantin, "Acceso," 33; Pino Iturrieta and Lange, coords., *Quimeras*, 222–24.

44. Carlos F. Duarte observes that some men in Caracas satisfied their vanity by requesting to be buried in their military uniforms with their arms. Duarte, *Historia del traje*, 161.

45. "Autoridades coloniales," 67.

46. Rodulfo Cortés, *Régimen*, 2:35.

47. In Spain the honorific was restricted to the nobility, but in Spanish America its use became less rigid after the mid-1700s, especially among professionals, master artisans, office holders, and prominent merchants. Among Indians in colo-

nial Mexico its usage conveyed high status. Kellogg, *Law and Transformation*, 221.

48. Waldron, "Social History," 72–73.

49. Blanco and Azpurúa, eds., *Documentos*, 1:268. Twinam argues that in Venezuela and Cuba, creole elites were less tolerant about passing in the last decades of the eighteenth century. *Public Lives*, 208–9, 313.

50. Pellicer, *Vivencia*, 92.

51. Stern, *Secret History*, 161.

52. Ferry, *Colonial Elite*, 229–33.

53. Ferry, *Colonial Elite*, 230.

54. For Caracas's established planters the new frontier was God-given, because cultivation along the Tuy Valley provided two to three times more *fanegas* of cacao than had their older coastal haciendas. From 1684 to 1744 there was a five-fold increase in the production of cacao, and 75 percent of the provincial harvest came from the Tuy Valley. See Ferry, *Colonial Elite*, 106. Ferry defines *fanegas* as "a dry measure; in Caracas' context 1.5 bushels" (*Colonial Elite*, 326).

55. Izard, *Miedo a la revolución*, 28; Pino Iturrieta, *Mentalidad venezolana*, 27.

56. López Bohórquez, *Ministros*, 71; Ferry, *Colonial Elite*, 4–5.

57. After 1778, when the position was created, the teniente del rey was in charge of replacing the governor when necessary. See López Bohórquez, *Ministros*, 78; Morón, *Historia* 4:195–226.

58. Sucre, *Gobernadores*, 251; Ferry, *Colonial Elite*, 160.

59. Ferry, *Colonial Elite*, 142.

60. Ferry offers the most complete analysis in English of the León insurrection in *Colonial Elite*. Two classic studies of the rebellion are Castillo Armas, *Aventura fundacional*, and Armas Chitty and Pinto, eds., *Juan Francisco de León*.

61. The inscription in the plaque stated, "May the destruction and spreading of salt stand to the perpetual memory of this infamy." This "reminder" of the consequences of conspiring against royal authorities lay in front of the ruins of the rebel's house until shortly after independence was declared in 1811. Ferry, *Colonial Elite*, 173.

62. Reforms were implemented in order to attract the support of the natives for the monopoly company. First, the creole elites would become shareholders of the company and even serve on the board of directors. In this way, the Basque company would lose its "foreign" image among the local people. Second, the prices of the company would be set jointly by the governor, a member of the cabildo, and the company factor. Third, the cacao planters would be free to market their cacao to Mexico as they did before the 1720s, as long as the Spanish demand for the bean was met.Finally, the prohibition against transporting cacao by sea was lifted. Ferry, *Colonial Elite*, 161, 165, 243.

63. Ferry, *Colonial Elite*, 175–76.

64. Ferry, *Colonial Elite*, 244.

65. By 1772 the amount collected for the alcabala tax amounted to 26 percent of the city's revenue, and six years later it constituted 40 percent of total revenue. A similar tax was placed on export goods such as cacao, sugar, tobacco, and hides. Ferry, *Colonial Elite*, 247–49.

66. Ferry, *Colonial Elite*, 245.

67. On Bishop Diez Madroñero's tenure, see Watters, *History of the Church*, 46–47; and *Diccionario de Historia*, s.v. "Diez Madroñero, Diego."

68. See his published personal diary, Martí, *Obispo Mariano Martí*. Another interesting piece on Martí is Waldron, "Sinners and the Bishop," 156–77. Watters points out the differing views of these two bishops in *History of the Church*, 41.

69. Waldron, "Social History," 200–201; Ferry, *Colonial Elite*, 320 n.14. A number of publications have analyzed the ecclesiastical lawsuits that were brought against transgressors of the good customs including Pino Iturrieta, *Contra lujuria*; Pino Iturrieta and Lange, coords., *Quimeras*; Pino Iturrieta, *Ventaneras*; and Rodríguez, *Babilonia de pecados*.

70. Pino Iturrieta, *Contra lujuria*, 63–89. Twinam found that this was a state policy for Spanish America. *Public Lives*, 277.

71. See Cruz, "Were Women's Gender Roles Constructed?"

72. See, for example, the cases analyzed by Pino Iturrieta in *Contra lujuria* and his conclusions on pages 119–31. I am borrowing the term "honor/shame complex" from Stern, *Secret History*, 13–15.

73. Duarte, *Historia del traje*, 181.

74. Sucre, *Gobernadores*, 280; Ferry, *Colonial Elite*, 254.

75. McKinley, *Pre-revolutionary Caracas*, 84.

76. *Diccionario de historia*, s.v. "Miranda Ravelo, Sebastián de."

77. The cédula also stated that "esta misma igualdad se ha debido y debe observar en todos los empleos militares del batallón de milicias nuevamente formado, y de las Compañías de Infantería y Caballería de Nobles Aventureros." López Bohórquez, *Ministros*, 79.

78. López Bohórquez, *Ministros*, 80; McKinley finds that only a few of the qualified Europeans were willing to serve in the Municipal council (*Pre-revolutionary Caracas*, 92).

79. Oficina de Compilación, *Toma de razón*, 33; Ferry, *Colonial Elite*, 193.

80. A good example of this revisionist writing is McKinley, *Pre-revolutionary Caracas*, 39–42.

81. McKinley reports that by 1809, foreign possessions in the Caribbean accounted for as much as 75 percent of coffee exports and approximately 35 percent of the indigo trade. Cacao continued to be sold primarily in the peninsular market. *Pre-revolutionary Caracas*, 43.

82. McKinley, *Pre-revolutionary Caracas*, 49–50, 111.

83. Waldron, "Social History," 3–4, 8, 21–25. Waldron asserts that external migration did not account for the increase in population in the eighteenth century, largely because Spanish migration was more conspicuous in the first half of the period than later. Most of this migration was linked to the establishment of the Compañía de Caracas and was heavily concentrated in 1728–40. Rather, Waldron believes that internal migration boosted population in Caracas.

84. Contrary to received wisdom, however, Venezuela experienced a strong increase in the presence of royal government after midcentury. Robert J. Ferry has convincingly argued that well before the Bourbon dynasty under Charles III resolved to reform the empire the colonial government in the province under the tenure of Felipe Ricardos (1751–57) tried out certain fiscal and administrative policies that would later characterize the centralizing zeal of the Bourbon regime. Ricardos's predecessor, Julián de Arriaga, was one of the prime architects of the policies later known as the Bourbon Reforms. As minister, Arriaga set new policies based on his experience in Venezuela from 1749 to 1751. For example, he stressed the need for excluding Basques, isleños, and creoles from administrative and judicial positions. His attitude, according to Ferry, had not changed since his tenure as governor of Caracas. See Ferry, *Colonial Elite*, 241–43.

85. The Real Cédula of 8 September 1777 created this new political entity. Before the creation of the new Captaincy-General, the provinces of Cumaná, Guayana, Maracaibo, Margarita, and Trinidad belonged to the Viceroyalty of Santa Fé de Bogotá in present-day Colombia. In 1786 Barinas split from Maracaibo, becoming a separate province, and in 1797 Trinidad came under British domination. Thus at the close of the century the new entity still consisted of six provinces. See García Chuecos, *Historia colonial*, 2:2–3. On the formation of the Captaincy-General, see also Zawisza, *Arquitectura*, 1:11.

86. Zawisza, *Arquitectura*, 1:11. García Chuecos traces the development of the Real Audiencia from its inception through the wars of independence in *Historia colonial*, vol. 2.

87. García Chuecos, *Historia colonial*, 2:5.

88. Although created by royal decree on 6 July 1786, this body did not have official status until 19 July 1787. French traveler Francisco Depons offers a firsthand account of the duties of the Caracas Audiencia in *Viaje*, 2:187–93.

89. As a high court of appeals, this body passed judgments on appeals from such lesser tribunals as the *corregidores*, who were the local governors. The discussion of the duties and operation of these tribunals is based on Bello Lozano, *Historia de las fuentes*, 184–89, 200–204; and Haring, *Spanish Empire*, 130–33.

90. García Chuecos, *Historia colonial*, 2:10, 14; Bello Lozano, *Historia de las fuentes*, 282–83. Instituted on 17 August 1788, the Colegio de Abogados of Caracas was

crudely analogous to a bar association. It was modeled after the one in Madrid and became the first professional organization in the country. See *Diccionario de historia*, s.v. "colegios profesionales."

91. Pérez Perdomo, *Abogados*, 60. In *Honorable Lives*, Uribe-Urán argues that in Colombia aristocrats and individuals with ties to high-ranking bureaucratic circles were well represented among the lawyers in the late colonial–early republican periods. A study of the economic and family links among members of the mantuanaje, high bureaucratic officials, and those who were part of the republican governments as well as a comprehensive political history of the nineteenth century is wanting for Venezuela. Unfortunately, the research and analysis of the biographies, ideologies, and relationships between men in these governments are beyond the scope of this book. It would be fair to say, however, that in Venezuela some members of the mantuanaje continued to participate in governmental positions but probably were not represented as strongly in the legal profession or in the government as they were in early-nineteenth-century Colombia. Many of the Venezuelan lawyers became important sponsors of liberal ideas throughout the process of nation-building, as also happened in Colombia and Brazil. See Kirkendall, *Classmates*.

92. McKinley, *Pre-revolutionary Caracas*, 94; Pérez Perdomo notes that the marqués del Toro graduated from law school in 1783, but he never practiced the profession (*Abogados*, 71). Given his status as the wealthiest and one of the most influential men in Venezuela, the legal practice would not have added to his prestige. A cursory glance at the list of lawyers who graduated from the University of Caracas and who actually practiced the profession (in Pérez Perdomo, *Abogados*, 300–307), along with biographical and professional information in García Chuecos, *Abogados de la colonia*, shows that many lawyers came from non-mantuano families from Caracas and other regions. Moreover, regarding the social origins of university students in Caracas, 31 percent were the sons of hacendados, 18 percent of a military man, 17 percent of a merchant, and 8 percent of a royal functionary. Pérez Perdomo, *Abogados*, 97 n.5.

93. See Leal, *Historia de la Universidad de Caracas*; and Kirkendall, *Classmates*.

94. See Liddle, "State, Masculinities, and Law."

95. López Bohórquez, *Ministros*. In *Pre-revolutionary Caracas*, McKinley downplays the anti-creole policy as a factor in the movement for independence.

96. Charles III also excluded creoles from high civil and military office in Spanish America. Burkholder and Chandler provide authoritative assessments of this anti-creole policy in *From Impotence to Authority*, 89–99.

97. López Bohórquez, *Ministros*, 86. One of the American creole appointees was Francisco de Berrío y Guzmán, born in Quito, who became the fiscal de real hacienda in 1798. In 1810 Berrío joined the pro-independence forces and was

rewarded with the position of intendant of the army and treasury. See García Chuecos, *Historia colonial*, 2:12–13.

98. López Bohórquez, *Ministros*, 93–95.

99. Before 1786 only one Venezuelan—José Rodríguez del Toro, son of the first marqués del Toro—became a judge (*oidor*) in Mexico, and between 1786 and 1815 only six Venezuelan-born magistrates held office in the audiencias of Guatemala, Guadalajara, Santa Fe, Mexico, and Charcas. López Bohórquez, *Ministros*, 143, 146.

100. *Diccionario de historia*, s.v. "Audiencia de Caracas," "Espejo Caamaño, Francisco Silvestre." On the political thinking of Espejo, see Pino Iturrieta, *Mentalidad venezolana*, 168–70. A thorough compilation of the exhibits and documentation gathered for the trial led by the Audiencia against the independence leader and former court official appears in *Causas de infidencia*, 2:83–306.

101. López Bohórquez, *Ministros*, 91–92; Dias, *Real Consulado*, 219; Rodulfo Cortés, *Régimen*, 1:313, 2:38, 76, 79, 82.

102. López Bohórquez, *Ministros*, 112–13; Quintero Montiel, "Autoridades en conflicto."

103. López Bohórquez, *Ministros*, 115–16.

104. López Bohórquez, *Ministros*, 120.

105. López Bohórquez, *Ministros*, 121–22.

106. According to McKinley, the hereditary aristocracy made up 55 percent of the consulado in 1786 and 40 percent in 1805–6. (Only one or two individuals from the most notable families were included on these lists). The surnames of the representatives of the most distinguished mantuanos include Alonso Gil, Jeréz de Aristeguieta, Ascanio, Berroterán, Blanco, Bolívar, Herrera, Ibarra, de la Madriz, Mijares de Solórzano, Martínez de Porras, Obelmexías, Pacheco, Palacios de Sojo, Plaza, Ponte, Rada, Rengifo, Toro, and Tovar. McKinley, *Pre-revolutionary Caracas*, 79.

107. Owners of vessels were also part of the consulado. See Alvarez, *Tribunal del Real Consulado*, 169. For a list of some merchants' last names, see McKinley, *Pre-revolutionary Caracas*, 80.

108. Mc Kinley, *Pre-revolutionary Caracas*, 88–90.

109. Alvarez, *Tribunal del Real Consulado*, 391–93.

110. Alvarez, *Tribunal del Real Consulado*, 285–92.

111. For a discussion of several conflicts involving the consulado, see López Bohórquez, *Ministros*, 127–39, and Alvarez, *Tribunal del Real Consulado*, 303–12.

112. López Bohórquez, *Ministros*, 139.

113. McKinley, *Pre-revolutionary Caracas*, 102–9.

114. Colonial historians often draw attention to the specific provision that allowed

pardos to switch racial categories through the purchase of a "certificate of whiteness," but they fail to examine the nature of this document and thus lose sight of the whole set of exemptions and dispensations enclosed in the gracias al sacar decree. Waldron, "Social History," 76–77; Izard, *Miedo a la revolución*, 129; Rout, *African Experience*, 156–60; and Wright, *Café con Leche*, 24, 26. Note-worthy exceptions are King, "Case of José Ponciano de Ayarza"; and Twinam, *Public Lives*.

115. Rodulfo Cortés, *Régimen*, 1:xvii. King translates the term as "concessions of ex-emptions" from existing laws ("Case of José Ponciano de Ayarza").

116. Rodulfo Cortés, *Régimen*, 1:xxiii, 107–8. Rodulfo Cortés offers interesting com-mentaries on the antecedents of the dispensations in medieval Spanish law and canon law and briefly discusses a similar practice in England (73–82, 104–20).

117. See Rodulfo Cortés, *Régimen*, 135–42, for a discussion of the complexities of the legal procedure to obtain a dispensation. See also Twinam, *Public Lives*.

118. Rodulfo Cortés, *Régimen*, 1:624. Before the introduction of the gracias al sacar, royal mercedes were given free of charge. Ann Twinam found that the gracias al sacar did not work, in practice, as a profiting scheme. See Twinam, *Public Lives*, 246.

119. These royal dispensations addressed all areas of social activity. The provisions included the purchase of noble titles, statements of *hidalguía* (gentry or the lesser nobility) and of pure blood, grants of encomienda rights, formation of entailed estates (*mayorazgo*), legitimation of extramarital offspring, rights to carry a sword, permits for residence and naturalization for foreigners, a dis-pensation of age to practice a trade or hold office, licenses for practicing certain trades and professions, and permission to hold more than one job—as, for ex-ample, allowing a priest trained in law to practice as a civil attorney in his par-ish. Some stipulations specifically governed the parental powers of widowed women under age twenty-five. Altogether, the 1795 cédula had seventy-one cat-egories of dispensation. The complete texts of the four diplomas are repro-duced in Rodulfo Cortés, *Régimen*, vol. 2. See also 1:209–14.

120. Rodulfo Cortés, *Régimen*, 1:xviii, 116, 120–27. The 1795 cédula was drafted by the Council of the Indies for application in the Americas and the Philippines. King points out that the 1801 decree prevailed through the independence pe-riod and lasted even longer in Cuba and Puerto Rico ("Case of José Ponciano de Ayarza," 643).

121. Rodulfo Cortés, *Régimen*, 1:124–26. On the political aims of the dispensations of color, see King, "Case of José Ponciano de Ayarza," 644; Rout, *African Expe-rience*, 159; and Rodulfo Cortés, *Régimen*, 1:624.

122. Blanco and Azpurúa, eds., *Documentos*, 1:265.

123. Haring, *Spanish Empire*, 122–23.

124. The quotation in English is reproduced in Domínguez, *Insurrection or Loyalty*, 37.

125. The Black Code of 31 May 1789 attempted to ameliorate the situation (working conditions, treatment, and instruction) of slaves in the Americas. Because of the opposition of masters in Havana, Santo Domingo, Caracas, and New Orleans, the Council of the Indies suspended its execution and ordered each province to draft its own regulations. Contrasting views on this code appear in Knight, *Slave Society*, 124–28; Rout, *African Experience*, 82–87; and Watson, *Slave Law*, 57–59. Klein offered a starkly different interpretation in *Slavery in the Americas*, 78–85. For events in Venezuela, see Leal, "Aristocracia criolla"; López Bohórquez, *Ministros*, 122; and Magallanes, *Luchas e insurrecciones*, 184. Interestingly, the Spanish crown liberalized the slave trade the same year that it issued and suspended the slave code of 1789. See Klein, *Esclavitud africana*, 59.

126. The ordeals of the Mejías Bejarano family are finely narrated and analyzed in Rodulfo Cortés, *Régimen*, 1:350–82, 410–47. The subsequent discussion is based on this work. On pardos and the medical profession in Venezuela during the late colonial period, see Texera Arnal, "Médicos y cirujanos pardos."

127. Rodulfo Cortés, *Régimen*, 1:377–78, 382, 430.

128. Rout, African experience, 157–58; Leal, *Historia de la Universidad de Caracas*, 326–32.

129. Rodulfo Cortés, *Régimen*, 1:103–4, 134, 310, 520, 527, 647.

130. Brito Figueroa, *Historia económica y social*, 1:166. See also Pérez Vila, *Los libros*, 29–35.

131. See Pino Iturrieta, *Mentalidad venezolana*, 21–63, 178–87.

132. Pino Iturrieta, *Mentalidad venezolana*, 28–31.

133. Duarte, *Testimonios*, 129, 131.

134. "Autoridades coloniales," 67; Blanco and Azpurúa, eds., *Documentos*, 1:247–48, 257–59, 327.

135. López, *Juan Bautista Picornell*, 354.

136. López, *Juan Bautista Picornell*, 375.

137. López, *Juan Bautista Picornell*, 386.

138. Pino Iturrieta, *Mentalidad venezolana*, 70.

139. Both lawyers occupied positions in the new republic. Ascanio was named teniente coronel de milicias de caballería. Peraza, who was also the lawyer for two different parda plaintiffs in 1794 and 1796 in my sample, was expelled from the Colegio de Abogados for his participation in the Gual and España conspiracy but was readmitted in 1811. He became a *diputado* in 1819. See Grases, *Preindependencia*, 249; Oficina de Compilación, *Toma de Razón*, 397.

140. Instituto Panamericano, ed., *Documentos relativos*, 96–98; Pino Iturrieta, *Mentalidad venezolana*, 64–66.

141. McKinley, *Pre-revolutionary Caracas*, 81–82.

142. Izard, *Miedo a la revolución*, 149; Parra Pérez, *Historia*, 1:228.

143. Parra Pérez, *Historia*, 2:15; Quintero Montiel, "Autoridades en conflicto," 128–29.

144. Parra Pérez, *Historia*, 1:260; Izard, *Miedo a la revolución*, 136–38.

145. Parra Pérez, *Historia*, 1:230.

146. Parra Pérez, *Historia*, 1:271.

147. Parra Pérez, *Historia*, 1:276.

148. Parra Pérez, *Historia*, 2:88–89.

149. Parra Pérez, *Historia*, 2:55 n.19; Izard, *Miedo a la revolución*, 143.

150. Parra Pérez, *Historia*, 2:90.

151. Parra Pérez, *Historia*, 2:90.

152. Parra Pérez, *Historia*, 2:90.

153. See Olívar, et al., *Ni monarquía ni república*.

154. Juan Germán Roscio was in charge of writing the Act of Independence, and Felipe Fermín Paúl wrote the oath of fidelity to the new regime. Both were lawyers. In addition, lawyers took active political and military roles in the early republic. Of the forty-two signatories to the Act of Independence, seventeen were lawyers. See López Bohórquez, *Ministros*, 148–49; and Parra Pérez, *Historia*, 2:51. Roscio was originally not admitted to the Colegio de Abogados due to his "sospechosa ascendencia parda." His father was white, but his mother was a mestiza-cuarterona. Rodulfo Cortés, *Régimen*, 1:343–48. Roscio was, allegedly, the principal author of the Constitution of 1811. See Blanco and Azpurúa, eds., *Documentos*, 1:236.

155. I am borrowing the phrase "una nación para los propietarios" from Pino Iturrieta, *Ideas*.

2. LAW AND ITS OPERATION

1. Ots y Capdequí, *Historia del derecho español*, 205–6; Borah, *Justice by Insurance*, 79–119; Kellogg, *Law and Transformation*, 8.

2. Watson, *Slave Law*, 43.

3. Escriche y Martín, *Diccionario razonado*, s.v. "esclavo"; Watson, *Slave Law*, 43, 46–50. As Watson argues, the fact that, according to the *Siete Partidas*, slaves could go directly to court to sue their masters represents a small recognition of the legal personality of slaves (*Slave Law*, 46).

4. Escriche y Martín, *Diccionario razonado*, s.v. "mujer casada."

5. I have preferred to use the term *padre de familia* because it was constantly used in court cases, regardless of social class. A padre de familia is defined as the man who rules and has power over the family, even if he has no children. His powers usually included those of the patria potestad, if he had children, and privileges as a husband. See Escriche y Martín, *Diccionario razonado*, s.v. "padre de familia." Richard Boyer has discussed the powers and legal rights of the padres de familia as they are laid out in the *Siete Partidas*. This code establishes five levels of authority: "1) that of the king, in possession of the 'clear and absolute right to judge and command the people of this country'; 2) that of lords of religions; 3) that of lords of estates; 4) that of the 'authority that fathers have over their children' and wives, and 5) the 'powers' of masters over slaves" (Boyer "Women, 'La Mala Vida,'" 254–55, quote on 254). See also Arrom, *Women of Mexico City*, 68–73. Elías Pino Iturrieta analyzes another definition of padre de familia as advocated by the Catholic church in its Sinodales de Santiago de León de Caracas of 1687. Here the padres de familia were fundamentally white Creole elite males. See Pino Iturrieta, *Contra lujuria*, 28–33. I find that the lower classes also used this term by the late eighteenth century.

6. "The Father can, in virtue of his parental power, keep, correct and punish his children with moderation; he can make them serve him without giving them a salary, for the father fulfills his duty of providing food and education to them. . . . Also the father can, by his right of potestad, have possession of the *bienes profeticios* of his son (goods acquired by a son who lives under his father's direction), and the usufruct of the *adventicios* (acquired by industry or inheritance, independent of a paternal fortune), but not the *bienes cuasi-castrenses* (children's goods earned from public position or profession) or *castrenses* (son's property acquired while in military service). . . . The husband is the head of the family and for this reason has some power over woman, because of his strength, moderation and aptitude. He is the administrator of the dowry and he can, therefore, alienate the marital estate without women's permission." Escriche y Martín, *Diccionario razonado*, s.v. "marido" and "patria potestad."

7. Stern, *Secret History*, 60.

8. Lavrin, "Sexuality in Colonial Mexico."

9. Ortega Noriega, "Discurso teológico," 17–19. Marilyn Stone's discussion of the fourth partida also attests to the influence of Saint Thomas Aquinas in the drafting of that code (Stone, *Marriage and Friendship*, 39–44).

10. Ortega Noriega, "Discurso teológico," 51.

11. See Stern, *Secret History*, 114.

12. Pino Iturrieta, *Contra lujuria*, 28–37.

13. A concise yet thorough assessment of the position of the church in colonial Venezuela can be found in Watters, *History of the Church*, 3–52.

14. Martínez-Alier, *Marriage, Class, and Colour*, 42–56.

15. Martínez-Alier, *Marriage, Class, and Colour*, 60–63.

16. Nazzari, "Concubinage in Colonial Brazil."

17. Among the few works dealing with marriage in colonial Venezuela, the best known are Almécija B., *La familia*; Waldron "Sinners and the Bishop"; Waldron, "Social History"; and Miller, "Bourbon Social Engineering."

18. In colonial Mexico, where the population of African descent was much lower than in Cuba, Brazil, or Venezuela, church policies did not seem to be very different. See Seed, *To Love, Honor, and Obey*, 149; and Cope, *Limits of Racial Domination*, 82.

19. In "American Law," Seed observes that women in Iberian America had far more legal control over property and the family than did women in Anglo-America, where the concentration of property and power within the family tended to fall into the hands of men. A similar situation occurred in Brazil. See Nazzari, "Widows as Obstacles."

20. On laws protecting the economic condition of women in Latin America, see Arrom, *Women of Mexico City*, 53–81; and Nazzari, *Disappearance*. According to Spanish law, "a person could dispose of only one-fifth of her property freely; the other four-fifths had to be divided among the legitimate heirs, with children of both sexes receiving equal shares from both parents. Widows normally received half of the community property, but an impecunious widow could inherit a larger share if the probate judge determined that she was in greater need of it than the other heirs. If a man died intestate and without other heirs, his widow inherited the entire estate." Arrom, *Women of Mexico City*, 63. See also Escriche y Martín, *Diccionario razonado*, s.v. "partición de herencia." The situation in Latin America contrasts with that in the United States, where testamentary freedom prevailed and thus male heads were not obliged to leave their property to their wives and children. See Shammas, "Anglo-American Household Government"; and Grossberg, *Governing the Hearth*. The difference in inheritance laws had implications for the accumulation of capital, as Nazzari suggests in "Widows as Obstacles."

21. Escriche y Martín, *Diccionario razonado*, s.v. "hombre."

22. For this reason defendants often questioned the sexual conduct of female plaintiffs. Good examples are [untitled: María Teresa Rengifo, parda libre, fue pretendida y deshonrada por Sebastián Agudelo, mulato libre], AANH, Civiles, 1786, Letra R, exp. 12, fol. 3v; and "Expediente por Leonardo Ponte y Francisca de Ortega, tío y sobrina, contra su legítima hija Bárbara Ponte sobre no quererse

sujetar," AANH, Civiles, 1789, Letra P, exp. 2, fol. 13v–14v. Stern qualifies the late-eighteenth-century Mexican discourse on violence against "unprotected women." He found that violence was gender-rooted and was more common to married than to single women. See *Secret History*, 60.

23. Stone, *Marriage and Friendship*, 62; Pino Iturrieta, *Ventaneras*, 13–32.

24. Escriche y Martín, *Diccionario razonado*, s.v. "adulterio"; Laws 1–2, title 16, Partida 7 (*Siete Partidas*).

25. Arrom observes a similar pattern in Mexico City (*Women of Mexico City*, 64).

26. Escriche y Martín, *Diccionario razonado*, s.v. "adúlteros," See also *Siete Partidas*, title 17, partida 7; *Novísima Recopilación*, laws 1–5, title 26, and laws 3, titles 27 and 28, lib. 12.

27. *Diccionario de derecho canónico*, s.v. "adulterio"; Sínodo Diocesano de Caracas of 1687, lib. 5, title 2, núm. 3.

28. Sínodo Diocesano of 1687, lib. 5, title 2, núm. 3.

29. *Novísima Recopilación*, law 2, title 26, bk. 12; Escriche y Martín, *Diccionario razonado*, s.v. "amancebado" and "concubina," I found that sending women accused of concubinage into exile was a common ruling by the church. See Martí, *Obispo Mariano Martí*.

30. Escriche y Martín, *Diccionario razonado*, s.v. "amancebamiento" and "concubinato." Nazzari defines concubinage as an unequal relationship ("Concubinage in Colonial Brazil," 108). The same definition applies to Caracas. According to Waldron, "Social History," most of those relationships were interracial. I also use the word *concubinage* to refer to these relationships because that was the term used in the late eighteenth century.

31. Ortega Noriega, "Discurso teológico," 47.

32. Sínodo Diocesano of 1687, lib. 6, title 8, item 63.

33. *Estupro* is different from the English *rape* in that it involves seduction and deceit but not necessarily violence. When violence was used, the crime was referred to in the documents as *estupro con violencia*. *Estupro* is different from the English *statutory rape* mainly because in Spanish America the term included females of age, whereas statutory rape implies that the victim is a female who is below an age set by the applicable law. The law against estupro also stipulated that the accused had to either marry the victim or give her monetary compensation as a dowry. On the legislation dealing with estupro, see Escriche y Martín, *Diccionario razonado*, s.v. "estupro"; and *Siete Partidas*, titles 19 and 20, partida 7.

34. This situation was common in Caracas and in Mexico. See Castañeda, *Violación, estupro y sexualidad*, 125–30, 143–44. See also Giraud, "Reacción social," 326–27.

35. *Diccionario de derecho canónico*, s.v. "estupro"; Ortega Noriega, "Discurso teológico," 30; and Giraud, "Reacción social," 335, 338–41.

36. Seed, *To Love, Honor, and Obey*, 101. See also Giraud, "Reacción social," 333–34.

37. Escriche y Martín, *Diccionario razonado*, s.v. "rapto" and "seducción"; *Siete Partidas*, laws 1–3, title 20, partida 7; laws 1–2, title 19, partida 7.

38. *Diccionario de derecho canónico*, s.v. "rapto"; and Lavrin, "Sexuality in Colonial Mexico," 51.

39. Escriche y Martín, *Diccionario razonado*, s.v. "patria potestad"; *Siete Partidas*, laws 1–19, title 18, partida 4.

40. Escriche y Martín, *Diccionario razonado*, s.v. "emancipación" and "divorcio"; *Siete Partidas*, law 18, title 18, partida 4; Boyer, "Women, 'La Mala Vida'"; Chambers, "To the Company of Man."

41. Escriche y Martín, *Diccionario razonado*, s.v. "marido."

42. Twinam, *Public Lives*, 91.

43. Escriche y Martín, *Diccionario razonado*, s.v. "filiación."

44. Twinam, *Public Lives*, 124; Martínez-Alier, *Marriage, Class, and Colour*, 111–12.

45. [María Tomasa Churión por esponsales], AAC, Matrimoniales, 1791, leg. 113, fol. 17r.

46. Arrom, *Women of Mexico City*, 65–97.

47. On this issue see Findlay, "Love in the Tropics," 141.

48. Ferry, *Colonial Elite*, 190. Lee Michael Penyak, for example, asserts that women used the courts to modify the conduct of men ("Criminal Sexuality," 180). See also Lavrin, "Sexuality in Colonial Mexico," 65.

49. Nader and Metzger, "Conflict Resolution"; Boyer, "Honor," 152.

50. Computed from data in Waldron, "Social History," 137 (table 14).

51. Gender ratios were computed from Lombardi, *People and Places*, 183–85. Waldron argues that Caracas was struck by devastating epidemics during the late eighteenth century ("Social History," 25–27). Robert McCaa points to the importance of high mortality levels during this period in Parral, Mexico, as a cause for the low number of grooms and brides who had a living parent to consent to their marriage ("Gustos de los padres.")

52. Escriche y Martín, *Diccionario razonado*, s.v. "equidad" and "interpretación de las leyes." Penyak argues that the "paternalistic nature" of Spanish law in Mexico explains why the courts used the sentences to correct antisocial behavior and to work for the good of the community. One important aspect of this policy was to reunite married couples and promote formal unions ("Criminal Sexuality," 226–27, 235–36). See also MacLaghlan, *Spanish Empire*, 12, 126.

53. Cf. Cutter, *Legal Culture*, 34–35.

54. Escriche y Martín, *Diccionario razonado*, s.v. "equidad."

55. *Siete Partidas*, laws 1 and 7, title 2, partida 4; Escriche y Martín, *Diccionario razonado*, s.v. "mujer casada."

56. *Siete Partidas*, laws 1 and 7, title 2, partida 4; Escriche y Martín, *Diccionario razonado*, s.v. "mujer casada."

57. *Siete Partidas*, laws 1 and 7, title 2, partida 4; Escriche y Martín, *Diccionario razonado*, s.v. "mujer casada."

58. *Siete Partidas*, laws 1 and 13, title 16, partida 6; Escriche y Martín, *Diccionario razonado*, s.v. "tutela," "tutor," and "tutora," Widows could be guardians of their children only if they did not marry again.

59. Escriche y Martín, *Diccionario razonado*, s.v. "curador" and "tutela."

60. Rodulfo Cortés, *Régimen*, 2:60, 164. Indeed, by 1801 the tariff increased from twenty-two hundred *reales de vellón* to twenty-seven hundred for each year until the widow reached the age of twenty-five. If a widow remarried and wanted to keep the guardianship of the children, she had to pay sixty-six hundred reales de vellón to the crown. These tariffs were significantly higher than the amount required for a pardo or a quinterón dispensation, which were worth five hundred and eight hundred reales de vellón respectively.

61. "Blasina Toledo contra su marido Matías Leguisamon sobre el ningún cumplimiento de sus obligaciones," AANH, Cajas Blancas, A12-C20-D2925.

62. Martín and Josefa were cousins from both their fathers' and mothers' sides. See Ladera de Díez, *Contribución al estudio*, 53–76. For a good summary of the divorce aspect of this case, see Dávila M., "Se tiraban fuertemente al honor."

63. "Divorcio Martín Geres contra Josefa Lovera," AAC, Judiciales, 1793, leg. 117.

64. "Don Martín Aristeguieta y doña Josefa Lovera sobre divorcio," AANH, Civiles, Letra A, núm. 2, exp. 2, fol. 2r. *Bienes parafernales* usually were clothes and jewels and any property the wife acquired through inheritance or donation. It seems that a husband customarily managed the bienes parafernales for his wife, although the law established that he could not dispose of those goods unless the wife agreed in writing. See Escriche y Martín, *Diccionario razonado*, s.v. "bienes estradotales" and "bienes parafernales"; and Arrom, *Women of Mexico City*, 67–68.

65. "Diligencias obradas a consecuencia de la Real Cédula ganada por doña Josefa sobre la libertad de su persona y desembargo de sus bienes," AANH, Civiles, 1786, Letra L, núm. 3, exp. 88, fol. 1v. Don Martín seems to have been interested in the fortunes of his paternal family as well. He filed a number of lawsuits against his father's second wife, María Josefa Blanco y Herrera, who received by testament the full administration of a fifth of the properties of her deceased husband. Dávila M., "Se tiraban fuertemente al honor," 92–95. Later on, doña María Josefa wanted to marry lawyer Juan José Mora, but don Martín also led the opposition to that marriage. After that opposition was approved by the authorities, don Juan José requested a royal cédula from the civil authorities so that his reputation would not be affected by the decision of the court. See "Real cedula a favor de don Juan Joseph Mora para que no perjudique a su calidad conducta estima-

cion y circunstancia el matrimonio que se le impidió con doña Josepha Maria Blanco y Herrera," AANH, Civiles, 1790, Letra M, exp. 27, fol. 4r.

66. Doña Josefa claimed that her husband had bribed the ecclesiastical judge, giving him five or six of her slaves. "Divorcio Martín Geres," fol. 22r.; Dávila M., "Se tiraban fuertemente al honor," 83.

67. "Sobre el Hospicio de mujeres," AAC, Obras Pías, 1793, tomo 9, núm. 12, , fol. 283r–283v; Dávila M., "Se tiraban fuertemente al honor," 70–71, 90.

68. See Albornoz de López, *La visita de Joaquín Mosquera y Figueroa*, 158. Although Gil was accused of socializing with mulattos, he, along with the mantuanos, signed a 1797 letter supporting the king after the Gual and España conspiracy. See Instituto Panamericano, ed., *Documentos relativos*, 96–98. Dr. Gerónimo de Windelvoxhel and Antonio Orenes also defended doña Josefa.

69. "Don Martín Aristeguieta y doña Josefa Lovera sobre divorcio," AANH, Civiles, 1786, Letra A, núm. 2, exp. 2, fol. 3r.

70. A *caución juratoria* is a "security or assurance given by one party to another that he [or she] shall perform an agreement, keep a promise or comply with an order," See Tejada y Sainz, *Diccionario de comercio*, s.v. "caución juratoria."

71. "Don Martín Aristeguieta," fol. 12r. This idea of the court performing the duties of a father is repeated in another case in which the male plaintiff requested a marriage license from a tribunal that "acts as a father," See "Licencia para conceder matrimonio entre don Domingo de Paz e doña Barbara de Mesa," AANH, Civiles, 1789, Letra P, núm. s/n, exp. 11.

72. "Diligencias obradas a consecuencia de la Real Cédula ganada por doña Josefa sobre la libertad de su persona y desembargo de sus bienes," AANH, Civiles, 1786, Letra L, núm. 3, exp. 8, fol. 1r–3v.

73. Real Cédula of March 22, 1787. See "Diligencias obradas," fol. 35r–35v.

74. "Diligencias obradas," fol. 1r–1v.

75. *Siete Partidas*, laws 3–4, title 19, partida 4.

76. The case of doña Maria and don Antonio was the only case of child custody among married people that I found in the colonial sample. *Litis expensas* is the money requested by litigants to pay legal costs. "Da. Maria del Rosario Burgos con su marido D. Antonio Aular por cobro de alimentos y litis expensas," AANH, Civiles, 1789, Letra B, núm. 2, exp. 22.

77. "Da. María del Rosario Burgos," fol. 73r.

78. *Siete Partidas*, law 6, title 1, partida 4; Escriche y Martín, *Diccionario razonado*, s.v. "matrimonio."

79. *Siete Partidas*, law 1, title 3, partida 4; Escriche y Martín, *Diccionario razonado*, s.v. "matrimonio."

80. *Siete Partidas*, law 1, title 3, partida 4; Escriche y Martín, *Diccionario razonado*, s.v. "matrimonio"; Real Pragmática, item 3.

81. Although pardos were not included in the pragmatic, some went to court to re-

quest a license. This is further discussed in chap. 3. I categorize as a special request, for example, one case in which a person petitioned the court to consider
her dead mother's consent as it appeared in her will and another in which the
parents submitted their permission for their daughter to marry and requested
the tribunal to give the license and incarcerate the groom to be certain that he
would marry their daughter. "Doña Juana Paula Gonzales sobre lo dispuesto en
testamento de la madre de su prometido don Ygnacio Palensuela en que declara
no haber causa para resistir el matrimonio," AANH, Civiles, 1788, Letra G, núm.
5, exp. 15; "Bruno de la Luz Muñoz solicita licencia para contraer matrimonio,"
AANH, Civiles, 1790, Letra M, exp. 19.

82. The priest of La Guaira cautioned the civil court that according to the pragmatic, the consent of two relatives (not one) was necessary to give a license. I did
not find this requirement in the law, however; the norm was that one license
from a relative was sufficient. See "Lizencia que pretende Francisco Miguel Nu-
ñez para contraer matrimonio con Thomasa Bermudes," AANH, Civiles, 1790,
Letra N, exp. 3.

83. The only case that was not approved had to do with a groom who requested that
the ecclesiastical authorities proceed with the proclamation of banns while he
obtained the licenses, in order to expedite the process. The civil judge, however,
had already cautioned the church not to proceed with this case without the appropriate paperwork. "Acuerdo de la Real Audiencia de esta ciudad sobre la pretensión matrimonial de Joseph de la Encarnación Gamarra y Andrea de la Concepción Alvares, presos en esta Real Carcel de Corte," AAC, Matrimoniales, 1787,
leg. 101.

84. See, for example, [untitled: Dispensa de dos exclavos de María de la Concepción
Nieves], AAC, Matrimoniales, 1792, leg. 115. See also "Dispensa de Parentesco de
José Alberto Esclavo de las Concepciones," AAC, Matrimoniales, 1789, leg. 109.

85. "Yncluyo á VSY Testimonio del auto proveido á consecuencia del oficio de 27 de
abril último en que me acompaño copia de la representación que le hizo al cura
de Tacarigua, sobre el impedimento que ponen algunos de esclavos que contraigan matrimonio siendo de distintos amos; y he calculado la providencia que en
aquel se cita," AAC, Matrimoniales, 1795, leg. 124, fol. 2r–3r.

86. "Yncluyo á VSY Testimonio," fols. 4v, 5v–6.

87. In this case the female plaintiff (a single mother) opposed the marriage of the father of her three children to another woman. The church heard her case and
gave her additional time to provide the licenses. She gave one license from her
father but did not include any from the parents of her ex-boyfriend. Moreover,
she did not return the records on time and, in addition, she did not further any
action in the lawsuit. For the fiscal, this confirmed the ill will of the plaintiff,
who wanted to delay the marriage of her ex-boyfriend. "Demanda matrimonial

puesta por Juana María Muñoz (morena libre) contra Josef Vicente Cordero (pardo)," AAC, Matrimoniales, 1787, leg. 102, fol. 50r.

88. [María Tomasa Churión por esponsales].

89. In Spanish America the judge's decision usually did not include a written explanation of the legal basis for the opinion. It is in the report by the fiscal that this reasoning is found. See Cutter, *Legal Culture*, 36, 53.

90. [María Tomasa Churión], Letter from the fiscal to the Vicario General, December 10, 1792, [n.p.], AAC, Matrimoniales, 1791, leg. 113.

91. "Demanda matrimonial de María de los Santos Márquez contra Juan de la Rox Diaz," AAC, Matrimoniales, 1789, leg. 106; "Testimonio de los autos seguidos por Juan Julián a nombre de su legítima hija María Josefa sobre que se cumpla la palabra de esponsales que con ella tiene celebrados," AAC, Matrimoniales, 1786, leg. 100.

92. "Interrogatorio por el cual se han de examinarse los testigos que presentare Pedro Ignacio Barguilla, en la causa que le ha promovido María del Carmen Blanco sobre cumplimiento de supuestos esponsales," AAC, Matrimoniales, 1788, leg. 106, fol. 44r–45v.

93. "Interrogatorio . . . Pedro Ignacio Barguilla," fol. 46r.

94. A similar verdict was given in "Juan Fernando Flores solicita dispensa para casarse con Juana María Aponte (ambos pardos libres)," AAC, Matrimoniales, 1787, leg. 102. The ruling on this lawsuit is found in another *legajo*. See untitled record, AAC, Matrimoniales, 1788, leg. 106.

95. Two cases of opposition to marriage that went to the church had to do with women claiming that the men who were about to marry other women had already promised to marry the plaintiffs. "Autos de ympedimento puesto por Ysabel Cathalina Cardoso al matrimonio que pretende contraher Manuel Ponte con Josepha Silva todos pardos libres y vecinos de esta ciudad," AAC, Matrimoniales, 1790, leg. 126; [untitled: Juan Miguel Fajardo, moreno libre de la Vega, residente en esta Ciudad—oposición a su matrimonio], AAC, Matrimoniales, 1795, leg. 124. In the other case of opposition to marriage heard in the church tribunals, after the Real Audiencia confirmed that his parents' opposition was irrational, the groom said that he had never asked the woman to marry him. The case has some pages missing, however, and I was unable to determine how the conflict ended. "Demanda matrimonial puesta por Josepha María Manson contra Joseph Miguel Castro," AAC, Matrimoniales, 1787, leg. 102.

96. The other case is that of Juan Joseph Mora, a mantuano who lodged a petition of "calidad," In reality, he was responding to an approved opposition to his marriage to doña María Josefa Blanco y Herrera, the stepmother of don Martín Jerez de Aristeguieta. See "Real cedula a favor de don Juan Joseph Mora."

97. "Jose Maria Arteaga solicita consentimiento al matrimonio con una joben exposita," AANH, Civiles, 1790, Letra A, exp. 25.

98. Paraphrased from "Real Cédula Pragmática para que se publique y tenga efecto en las Indias en los términos que se expresa a fin de que los hijos de familia no contraigan esponsales, ni matrimonio sin el consentimiento de sus padres, parientes o tutores," AAC, Reales Cédulas, Carpeta 4, núm. 24, 7 de abril de 1778, fol. 189r. A similar rationale seems to have been practiced in nineteenth-century Cuba. See Martínez Alier, *Marriage, Class, and Colour*, 21–22.

99. "The Jamaica Letter," in Bolívar, *Political Thought*, 34.

100. Dávila M., "Se tiraban fuertemente al honor," 69–70; Pino Iturrieta, *Contra lujuria*, 28–33.

101. "Divorcio Martín Geres," fol. 3r.

102. "Sobre el Hospicio de mujeres," fol. 283r–283v; Dávila M., "Se tiraban fuertemente al honor," 70–71, 90.

103. Dávila M., "Se tiraban fuertemente al honor," 80–81.

104. "Divorcio Martín Geres," fol. 121r.

105. "Divorcio Martín Geres," fol. 121r–121v.

106. "Divorcio Martín Geres," fol. 202r–202v.

107. This runs contrary to the vision of a harmonious legal system described by Cutter in *Legal Culture*, 148.

108. Dávila M., "Se tiraban fuertemente al honor," 82–84; "Divorcio Martín Geres," fol. 6r–6v, 15r–16r, 22r, 48r–48v; "Autos seguidos por Petrona y Angela Lovera esclavas de doña Josepha Lovera pretendiendo aquellas su venta," AANH, Civiles, 1790, Letra L, exp. 2, fol. 8r.

109. "Autos de divorcio que sigue doña Rosalía Hernández contra su legítimo marido don Juan Truxillo," AAC, Matrimoniales, 1794, leg. 120, fol. 46v–47r.

110. [untitled: Blasina Toledo contra Matías Leguisamon por divorcio], AAC, Matrimoniales, 1799, leg. 105, fol. 101r.

111. These are the words of the husband's lawyer, don Andrés Martínez. "Separación que pretende doña Ana María López Infante de su marido, don Pedro Landin, vecinos del puerto de La Guaira," AAC, Matrimoniales, 1790, leg. 110, fol. 35v. On Martínez, see Oficina de Compilación, *Toma de razón*, 126.

112. This reasoning is clearly exposed by a female slave owner in "Expediente formado por el Dr. don Domingo Gil a nombre de sus hermanas y tias sobre queja de su esclava que dio en este tribunal," AANH, Civiles, 1790, Letra G, exp. 25, fol. 9v.

113. "Ana Josefa Freytes esclava de doña Ana María Castro sobre su venta," AANH, Civiles, 1790, Letra F, exp. 7, fol. 6r–7r. See also "Autos que sigue Ines María con su amo don Juan Matías Ramos sobre su libertad," AANH, Civiles, 1790, Letra V, exp. 2; "Información ofrecida por Da. Josefa de la Plaza sobre hacer constar

que dos esclavos que se profugaron fue por no trabajar," AANH, Civiles, 1790, Letra P, exp. 11.

114. "Autos seguidos por Juana Bautista Páez contra don Josef Quintero sobre su libertad," AANH, Civiles, 1788, Letra P, núm. 1, exp. 4.

115. "Autos seguidos por Juana Bautista Páez," fol. 16r.

116. "Rita Antonia Dias esclava de doña Maria Antonia Dias sobre su libertad," AANH, Civiles, 1789, Letra D.

117. "Autos que sigue Ygnes Maria con su amo Dn. Juan Matias Ramos sobre su libertad," AANH, Civiles, 1790, Letra V, exp. 2.

118. "Autos seguidos por Petrona y Angela Lovera."

119. For a similar case, see "Información ofrecida por Da. Josefa de la Plaza."

120. [untitled: Esclava pidiendo la libertad de su hijo], AANH, Civiles, 1786, Letra L, núm. 2, exp. 5.

121. I have no sexual crime lawsuits against elite males in my two samples. Divorce cases, however, are replete with references to such crimes. In these cases, elite males consistently tried to manipulate the witnesses and the court to avoid a trial and major embarrassment. Pino Iturrieta studies three lengthy cases among the creole elites of Caracas and finds that the church sought justice but ostensibly preferred to give the elites special treatment to avoid major social scandals that would question the morality of the ruling classes of caraqueño society (*Contra lujuria*).

122. Penyak makes a similar argument in "Criminal Sexuality," 204.

123. I am grateful to Juan Carlos Reyes, a historian at the Academia Nacional de la Historia, who kindly furnished me with an unpublished paper in which he discusses this case. See "Estupro," Departamento de Investigaciones Históricas, Academia Nacional de la Historia (Caracas), unpublished manuscript.

124. AANH, A10-C43-D408 (1789).

125. "Expediente por Leonardo Ponte," fol. 25r.

126. "Autos seguidos de oficio sobre el Yncesto que cometio Juan Nicolas Sisneros con su hija Lucia," AANH, Civiles, 1790, Letra S, exp. 3.

127. In the case of New Spain, Castañeda concludes that "La protección que una mujer violada podía recibir de la sociedad de las autoridades dependía más que nada de la situación de su familia.... era necesario que su familia tuviera riquezas para que su casa pidiera castigo al violador" (*Violación, estupro y sexualidad*, 144).

128. Depons, *Viaje*, 1:209.

129. "Autos promovidos por Da. María Manuela Roxas contra Dn. Josef María Rivera [*sic*] sobre que contraiga matrimonio con ella," AAC, Matrimoniales, 1790, leg. 110; "Manuela Roxas con don Luis Ruiz Rivera solicita su captura por haberla burlado bajo palabra de matrimonio," AANH, Civiles, 1790, Letra R, exp. 7r.

130. "Juan Fernando Flores solicita dispensa para casarse con Juana María Aponte (ambos pardos libres)," AAC, Matrimoniales, 1787, leg. 102 and 106. From a reading of this case, I believe that Juana María initiated this lawsuit.

131. "Interrogatorio por el cual han de examinarse los testigos que presentare Pedro Ignacio Varguilla, en la causa que le ha promovido María del Carmen Blanco sobre sumplimiento de supuestos esponsales," AAC, Matrimoniales, 1788, leg. 106.

132. "Don Martin Aristeguieta con doña Josefa Lovera su mujer, por varios excesos," AANH, Criminales, 1786, Libro ADE, Letra A, exp. 1r.

133. [Blasina Toledo contra Matías Leguisamon por divorcio].

134. French traveler Depons observed that being in jail was a common occurrence in Caracas.

135. See, for example, "Don Francisco Solorsano a nombre de su hija Da. Francisca sobre la entrega de una muchacha llamada Ana Francisca," AANH, Civiles, 1789, Letra S, exp. 4; "Sobre el casamiento de José Miguel Herrera con Juana Evangelista de Ramos," AAC, Matrimoniales, 1796, leg. 126; "Vicente Hernández sobre que se saque del depósito en que se haya su legitima hija María Joaquina en la casa de corrección," AANH, Civiles, 1790, Letra H, exp. 5.

3. WOMEN AND MEN AT THE TRIBUNALS

1. [untitled: María Tomasa Churión, por esponsales], AAC, Matrimoniales, 1791, leg. 113.

2. "Autos que sigue Ygnes Maria con su amo Dn. Juan Matias Ramos sobre su livertad," AANH, Civiles, 1790, Letra V, exp. 2.

3. Waldron, "Sinners and the Bishop," 169–70.

4. See, for example, "Demanda matrimonial puesta por María del Carmen Quintero contra Nicolás Crespo y Ramírez, ambos mulatos," AAC, Matrimoniales, 1789, leg. 109; "Testimonio de los autos seguidos por Juan Julian Arias a nombre de su legítima hija Maria Jossepha sobre que se cumpla la palabra de esponsales que con ella tiene celebrados," AAC, Matrimoniales, 1786, leg. 100; and "Demanda matrimonial puesta por Juana María Muñoz (morena libre) contra Josef Vicente Cordero (pardo)," AAC, Matrimoniales, 1787, leg. 102.

5. "Autos de divorcio que sigue Da. Francisca Rosalía Hernández contra su legítimo marido don Juan Truxillo," AAC, Matrimoniales, 1794, leg. 120. In divorce cases the depósito sought to provide temporary custody to female plaintiffs for the length of the trial. Its purpose was to grant women freedom to litigate without the husband's obstruction. It upheld the man's honor by guaranteeing the woman's honesty during the trial process. The depósitos also functioned as an extension of the secular courts. Arrom, *Women of Mexico City*, 212–17.

Depósitos also had other uses, as explained by Penyak in "Protecting and Punishing Deviant Women" and "Criminal Sexuality," 181. See also Deborah Kanter, "Correction of Sins."

6. "Autos que sigue Ygnes Maria."

7. See, for example, "Rita Antonia Dias esclava de doña Maria Antonia Dias sobre su libertad," AANH, Civiles, 1789, Letra D, exp. 5.

8. "Demanda matrimonial puesta por Juana María Muñoz," fol. 19r.

9. Tribunals honored petitions from the poor based on Spanish law of the *Novísima Recopilación*, under which a person without money to pursue a complaint could be exempt from the costs of justice after a "Certificate of Poverty" was issued. See *Novísima Recopilación*, law 7, title 19, lib. 5. I found only six cases for which such petitions were requested and granted between 1786 and 1790.

10. [María Tomasa Churión, por esponsales].

11. "Demanda matrimonial de María de los Santos Marques contra Juan de la Rox Dias," AAC, Matrimoniales, 1789, leg. 106, fol. 1v–2r. See also "Ynterrogatorio por el qual han de examinarse los testigos que presentare Pedro Ygnacio Barquilla, en la causa que le ha movido María del Carmen Blanco sobre cumplimiento de supuestos esponsales," AAC, Matrimoniales, 1788, leg. 106; "Demanda matrimonial puesta por Juana María Muñoz"; "Autos promovidos por Da. María Manuela Roxas contra Dn. Josef María Rivera sobre que contraiga matrimonio con ella," AAC, Matrimoniales, 1790, leg. 110; "Autos de ympedimento puesto por Ysabel Cathalina Cardoso al matrimonio que pretende contraher Manuel Ponte con Josepha Silva todos pardos libres y vecinos de esta ciudad," AAC, Matrimoniales, 1790, leg. 126; [untitled: Juan Miguel Fajardo — oposición a su matrimonio] AAC, Matrimoniales, 1795, leg. 124; "Autos seguidos por Maria Vicenta Gonzalez con Pablo Echevarria sobre asunto de matrimonio," AANH, Civiles, 1790, Letra G, exp. 17; and "Demanda matrimonial puesta por María del Carmen Quintero."

12. "Demanda matrimonial puesta por Juana María Muñoz," fol. 6r. See also "Demanda matrimonial puesta por María del Carmen Quintero"; "Testimonio de los autos seguidos por Juan Julian Arias."

13. McCaa, "Calidad, Clase, and Marriage"; see also Twinam, *Public Lives*.

14. Boyer, "Honor," 162–63.

15. Waldron, "Sinners and the Bishop," 158, 163.

16. "Ynterrogatorio . . . Pedro Ygnacio Barquilla," fol. 20r–20v.

17. "Ynterrogatorio . . . Pedro Ygnacio Barquilla," fol. 42. Another example is [Juan Miguel Fajardo . . . — oposición a su matrimonio].

18. [untitled: Maria Teresa Rengifo, parda libre, fue pretendida con palabra de casamiento y fue deshonrada por Sebastián Agudelo, mulato libre], AANH, Civiles, 1786, Letra R, núm. 1, exp. 12, fol. 3v.

19. "Separación que pretende Da. Ana María Lopez Ynfante de su marido, Dn. Pedro Landin, vecinos del puerto de La Guaira," AAC, Matrimoniales, 1790, leg. 110; "Ynterrogatorio . . . Pedro Ygnacio Barguilla."

20. "Doña Josefa Maria Soriano y Durán contra don Matías Fortunato Sublet sobre querer aquella se le reedifique su cuarto y la casa que alquila a dicho Sublet por haber muerto en él suponiendo fue contagioso el mal," AANH, Civiles, 1787, Letra S, núm. 2, exp. 4.

21. See, for example, "Dispensa de parentesco de José Alberto (esclavo de las Concepciones)," AAC, Matrimoniales, 1789, leg. 109; "Demanda matrimonial puesta por María del Carmen Quintero"; "Demanda matrimonial de Francisco García contra Pasquala N.," AAC, Matrimoniales, 1787, leg. 102; "Doña Rufina Sandoval con don Diego Navarro sobre oponerse al matrimonio que su hijo pretende contraer," AANH, Civiles, 1786, Letra S, núm. 1, exp. 3.

22. [Maria Tomasa Churión, por esponsales], fol. 1–3, 10. See also "Autos promovidos por Da. María Manuela Roxas," in which the female plaintiff requested the tribunal to alter the order in which she should present her case so that the accused had no time to run away.

23. On this issue, see Pino Iturrieta, *Ventaneras*.

24. See, for example, "Separación que pretende Da. Ana María Lopez Ynfante"; "Auto que sigue don Juan de Soto y Monasterios para que Joseph Ignacio Escalona novio de su hija D. Ana Josefa obtenga un disenso para casarse con ella," AANH, Civiles, 1787, Letra S, núm. 2, exp. 8; "Autos que sigue doña Juana Lorenza Dominguez contra don Josef Antonio Vaez su marido sobre alimentos," AANH, Civiles, 1788, Letra D, núm. 7, exp. 8.

25. [untitled: Don Ygnacio González — su mujer se resiste a cumplir con las obligaciones de su estado], AAC, Matrimoniales, 1795, leg. 124, fol. 27r–27v.

26. [untitled: Divorcio — Juana Feliciana Dias con Juan Domingo Moreno], AAC, Matrimoniales, 1794, leg. 120, fol. 8r.

27. Stern, *Secret History*, 78–79, 162–63.

28. [Don Ygnacio González — su mujer se resiste a cumplir], fol. 72–73.

29. See, for instance, "Demanda matrimonial de María de los Santos Marques"; "Demanda matrimonial puesta por Juana María Muñoz"; "Separación que pretende Da. Ana María Lopez Ynfante"; "Autos seguidos por Da. Luisa de Ochoa sobre que se extraigan del poder de su marido don Bernardo Riso todos y cualesquiera bienes que mantenga en su poder por ser propios suyos y estarlos disipando," AANH, Civiles, 1790, Letra O, exp. 6.

30. [Divorcio — Juana Feliciana Dias con Juan Domingo Moreno], fol. 8.

31. "Separación que pretende Da. Ana María Lopez Ynfante," fol. 23.

32. "Autos de divorcio que sigue Da. Francisca Rosalía Hernández contra su legítimo marido don Juan Truxillo," AAC, Matrimoniales, 1794, leg. 120, fol. 14v.

33. Depons, *Viaje*, 1:88–91.

34. "Real Cédula Pragmática para que se publique y tenga efecto en la Indias en los términos que se expresa a fin de que los hijos de familia no contraigan esponsales, ni matrimonio sin el consentimiento de sus padres, parientes o tutores," AAC, Reales Cédulas, Carpeta 4, núm. 24, 7 de abril de 1778; Twinam, *Public Lives*, 311.

35. See Seed, *To Love, Honor and Obey*, 205–25.

36. Mago de Chópite, *Caracas*, 188.

37. This refers to article 9 of the Royal Pragmatic of 1776, which was not modified when the pragmatic was extended to Spanish America in 1778.

38. These cases include lawsuits over issues such as divorce, abuse, family support, seduction, breach of betrothal, unlawful clandestine marriages, and opposition to marriage.

39. "Jose Maria Arteaga solicita consentimiento al matrimonio de una joben exposita," AANH, Civiles, 1790, Letra A, exp. 25.

40. "Auto que sigue don Juan de Soto y Monasterios para que Joseph Ignacio Escalona novio de su hija D. Ana Josefa obtenga un disenso para casarse con ella," AANH, Civiles, 1787, Letra S, Libro 2, exp. 8.

41. See Twinam, "Honor, Sexuality, and Illegitimacy"; and Johnson and Lipsett-Rivera, eds., *Faces of Honor*.

42. "Jose Maria Arteaga solicita consentimiento al matrimonio con una joben exposita," AANH, Civiles, 1790, Letra A, exp. 25. See also Twinam, *Public Lives*, 66–73.

43. "Doña Rufina Sandoval con don Diego Navarro sobre oponerse al matrimonio que su hijo pretende contraer," AANH, Civiles, 1786, Letra S, núm. 1, exp. 3.

44. "Real cedula a favor de don Juan Joseph Mora para que no perjudique a su calidad conducta estimacion y circunstancia el matrimonio que se le impidió con doña Jossepha Maria Blanco y Herrera," AANH, Civiles, 1790, Letra M, exp. 27, fol. 4r.

45. See "Demanda matrimonial puesta por María del Carmen Quintero"; "Demanda matrimonial puesta por Juana María Muñoz"; "Autos de ympedimento puesto por Ysabel Cathalina Cardoso"; and "Contra José Urvina por el matrimonio que contrajo en la Parroquia de Santa Rosalía siendo feligreses de Altagracia," AAC, Matrimoniales, 1790, leg. 126.

46. An unlawful clandestine marriage was one in which there was no publication of banns or ceremonies as determined by the Council of Trent. The couple was married in secrecy with only a priest and two witnesses present.

47. "Demanda matrimonial puesta por Juana María Muñoz."

48. See, for example, "Licencia que pretende don Juan Gonzalez Hernandez para contraer matrimonio con doña Maria Josef Padrón," AANH, Civiles, 1790, Letra

G, exp. 14; "Acuerdo de la Real Audiencia de esta ciudad sobre la pretensión matrimonial de Joseph de la Encarnación Gamarra y Andrea de la Concepción Alvares, presos en esta Real Carcel de Corte," AAC, Matrimoniales, 1787, leg. 101, fol. 3r.

49. See "Instancia que hace Don Antonio del Castillo sobre lo que pretende contraer metrimonio con Doña Josefa Navarro y solicita lizencia de Don Antonio Perez," AANH, Civiles, 1790, Lera C, exp. 24; "Autos seguidos por Maria Nicolasa Tovar con Bernardino Cuebas sobre contracción de matrimonio," AANH, Civiles, 1790, Letra T, exp. 2; "Maria Nicolasa Tovar pretende ponerse en estado matrimonial con Pedro Vernardino Cueva," AANH, Civiles, 1790, Letra T, exp. 13.

50. "Contra José Urvina por el matrimonio que contrajo en la Parroquia de Santa Rosalía siendo feligreses de Altagracia," AAC, Matrimoniales, 1790, leg. 126.

51. "Sobre el casamiento de José Miguel Herrera con Juana Evangelista de Ramos," AAC, Matrimoniales, 1790, leg. 126; "Causa seguida contra Francisco E. Gomez por el matrimonio clandestino que quiso contraer con Rosario María Hernández," AAC, Matrimoniales, 1790, leg. 114; "Sobre cumplimiento de la Real Cedula de su Magestad presentada por Dn Felipe Madrid contra Joseph Manuel Moron por el clandestino que contrajo con Da Rosalia de la Madrid, su hermana," AANH, Civiles, 1800, Letra M; "Contra José Urvina por el matrimonio que contrajo"; Depons's account validates this interpretation (Viaje, 1:88–89).

52. McCaa finds that high mortality rates limited the effectiveness of the pragmatic. In Caracas this was another important factor in complicating the process of formalizing unions, because the courts might request proof of the lack of parents or relatives before granting any license. See McCaa, "Gustos de los padres."

53. See "Nicolasa Antonia Graterón sobre oponerse al matrimonio que pretende contraer su hija natural Maria Josepha Grateron con Ramón Ortiz," AANH, Civiles, 1790, Letra G, exp. 37; "Maria Francisca Meza sobre pretender casarse con Ylario Ruis esclavo de los herederos de don Christobal Ruiz," AANH, Civiles, 1790, Letra M, exp. 20.

54. See "Ynformación evacuada a instancia de doña Maria Alexander," AAC, Matrimoniales, 1785, leg. 100; "Doña Maria Agustina y doña Maria Micaela Perez para hacer constar en Tribunal Real su calidad y limpieza de sangre," AANH, Civiles, 1790, Letra P, exp. 14.

55. "Doña Rufina Sandoval con don Diego Navarro."

56. See Martínez-Alier, Marriage, Class, and Colour, 15–18.

57. "Nicolasa Antonia Graterón sobre oponerse al matrimonio que pretende contraer su hija natural Maria Josepha Grateron con Ramón Ortiz," AANH, Civiles, 1790, Letra G, exp. 37.

58. "Demanda matrimonial puesta por Juana María Muñoz," fol. 59r.

59. Pellicer discusses how the privilege of belonging to the Batallón de Pardos gave

social status to its members in *Vivencia*. See also Rodulfo Cortés, "Milicias de pardos."

60. Corominas, *Diccionario crítico*, s.v. "pardo" and "mulato."

61. "Don Andres Mosquera por Josef Antonio Guillen sobre acreditar su calidad de pardo," AANH, Civiles, 1800, Letra M, exp. 29. See also "Don Nicolas Gonzales Palma contra Geronima Olivares sobre desocupar una casa," AANH, Civiles, 1788, Letra G, núm. 5, exp. 12, in which Geronima complains that don Nicolas called her a mulatta when she is a parda.

62. See "Traslado de la Real Cédula sobre matrimonios — Maracay, 30 de septiembre de 1806," AGN, Colección Aragua, Tomo 61, fol. 1–17. This document clarifies certain doubts that the 1803 law raised, especially the item that stated that people older than the indicated ages could marry at their discretion. In this 1806 writing the Spanish crown made clear that it would not allow any marriage between white people (of known purity of blood and nobility) and people of African ancestry, even if they were of age (fol. 14). This piece also takes note of problems that people encountered while trying to comply with the marriage laws in the Venezuelan parishes. Some of the difficulties included distance from the ecclesiastical and civil authorities, poverty, and the lack of parents or relatives, particularly among foreigners and newly arrived African slaves.

63. As Pablo Rodríguez notes in *Seducción*, after the Council of Trent promises of marriage became formalized in contracts regulated by parents and the church.

64. In "Marriageways in Mexico and Spain" McCaa argues that scholarly works have given less attention to the 1803 edict than to that of 1778, although the 1803 law was much more significant because the republican civil codes adopted many of its provisions.

65. Cf. Almécija B., *La familia*, 197–207.

66. Johnson and Lipsett-Rivera, introduction to Johnson and Lipsett-Rivera, eds., *Faces of Honor*, 11.

67. Boyer, "Honor," 156.

68. [Maria Teresa Rengifo, parda libre, fue pretendida con palabra de casamiento], fol. 12r. Cope also notes differences among the lower classes' ideas on race (*Limits of Racial Domination*).

4. A NATION FOR THE LANDOWNERS

1. Liddle, "State, Masculinities, and Law."

2. Montesquieu's writings made clear to Bolívar that any form of government had to be adapted to the local culture and conditions of the communities. See Pagden, *Spanish Imperialism*; and "Discurso pronunciado . . . de Angostura."

3. Bolívar did not hold a high opinion of Indians. To him, the actions of Tupac

Amaru and Morelos were motivated by an illusory patriotism and a fervent Catholicism that led to anarchy and tyranny in both Peru and Mexico. Although Bolívar's writings mentioned positive aspects of the native population, such as Indians' natural love for liberty, he did not concede them much will for work and for implementing change. Pagden, *Spanish Imperialism*, 134, 138.

4. Chambers, "Gender." Chambers also identifies other meanings for *pasiones* in Bolívar's writings, such as passions of "productive emotions," as well as "lacking reason," "jealousy," and "being out of control."

5. "Discurso pronunciado . . . de Angostura," 214–15, 226–27.

6. Pagden, *Spanish Imperialism*, 150.

7. Pagden, *Spanish Imperialism*, 147.

8. Picón-Salas and Fundación Eugenio Mendoza, *Venezuela independiente*, 210.

9. Skurski, "'Leader' and the 'People,'" 19.

10. Pino Iturrieta, *Mentalidad venezolana*; Skurski, "'Leader' and the 'People,'" 18.

11. "Discurso pronunciado . . . de Angostura," 216.

12. This is comparable to the situation in early republican Bolivia. See Barragán "Spirit of Bolivian Laws."

13. Skurski, "'Leader' and the 'People,'" 19.

14. See Landes, *Women and the Public Sphere*, 202–6; and Carol Pateman, *Sexual Contract*.

15. "Discurso pronunciado . . . de Angostura," 220, 232–33.

16. Skurski, "'Leader' and the 'People,'" 15.

17. Skurski, "'Leader' and the 'People,'" 15.

18. Skurski, "'Leader' and the 'People,'" 15–17; Carrera Damas, *Culto a Bolívar*.

19. Skurski, "'Leader' and the 'People,'" 18, 29; "Discurso pronunciado . . . de Angostura," 228–29.

20. Quoted in Olívar, et al., *Ni monarquía ni república*, 47.

21. "Juan José Espinosa solicitando que Micaela Ravelo se restituya con los hijos que ha ocultado a la casa de su madre donde aquel la tenía," ARPDF, Civiles, 1836, Letra E, exp. 15, fol. 17v.

22. Cherpak, "Participation of Women," 220–21; Cherpak, "Women and the Independence of Gran Colombia," 81, 89–98, 112–15, 122–47.

23. Cherpak, "Participation of Women," 222. Troconis de Veracoechea also mentions the case of a free black woman who was sent to jail for four years for being a conspirator and was later prohibited from returning to Caracas and La Guaira (*Indias*, 128). For other examples of higher- and lower-class women participating in the wars, see Troconis de Veracoechea, *Indias*, 132–52. See also Troconis de Veracoechea, *Gobernadoras*; and Quintero Montiel, *Mirar tras la ventana*, for a traveler's descriptions of women's participation in the independence wars. Carmen Perdomo Escalona includes some biographies of women who partici-

pated in the Independence Wars in *Heroínas y mártires*. For a Latin American perspective, see Coelho Prado, "Em busca."

24. Earle, "Rape."

25. Skurski, "'Leader' and the 'People,'" 18.

26. Skurski, "'Leader' and the 'People,'" 22. In revolutionary France, the female figure represented liberty, revolution, and the republic itself. See Landes, *Women and the Public Sphere*, 159–66; and Carvalho, *A formaçao das almas*, 75–76.

27. Landes, *Women and the Public Sphere*, 159.

28. Earle, "Rape," 138–39.

29. See Landes, *Women and the Public Sphere*, 164; and Castro Leiva, *De la patria boba*, 19–83.

30. Skurski, "'Leader' and the 'People,'" 9, 22.

31. Hunt, *Politics, Culture, and Class*, 31, 62; also cited by Landes, *Women and the Public Sphere*, 161.

32. Skurski, "'Leader' and the 'People,'" 18.

33. Picón-Salas and Fundación Eugenio Mendoza, *Venezuela independiente*, 213.

34. Skurski, "'Leader' and the 'People,'" 22.

35. These ideas were reinforced by nineteenth-century biological discourse in Europe. Nye, *Masculinity*, 49.

36. Nye, *Masculinity*, 49; Landes, *Women and the Public Sphere*, 68–71, 85–87.

37. Pino Iturrieta, *Ventaneras*, 16–17.

38. Pino Iturrieta, *Ventaneras*, 69.

39. See the appendix to the Constitution of 1819, sec. 3, art. 2. This is also discussed in Earle, "Rape," 141.

40. See, for example, "La lactancia," *Crónica Eclesiástica de Venezuela*, 14 December 1855; "Palabras de una madre á su hija," *Crónica Eclesiástica de Venezuela*, 2 April 1856; "¿A dónde vamos a parar? El divorcio," *Crónica Eclesiástica de Venezuela*, 14 November 1855; "Religión y moral," *Crónica Eclesiástica de Venezuela*, 31 October 1855; "La familia," *Crónica Eclesiástica de Venezuela*, 12 August 1857.

41. Chambers, *From Subjects to Citizens*, 192–93. Chambers argues that virtue became one central argument among plebeian men in their defense at the courts of Arequipa, Peru. Men used military service to the state as well as their hard work to justify their rights as citizens.

42. See Chambers, "Gender"; Zerilli, *Signifying Woman*; Hufton, *Women and the Limits of Citizenship*; and Levy and Applewhite, "Women and Militant Citizenship," For a discussion on how these ideas affected women in the United States, see Kerber, *Women of the Republic*.

43. Gil Fortoul, *Historia constitucional*, 1:559.

44. A terse statement by Páez's wife speaks eloquently of the independence hero's

rise to riches: "My husband brought nothing to this marriage," Doña Dominga did state, however, that her former husband was a good administrator of her properties. The couple lost all of their assets to confiscation by the royalists during the independence wars. See "No contencioso. Apertura del testamento de Dominga Ortiz de Páez," ARPDF, Civiles, 1876, Letra O, exp. 8, fol. 9v. See also Bushnell, *Santander Regime*, 276–79; and Friedman, "City of Caracas," 78–79.

45. Gil Fortoul, *Historia constitucional*, 1:561; Lombardi, *Venezuela*, 158–59.

46. Gil Fortoul, *Historia constitucional*, 1:652; Banko, *Luchas federalistas*, 91–94.

47. Friedman, "City of Caracas," 61.

48. Friedman, "City of Caracas," 57–58.

49. Pino Iturrieta, *Ideas*, 16.

50. Pino Iturrieta, *Ideas*, 167.

51. Banko, *Luchas federalistas*, 121–22.

52. Pino Iturrieta, *Ideas*, 170.

53. Pino Iturrieta, *Ideas*, 15.

54. Lombardi, *Venezuela*, 162–82. A coffee boom coincided with the emergence of what Venezuelan historians call the Conservative Oligarchy (1830–48), with General Páez as the leading political figure. An excellent overview of political developments leading to the consolidation of the Conservative Oligarchy appears in Lombardi, *Decline and Abolition*, 16–24. Other works that provide a wealth of information on the period are González Guinán, *Historia contemporánea*; Gil Fortoul, *Historia constitucional*; and Díaz Sánchez, *Guzmán*.

55. Pino Iturrieta, *Ideas*, 23.

56. Pino Iturrieta, *Ideas*, 44, 47.

57. On the reasons for its promulgation and the economic and political impact of this law, see Lombardi, *Decline and Abolition*, 19–20, 99–100; Friedman, "City of Caracas," 120–30; González Guinán, *Historia contemporánea*, 2:329–31; and Floyd, *Guzmán Blanco*. Other laws that were enacted include the manumission law of 1830; the abolition of the alcabala tax (*alcabala de tierra*) on goods for internal consumption (1831); the elimination of all export duties (*alcabala de mar*) on cotton, indigo, and coffee; and the reduction of duties for hides and cattle. Planters welcomed these measures, which were followed by the abolition of church tithe in 1833 and the abolition of the tobacco monopoly (*estanco*) in 1833. *Diccionario de historia*, s.v. "Páez, José Antonio, Gobiernos de" and "alcabala"; Watters, *History of the Church*, 146.

58. By 1839, however, a board was created to censor criticism against the government. See Pino Iturrieta, *Ideas*, 55.

59. Articles 188 and 215 of the Constitution of 1830 abolished all special privileges of the church and the military, including fiscal immunity from taxation. In addition, on 16 April 1833 another law abolished tithes so that those monies could be

used to boost agriculture. On the debates surrounding the passage of the law, see Bushnell, *Santander Regime*, 229–37. The law is reproduced in González Oropeza, ed., *Iglesia y Estado*, 71–88. Watters thoroughly examines church-state relations during the Conservative Oligarchy period in *History of the Church*, 125–62.

60. Pino Iturrieta, *Ideas*, 58–59, 170.

61. Pino Iturrieta, *Ideas*, 59. This comes from a manifesto written by critics of Páez and, since it was written in 1836, when the death sentence of Vicenta Ochoa was publicly debated, they may be referring to their opposition to the execution of that pregnant woman in their claim that the regime was "insulting the female sex." That case is discussed later in this chapter and in chap. 5. Moreover, Páez was criticized for his growing wealth, for the free contract law of April 1834 that made many lose their properties, and for the *ley de azotes*.

62. Banko, *Luchas federalistas*, 121–23.

63. Banko, *Luchas federalistas*, 123; Pino Iturrieta, *Ideas*, 60–61.

64. Floyd, *Guzmán Blanco*, 25; Toro, "Reflexiones."

65. Pino Iturrieta, *Ideas*, 55.

66. Pino Iturrieta, *Ideas*, 54–55, 62–64, 170–71.

67. Pino Iturrieta, *Ideas*, 17.

68. The presidencia de la república published these debates in the collection *Pensamiento político venezolano del siglo XIX*.

69. The flyers were titled "Vicenta Ochoa and Her Constitutional Rights" and "Vicenta Ochoa, muchas veces muerta" (Vicenta Ochoa, dead many times), and were included in the "Testimonio de la sentencia pronunciada en la causa criminal seguida de oficio contra Guillermo Castell, su muger Vicenta Ochoa y sirvienta Manuela Benavides por el homicidio cometido en la persona de María de la Cruz, sierva de la señora Ana Salías el dia 28 de octubre del año pasado de 1834," ARPDF, Criminales, 1836, Letra O, exp. 3, fol. 26, 33–33v.

70. Pino Iturrieta, *Ideas*, 62–63; Oficina de Compilación, *Toma de razón*, vol. 4, *Pensamiento político*.

71. Levit, *Gender Line*, 54–57. Indeed, the letters of lawyers in the lawsuits studied show these men's preoccupation in demonstrating legal knowledge. The letters quote Roman, Spanish, and republican laws and decrees as well as the jurisprudence of Venezuela and other Latin American countries. Such expositions are not as common in the other two samples.

72. Due to José María Vargas's resignation as president on 24 April 1836, Vice President Andrés Narvarte was in charge of the government until 1837.

73. "Testimonio de la sentencia," fl. 26.

74. "Testimonio de la sentencia," 33–33v.

75. Salvatore, "Death and Liberalism," 333.

76. A similar argument was made by a member of the elite, Martín Echegarreta, in defense of his son who was accused of estupro of a freed woman. In his letter Echegarreta not only expounded on Roman, Spanish, and republican laws but also repeated the idea of women's power over men: "parece casi imposible que un sólo hombre pueda cometerlo, teniendo la muger mas medios para oponerse á la violencia que el hombre para vencer su resistencia." See "Criminales contra Francisco de Paula Echagarreta por estupro inmaturo," ARPDF, 1837, Criminales, Letra E, exp. 5, fol. 12.

77. Escriche, *Diccionario*, s.v. "madre de familia" and "padre de familia."

78. Pino Iturrieta, *Ideas*, 27.

79. "Educación de la mujer," *El Foro*, 1857.

80. "Conmutación de la pena de muerte impuesta a Vicenta Ochoa, en la de seis años de confinación en la Isla de Margarita," AGN, Secretaría del Interior y Justicia, 1836, Tomo 133, fol. 146.

81. "Conmutación de la pena," fol. 146–47.

82. Chiossone, *Formación jurídica*, 174.

83. Affonso Romano de Sant'Anna is borrowing the ideas of Simone de Beauvoir in this passage. See his *O canibalismo amoroso*, 39–40.

84. The execution of Camila O'Gorman and her priest lover when she was allegedly eight months pregnant also produced much political discussion in 1848 in Argentina. According to Donald F. Stevens, the executions "were meant to warn others not to keep secrets from him [dictator Juan Manuel de Rosas], not to doubt patriarchal authority, and not to accept passion as an acceptable guide to choosing a mate." See Stevens, "Passion and Patriarchy." In "Death and Liberalism," Salvatore discusses the effects that the death sentence of an allegedly pregnant murderer, Clorinda Sarracán (1856), had in promoting the gradual and effective decline of the death penalty in post-Rosas Argentina.

85. "Vicenta Ochoa pide al jefe de las reformas que le conmute la pena de muerte a que ha sido condenada por delitos comunes," AGN, Secretaría del Interior y Justicia, Tomo 108, fol. 105.

86. "Vicenta Ochoa pide al jefe," fol. 106.

87. *Diccionario de Historia*, s.v. "revolución de las reformas."

88. "Vicenta Ochoa pide al jefe," fol. 107.

89. "Conmutación de la pena," fl. 140.

90. Brown, "Princess of Monaco's Hair." *Diccionario de Legislación*, s.v. "muerte."

91. It is important to note that most of the women who signed the letter included their husband's last name to acknowledge their married status. Because this was an upper-class convention, it can be surmised that these women belonged to or identified themselves as upper-class. See ch. 9.

92. "Conmutación de la pena," fol. 142v. The words *humano* and *filantrópico* were written in larger letters in the original.

93. "Conmutación de la pena," fol. 111–60; "Vicenta Ochoa pide al jefe," fol. 105–7.

94. "Conmutación de la pena," fol. 144v.

95. See Lavrin, *Women, Feminism, and Social Change*, 5.

96. On how the emphasis on motherhood undermined a redefinition of women's social role, see, for example, Besse, *Restructuring Patriarchy*, 109; and Lavrin, *Women, Feminism, and Social Change*.

5. EQUALITY BEFORE THE LAW

1. Constitution of 1811, art. 154, 226. The Constitution of 1811 lasted for only one year due to the independence wars, but it set the framework for future constitutions. It abolished the slave trade (art. 202), although slavery was not abolished until 1854. Slaves were not included in the right of citizenship. See Brewer-Carías, *Constituciones de Venezuela*, 15–52. The Brazilian Constitution of 1824 also hedged its language where the rights of free mixed-race people were concerned. See Flory, "Race and Social Control."

2. See Constitution of 1811, chap. 9, art. 201–26.

3. John Hawkshaw, quoted in Friedman, "City of Caracas," 108, 238. Hawkshaw visited Caracas in 1838. Another traveler, Edward B. Eastwick, enthusiastically remarked how well the doctrine of equality was practiced in Venezuela in the 1800s. See Pino Iturrieta and Calzadilla, comps., *Mirada del otro*, 148.

4. Chiossone, *Formación jurídica*, 133–34.

5. Merryman, *Civil Law Tradition*, 48–55. See also Pérez Perdomo, "Teoría y práctica."

6. According to the Constitution of 1811, chap. 2, sec. 2, art. 26, a voter is a free male, married or over twenty-one years of age, who has wealth of six hundred pesos if single and four hundred pesos if married (even if the money belongs to the wife).

7. See Constitution of 1811, art. 151–65; Constitution of 1819, title 1, sec. 1, art. 1–16; Constitution of 1821, preamble and art. 156–84; Constitution of 1830, art. 187–219.

8. *Cuerpo de leyes, decretos y resoluciones*, 90–93.

9. This is similar to Mexico. See McCaa, "Marriageways."

10. I owe this observation to Asunción Lavrin.

11. Decree of 21 June 1823. See *Cuerpo de leyes de la República de Colombia*, 129.

12. The law of August 1828 that prohibited marriages between Spaniards and Colombians was revoked on June 1831. *Cuerpo de leyes, decretos y resoluciones*, 140–

41. Another restriction, which was actually a continuation of the pragmatics, obliged members of the military to request a license from the government (28 July 1828). See Sociedad Bolivariana de Venezuela, *Decretos*, 3:121.

13. Bolívar, "Proyecto de Decreto," 71–74.

14. "Ordenanza de 10 de diciembre de 1838. Sobre empadronamiento de los jornaleros y sirvientes," in Universidad Central de Venezuela, *Materiales para el estudio*, 171–74.

15. Matthews, *Violencia rural*, 42.

16. Guy, "Lower-Class Families," 319.

17. Decree of 6 September 1813, in Sociedad Bolivariana de Venezuela, *Decretos*, 1:12.

18. Chiossone, *Formación jurídica*, 149; Sociedad Bolivariana de Venezuela, *Decretos*, 1:283.

19. See, for example, "Divorcio que prepara doña María Antonia Pérez a su legítimo marido don Ramón Maucó," AAC, Matrimoniales, 1811, leg. 187; "Segunda pieza de los autos de divorcio que sigue María Ignacia Sanavria contra su legítimo marido Juan Nepomuceno Ascanio," AAC, Matrimoniales, 1820, leg. 230; "Divorcio que pretende la Sra. Josefa Antonia Castro contra su legítimo marido el Sr. Francisco Morales," AAC, Matrimoniales, 1837, leg. 270; and "María Jesús Menéndez proponiendo demanda de divorcio contra su marido Vicente Egui," ARPDF, Civiles, 1840, Letra M, exp. 30.

20. Chiossone, *Formación jurídica*, 123–24.

21. Bushnell, *Santander Regime*, 46–47, 49.

22. Chambers, *From Subjects to Citizens*, 141–45. Twinam also found that cases increased in the last two decades of the eighteenth century. See *Public Lives*.

23. Socolow found that women involved in criminal cases in Buenos Aires in the 1757–97 period were mostly victims or accomplices; she interprets this finding as a reflection of women's generally passive role in society. See Socolow, "Women and Crime."

24. The percentage is higher if I add the number of cases in categories in which women were contending against other women; I analyzed those cases as a different category.

25. [untitled: Tomasa Ramírez contra su marido Gregorio Acosta por divorcio], AAC, Matrimonales, 1840, leg. 271. See also [untitled: Divorcio de María Ignacia Sanabria y Juan Nepomuceno Ascanio], AAC, Matrimoniales, 1835, leg. 264; "Para averiguar la persona que causó una contusión a María Josefa Barrios" ARPDF, Criminales, 1839, Letra A, exp. 2. María Josefa was involved in several demands against the father of her natural child, who was planning to marry another woman. See, for instance, the complaint María Josefa filed at the ecclesiastical court, [untitled] AAC, Matrimoniales, 1837, leg. 270.

26. The percentage of women who initiated the legal procedure in court (50.1 per-

cent) is the sum of the number of women plaintiffs, victims, and women who later were represented by men. See Escriche y Martín, *Diccionario razonado*, s.v. "mujer casada," and "mujer pública."

27. See "Lista de los ciudadanos del Cantón Caracas, que reúnen las cualidades para ser electores," BN, Colección de Libros Raros y Manuscritos, Colección de Hojas Sueltas, 1 de julio de 1850.

28. Friedman, "City of Caracas," 90, 96–98, 192–96.

29. Luis Sanojo, "Arancel judicial," *El Foro* 9 (1856), cited in Pérez Perdomo, "Teoría y práctica," 359.

30. Pérez Perdomo, "Teoría y práctica," 359.

31. See *Novísima Recopilación*, law 7, title 19, lib. 5; Escriche y Martín, *Diccionario razonado*, s.v. "litigante" and "pobre." Escriche writes: "El pobre que, aunque tenga lo suficiente para vivir, carece de lo necesario para litigar, no ha de ser compelido a pagar las costas y derechos que devengue en defenderse, con tal que haga constar su pobreza mediante información ante cualquier juez, presentando además un testigo fidedigno ante el tribunal en que se sigue el pleito."

32. *Cuerpo de leyes, decretos y resoluciones*, 32–36 (Ley de 13 de mayo de 1825, Capt. I, II, and III). See also Matos Rodríguez "La mujer y el derecho."

33. "Luiza Blanco solicitando licencia judicial para la venta de la hacienda," ARPDF, Civiles, 1836, Letra B, exp. 17.

34. "Luiza Blanco solicitando licencia judicial," fol. 1v.

35. "Luiza Blanco solicitando licencia judicial," fol. 2v. Luiza refers to law 13, title 1, bk. 10, and law 15, title 1, bk. 10 of the *Novísima Recopilación*.

36. "Luiza Blanco solicitando licencia judicial," fol. 2r.

37. "Marcelina Medina solicitando habilitación judicial para administrar sus intereses, y que se le nombre curador ad bona a su legítimo marido Ramón Gusman, por hallarse constituido en la demencia," ARPDF, Civiles, 1839, Letra M, exp. 32.

38. *Código de Procedimiento Judicial de 19 de mayo de 1836*, art. 8, law 1a, title 1a; "María Ygnacia Sanavria, legítima muger de Juan Nepomuceno Ascanio, pidiendo que se la habilite para obrar sin la intervención de su marido," ARPDF, Civiles, 1838, Letra S, exp. 6, fol. 2v.

39. A natural child was entitled to receive at least a fifth of the properties of his or her father or mother as alimentos. If the child was the product of an adulterous relationship, then the father could leave the child a fifth of his properties as alimentos. Yet such a child would always inherit from his or her mother. See Escriche y Martín, *Diccionario razonado*, s.v. "hijo natural," "hijo espurio o bastardo," and "hijo adulterino o noto."

40. "El Dr. Medardo Medina como curador ad litem de Rosalía Mayora contra Juan José Sosa sobre alimentos," ARPDF, Civiles, 1839, Letra M, exp. 25.

41. "El Dr. Medardo Medina como curador," fol. 19v.

42. "Demanda por Nicolás Martines endosatario de Antonio Madrigal contra Micaela Ravelo por cobro de pesos, disese ahora contra Juan Jose Espinosa," ARPDF, Civiles, 1837, Letra M, exp. 41. The case of Micaela Ravelo's divorce is discussed in chap. 6.

43. "Demanda por Nicolás Martines," fol. 20r.

44. "Demanda por Nicolás Martines," fol. 21v.

45. Escriche y Martín, *Diccionario razonado*, s.v. "alimentos." See also *Siete Partidas*, law 2–5, title 19, partida 4.

46. [untitled: Juicios verbales de conciliación; Bacilia Ayala reclama pago de alimentos al padre de su hijo natural], ARPDF, Civiles, 1836, Letra C, exp. 10, fol. 30v–31v.

47. "Juan José Espinosa solicitando que Micaela Ravelo se restituya con los hijos que ha ocultado a la casa de su madre donde aquel la tenía," ARPDF, Civiles, 1836, Letra E, exp. 15, fol. 18r.; "Expediente promobido por la Señora Rosalía Canosa, contra su marido el Señor Ygnacio Hernández, sobre alimentos y litis expensas y entrega de bienes," ARPDF, Civiles, 1837, Letra C, exp. 253, fol. 43r.

48. See, for example, "Santiaga Torres pidiendo licencia judicial para contraer matrimonio," ARPDF, Civiles, 1837, Letra T, exp. 8, in which the tribunal made clear that they did not want to promote any scandals because the Torres family was "a very virtuous one."

49. See, for example, "No contensioso, Serafina España solicitando habilitación para casarse," ARPDF, Civiles, 1837, Letra E, exp. 15, fol. 3r; "Felipe Ponte pretendiendo esposarse con la señorita Manuela Ysabel Aldrei," ARPDF, Civiles, 1838, Letra P, exp. 21, fol. 1r.

50. See, for example, "Criminales contra José Yrrizarri por heridas," ARPDF, Civiles, 1838, Letra Y, exp. 3; "Criminales contra Teodora Castro por heridas," ARPDF, Civiles, 1839, Letra C, exp. 6.

51. See "Criminales contra Antonio Romero por aporreo," ARPDF, Civiles, 1837, Letra R, exp. 12; "Demandas de injurias propuesta por el podatario de Victorio Quevedo contra Josefa Jimenes," ARPDF, Civiles, 1838, Letra Q, exp. 1; "Criminales contra Teodora Castro."

52. These lawsuits include cases of theft, bodily harm, cutting and wounding, murder, and poisoning. All the victims and people accused of these crimes belonged to the lower classes, except in cases of theft, where four out of seven plaintiffs belonged to the upper classes.

53. "Testimonio de la sentencia pronunciada en la causa criminal seguida de oficio contra Guillermo Castell, su muger Vicenta Ochoa y sirvienta Manuela Benavides por el homicidio cometido en la persona de María de la Cruz, sierva de la señora Ana Salías, el dia 28 de octubre del año pasado de 1834," ARPDF, Criminales, 1836, Letra O, exp. 3.

54. "Conmutación de la pena de muerte impuesta a Vicenta Ochoa, en la de seis

años de confinación á la Isla de Margarita," AGN, Secretaría del Interior y Justicia, 1836, Tomo 133, fol. 111–60; "Vicenta Ochoa pide al Jefe de las reformas se le conmute la pena de muerte a que ha sido condenada por delitos comunes," AGN, Secretaría del Interior y Justicia, 1835, Tomo 108, fol. 105–7. Flyers entitled "Vicenta Ochoa y las garantías constitucionales" and "Vicenta Ochoa: muchas veces muerta" were distributed in the streets of Caracas arguing about the constitutionality of this death sentence. See "Testimonio de la sentencia," fol. 26r, 33r–33v. See also chap. 4.

55. "Criminales seguidos contra el siervo José Agustín por haber asecinado a la esclava Juliana en 23 de octubre de 1837," ARPDF, Criminales, 1837, Letra S, exp. 28.

56. "Sobre averiguar los autores y cómplices en el asesinato perpetrado en la persona del extranjero Miguel Muñoz, la noche del 19 de enero del presente año," ARPDF, Civiles, 1835, Letra H, exp. 7.

57. "Sobre averiguar los autores y cómplices," fol. 350r.

58. See "Contra Tomás Rodríguez por heridas y porrazos," ARPDF, Criminales, 1840, Letra R, exp. 6; "Criminales contra Teodora Castro por heridas," ARPDF, Criminales, 1839, Letra C, exp. 6; "Criminales contra Josefa Blanco por heridas y aporreos que dio a Josefa Carrasco," ARPDF, Criminales, 1836, Letra B, exp. 14; "Criminal contra Marcelina Pimentel por haber herido a José Santana Machado," ARPDF, Criminales, 1839, Libro NOP, Letra P, exp. 4. Penyak observed a similar pattern for Mexico City in his study of criminal sexuality between 1750 and 1850. Specifically, he found that men and women accused of adultery received comparable sentences ("Criminal Sexuality," 144–47).

6. CIUDADANAS VERSUS PADRES DE FAMILIA

1. Between 1796 and 1829 the gender ratios in Caracas remained rather constant, with an average of 1.6 women for every man. Computed from data in Lombardi, *People and Places*, 183–85, and Sociedad Económica de Amigos del País, *Anuario de la Provincia*, 32–35.

2. Waldron, "Social History," 127–37.

3. On the "race and class war," see Izard, *Miedo a la revolución*; Carrera Damas, *Boves*; and Vallenilla Lanz and Harwich Vallenilla, *Cesarismo democrático*, 19–37. These authors challenge the dominant historiography on independence, arguing that this period was one of many civil wars in which political independence was only one of the motives.

4. "La Sra. Micaela Ravelo solicitando se le habilite judicialmente para administrar por si los bienes que heredó de su padre Miguel Ravelo y sin la intervención de su marido el Sr. Juan José Espinoza," ARPDF, Civiles, 1836, Letra R, exp. 14, fol. 14r.

5. "La Sra. Micaela Ravelo solicitando," fol. 17v.

6. "Juan José Espinosa solicitando que Micaela Ravelo se restituya con los hijos que ha ocultado a la casa de su madre donde aquel la tenía," ARPDF, Civiles, 1836, Letra E, exp. 15, fol. 6v.

7. "Juan José Espinosa solicitando," fol. 6v.

8. "Juan José Espinosa solicitando," fol. 7r.

9. On *bienes parafernales*, see chap. 2, n. 64.

10. "Juan José Espinosa solicitando," fol. 8r.

11. "Juan José Espinosa solicitando," fol. 17v.

12. See Daitsman, "Unpacking the First Person Singular," código de procedimiento judicial de 19 de mayo de 1836, art. 18, law 1a, title 1a.

13. "Juan José Espinosa solicitando," fol. 18r.

14. "La Sra. Micaela Ravelo solicitando," fol. 37v–39r.

15. "Juan José Espinosa solicitando," fol. 7r; Escriche y Martín, *Diccionario razonado*, s.v. "bienes dotales," and "bienes estradotales."

16. "La Sra. Micaela Ravelo solicitando," fol. 42r.

17. "La Sra. Michaela Alcantara y Ravelo con su marido el Sr. Juan José Espinoza, sobre que se le prohiba la administración y manejo de sus bienes parafernales por las razones que ella alega," ARPDF, Civiles, 1836, Letra A, exp. 15, fol. 3v.

18. I did not find the Ravelo-Espinosa divorce lawsuit at the ecclesiastical archive, where the adultery claim would have been investigated.

19. Escriche y Martín, *Diccionario razonado*, s.v. "mujer casada" and "mujer pública"; Arrom, *Women of Mexico City*, 66–67.

20. "La Sra. Michaela Alcantara y Ravelo," fol. 7r.

21. "La Sra. Micaela Ravelo solicitando," fol. 38r.

22. Brown, *Good Wives*, 171.

23. "Criminales seguidos contra Rosario Canino y Ramón Yanes por haber sorprendido en el camino de la Vega al Sr. Crispín Oquendo para quitarle su mujer," ARPDF, Civiles, 1835, Letra C, exp. 27.

24. See "Juan José Espinosa solicitando," fol. 18v; "Expediente promobido por la Señora Rosalía Canosa," fol. 43r.

25. "Divorcio que prepara doña María Antonia Pérez á su legítimo marido don Ramón Maucó," AAC, Matrimoniales, 1811, leg. 187, fol. 2r.

26. According to Elías Pino Iturrieta, who studied one ecclesiastical lawsuit from him, Maucó accused María Antonia of adultery with a priest. See Pino Iturrieta, *Ventaneras*, 115–17.

27. *Litis-expensas* are the court costs. See Escriche y Martín, *Diccionario razonado*, s.v. "litisespensas."

28. "Expediente promobido por la Señora Rosalía Canosa," fol. 35r.

29. "Expediente promobido por la Señora Rosalía Canosa," fol. 35r.

30. "Josefa Maria Albelo con su marido Manuel Franco sobre que este se separe de

la administración de los bienes que ella aportó al matrimonio," ARPDF, Civiles, 1839, Letra A, exp. 10, pieza 1, fol. 2r.

31. See Porter, *Caracas Diary*; and De Grummond, *Caracas Diary*.

32. Arrom, *Women of Mexico City*, 111–21, 143–53.

33. "Divorcio que prepara doña María Antonia Pérez."

34. "Divorcio que prepara doña María Antonia Pérez," fol. 46–47.

35. "Expediente promobido por la Señora Rosalía Canosa," fol. 91–92.

36. "Expediente promobido por la Señora Rosalía Canosa," fol. 43r.

37. "Rosalía Canoso solicitando la posesión y entrega de una casa y esclava que aportó á su marido con Ygnacio Hernández," ARPDF, Civiles, 1838, Letra C, exp. 253, pieza 6.

38. "Josefa Maria Albelo con su marido Manuel Franco," fol. 109r.

39. "Incidencia sobre rendimiento de cuentas por Dionicia Albelo como depositaria de los bienes de su difunta hermana Josefa María en la causa seguida por esta sobre separación de la administración de aquellos, con su marido Manuel Franco Moreno," ARPDF, Civiles, 1840, Letra C, exp. 106, pieza 3.

40. "Manuel Franco Moreno con Dionicia Albelo sobre gananciales en el matrimonio del primero con Josefa Albelo de quien es heredera la segunda," ARPDF, Civiles, 1840, Letra M, exp. 30.

41. Hünefeldt, *Liberalism in the Bedroom*, 261, 362.

42. Boyer, "Women, 'La Mala Vida,' " 257.

43. Boyer, "Women, 'La Mala Vida,' " 279. See also Stern, *Secret History*.

44. Patricia Seed argues that by the eighteenth century changes in attitudes about control of property and acquisitiveness that accompanied capitalism provided for the reevaluation of the role of fathers, allowing them more authoritarian ways than they had had in the previous two centuries. Her work provides evidence of the changes in attitudes toward marriage by the early nineteenth century. The patriarchal and individual ideology was not universal; it applied most saliently to adult males involved in capitalist economic institutions. See Seed, *To Love, Honor and Obey*, 235–36.

45. I agree with Muriel Nazzari that, by the middle of the nineteenth century, marriage came to be viewed more as a tie between individuals, with love as an important aspect of the relationship. These relationships were mostly supported by the husband's work, as productive enterprises became entities separate from the family business by the second half of the 1800s. In this process the authority of husbands over wives may have increased. See Nazzari, *Disappearance*, 130–48. As I will discuss in the remainder of this chapter, this does not mean that material aspects of the relationships were not important. Both emotional and material aspects were vital in the relationships I studied in Caracas. Moreover, my findings show that patriarchal authority did increase in the late eighteenth and

early nineteenth centuries, but it was more evident in state policies than in the behavior of individuals.

46. See Lavrin, "Lo femenino."

47. See McCaa, "Gustos de los padres."

48. "Seguidos contra Ignacio Padrón por atribuirsele el hurto de diez mil pesos," ARPDF, Criminales, 1836, Letra P, exp. 7, pieza 1, fol. 101.

49. "Seguidos contra Ignacio Padrón," fol. 20v–21r.

50. "Pruebas de José Ignacio Padrón," fol. 3, 4.

51. "Pruebas de José Ignacio Padrón," fol. 15r.

52. "Pruebas de José Ignacio Padrón," fol. 108v–109r.

53. I thank Ricardo Salvatore for bringing this to my attention.

54. Pablo Rodríguez discusses the importance of these symbolic exchanges in *Seducción*, 29–30.

55. The fact that I am presuming a material link affecting female-male relationships does not mean that this was the only tie or reason for a couple to be together. See Stern, *Secret History*, 75–77. Muriel Nazzari has argued that the dowry was the foremost material incentive for men to contract marriage in colonial São Paulo. With the decline of the dowry, people's perception of marriage changed as well. See Nazzari, *Disappearance*, 159–61.

56. For a discussion of the issue of verbal deference and economic obligation, see Stern, *Secret History*, 70–75.

57. "Criminales contra Dionisio Vega por heridas," ARPDF, Civiles, 1840, Letra V, exp. 10.

58. "Criminales seguidos contra Ysabel Freytes por imputársele complicidad en el hurto de unas botellas de rapé a M.A. [Yeseirum]," ARPDF, Criminales, 1837, Letra F, exp. 2.

59. Arrom finds that the same holds true for poor women in Mexico City (*Women of Mexico City*, 176–84).

60. "Demanda propuesta por Cecilia Baraniz para que se obligue a su marido a acreditar que la sostiene con todo lo necesario, o a que no la impida trabajar en su profesión," ARPDF, Civiles, 1836, Letra B, exp. 6.

61. "Agustina Arnal demandando en conciliación a su legítimo marido Dionisio Acosta," ARPDF, Civiles, 1835, Letra M, exp. 10; "Sumaria información contra Dionicio Acosta instruida por el Juez de Paz 1° de la Parroquia de Sta. Rosalía por ante el escribano Juan José Medina," ARPDF, Civiles, 1836, Letra A, exp. 5; "Criminales contra Dionicio Acosta por vagancia," ARPDF, Civiles, 1836, Letra A, exp. 31; "Agustina Arnal se divorcia de su legítimo marido Dionicio Acosta," AAC, Matrimoniales, 1835, leg. 264.

62. "Juana Rafaela Casares quejándose de su marido," AAC, Matrimoniales, 1830, leg. 254.

63. Stern, *Secret History*, 78–85.

64. See, for example, "Demanda de divorcio de José de la Cruz Parra contra su muger Rosa María Pérez," AAC, Matrimoniales, 1832, leg. 257.

65. "Pedro Pablo Herrera contra su mujer Escolástica Gutierres por hebria," ARPDF, Civiles, 1839, Letra H, exp. s/n.

66. "Criminales contra Antonio Romero por aporreo," ARPDF, Civiles, 1837, Letra R, exp. 12. See also "Averiguación sumaria por la que resulta que la Sra. Aureliana Silvera vecina de esta parroquia, en uso de su defensa natural [illegible] repelendo, hirió a Cosme Orosco, vecino de la de Chacao," ARPDF, Criminales, 1836, Libro RS, Letra S, exp. 3.

67. See Stern, *Secret History*, 84–87. Kimberly Jane Morse also finds that many female litigants were quite assertive in nineteenth-century Aragua, Venezuela. See Morse, "Aún en la muerte separados," chap. 4.

68. I use James C. Scott's concept of dual "public" and "hidden" transcripts to uncover and discern actions through which Venezuelan women resisted domination from above. These actions range from highly visible ones that directly challenged those in power to less conspicuous acts of resistance expressed in everyday behavior. See Scott, *Domination*.

69. "Divorcio que prepara doña María Antonia Pérez a su legítimo marido don Ramón Maucó," AAC, Matrimoniales, 1811, leg. 187, fol. 46r–47r, my emphasis.

70. "Barbara Jedler quejándose contra el gobernador de la Provincia por el cruel castigo que ha hecho dar a su hijo Antonio Madriz, esclavo del Sr. Juan Pablo Huizi, por indicios de estar comprendido en una revolución que tramara," ARPDF, Civiles, 1835, Letra J, exp. 22, fol. 11r, my emphasis.

71. Cf. Cherpak, "Participation of Women," 230; Arrom, *Women of Mexico City*, 14–52.

7. BOURGEOIS CARACAS

1. Rafael Villavicencio, "Discurso pronunciado en el acto de repartición de premios de la ilustre universidad, el 8 de enero de 1869," in *Pensamiento político venezolano*, 13:70. This lecture was also published in the newspaper *El Federalista* between January and February 1869.

2. See Gil Fortoul, "Filosofía constitucional," 151–52, 188.

3. See Rafael Villavicencio, "Discurso pronunciado ante la ilustre universidad en el acto de repartición de premios, el dia 8 de diciembre de 1866," in *Pensamiento político venezolano*, 13:45–60.

4. Rafael Villavicencio, "Discurso de incorporación a la Academia Nacional de la Historia," in *Pensamiento político venezolano*, 13:101. On the instability between 1840 and 1870, see Matthews, *Violencia rural* and "La turbulenta década"; Pérez

Vila, "El gobierno deliberativo"; Frankel, "La Guerra Federal"; Gilmore, *Caudillism and Militarism*; Floyd, *Guzmán Blanco*; and Lombardi, *Venezuela*, 187–90.

5. Guzmán Blanco ruled directly during the years 1870–77 (the Septenio), 1879–84 (the Quinquenio), and 1886–88 (the Bienio). Two appointees of Guzmán Blanco (Francisco Linares Alcántara and Joaquín Crespo) governed during the interregnum years while he was in Europe. During Guzmán Blanco's last years as president Gen. Hermógenes López was in charge. See Wise, *Caudillo*, 65–76. *Diccionario de historia*, s.v. "Guzmán Blanco, Antonio," and "Guzmán Blanco, Antonio, Gobiernos de"; Quintero Montiel, coord., *Antonio Guzmán Blanco*.

6. Polanco Alcántara, *Guzmán Blanco*, 1–7.

7. Lombardi, *Venezuela*, 190–97.

8. Díaz Sánchez, *Guzmán*, 569.

9. Floyd, *Guzmán Blanco*, 80–83. The Compañía de Crédito was transformed into the Banco de Caracas, which merged with the Banco Comercial in 1885. See also González Deluca, *Negocios y política*.

10. Floyd, *Guzmán Blanco*, 80–96.

11. Floyd, *Guzmán Blanco*, 138–56.

12. Although Guzmán Blanco publicly identified himself with federalism, he did more than any other president to establish a centralized government. See Floyd, *Guzmán Blanco*, 197–99.

13. Floyd, *Guzmán Blanco*, 103–23.

14. Hale, "Political and Social Ideas," 240–41.

15. Carvalho, *Formação das almas*, 130. Carvalho provides an authoritative analysis of the political implications of Comtean philosophy in Brazil.

16. Carvalho, *Formação das almas*, 130.

17. Carvalho, *Formação das almas*, 9–15.

18. For an excellent synthesis of the cultural context of this period and an analysis of the hegemonic project and political discourse, see Skurski, "'Leader' and the 'People.'"

19. Vannini, *Influencia francesa*; Pino Iturrieta, *Mentalidad venezolana*.

20. Skurski, "'Leader' and the 'People,'" 56.

21. Wise, *Caudillo*, 163; Skurski, "'Leader' and the 'People,'" 55.

22. Wise, *Caudillo*, 168.

23. See Skurski, "'Leader' and the 'People,'" chap. 3.

24. Skurski, "'Leader' and the 'People,'" 76–79.

25. Skurski, "'Leader' and the 'People,'" 77.

26. See Germán Carrera Damas, *Culto a Bolívar*.

27. Skurski, "'Leader' and the 'People,'" 74.

28. Díaz Sánchez, *Guzmán*, 573.

29. O'Malley, *Myth of the Revolution*, 113, 141.

30. Julián Nava, "Illustrious American," 543.

31. See Esteva Grillet, *Guzmán Blanco*, 33–49.

32. Skurski, "'Leader' and the 'People,'" 78.

33. On the construction of national monuments, public works, and the promotion of the arts during the Guzmanato, see Esteva Grillet, *Guzmán Blanco*, 95–151; Skurski, "'Leader' and the 'People,'" 66; and Zawisza, *Arquitectura y obras públicas*, vol. 3.

34. Curtis, *Venezuela*, 153.

35. Skurski, "'Leader' and the 'People,'" 71.

36. González Ordosgoitti, "Estudio de la lucha cultural."

37. González Ordosgoitti, "Estudio de la lucha cultural," 193.

38. González Ordosgoitti, "Estudio de la lucha cultural," 194; Polanco Alcántara, *Guzmán Blanco*, 385–404; *Diccionario de historia*, s.v. "Guzmán Blanco, Antonio, Gobiernos de."

39. Decree of 28 September 1870; González Ordosgoitti, "Estudio de la lucha cultural," 194; *Diccionario de historia*, s.v. "Guzmán Blanco, Antonio, Gobiernos de."

40. For the text of all the decrees pertaining to the church, see González Oropeza, ed., *Iglesia y Estado*, 193–227.

41. As a freemason Guzmán Blanco disapproved of having different churches of various religions, because that situation could only produce more discord. In this period the masons flourished in Caracas. See Wise, *Caudillo*, 118–19; and Skurski, "'Leader' and the 'People,'" 69.

42. González Ordosgoitti, "Estudio de la lucha cultural," 201.

43. Ernst created the School of Natural History in 1874 and was in charge of the National Museum and the National Library, also founded in that decade. Villavicencio became Ministro de Fomento in 1870. Arturo Sosa considers the last three decades of the nineteenth century to be a transition period preceding the fulfillment of positivist thinking during Juan Vicente Gómez's regime (1908–35). See Sosa, *Ensayos*, 3–15.

44. Lemmo, *Educación en Venezuela*; Zawisza, *Arquitectura y obras públicas*, 3:16, 239–51.

45. The writing of an official history of Venezuela was undertaken by the regime. The official account of events gave most importance to independence and its leaders, especially Bolívar, while almost neglecting Venezuela's colonial and early republican history. As Skurski argues, "Bolívar and his fellow independence leaders thus were placed in the pantheon of providential heroes occupied by Greek heroes, figures of legend, and saints. Through the memorization of their deeds by students, particularly by girls, these tales of heroism and of

Christian sacrifice to the nation became part of the body of oral literature through which children were instructed at home" ("'Leader' and the 'People,'" 78–79).

46. Decree of 27 June 1870 and Decree of 23 May 1881, in Venezuela, *Recopilación de leyes y decretos de Venezuela*; *Diccionario de historia*, s.v. "educación."

47. Zawisza, *Arquitectura y obras públicas*, 3:17–18, 239–53; Lemmo, *Educación en Venezuela*; Leal, *Historia de la Universidad Central*.

48. "Diversiones y juegos públicos," *La Opinión Nacional*, 6 February 1869, p. 1.

49. "Un reclamo a la civilización del pueblo de Caracas," *La Opinión Nacional*, 9 February 1872, p. 2. See also "El carnaval venezolano," *La Opinión Nacional*, 14 February 1874, p. 2.

50. Rondón Márquez, *Guzmán Blanco*, 2:158–59. One newspaper article reported that the Caracas police shut off public water fountains to hamper the popular carnival games. But muleteers quickly brought water back into the city for the traditional carnival water battle. See "Agua va: Artículo escrito sobre el campo de batalla," *La Opinión Nacional*, 14 February 1872, p. 2.

51. Nava, "Illustrious American," 537.

52. The government avoided any reference to race and color, but this did not hinder racial prejudice in Venezuela. Racist views were expressed in other ways. On the one hand, urban elites kept using pejorative folk sayings to reinforce their racist views, and on the other, the construction of a discourse of racial improvement and government policies of European immigration gained stronger support in the late nineteenth and early twentieth centuries. Wright, *Café con Leche*, 43–68; Nava, "Illustrious American," 530–31.

53. European immigration had been fostered since the early republic without much success. For a further discussion on immigration, the church, and civil marriage, see chap. 8. Also see Wright, *Café con Leche*, 59–62.

54. Skurski, "'Leader' and the 'People,'" 53–54; Wright, *Café con Leche*, 62.

55. González Deluca, *Negocios y política*, 38; Lavenda, "First Modernizing Attempt," 153.

56. Sánchez-Albornoz, "Population of Latin America," 4:130.

57. Skurski, "'Leader' and the 'People,'" 68.

58. "Francisca Lameda de Vázquez contra su consorte Féliz Vázquez por divorcio," ARPDF, Civiles, 1878, Letra L, exp. 12, fol. 1r–2r.

59. Wise, *Caudillo*, 85.

60. Skurski, "'Leader' and the 'People,'" 84–85; Wise, *Caudillo*, 108–9; *Diccionario de Historia*, s.v. "La Delpiniada" and "Delpino y Lamas, Francisco Antonio."

61. Landes, *Women and the Public Sphere*, 172.

62. "La idea de lo futuro I," *La Opinión Nacional*, 18 November 1868, p. 1. Published from 1868 to 1892, *La Opinión Nacional* was the self-proclaimed printed advo-

cate of the regime. In addition to preaching a certain morality, the editorials also touched on more prosaic issues, like labor discipline and its relation to achieving peace. Remarking that a small population in a country as big as Venezuela did not allow for the consolidation of peace, the paper called for expedient economic and migration policies. In a land blessed with rich natural resources, the paper stated, peasants did not feel the need to work regularly (i.e., for wages) or to develop the industries because they could earn a livelihood from the irregular tilling of the land. The paper claimed that it was time for free peasants and urban peddlers to earn their living with their own work. The principle of private property became a relevant issue: limiting access to land could curb vagrancy, forcing people to work for the acquisition of their own property. The paper called for encouraging such work habits by increasing the population through foreign immigration, especially from Europe (preferably Germany) and from the southern United States. In the minds of newspaper commentators, Venezuelan laborers had to be disciplined and educated in good domestic habits by placing them in an atmosphere that forced them to work for a wage and through the good example provided by foreigners. See "La idea de lo futuro VIII. Vías de comunicación—Hábitos de órden y trabajo—Conclusión," *La Opinión Nacional*, 16 December 1868, p. 2; *Diccionario de historia*, s.v. "Guzmán Blanco, Antonio, Gobiernos de."

63. "Decadencia de la República," *La Opinión Nacional*, 9 January 1869, p. 1.

64. "Decadencia de la República," 1.

65. According to Carl Sach, who traveled across Venezuela between 1867 and 1877, Guzmán Blanco's title of "Regenerador" or the concept of "Regeneración" refer to the renaissance or pacification in Venezuela during his tenure. See Pino Iturrieta and Calzadilla, comps., *Mirada del otro*, 263, 258; Floyd, *Guzmán Blanco*, 36. One must point out, however, that Comtean philosophy also stressed the idea of "moral regeneration." Given Guzmán Blanco's leanings toward positivism, the borrowing of the idea of regeneración is not a coincidence. See Landes, *Women and the Public Sphere*, 177; Carvalho, *Formação das almas*, 129–30.

66. *La Opinión Nacional*, 15 December 1873.

67. In 1873 civil, penal, commercial, and military codes were established, as were rules of procedure for the effective application of the law. Corresponding to the cultural environment of the times, the Civil Code of 1873 was modeled after the Italian Code, which was considered an advanced version of the French Napoleonic Code. See Rangel Lamus, "Código Civil de 1873"; Bastidas "Historia del Código Civil," 41–42.

68. Skurski, "'Leader' and the 'People,'" 72–73.

69. "La idea de lo futuro II: Por dónde debe comenzar la reorganización del país," *La Opinión Nacional*, 21 November 1868, p. 1.

70. "Sermón: Sobre la misión cristiana de la mujer," *La Opinión Nacional*, 18 November 1868, p. 2. The sermon was delivered at the Santa Rosalía parish, which, along with Cathedral and Santa Teresa, were the three most prestigious parishes in Caracas in the late nineteenth century. Lavenda, "First Modernizing Attempt," 302–3. There are similarities between the way that priests in Michoacán portrayed the Virgin Mary during the Mexican Revolution and the case of Caracas. See Becker, *Setting the Virgin on Fire*, 13–19.

71. Indeed, although he was a clergyman, Father Riera always had liberal inclinations. The holder of a doctorate in theology from the University of Caracas, Riera had the reputation of being an accomplished speaker. He was active in the Federal Wars as chaplain of Gen. Ezequiel Zamora's army, which fought on the side of the liberals led by Antonio Leocadio Guzmán, the father of the future Regenerador. The Venezuelan Congress appointed Presbítero Riera to the bishoprics of Barquisimeto (1864) and Calabozo (1867), but on both occasions the Vatican rejected his candidacy. *Diccionario de historia*, s.v. "Riera Aguinagalde, Andrés Manuel."

72. Carvalho, *Formação das almas*, 130.

73. Riera set out a distinction between the condition of women in ancient and Christian times, one that resembled the dichotomy of *civilización* and *barbarie* so popular at the time. See, for example, "Cuestión de urbanidad," *La Opinión Nacional*, 13 May 1869, p. 1; and "Recreaciones del hogar," *La Opinión Nacional*, 5 May 1871, p. 1.

74. See Zagarri, "Rights of Man and Woman," 218. It is questionable, however, whether in Venezuela, as in the United States, this religious change gave women "spiritual equality" with men.

75. There are a number of examples in *La Opinión Nacional* in which the fear of women's struggles could be perceived. See, for example, "Derechos de las mujeres en Cuba," *La Opinión Nacional*, 24 March 1870, p. 2.

76. For analysts who have argued that Marianismo is a cult of female superiority, see Stevens, "Marianismo"; Jaquette, "Literary Archetypes"; and Arrom, *Women*, 259–68. In this chapter I stress briefly the links between religious ideas such as Marianismo and the political agenda with respect to women up to the late nineteenth century. The effects of Marianismo in its religious dimension in Venezuela as well as how it changed over time require further study.

77. "La madre y el niño," *La Opinión Nacional*, 7 March 1877, p. 1. These ideas mirrored those of Comte, who believed that, ideally, the woman who represented humanity was a thirty-year-old with a child in her arms. Carvalho, *Formação das almas*, 81.

78. On this issue, see Landes, *Women and the Public Sphere*, 169–200; Carvalho, *Formação das almas*, 130; and Soihet, *Condição feminina*, 111–13.

79. Research on the family in the nineteenth-century United States has shown similar patterns. An essential reading is Grossberg, *Governing the Hearth*, 289–307.

8. WOMEN, ORDER, AND PROGRESS

1. For an analysis of politics during the Guzmán Blanco period, see Floyd, *Guzmán Blanco*; González Deluca, *Negocios y política*; Lavenda, "First Modernizing Attempt"; and Lombardi, *Venezuela*.
2. Lavenda, "First Modernizing Attempt," 149, 246, 249.
3. I checked the elite status of some litigants by means of a list of wills and property values for the late nineteenth century. The list was compiled and kindly furnished to me by Dr. Derwin Munroe.
4. In the context of late-nineteenth-century Venezuela, rapto is the abduction of a female from her parental home for the purpose of living together but not necessarily getting married.
5. An exception is the case of "El General Nicomedes Ramírez en representación de Juana Bautista Córdova demanda a Pedro Pérez hijo, por esponsales," ARPDF, Civiles, 1879, Letra C, exp. 38. In this case the female victim of a seduction was an orphan who spent most of the day in the home without the guidance of her father. Yet the father found a legal representative who was successful in court. That was not the case in three other suits dealing with sex crimes involving the elites (two of them submitted by the same person). See "María del Carmen Benítez de Quintero en representación de su menor hija Magdalena Quintero contra Gregorio Domínguez por promesa de matrimonio," ARPDF, Civiles, 1879, Letra B, exp. 14; "Averiguación del rapto de la niña Magdalena Quintero," ARPDF, Criminales, 1879, Letra D, exp. 1; "María Catalina Hulpisch contra Matías Reverón, por esponsales," ARPDF, Civiles, 1877, Letra H, exp. 3.
6. See, for example, "Mercedes Mota contra Angel Acosta, por esponsales," ARPDF, Civiles, 1879, Letra M, exp. 47, fol. 10r; "María del Rosario León contra su marido Ramón López, por divorcio," ARPDF, Civiles, 1879, Letra L, exp. 12, fol. 7r.
7. In *Liberalism in the Bedroom*, Hünefeldt found that lawsuits filed by married women declined over the course of the nineteenth century (p. 350). There was also a drop in the number of ecclesiastical cases filed and won by women, while those by men increased between 1840 and 1910 (p. 346–47). She argues that although these trends have multiple explanations it is clear that men's power was reaffirmed in Lima's courts by the turn of the twentieth century. In Caracas, however, women from the lower classes increasingly sued men throughout the nineteenth century, even as the courts increasingly defended men's power in society. Eugenia Rodríguez Sáenz also found that the vast majority of lawsuits

were placed by lower-class women in Costa Rica between 1750 and 1850 and that the number of such suits increased over the course of the period. She relates this increase to the expansion of the judicial institutions. Rodríguez Sáenz, *Novias*, 111–54.

8. Women in Peru, Mexico, and the Southern Cone had a similar experience. See Hünefeldt, *Liberalism in the Bedroom*, 148–49, 185–78, 346–48; Arrom, "Changes in Mexican Family Law"; and Lavrin, *Women, Feminism, and Social Change*, 193–226.

9. See "José Prágedes Nuéz contra su consorte Ana Pérez, para que viva con él consumando [su] matrimonio o por la nulidad de éste," ARPDF, Civiles, 1876, Letra P, exp. 2; "Copia de la sentencia pronunciada en el juicio seguido por José Prágedes Nuez contra su consorte Ana Pérez para que convenga en la nulidad de su matrimonio," ARPDF, Civiles, 1876, Letra N, exp. 5; "Emilio Roo solicitando que su consorte María de Jesús Mejías le entregue sus hijas Ines, Luisa y Trinidad Roo," ARPDF, Civiles, 1876, Letra R, exp. 18; and "Juan Guillermo Castillo contra su consorte Merced María García para que se le obligue a volver a su consorte a llevar sus deberes conyugales," ARPDF, Civiles, 1877, Letra C, exp. 27.

10. Civil Code of 1873, art. 183. This practice, in which women had to request permission from a judge before doing any transaction, had been common since colonial times. For the late nineteenth century, see "María de las Nieves González sobre autorización para administrar sus bienes y los matrimoniales," ARPDF, Civiles, 1878, Letra G, exp. 20, fol. 5v; "María de la Merced Goicoechea de Herrera sobre autorización para administrar bienes," ARPDF, Civiles, 1877, Letra G, exp. 29; and "Brígida Isabel Gascón solicitando licencia de su marido para aceptar una donación," ARPDF, Civiles, 1876, Letra G, exp. 1.

11. Arrom has argued similarly for Mexico in "Changes in Mexican Family Law."

12. In 1867 the age of majority was lowered to twenty-three for males and twenty for females (art. 54). The ages established in 1873 remained the same in the 1896 code. Unlike Mexico, in subsequent codes Venezuela did not retain the 1862 requirement that women stay at home until age thirty. See Civil Code of 1862, bk. 1, title 3, law 2, chap. 2, art. 6; Arrom, *Women of Mexico City*, 33; Pérez Perdomo and San Juan, "Iguales."

13. Civil Code of 1873, art. 232, 285.

14. Civil Code of 1873, art. 231–54; "Juana Guevara contra Manuel Lugo por la entrega de su menor hija Dolores Guevara," ARPDF, Civiles, 1875, Letra G, exp. 7, fol. 65r–65v.

15. Grossberg, "Who Gets the Child?"

16. Article 208 of the Civil Code of 1873 established: "Queda prohibida toda inquisición acerca de la paternidad ilegítima, y ningún tribunal podrá admitir demanda ó gestión sobre ella." A similar law was enacted in the Civil Code of 1862

(bk. 1, title 5, law 4) and in the Civil Code of 1896 (art. 211), although the later code continues a special consideration that appeared in 1873 for cases of elopement or violent estupro. Republican paternity laws were influenced by the Spanish requirement for proof of paternity. Either the father had to recognize the child formally or there had to be positive proof of his cohabitation with the child's mother. See Escriche y Martín, *Diccionario razonado*, s.v. "paternidad"; and *Siete Partidas*, bk. 7, title 7, partida 4. In the nineteenth century the only way to verify paternity was by the father's recognition in a public document or by the later marriage of the child's parents.

17. The juridical system excluded modes of family organization other than formal marriage. The Penal Code of 1873 (art. 423) made concubinage a crime, especially if the couple lived a licentious life.

18. Sanojo discussed the need for a civil marriage law as early as 1858, when he was editor of the legal journal *El Foro*. At that time Sanojo held that a civil marriage law was needed to facilitate the lives of immigrants in Venezuela, because Venezuelan marriage laws at that time pertained only to Catholics. His article received a fierce response from Father Henrique María Castro in a publication titled *El matrimonio civil en Venezuela*.

19. Antonio José Sucre (Arcediano), "Matrimonio Civil," *La Opinión Nacional*, 12 February 1869, p. 2; "Matrimonio Civil," *La Opinión Nacional*, 24 February 1869, p. 2; and "Matrimonio Civil," 27 February 1869, p. 2.

20. Sanojo, *Instituciones de derecho*, 1:viii–ix.

21. "El sistema de colonización: Influencia en ella de la lei de matrimonio civil," *La Opinión Nacional*, 2 September 1873, p. 2.

22. "El sistema de colonización."

23. Polanco Alcántara, *Guzmán Blanco*, 385–404.

24. "El sistema de colonización."

25. Lavenda, "First Modernizing Attempt," 302.

26. The reforms implemented by one member of the second generation of positivists, José Gil Fortoul, are discussed in the conclusion.

27. Article 92 of the Civil Code of 1873 established that banns had to be posted for fifteen days.

28. Sanojo, *Instituciones de derecho*, 1:152–63.

29. Lavenda argues, "the total cost was to be Bs. 2, and although no one ever gives the exact figure for church marriage, all agree it was much too expensive for a poor man to afford" ("First Modernizing Attempt," 283). In 1915 Dr. Pedro Manuel Arcaya held that civil marriage was financially out of reach of proletarians and salaried workers. See Pérez Perdomo and San Juan, "Iguales."

30. Lavenda, "First Modernizing Attempt," 246, 300.

31. Civil Code of 1873, art. 118.

32. Lavenda, "First Modernizing Attempt," 287–89, also supports this argument.

33. Civil Code of 1873, art. 60–67.

34. This was the first time that a republican code allowed breach of promise claims, as the Civil Code of 1862 did not do so (title 3, law 1, art. 1–3). See *El Código Civil de Páez*. Authorities enforced the Civil Code of 1862 only briefly, however—from April to August 1863.

35. Pérez Perdomo and San Juan, "Iguales," 265.

36. Sanojo, *Instituciones de derecho*, 1:126.

37. Sanojo, *Instituciones de derecho*, 1:120–26. I found no lawsuit in which this situation occurred.

38. In two of these nine cases, at least one party was upper or middle class. In five cases the female plaintiffs had legally married parents. The middle class used the law on "breach of promise" successfully, because they valued marriage for keeping or improving their social position. This fact emerges clearly from the other thirty-four cases: where the female plaintiffs were lower class and had unmarried parents, adverse decisions usually resulted. "Zoila Antonia Mosquera contra Ricardo Lezama por esponsales," ARPDF, Civiles, 1876, Letra M, exp. 19; "Sofía Díaz contra Miguel Gerónimo Velázquez por esponsales," ARPDF, Civiles, 1875, Letra D, exp. 10; "Sofía Domínguez contra Francisco Aguiar, por esponsales," ARPDF, Civiles, 1877, Letra D, exp. 10; "Ursula Key por su menor hija Susana contra Antolín Iriarte, por esponsales," ARPDF, Civiles, 1877, Letra K, exp. 1; "Tomasa Muñoz contra Ramón Montilla, por esponsales," ARPDF, Civiles, 1877, Letra M, exp. 2; "Augusta Velázquez contra Félix María Bosa, por promesa de matrimonio," ARPDF, Civiles, 1878, Letra V, exp. 14; "Carmen Figuera a nombre de su hija Rosario Díaz demanda a Rafael E. Alvarado por esponsales," ARPDF, Civiles, 1879, Letra F, exp. 16; "Luisa López contra Juan Antonio Sucre, por esponsales," ARPDF, Civiles, 1879, Letra L, exp. 6; and "Mercedes Mota contra Angel Acosta, por esponsales," ARPDF, Civiles, 1879, Letra M, exp. 47.

39. "Mercedes Mota contra Angel Acosta," fol. 17r.

40. "Zoila Antonia Mosquera contra Ricardo Lezama."

41. "Candelaria Manzo contra Ricardo Lezama por esponsales," ARPDF, Civiles, 1875, Letra M, exp. 26, fol. 41v.

42. "Zoila Antonia Mosquera contra Ricardo Lezama," fol. 20r, 21r.

43. "Basilia Domínguez contra Francisco Aguiar, por esponsales," ARPDF, Civiles, 1877, Letra D, exp. 10; and "Carmen Figuera a nombre de su hija Rosaura Díaz demanda a Rafael E. Alvarado por esponsales," ARPDF, Civiles, 1879, Letra F, exp. 16.

44. "El General José Nicomedes Ramírez en representación de Juana Bautista Córdova demanda a Pedro Pérez hijo por esponsales," ARPDF, Civiles, 1879, Letra C, exp. 38.

45. "El General José Nicomedes Ramírez," fol. 47v–48r.

46. "El General José Nicomedes Ramírez," fol. 63r.

47. "Luisa López contra Juan Antonio Sucre," fol. 28r.

48. Among colonial Spanish American male elites, multiple relationships did happen with some frequency and, as a consequence, they encountered legal complications. In these cases, the Cámara, a body within the Council of the Indies in Spain in charge of dispensing legitimations among other special favors, did take into consideration the plight of the other women who had been offered marriage and the legitimation of their natural children. Twinam, *Private Lives*, 101–2.

49. "Candelaria Manzo," fol. 42r. See also "Tomasa Muñoz contra Ramón Montilla."

50. While illegitimacy was common in Venezuela, a child born outside marriage but recognized by the father did not bear the same social stigma as an unacknowledged child. The latter case could imply that the child was a bastard, born of a mother and father unable to marry (i.e., in an adulterous, incestuous, or sacrilegious union), suggesting that the woman had an immoral and illegal relationship. We see this situation in a word used in colonial and nineteenth-century Venezuela: *botado*, or throwaway. The term disparages foundlings, who often were born of illegal relationships. Moreover, natural and illegitimate children had different legal rights. Three sources discuss the distinctions: for Brazil, see Lewin, "Natural and Spurious Children"; for Spanish America, see Twinam, *Public Lives*, 133–39; and Escriche y Martín, *Diccionario razonado*, s.v. "hijo legítimo," "hijo natural," and "hijo espúrio o bastardo."

51. In terms of the juridical procedure, a divorce lawsuit followed the same steps as an ordinary trial, with the exception that the court was required to promote conciliation between the parties. After the suit was brought to court, the judge summoned both parties to an initial hearing in ten days, where he invited them to reconcile. If that was not possible, a new citation was issued one hundred days after a reply to the lawsuit was made. If a settlement was impossible in that time, a marriage counselor for the defense was appointed and the trial continued as usual. See Code of Civil Procedure of 1873, art. 37.

52. *Siete Partidas*, law 7, title 9, partida 4.

53. Civil Code of 1873, art. 152, number 1. In Paez's Penal Code of 1862 adultery could be committed by both women and men. (title II, law 1, art. 1); see Biblioteca Nacional de la Historia, *Codificación de Páez*, 333. This innovation was carried on to the Penal Code of 1873 (art. 415).

54. Voluntary abandonment of the marital home was not a cause for divorce under Spanish law. In the 1875–80 sample seventeen cases claimed divorce on grounds of adultery and thirty for abuse and/or abandonment.

55. Escriche y Martín, *Diccionario razonado*, s.v. "disolución de matrimonio" and "divorcio"; *Siete Partidas*, bk. 1, laws 12, 15, and 17 title 5, partida 4; and Civil Code of 1873, art. 126, 130.

56. Civil Code of 1873, art. 127, 131. The latter article put an official end to clandestine marriages, which were possible under canon law.

57. "Jesús María González Bello contra José de la Presentación Sánchez y Carolina Ragas por la nulidad del matrimonio contraído por éste," ARPDF, Civiles, 1877, Letra G, exp. 44; and "Isabel Hernández de Mendivil contra Antonio de Mendivil y Salomé Mendivil por la nulidad de matrimonio contraído por éstos," ARPDF, Civiles, 1878, Letra H, exp. 17.

58. "Copia de la sentencia pronunciada . . . José Prágedes Nuez contra su consorte."

59. The colonial sample (1786–91) showed 8 divorce cases (out of a sample of 139 cases), in which the court granted only 2 temporal divorces and 1 perpetual divorce. Two were withdrawn, and 3 records were incomplete. The early republican sample (1835–40) shows 22 different claims out of a total of 240. Of these 22, only 9 had a verdict and only 6 were approved.

60. The story of the world-acclaimed Venezuelan pianist and composer Teresa Carreño reveals the elite stance toward divorce. In 1886 Guzmán Blanco asked her to organize the opera season in Caracas. Because Carreño was divorced and had even remarried in Europe, a great scandal at the time, Venezuelan elites shunned her and boycotted her shows and performances, making the season a complete failure. Because her extraordinary talents were not matched by morally acceptable behavior, Carreño could not be acceptable to the elite. *Diccionario de historia*, s.v. "Carreño, Teresa."

61. Wives litigated most of the divorce cases (76 percent), as in the earlier samples. Yet by the late nineteenth century more men sued for divorce, all accusing their wives of adultery.

62. "María Teresa Belsinger contra Juan Bautista Acereto por divorcio," ARPDF, Civiles, 1875, Letra B, exp. 5, fol. 32v–33r.

63. "María Teresa Belsinger contra Juan Bautista Acereto," fol. 39r.

64. "María Teresa Belsinger contra Juan Bautista Acereto," fol. 51v–52r.

65. "María Teresa Belsinger contra Juan Bautista Acereto," fol. 52v.

66. "María Teresa Belsinger contra Juan Bautista Acereto," fol. 52v–53r.

67. See Scott, *Gender and the Politics of History*, 47.

68. "Manuela Blandín de López contra su marido Juan Evangelista, por divorcio," ARPDF, Civiles, 1880, Letra B, exp. 33; and "Luis Felipe Delgado contra su consorte Teolinda Hernández por divorcio," ARPDF, Civiles, 1879, Letra D, exp. 17. The Corte de Casación is roughly equivalent to an appellate court in the United States, although the Venezuelan institution is based on the French model. The term *cassation* derives from the French *casser*, which means "to quash." This re-

fers to the nullification of judicial decisions by lower courts based on erroneous interpretations of the statutes. See Merryman, *Civil Law Tradition*, 39–41. On the evolution of this judicial organ in Venezuela, see *Diccionario de historia*, s.v. "poder judicial."

69. "Luis Felipe Delgado contra su consorte," fol. 36r.

70. "Mercedes García contra Juan Bautista Castillo por divorcio," ARPDF, Civiles, 1878, Letra G, exp. 52; and "Serapio Martínez contra su consorte Ramona Delgado por divorcio," ARPDF, Civiles, 1878, Letra M, exp. 3.

71. The word *estupro* disappeared in the 1897 Penal Code, and jail sentences for violación became harsher. See 1897 Penal Code, art. 338–46.

72. See articles 428–31 on estupro and articles 423–27 on violación in the Civil Code of 1873. Although article 428 establishes that estupro is sexual intercourse with a virgin older than twelve years of age, article 423 (number 3) includes under estupro the nonviolent crime against girls who are older than ten.

73. If the aggressor was a close relative, the Civil Code of 1873 (art. 430) specified that a harsher punishment would be considered.

74. See Pino Iturrieta, *Ventaneras*.

75. "Proceso de estupro. Inculpado: Juan Machado," ARPDF, Criminales, 1879, Letra M, exp. 39.

76. This contrasts with the questions asked of the defendant, Juan Machado. The tribunal queried him about the victim—if he knew where she worked, who raped her, and why he was arrested. "Proceso de estupro," fol. 6v–7r.

77. This happened, for instance, in the claim against Juan Machado discussed and in "Criminal contra Felipe Kuey por imputársele el delito de estupro por fuerza," ARPDF, Criminales, 1878, Letra K, exp. 1.

78. See "Criminal contra Vicente Berthier Tompson por violación," ARPDF, Criminales, 1875, Letra B, exp. 2; "Proceso de estupro"; and "Sumario seguido contra Ildefonso León por violación perpetrado en la persona de Trinidad Bigot," ARPDF, Criminales, 1877, Letra L, exp. 2.

79. "Contra Juan Ramón Gómez por violación de la impúber Isabel Hernández," ARPDF, Criminales, 1880, Letra G, exp. 9, fol. 30v–31r.

80. This is clear in the law dealing with bodily injuries in which only serious, handicapping injuries would carry a punishment. Causing minor lesions would not be punished, even if they were caused by a padre de familia. See Civil Code of 1873, art. 368–78.

81. See "Contra Juan Ramón Gómez"; "Sumario seguido contra Ildefonso León," fol. 28; and "Contra Ricardo Ramos por el delito de violación," ARPDF, Criminales, 1876, Letra R, exp. 5, fol. 36–37r.

82. Ildefonso León admitted that he was "embromándola pretendiendo ofenderla, pero no resultó," and Juan Ramón Gómez said that "se abstuvo de hacer lo que

se había prometido." "Sumario seguido contra Ildefonso León," fol. 8v; "Contra Juan Ramón Gómez," fol. 2r.

83. The terms *fianza de cárcel segura* and *libertad provisional* are not equivalent to *probation* in English. In Venezuela, someone under libertad provisional in the late nineteenth century was not necessarily convicted of a crime; the person had been accused of committing an offense, and a judgment on the guilt of the defendant had not necessarily been issued.

84. Code of Criminal Procedure, art. 110. This type of outcome, in which an aggressor was freed on bail because the injuries were not severe, was common in cases of physical abuse, bodily harm, and injuries. See, for example, "Criminal contra Pedro Pablo Vera por golpes," ARPDF, Criminales, 1878, Libro UV, Letra V, exp. 2; "Lucia Acosta, heridas," ARPDF, Criminales, 1879, Letra A, exp. 2; "Averiguación contra Julián Acosta, por golpes dados a su padre natural Víctor Aguilar," ARPDF, Criminales, 1879, Letra A, exp. 4; "Averiguación sobre unos golpes que dice la Sra. Rafaela Arias de Llaguno le infirió su marido Emiliano Llaguno," ARPDF, Criminales, 1880, Libro LM, Letra ll, exp. 1; "Ynstrucción sumaria sobre una herida inferida a Reyes Madera," ARPDF, Criminales, 1878, Libro HJK, Letra H, exp. 6; "Contra Santos Machado por herida," ARPDF, Criminales, 1878, Letra M, exp. 6; and "Averiguación sobre una herida que le fue inferida por Andrés Sánchez a Rosaura González," ARPDF, Criminales, 1880, Letra S, exp. 2.

85. Code of Criminal Procedure, art. 112, 117.

86. Code of Criminal Procedure, art. 113–114. Men under age twenty-one and women were not entitled to be sponsors according to this code.

87. Eileen J. Findlay argues similarly for Puerto Rico. During the early years of U.S. rule on the island, the colonial government intended to promote formal marriages among Puerto Ricans by making full divorce possible. See Findlay, "Love in the Tropics."

9. CONTESTING GENDER MEANINGS FROM BELOW

1. "María Teresa Belsinger contra Juan Bautista Acereto por divorcio," ARPDF, Civiles, 1875, Letra B, exp. 5, fol. 58v. María Teresa seemed to have written the letter herself with the help of a scribe, because she did not know how to read or write. According to the record she personally brought the letter to the court.

2. "Mercedes García contra Juan Bautista Castillo por divorcio," ARPDF, Civiles, 1878, Letra G, exp. 52, fol. 15r–15v. The term *natural law* in this context refers, according to Escriche, to "el que la naturaleza ha enseñado á [*sic*] los hombres y á [*sic*] todos los animales; como por ejemplo la union [*sic*] del macho y la hembra, el deseo de la conservación de la especie, la crianza de los hijos, el amor de la li-

bertad, y la defensa personal. Pero aquí la palabra derecho no se toma sino en un sentido impropio y extenso; pues los brutos, como incapaces de raciocinio, lo son tambien [*sic*] de derecho." See Escriche y Martín, *Diccionario razonado*, s.v. "derecho natural."

3. An important goal of many Caribbean historians has been to understand the ways in which the lower classes, especially Afro-Caribbean peoples, have creatively dealt with and participated in their history. See, for example, Mintz, *Caribbean Transformations*; and Price, "An Absence of Ruins?"

4. See Lazarus-Black and Hirsh, eds., *Contested States*.

5. Johnson and Lipsett-Rivera, eds., *Faces of Honor*.

6. See Scott, *Domination*, 196–97.

7. I found only two cases (one upper class and one lower class) in which women used their husband's last name in the early nineteenth century and none for the late colonial period.

8. Examples of cases in which married female plaintiffs mentioned dominant feminine values and expected men to change their conduct include: "Rosalía Azcárate contra su marido Tomás González Silva, por divorcio," ARPDF, Civiles, 1878, Letra A, exp. 31; and "Belén María Rodríguez contra Gregorio López por divorcio," ARPDF, Civiles, 1879, Letra R, exp. 22, fol. 1v.

9. "Francisca Lameda de Vázquez contra su consorte Féliz Vázquez por divorcio," ARPDF, Civiles, 1878, Letra L, exp. 12, fol. 14v–15r.

10. "Francisca Lameda de Vázquez contra su consorte Féliz Vázquez."

11. See Stern, *Secret History*, 70–75.

12. For a discussion on how feminists used their roles as mothers to legitimize the struggle for better rights for women, see Lavrin, *Women, Feminism, and Social Change*.

13. "Juana Rita Buerta de Pompa contra Tomás Ramón Hernández por rapto," ARPDF, Criminales, 1880, Libro GH, Letra H, exp. 2, fol. 8v.

14. Manuela Méndez de Navarro also invoked her rights as a mother in "Averiguación sumaria seguida contra José María Olivo hijo por rapto y estupro," ARPDF, Criminales, 1878, Libro OPQ, Letra O, exp. 1, fol. 12v. See also "María Teresa Belsinger contra Juan Bautista Acereto," fol. 2.

15. "Bernardo Quintero contra Amalia Bolívar, por la entrega de su hija natural Luisa Quintero," ARPDF, Civiles, 1876, Letra Q, exp. 54, fol. 11r–11v.

16. "Luisa Piñango de Morales contra su marido Juan Cleofe Morales, por divorcio," ARPDF, 1879, Civiles, Letra P, exp. 1, fol. 6r.

17. "Brígida Isabel Gascón solicitando licencia de su marido para aceptar donación," ARPDF, Civiles, 1876, Letra G, exp. 1, fol. 5r–6r.

18. "Diligencias practicadas por la Gobernación con motivo de varias contusiones que le infirió José Tomás Gil a su esposa Isolina Hernández de Gil," ARPDF,

Criminales, 1878, Libro ABCFGHI, Letra G, exp. 20, fol. 5r–5v. See also "Mercedes García contra Juan Bautista Castillo," fol. 32r–32v.

19. "Belén María Rodríguez contra Gregorio López por divorcio," ARPDF, Civiles, 1879, Letra R, exp. 22, fol. 15r–15v. See also the case of Serapio Martínez, whose legal representative claimed that Serapio's wife had become "a rebellious woman who does not fulfill her duties." "Serapio Martínez contra su consorte Ramona Delgado por divorcio," ARPDF, Civiles, 1876, Letra M, exp. 3, fol. 25r.

20. See, for example, "Autos promovidos por doña María Manuela Roxas contra don Josef María Rivera sobre que contraiga matrimonio con ella," AAC, Matrimoniales, 1790, leg. 110, fol. 7r.

21. This was common not only in Venezuela but also in Cuba and in the Mediterranean world. See Pino Iturrieta and Lange, coords., *Quimeras*; and Martínez-Alier, *Marriage, Class, and Colour*, 120–21.

22. See chap. 6. For an excellent discussion of the male code of honor in colonial Mexico, see Stern, *Secret History*, 11–16.

23. "Daniel Martínez en representación de su hija Mercedes, contra Vicente Sanabria por esponsales," ARPDF, Civiles, 1875, Letra M, exp. 7, fol. 1v.

24. "Brígida Isabel Gascón solicitando licencia," fol. 5r–6r.

25. Lavenda, "First Modernizing Attempt," 232–33; and Nava, "Illustrious American," 533–34.

26. Lavenda, "First Modernizing Attempt," 227.

27. From Bolívar, who was known for having various lovers (in particular, the Ecuadorian Manuelita Sáenz), and José Antonio Páez, who abandoned his wife, doña Dominga Ortiz de Páez, to be with his lover, to recent president Carlos Andrés Pérez, presidents and their lovers are publicly known in Venezuela. (During his reelection campaign President Rafael Caldera took pride in having one stable family.) See Troconis de Veracoechea, *Indias*, 190; and Troconis de Veracoechea, *Gobernadoras*.

28. Lavenda, "First Modernizing Attempt," 226.

29. See, for example, "María de los Santos Yanes contra su consorte Encarnación Blanco por divorcio," ARPDF, 1876, Letra Y, exp. 7, fol. 1r; "Francisca Lameda de Vázquez contra su consorte Féliz Vázquez"; and "María Evarista Pérez contra su marido Jesús María Romero, por alimentos," ARPDF, Civiles, 1879, Letra P, exp. 4.

30. See "Sumario seguido contra Ildefonso León," fol. 1v, 8v; "Contra Juan Ramón Gómez," fol. 2r.

31. "Juana Rita Buerta de Pompa," fol. 3v. See also "Luisa López contra Juan Antonio Sucre," fol. 28r.

32. "El General José Nicomedes Ramíres," fol. 27r.

33. One thing that caught the attention of some late-nineteenth-century travelers

in Caracas was how women and men socialized in separate spheres. See Pino Iturrieta and Calzadilla, comps., *Mirada del otro*, 302; and Lavenda, "First Modernizing Attempt," 228.

34. See "Contra Antonio Mendivil por el delito de bigamia," ARPDF, Criminales, 1877, Letra M, exp. 1, fol. 37r; "Juana Rita Buerta de Pompa," fol. 2r; and "Mercedes García contra Juan Bautista Castillo," fol. 1v.

35. "Mercedes Mota contra Angel Acosta." The verdict of this case was discussed in chap. 8.

36. *Negra* or *mi negra*, literally "my black one," is a term of endearment frequently used in the Spanish Caribbean and Brazil (*nego* or *neguinho*). This phrase was used by lower classes in my late-nineteenth-century sample usually to demonstrate love to someone of mixed-race or black ancestry. Nowadays everyone uses this term of endearment, regardless of the color of the person to whom the affection is addressed. It is used to express love to a partner, a son or daughter, a relative, or even a friend. Winthrop R. Wright discusses the sexual meaning of the word *negrita*: "Ironically, black and pardo women epitomized sexuality, sensuality, and beauty in Venezuela, and lovers often used the words negrita and *morena* (female black) as terms of endearment. In fact, even to this day, Venezuelan men consider tan-skinned women, or morenas, the most appealing type of beauty. As one refrain put it: 'The man who might die / Without loving a morena / Leaves this world for another / without having known a good thing'" (*Café con Leche*, 45).

37. "Luisa López contra Juan Antonio Sucre."

38. Several authors and travelers have highlighted the "window culture" of Caracas. See Pino Iturrieta and Calzadilla, comps., *Mirada del otro*, 257. The window as a place of socialization was mentioned in the cases in my sample. See, for example, "Ursula Key por su menor hija Susana contra Antolín Yriarte, por esponsales," ARPDF, Civiles, 1877, Letra K, exp. 1, fol. 23r.

39. "Contra Isidoro Jocko por rapto," ARPDF, Criminales, 1880, Letra J, exp. 2.

40. "Contra Isidoro Jocko por rapto," fol. 21r.

41. "Contra Isidoro Jocko por rapto," fol. 9r.

42. "Contra Isidoro Jocko por rapto," fol. 87r–88r. In Spanish America as well as in republican Venezuela, the criminal prosecutor or *fiscal en lo criminal* is a qualified attorney who gives his opinion on the merits of the case to the court. In particular, the fiscales point out any error in the technical aspects of legal procedure. See Cutter, *Legal Culture*, 53, 105.

43. "Mercedes García contra Juan Bautista Castillo," fol. 1r.

44. "Simón Avilán a nombre de su hija María Antonia contra Leandro Orta por esponsales," ARPDF, Civiles, 1880, Letra A, exp. 32, fol. 2v.

45. "Simón Avilán a nombre de su hija María Antonia," fol. 5r.

46. "Violante Mijares contra Carlos Ascanio, por esponsales," ARPDF, Civiles, 1877, Letra M, exp. 15.

47. "Violante Mijares contra Carlos Ascanio," fol. 1r.

48. "Violante Mijares contra Carlos Ascanio," fol. 18.

49. "Violante Mijares contra Carlos Ascanio," fol. 21r.

50. "Candelaria Manzo," fol. 42r.

51. "María Teresa Belsinger contra Juan Bautista Acereto," fol. 1v. Similar arguments appear in "Bibiana Aponte conta su consorte Juan José Fuentes por divorcio," ARPDF, Civiles, 1875, Letra A, exp. 7.

52. "Averiguación sumaria contra José María Olivo por rapto y estupro," ARPDF, Criminales, 1878, Libro OPQ, Letra O, exp. 1.

53. "Averiguación sumaria contra José María Olivo," fol. 7v.

54. "Averiguación sumaria contra José María Olivo," fol. 11r–11v.

55. "Averiguación sumaria contra José María Olivo," fol. 12v.

56. "Contra Jesús María Jiménez por rapto," ARPDF, Criminales, 1879, Libro JL, Letra J, exp. 1, fol. 2v–3r.

57. "Santos Ojeda de Monasterios contra Juan Hernández por el rapto de su sobrina Salomé Cabrera," ARPDF, Criminales, 1880, Libro GH, Letra H, exp. 3.

58. "Santos Ojeda de Monasterios contra Juan Hernández," fol. 3r–3v.

59. "Santos Ojeda de Monasterios contra Juan Hernández," fol. 4v–5r.

60. See "Criminal contra Felipe Kuey por imputársele el delito de estupro con fuerza," ARPDF, Criminales, 1878, Libro HJK, Letra K, exp. 1, fol. 23r; "Proceso de rapto inculpado, Rafael Chapellín," ARPDF, Civiles, 1879, Letra Ch, exp. 5, fol. 4r.

61. See "Proceso de rapto inculpado, Rafael Chapellín"; and "Averiguación del rapto de la niña Magdalena Quintero," ARPDF, Criminales, 1879, Letra D, exp. 1. See also the case of the three young daughters (ages twelve, fourteen, and seventeen) of a French carpenter who were socially recognized as "hijas de familia." The girls left their home to be with their boyfriends but confessed that they had previously lost their virginity to other men. The three accused lovers had offered marriage to them. "Juan Mec por el rapto de tres hijas suyas contra Jacinto González, Carlos Vera y Leopoldo Hernández," ARPDF, Criminales, 1880, Libro GH, letra G, exp. 11.

62. See "Isabel Cásares contra su consorte José Dolores Alvarado, por divorcio," ARPDF, Civiles, 1876, Letra L, exp. 2, fol. 13v; "Francisca Lameda de Vázquez contra su consorte Féliz Vázquez," fol. 4v, 6v; "María de Jesús Romero contra su marido Pedro Celestino Ruiz por divorcio," ARPDF, Civiles, 1879, Letra R, exp. 20, fol. 1r; "Belén María Rodríguez contra Gregorio López por divorcio," ARPDF, Civiles, 1879, Letra R, exp. 22, fol. 2v; "Criminal contra Pedro Pablo Vera por golpes," ARPDF, Criminales, 1878, Libro UV, Letra V, exp. 2; and "Lucía Acosta herida," ARPDF, Criminales, 1879, Letra A, exp. 2.

63. Lavenda, "First Modernizing Attempt"; "Legitimación de José Vicente del Carmen, hijo de Juan Ramón García y María del Rosario Requez," AAC, Matrimoniales, 1872, leg. 329; "Legitimación de Francisca Amalia, hija de Federico Parra y Soledad Echeverría, antes del matrimonio que después cotrajeron," AAC, Matrimoniales, 1872, leg. 329; "Legitimación de José de la Merced y María Dolores hijos de Antonio Perez y Josefa Avila antes del matrimonio que contrajeron," AAC, Matrimoniales, 1872, leg. 329; "Legitimación de Rafael Gregorio, Federico, Elidoro, Josefa Eugenia y Clara Dolores hijos de los Sres. Federico Alvarez y Josefa Benitez antes del matrimonio," AAC, Matrimoniales, 1872, leg. 329; "Legitimación de Angel María y Rafael María hijos de Manuel Rivas y Belen Rosales, antes el matrimonio que contrajeron," AAC, Matrimoniales, 1876, leg. 331; "Legitimación de Dolores Bernarda de Jesus," AAC, Matrimoniales, 1876, leg. 331; "Legitimación de Juan Evangelista, Ysabel María de los Remedios, Juan de Dios y José Norberto Espinosa," AAC, Matrimoniales, 1878, leg. 333; [untitled: Legitimación de Felipa Navarro], AAC, Matrimoniales, 1879, leg. 333; and "Legitimaciones", AAC, Matrimoniales, 1879, leg. 333. I suspect that there are more legitimations in another collection of the AAC.

64. "Contensioso. Justo Ubisco contra su esposa por divorcio," ARPDF, Civiles, 1879, Letra U, exp. 4, fol. 52v.

65. "Carolina Hernández contra Juan Nepomuceno Alcántara por esponsales," ARPDF, Civiles, 1876, Letra H, exp. 6.

66. There are a number of cases of breach of promise in which women sued their male partners because they were going to marry other women, leaving the plaintiffs with their natural children. Of ten such cases, five were settled by the men agreeing to provide support, two were dropped for unknown reasons (probably the couple reached an agreement), two were incomplete or inconclusive, and in only one case was a verdict pronounced (and it favored the defendant because the woman was considered not virtuous). See, for example, "Carolina Hernández contra Juan Nepomuceno Alcántara"; "Mercedes Sojo contra Alejandro Bolívar, por esponsales," ARPDF, Civiles, 1875, Letra S, exp. 24; "Agueda Herrera en representación de su hija Dominga contra Mamerto Tovar y Banderlinder, por esponsales," ARPDF, Civiles, 1878, Letra H, exp. 29; and "Asención García contra Gregorio Rodríguez, por esponsales," ARPDF, Civiles, 1877, Letra G, exp. 38. Although money was an important aspect for poor women, the cases lead me to believe that women felt it was crucial to make men comply with their part of the responsibilities. Mindie Lazarus-Black makes a similar argument for Antigua in "Why Women Take Men to Magistrate's Court."

67. Lavenda, "First Modernizing Attempt," 288.

68. See, for example, "Tomasa Muñoz contra Ramón Montilla, por esponsales,"

ARPDF, Civiles, 1877, Letra M, exp. 2. In this case Tomasa Muñoz filed a suit against her boyfriend, Ramón Montilla, whom she had been with for seven years. Ramón got engaged to another woman named María de Jesús. Tomasa aspired to a marriage with him so that their two children would become legitimate and enjoy "social representation" (fol. 5r). The court decided that Ramón was obliged to marry María de Jesús and not Tomasa. See also "Casimira Palacios contra Concepción Turipe, por esponsales," ARPDF, Civiles, 1876, Letra S, exp. 6, fol. 1v. Casimira Palacios also aspired to legitimate her children by persuading her boyfriend to honor his promise of marriage.

69. Lavenda, "First Modernizing Attempt," 289.

70. See, for example, "Contensioso. Justo Ubisco"; and "Dominga Monasterios contra Silverio Mujica, por esponsales" ARPDF, 1877, Letra M, exp. 54, fol. 1r.

71. See "María de los Santos Yanes"; "Rosalia Azcarate contra su marido Tomas González Silva, por divorcio," ARPDF, Civiles, 1878, Letra A, exp. 31; "Averiguación sobre unos golpes que dice la señora Rafaela Arias de Llaguno le infirió su marido Emiliano Llaguno," ARPDF, Criminales, Libro LM, Letra ll, exp. 1; "Bibiana Aponte contra su consorte Juan Jose Fuentes por divorcio," ARPDF, Civiles, 1875, Letra A, exp. 7; and "Eusebia Hernández de Hijuelo contra su consorte Andrés Hijuelo Llaguno, por divorcio," ARPDF, 1878, Fondo: Civiles, Letra H, exp. 30.

72. "Bibiana Aponte," fol. 1r.

73. "Contra Pedro Pablo por Heridas," ARPDF, Criminales, 1877, Letra A, exp. 4.

74. "Criminal contra Pedro Pablo Vera por golpes," ARPDF, 1878, Letra V, exp. 2.

75. See also "María del Rosario Hernández contra su consorte Daniel Legueto por divorcio," ARPDF, Civiles, 1875, Letra H, exp. 8, in which the plaintiff claimed that "pretendiendo en muchísimas ocasiones descargarme golpes y aporrearme como a una miserable sierva, lo que no ha llegado a verificar porque vivo bajo el amparo de mis padres y de mis tías en una misma casa, que hasta ahora se lo han estorbado con su personal interposición" (fol. 1v).

76. "María del Rosario Hernández," fol. 1r.

77. "María Teresa Belsinger contra Juan Bautista Acereto," fol. 1r.

78. "Mercedes Borges de Burgos contra su marido José Ignacio Burgos por divorcio," ARPDF, Civiles, 1878, Letra B, exp. 23. See also "María Evarista Pérez contra su marido Jesús María Romero, por alimentos," ARPDF, Civiles, 1879, Letra P, exp. 9.

79. "Guadalupe Obregón contra su consorte Juan de Jesús Acosta por divorcio," ARPDF, Civiles, 1876, Letra O, exp. 1, fol. 20r.

80. "Eusebia Hernández de Hijuelo," fol. 1r. See also "Josefa León de Bolívar contra su consorte Alejandro Bolívar por divorcio," ARPDF, Civiles, 1878, Letra L, exp.

18. Josefa lodged a claim because of her husband's verbal and physical abuse, including his intent to make her abort the child she was expecting by him.

81. "Contra Pedro Figueroa y los rondas de policía Nos. 73, 74 y 104 por golpes inferidos a María Rodríguez Díaz," ARPDF, Criminales, 1878, Libro DEF, Letra F, exp. 3. Six of the ten cases for bodily injury did not have an ending, usually because the law stipulated that only debilitating injuries would carry some type of punishment and victims may have recuperated and lost interest in pursuing the lawsuit. Indeed, three were dismissed because the injuries were not serious, and one was acquitted.

82. Hünefeldt arrived at a similar conclusion for late-nineteenth-century Lima. See *Liberalism in the Bedroom*, 360.

83. This contrasts with Kristin Ruggiero's findings about infanticide as a way in which single, working-class mothers in late-nineteenth-century Argentina sought to preserve their honor. There are similarities, however, with Martha de Abreu Esteves and Sueann Caufield's findings drawn from rape cases in Rio de Janeiro for the early twentieth century. See Ruggiero, "Honor, Maternity"; Esteves, *Meninas perdidas*; and Esteves and Caufield, "Fifty Years of Virginity."

10. CONCLUSION

1. Costa Rica was the first country in nineteenth-century Spanish America to have a divorce law that allowed both the dissolution of the bond of union (divortium quaod vinculum) and the separation of bed and board (divortium quaod thorum et cohabitationem) without interruption since its enactment on 26 April 1876. Another overlooked situation is Haiti, which regulated divorce matters in its Civil Code of 1825. See Gatti, *Disolución*, 52–53, 56. On the case of Puerto Rico, see Findlay, "Love in the Tropics."

2. José Gil Fortoul, "Sección Neutral: El Divorcio II," *La Opinión Nacional*, 14 September 1883, p. 3.

3. Pedro M. Arcaya, "Exposición del Ministro de Relaciones Interiores a la Cámara del Senado sobre el proyecto de código civil," foreword to Pietri, *Código Civil de 1916*, xi.

4. See Gil Fortoul, *El humo de mi pipa*, 455–69, 495–515.

5. Findlay, "Love in the Tropics," 141.

6. Gil Fortoul, "Cartas a Pascual," 13:225, 232. These letters were published in 1898.

7. Positivist intellectuals' support for the dictatorship of Juan Vicente Gómez in 1908 was seen as a historical necessity for the advancement of civilization and progress in Venezuela. See Sosa, *Ensayos*, 28–29.

8. Gil Fortoul, *El humo de mi pipa*, 455–69, 495–515; Pietri, *Código Civil de 1916*, 81–

84. See also article 242 of the Civil Code of 1922, which prohibited inquiries about the paternity of natural children.

9. Lavrin, *Women, Feminism, and Social Change*, 208. Susan K. Besse studies how social and legal changes in the period 1914–40 in Brazil created an "illusion of change" and helped to perpetuate male dominance, in *Restructuring Patriarchy*.

10. Pateman, *Sexual Contract*, 1–8.

11. Constitution of 1811, art. 27; Constitution of 1819, title 3, sec. 1, art. 8, num. 5; Constitution of 1830, title 5, art. 15.

12. On the Federal Wars see Matthews, *Violencia rural*; and Banko, *Luchas federalistas*.

13. Constitution of 1864, title 1, sec. 2, art. 8; Pérez Perdomo and San Juan, "Iguales," 261.

14. Constitution of 1864, title 3, art. 11; Constitution of 1874, title 3, art. 11; Constitution of 1891, title 3, art. 11; Constitution of 1893, title 4, art. 11.

15. Constitution of 1901, title 3, sec. 2, art. 11.

16. Gil Fortoul, *El humo de mi pipa*, 507.

17. Perdomo and San Juan, "Iguales," 261.

18. Ochoa, *Estudios jurídicos*, 152. See also Perdomo and San Juan, "Iguales."

19. On the ways in which French feminists used the arguments of equality and difference in their struggle for political rights, see Scott, *Only Paradoxes to Offer*.

20. *Nosotras* (without the hyphen) is the feminine of "we" in Spanish. With the hyphen, *Nos-Otras* suggestively means "we, the others [feminine form]." Unfortunately Venezuela's early feminist movements remain understudied. For an analysis of the post-1936 period see Friedman, *Unfinished Transitions*.

21. Scott, *Only Paradoxes to Offer*, 173.

22. Friedman, *Unfinished Transitions*; and Friedman, "Paradoxes."

23. Friedman, "Paradoxes," 88.

24. See McGee-Deutsch, "Gender and Sociopolitical Change," and Besse, *Restructuring Patriarchy*, 202.

Bibliography

ARCHIVES

Archivo Arquidiocesano de Caracas, Caracas, Venezuela (AAC)
  Judiciales
  Matrimoniales
  Obras Pías
  Reales Cédulas
Archivo de la Academia Nacional de la Historia, Caracas, Venezuela (AANH)
  Cajas Blancas
  Civiles
  Criminales
Archivo del Registro Principal del Distrito Federal, Caracas, Venezuela (ARPDF)
  Civiles
  Criminales
Archivo General de la Nación, Caracas, Venezuela (AGN)
  Colección Aragua
  Secretaría del Interior y Justicia
Biblioteca Nacional, Caracas, Venezuela (BN)
  Colección de Libros Raros y Manuscritos
  Colección de Hojas Sueltas

NEWSPAPERS AND MAGAZINES

El Alba
El Album del Hogar
El Constitucional
Crónica Eclesiástica de Venezuela
El Federalista
El Foro
La Opinión Nacional

Albornoz de López, Teresa. *La visita de Joaquín Mosquera y Figueroa a la Real Audiencia de Caracas (1804–1809): Conflictos internos y corrupción en la administración de justicia.* Caracas: Academia Nacional de la Historia, 1987.

Almécija B., Juan. *La familia en la provincia de Venezuela, 1745–1798.* Madrid: Editorial MAPFRE, 1992.

Alvarez F., Mercedes M. *Comercio y comerciantes y sus proyecciones en la independencia venezolana.* Caracas: Tipografía Vargas, 1963.

———. *El Tribunal del Real Consulado de Caracas: Contribución al estudio de nuestras instituciones.* Caracas: Comisión Nacional del Cuatricentenario de la Fundación de Caracas, Comité de Obras Económicas, 1967.

Arcaya, Pedro Manuel. *Observaciones al proyecto de Código Civil.* Caracas: Tipografía La Nación, 1942.

Armas Chitty, José Antonio de, and Manuel Pinto, eds. *Juan Francisco de León: Diario de una insurgencia.* Caracas: Tipografía Vargas, 1971.

Arrom, Silvia M. "Changes in Mexican Family Law in the Nineteenth Century: The Civil Codes of 1870 and 1884." *Journal of Family History* 10, no. 3 (fall 1985): 305–17.

———. *The Women of Mexico City, 1790–1857.* Stanford CA: Stanford University Press, 1985.

"Las autoridades coloniales venezolanas ante la propaganda revolucionaria de 1795," *Boletín del Archivo Nacional* (Caracas) 32, no. 126 (January–February 1945): 65–72.

Banko, Catalina. *Las luchas federalistas en Venezuela.* Caracas: Monte Avila Editores, 1996.

Barragán, Rossana. "The Spirit of Bolivian Laws: Citizenship, Infamy, and Patriarchal Hierarchy." Paper presented at the conference Honor, Status and Law in Modern Latin America, University of Michigan, Ann Arbor, December, 1998.

Bastidas, Luis I. "Historia del Código Civil venezolano, (1862–1896)." *Revista del Colegio de Abogados del Distrito Federal* 14 (September–October 1939): 3–38.

Becker, Marjorie. *Setting the Virgin on Fire.* Berkeley: University of California Press, 1995.

Behar, Ruth. "Sexual Witchcraft, Colonialism, and Women's Powers: Views from the Mexican Inquisition." In Lavrin, ed., *Sexuality and Marriage,* 178–208.

Belaúnde, Víctor Andrés. *Bolívar and the Political Thought of the Spanish American Revolution.* Baltimore MD: John Hopkins Press, 1938.

Bello Lozano, Humberto. *Historia de las fuentes e instituciones jurídicas venezolanas.* Caracas: Editorial Estrados, 1966.

Besse, Susan K. *Restructuring Patriarchy: The Modernization of Gender Inequality in Brazil, 1914–1940.* Chapel Hill: University of North Carolina Press, 1996.

Biblioteca Nacional de la Historia. *Codificación de Páez (Códigos de Comercio, Penal, de Enjuiciamiento y Procedimieno—1862–63)*. Caracas: Academia Nacional de la Historia, 1975.

Blanco, José Félix, and Ramón Azpurúa, eds. *Documentos para la historia de la vida pública del Libertador de Colombia, Perú, y Bolivia.* 14 vols. Caracas: Imprenta de la Opinión Nacional, 1875.

Bolívar, Simón. *The Political Thought of Bolívar: Selected Writings.* The Hague, Netherlands: Martinus Nijhoff, 1971.

———. "Proyecto de Decreto sobre policía general que somete al exámen público el Libertador." In Universidad Central de Venezuela, *Materiales para el estudio,* 71–74.

Borah, Woodrow. *Justice by Insurance: The General Indian Court of Colonial Mexico and the Legal Aides of the Half-Real.* Berkeley: University of California Press, 1983.

Boyer, Richard. "Honor among Plebeians: Mala Sangre and Social Reputation." In Johnson and Lipsett-Rivera, eds., *Faces of Honor,* 152–78.

———. *Lives of the Bigamists: Marriage, Family, and Community in Colonial Mexico.* Albuquerque: University of New Mexico Press, 1995.

———. "Women, 'La Mala Vida,' and the Politics of Marriage." In Lavrin, ed., *Sexuality and Marriage,* 252–86.

Brading, D. A. *Classical Republicanism and Creole Patriotism: Simon Bolívar (1783–1830) and the Spanish American Revolution.* Cambridge: Centre of Latin American Studies, University of Cambridge, 1983.

Brewer-Carías, Allan R. *Las constituciones de Venezuela.* Madrid: Universidad del Táchira y Centro de Estudios Constitucionales, 1985.

Brito Figueroa, Federico. *Historia económica y social de Venezuela: Una estructura para su estudio.* 2 vols. Caracas: Universidad Central de Venezuela, 1966.

Brown, Kathleen M. *Good Wives, Nasty Wenches, and Anxious Patriarchs.* Chapel Hill: University of North Carolina Press, 1996.

Brown, Stephanie. "The Princess of Monaco's Hair: The Revolutionary Tribunal and the Pregnancy Plea." *Journal of Family History* 23 (April 1998): 136–58.

Burkholder, Mark A., and D. S. Chandler. *From Impotence to Authority: The Spanish Crown and the American Audiencias, 1687–1808.* Columbia: University of Missouri Press, 1977.

Burton, Richard D. E. *Afro-Creole: Power, Opposition, and Play in the Caribbean.* Ithaca NY: Cornell University Press, 1997.

Bushnell, David. *The Santander Regime in Gran Colombia.* Newark: University of Delaware Press, 1954.

Butler, Judith. *Gender Trouble: Feminism and the Subversion of Identity.* New York: Routledge, 1990.

Carrera Damas, Germán. *Boves: Aspectos socioeconómicos de la Guerra de Independencia*. Caracas: Universidad Central de Venezuela, 1972.

———. *El culto a Bolívar: Esbozo para un estudio de la historia de las ideas en Venezuela*. Caracas: Universidad Central de Venezuela, 1969.

Carvalho, José Murilo de. *A formação das almas: O imaginário da república no Brasil*. São Paulo: Companhia das Letras, 1990.

Castañeda, Carmen. *Violación, estupro y sexualidad en Nueva Galicia, 1790–1821*. Guadalajara: Editorial Hexágono, 1989.

Castillo, Pedro del. *Teatro de la legislación colombiana y venezolana vigente*. 3 vols. Valencia, Spain: Imprenta del Teatro de Legislación, 1852.

Castillo Armas, Lucas Guillermo. *La aventura fundacional de los isleños*. Caracas: Academia Nacional de la Historia, 1983.

Castro, Henrique María. *El matrimonio civil en Venezuela*. Barinas, Venezuela: Imprenta Independiente de Luis Avril e hijo, 1858.

Castro Leiva, Luis. "The Ironies of the Spanish-American Revolutions." *International Social Science Journal*, 119 (February 1989): 53–67.

———. *De la patria boba a la teología bolivariana*. Caracas: Monte Avila Editores, 1991.

Caufield, Sueann. *In Defense of Honor: Sexual Morality, Modernity, and Nation in Early-Twentieth-Century Brazil*. Durham NC: Duke University Press, 2000.

Causas de infidencia. 2 vols. Caracas: Academia Nacional de la Historia, 1960.

Chalhoub, Sidney. *Trabalho, lar e botequim: O cotidiano dos trabalhadores no Rio de Janeiro da Belle Epoque*. São Paulo: Brasiliense, 1986.

Chambers, Sarah Clarke. "Gender in Bolívar's Virtuous Republic." Paper presented at the Latin American Studies Association meeting, Guadalajara, Mexico, 1997.

———. *From Subjects to Citizens: Honor, Culture, and Politics in Arequipa, Peru, 1780–1854*. University Park PA: Pennsylvania State University Press, 1999.

———. "To the Company of Man Like My Husband, No Law Can Compel Me: The Limits of Sanctions against Wife Beating in Arequipa, Peru, 1780–1850." *Journal of Women's History* 11, no.1 (1999): 31–52.

Cherpak, Evelyn M. "The Participation of Women in the Independence Movement in Gran Colombia, 1780–1830." In Lavrin, ed., *Latin American Women*, 219–34.

———. "Women and the Independence of Gran Colombia, 1780–1830." Ph.D. diss., University of North Carolina at Chapel Hill, 1973.

Chiossone, Tulio. *Formación jurídica de Venezuela en la colonia y en la república*. Caracas: Universidad Central de Venezuela, 1980.

Clagett, Helen L. *A Guide to the Law and Legal Literature of Venezuela*. Washington DC: Library of Congress, 1947.

Clemente Travieso, Carmen. *Mujeres de la independencia: Seis biografías de mujeres venezolanas*. México: Talleres Gráficos de México, 1964.

Codificación de Páez (códigos de comercio, penal, de enjuiciamiento y procedimiento, 1862–63). Caracas: Academia Nacional de la Historia, 1975.

El código civil de Páez. Caracas: Academia Nacional de la Historia, 1974.

"Código de procedimiento criminal de 1873." In *Recopilación de leyes y decretos de Venezuela*. Vol. 5. Caracas: Imprenta de "La Concordia," 1874.

Código de procedimiento judicial. Caracas: Imprenta de Valentín Espinal, 1845.

Código de procedimiento judicial de 19 de mayo de 1836. Caracas: Imprenta de Valentín Espinal, 1845.

Códigos civil, penal, de procedimiento civil, de enjuiciamiento criminal y de instrucción pública de los Estados Unidos de Venezuela. Madrid: Centro Editorial de Góngora, 1901.

Coelho Prado, Maria Lígia. "Em busca da participação das mulheres nas lutas pela independencia política da América Latina." *Revista Brasileira de História* 12, no. 23/24 (September 91/August 92): 77–90.

Comaroff, Jean, and John Comaroff. *Of Revelation and Revolution: Christianity, Colonialism, and Consciousness in South Africa*. Vol. 1. Chicago: University of Chicago Press, 1997.

Los comuneros de Mérida: Edición conmemorativa del bicentenario del movimiento comunero. 2 vols. Caracas: Academia Nacional de la Historia, 1981.

Cope, Douglas. *The Limits of Racial Domination: Plebeian Society in Colonial Mexico City, 1660–1772*. Madison: University of Wisconsin Press, 1994.

Corominas, Joan. *Diccionario crítico etimológico castellano e hispánico*. 5 vols. Madrid: Editorial Gredos, 1981.

Correa, Mariza. *Morte en família: Representações jurídicas de papéis sexuais*. Rio de Janeiro: Graal, 1983.

Costa, Emília da Viotti. *Crowns of Glory, Tears of Blood*. New York: Oxford University Press, 1994.

Cruz, Marie. "Were Women's Gender Roles Constructed?: The Chasm between Official Discourse and Practice in Late Colonial Venezuela." Paper presented at the Summer Research Opportunity Program, Indiana University, Bloomington, 1998.

Cuerpo de leyes, decretos y resoluciones sancionados por los Congresos de Venezuela en los años de 1830, 31, 32 y 33. 2d ed. Caracas: Valentín Espinal, 1833.

Cuerpo de leyes de la República de Colombia. Caracas: Universidad Central de Venezuela, 1961.

Cuerpo de leyes de Venezuela. Caracas: Valentín Espinal, 1851.

Cunill Grau, Pedro. *Geografía del poblamiento venezolano en el siglo XIX*. 3 vols. Caracas: Ediciones de la Presidencia de la República, 1987.

Curtis, William Eleroy. *Venezuela: The Land Where It's Always Summer*. London: Osgood, McIlvaine, 1896.

Cutter, Charles R. *The Legal Culture of Northern New Spain*. Albuquerque: University of New Mexico Press, 1995.

Daitsman, Andy. "Unpacking the First Person Singular: Marriage, Power and Negotiation in Nineteenth-Century Chile," *Radical History Review* 70 (winter 1998): 26–47.

Dávila M., Dora. "Se tiraban fuertemente al honor: La separación de dos aristócratas a fines del siglo XVIII venezolano." In Pino Iturrieta and Lange, coord., *Quimeras*, 65–100.

De Grummond, Jane Lucas. *Caracas Diary, 1835–1840*. Baton Rouge LA: Camellia, 1954.

Depons, Francisco. *Viaje a la parte oriental de Tierra Firme en la América Meridional*. 2 vols. Caracas: Banco Central de Venezuela, 1960.

Desan, Suzanne. "Religious Riots and Ritual during the French Revolution." *Proceedings of the Annual Meeting of the Western Society for French History* 14 (1987): 171–79.

———. "War between Brothers and Sisters: Inheritance Law and Gender Politics in Revolutionary France." *French Historical Studies* 20, no. 4 (autumn 1997): 597–634.

Dias, Manuel Nunes. *El Real Consulado de Caracas (1793–1810)*. Caracas: Academia Nacional de la Historia, 1984.

Díaz Quiñonez, Arcadio. *El arte de bregar*. San Juan, Puerto Rico: Ediciones Callejón, 2000.

Díaz Sánchez, Ramón. *Guzmán: Elipse de una ambición de poder*. Caracas: Ministerio de Educación Nacional, 1950.

Diccionario de derecho canónico arreglado a la jurisprudencia eclesiástica española antigua y moderna. París: Librería de Rosa y Bouret, 1854.

Diccionario de historia de Venezuela. Caracas: Fundación Polar, 1988.

"Discurso pronunciado por el Libertador ante el Congreso de Angostura el 15 de febrero de 1819, día de su instalación." In Vicente Lecuna, *Proclamas y discursos del Libertador*, 202–35. Caracas: Lit. y Tip. del Comercio, 1939.

Domínguez, Jorge I. *Insurrection or Loyalty: The Breakdown of the Spanish American Empire*. Cambridge: Harvard University Press, 1980.

Duarte, Carlos F. *Historia del traje durante la época colonial venezolana*. Caracas: Ernesto Armitano Editor, 1984.

———. *Testimonios de la visita de los oficiales franceses a Venezuela en 1783*. Caracas: Academia Nacional de la Historia, 1998.

Earle, Rebecca. "Rape and the Anxious Republic: Revolutionary Columbia, 1810–1830." In *Hidden Histories of Gender and the State in Latin America*, ed. Elizabeth Dore and Maxine Molyneaux, 127–46. Durham NC: Duke University Press, 2000.

Escriche y Martín, Joaquín. *Diccionario razonado de legislación civil, penal, comercial y forense.* Caracas: Imprenta de Valentín Espinal, 1840.

Esteva Grillet, Ramón. *Guzmán Blanco y el arte venezolano.* Caracas: Academia Nacional de la Historia, 1986.

Esteves, Martha de Abreu. *Meninas perdidas: Os populares e o cotidiano do amor no Rio de Janeiro da "Belle Epoque."* Rio de Janeiro: Paz e Terra, 1989.

Esteves, Martha de Abreu, and Sueann Caufield. "Fifty Years of Virginity in Rio de Janeiro: Sexual Politics and Gender Roles in Juridical and Popular Discourse, 1890–1940." *Luso-Brazilian Review* 30, no. 1 (1993): 47–74.

Fausto, Boris. *Crime e cotidiano: A criminalidade em São Paulo (1880–1924).* São Paulo: Brasiliense, 1984.

Felstiner, Mary Lowenthal. "Family Metaphors: The Language of an Independence Revolution." *Comparative Studies in Society and History* 25, no. 1 (January 1983): 154–80.

———. "Kinship Politics in the Chilean Independence Movement." *Hispanic American Historical Review* 56, no. 1 (February 1976): 58–80.

Ferry, Robert J. *The Colonial Elite of Early Caracas: Formation and Crisis, 1567–1767.* Berkeley: University of California Press, 1989.

Findlay, Eileen. *Imposing Decency: The Politics of Sexuality and Race in Puerto Rico, 1870–1920.* Durham NC: Duke University Press, 1999.

———. "Love in the Tropics: Marriage, Divorce, and the Construction of Benevolent Colonialism in Puerto Rico, 1898–1910." In *Close Encounters of Empire,* ed. G. M. Joseph, Catherine LeGrand, and Ricardo Donato Salvatore, 139–72. Durham NC: Duke University Press, 1998.

Fliegelman, Jay. *Prodigals and Pilgrims: The American Revolution against Patriarchal Authority.* Cambridge: Cambridge University Press, 1982.

Flores, Juan. *Divided Borders: Essays on Puerto Rican Identity.* Houston TX: Arte Público, 1991.

Flory, Thomas. "Race and Social Control in Independent Brazil." *Journal of Latin American Studies* 9, no. 2 (1977): 199–224.

Floyd, Mary B. *Guzmán Blanco: La dinámica de la política del Septenio.* Caracas: Instituto Autónomo Biblioteca Nacional and FUNRES, 1988.

———. "Política y economía en tiempos de Guzmán Blanco: Centralización y desarrollo, 1870–1888." In *Política y economía en Venezuela, 1810–1976,* ed. Fundación John Boulton, 163–201.

Foyster, Elizabeth. *Manhood in Early Modern England: Honor, Sex, and Marriage.* London: Longman, 1999.

Frankel, Benjamin A. "La Guerra Federal y sus secuelas." In *Política y economía en Venezuela, 1810–1976,* ed. Fundación John Boulton, 131–62.

Friedman, Elisabeth J. "Paradoxes of Gendered Political Opportunity in the Venezuelan Transition to Democracy." *Latin American Research Review* 33, no. 3 (1998): 87–135.

——. *Unfinished Transitions: Women and the Gendered Development of Democracy in Venezuela, 1936–1996.* University Park: Pennsylvania State University Press, 2000.

Friedman, Stephen Joel. "City of Caracas: 1830–1846." Ph.D. diss., New York University, 1976.

Fundación, John Boulton. *Política y economía en Venezuela, 1810–1976.* Caracas: Italgráfica, 1976.

García Chuecos, Héctor. *Los abogados de la colonia.* Madrid: Imp. Juan Bravo, 1965.

——. *Historia colonial de Venezuela.* 3 vols. Caracas: Archivo General de la Nación, 1985.

García Maldonado, Ana Lucina, ed. *La mujer en la historia de América: Obra enciclopédica.* Caracas: Asociación Civil la Mujer y el Quinto Centenario de América y Venezuela, 1995.

Gatti, Hugo E. *La disolución del vínculo matrimonial.* Montevideo: Centro Estudiantes de Derecho, 1967.

Gil Fortoul, José. "Cartas a Pascual." In *Pensamiento político venezolano del siglo XIX*, 13: 217–42.

——. *Historia constitucional de Venezuela.* 5th ed. 3 vols. Caracas: Librería Piñango, 1967.

——. *El humo de mi pipa.* Vol. 5 of *Obras completas.* Caracas: Ministerio de Educación, Dirección de Cultura y Bellas Artes, 1956.

Gilmore, Robert L. *Caudillism and Militarism in Venezuela, 1810–1910.* Athens: Ohio University Press, 1964.

Giraud, François. "La reacción social ante la violación: Del discurso a la práctica (Nueva España, siglo XVIII)." In *El placer de pecar & el afán de normar*, by Seminario de Historia de las Mentalidades y Religión en el México Colonial, Instituto de Antropología e Historia, 295–352.

——. "Viol et société coloniale: Le cas de la Nouvelle-Espagne au XVIII siècle." *Annales esc*, 3 (May–June 1986): 625–37.

Godineau, Dominique. *The Women of Paris and Their French Revolution.* Berkeley: University of California Press, 1998.

González Deluca, María Elena. *Negocios y política en tiempos de Guzmán Blanco.* Caracas: Universidad Central de Venezuela, 1991.

González Guinán, Francisco. *Historia contemporánea de Venezuela.* 15 vols. Caracas: Tipografía Empresa El Cojo, 1909.

González Ordosgoitti, Enrique. "Para un estudio de la lucha cultural durante la presidencia de Guzmán Blanco de 1870–1876." *Tierra Firme* 6, no. 22 (April–June 1988): 187–212.

González Oropeza, Hermann, ed. *Iglesia y estado en Venezuela.* Caracas: Universidad Católica Andrés Bello, 1977.

Gould, Jeffrey L. *To Lead as Equals: Rural Protest and Political Consciousness in Chinandega, Nicaragua, 1912–1979.* Chapel Hill: University of North Carolina Press, 1990.

Grases, Pedro. *Derechos del hombre y del ciudadano.* Caracas: Academia Nacional de la Historia, 1959.

———. *Libros y libertad.* Caracas: Ediciones de la Presidencia de la República, 1974.

———. *Pensamiento político de la emancipación venezolana.* Caracas: Biblioteca Ayacucho, 1988.

Grossberg, Michael. *Governing the Hearth: Law and the Family in Nineteenth-Century America.* Chapel Hill: University of North Carolina Press, 1985.

———. "Who Gets the Child? Custody, Guardianship, and the Rise of a Judicial Patriarchy in Nineteenth-Century America." *Feminist Studies* 9 (summer 1983): 235–60.

Guardino, Peter F. *Peasants, Politics, and the Formation of Mexico's National State: Guerrero, 1800–1857.* Stanford CA: Stanford University Press, 1996.

Gutiérrez, Ramón A. *When Jesus Came, the Corn Mothers Went Away: Marriage, Sexuality, and Power in New Mexico.* Stanford CA: Stanford University Press, 1991.

Gutiérrez de Arce, Manuel. *El Sínodo de Santiago de León de Caracas de 1687.* 2 vols. Caracas: Academia Nacional de la Historia, 1975.

Gutwirth, Madelyn. "Citoyens, Citoyennes: Cultural Regression and the Subversion of Female Citizenship in the French Revolution." In *The French Revolution and the Meaning of Citizenship*, ed. Renée Waldinger et al., 17–28. Westport CT: Greenwood, 1993.

Guy, Donna J. "Lower-Class Families, Women, and the Law in Nineteenth-Century Argentina." *Journal of Family History* 10, no. 3 (fall 1985): 318–31.

Hale, Charles A. "Political and Social Ideas." In *Latin America: Economy and Society, 1870–1930*, ed. Leslie Bethell, 225–99. Cambridge: Cambridge University Press, 1989.

Haring, Clarence, H. *The Spanish Empire in America.* New York: Oxford University Press, 1947.

Hufton, Olwen H. *Women and the Limits of Citizenship in the French Revolution.* Toronto: University of Toronto Press, 1992.

Hünefeldt, Christine. *Liberalism in the Bedroom: Quarreling Spouses in Nineteenth-Century Lima.* University Park PA: Pensylvania State University Press, 2000.

Hunt, Lynn. *The Family Romance of the French Revolution*. Berkeley: University of California Press, 1992.

———. *Politics, Culture, and Class in the French Revolution*. Berkeley: University of California Press, 1984.

Instituto Panamericano de Geografía e Historia, ed. *Documentos relativos a la revolución de Gual y España*. Buenos Aires: Imprenta López, 1949.

Iturriza Guillén, Carlos. *Algunas familias caraqueñas*. 2 vols. Caracas: n.p., 1967.

Izard, Miguel. *El miedo a la revolución: La lucha por la libertad en Venezuela (1777–1830)*. Madrid: Editorial Tecnos, 1979.

———. *Series estadísticas para la historia de Venezuela*. Mérida: Universidad de Los Andes, 1970.

Jaquette, Jane. "Literary Archetypes and Female Role Alternatives: The Woman and the Novel in Latin America." In *Female and Male in Latin America: Essays*, ed. Ann Pescatello, 89–101. Pittsburgh PA: University of Pittsburgh Press, 1973.

Johnson, Lyman L., and Sonya Lipsett-Rivera, eds. *The Faces of Honor: Sex, Shame, and Violence in Colonial Latin America*. Albuquerque: University of New Mexico Press, 1998.

Joseph, Suad. "Gendering Citizenship in the Middle East." In *Gender and Citizenship in the Middle East*, ed. Suad Joseph, 3–30. Syracuse NY: Syracuse University Press, 2000.

Kanter, Deborah. " 'Correction of Sins Is My Obligation': Priests and the Enclosure of Women in Late Colonial Mexico." Paper presented at the Second Conference on the History of the Family, Carleton University, Ottawa, Ontario, May 11–14, 1994.

Kellogg, Susan. *Law and the Transformation of Aztec Culture, 1500–1700*. Norman: University of Oklahoma Press, 1995.

Kerber, Linda. *No Constitutional Right to Be Ladies*. New York: Hill and Wang, 1998.

———. *Women of the Republic*. New York: Norton, 1986.

King, James F. "The Case of José Ponciano de Ayarza: A Document on 'Gracias al Sacar.'" *Hispanic American Historical Review* 21, no. 4 (November 1951): 640–47.

Kirkendall, Andrew J. *Classmates: Male Student Culture and the Making of a Political Class in Nineteenth-Century Brazil*. Lincoln: University of Nebraska Press, 2002.

Klein, Herbert S. *La esclavitud africana en América Latina y el Caribe*. Madrid: Alianza Editorial, 1986.

———. *Slavery in the Americas: A Comparative Study of Virginia and Cuba*. Chicago: University of Chicago Press, 1967.

Knight, Franklin W. *Slave Society in Cuba during the Nineteenth Century*. 1970. Reprint, Madison: University of Wisconsin Press, 1986.

Kuznesof, Elizabeth Ann. *Household Economy and Urban Development: São Paulo, 1765–1836*. Boulder: Westview, 1985.

Ladera de Díez, Elizabeth. *Contribución al estudio de la "aristocracia territorial" en Venezuela colonial: La familia Xeres de Aristeguieta, siglo XVIII*. Caracas: Academia Nacional de la Historia, 1990.

Landes, Joan B. *Women and the Public Sphere in the Age of the French Revolution*. Ithaca NY: Cornell University Press, 1988.

Lavenda, Robert H. "The First Modernizing Attempt: Modernization and Change in Caracas, 1870–1908." Ph.D. diss., Indiana University, 1977.

Lavrin, Asunción, "'Lo femenino': Women in Colonial Historical Sources." In *Coded Encounters: Writing, Gender, and Ethnicity in Colonial Latin America*, ed. Francisco Javier Cevallos-Cadau et al., 153–76. Amherst: University of Massachusetts Press, 1994.

———. "Sexuality in Colonial Mexico: A Church Dilemma." In Lavrin, ed., *Sexuality and Marriage*, 47–95.

———. *Women, Feminism, and Social Change in Argentina, Chile, and Uruguay, 1890–1940*. Lincoln: University of Nebraska Press, 1995.

Lavrin, Asunción, ed. *Latin American Women: Historical Perspectives*. Westport CT: Greenwood, 1978.

———. *Sexuality and Marriage in Colonial Latin America*. Lincoln: University of Nebraska Press, 1989.

Lazarus-Black, Mindie. "Why Women Take Men to Magistrate's Court: Caribbean Kinship Ideology and Law." *Ethnology* 30, no. 2 (1991): 119–33.

Lazarus-Black, Mindie, and Susan F. Hirsch, eds. *Contested States: Law, Hegemony and Resistance*. New York: Routledge, 1994.

Leal, Ildefonso. "La aristocracia criolla venezolana y el Código Negrero de 1789." *Revista de Historia* 6 (1981): 61–81.

———. *Historia de la Universidad Central de Venezuela*. Caracas: Universidad Central de Venezuela, 1981.

———. *Historia de la Universidad de Caracas (1721–1827)*. Caracas: Universidad Central de Venezuela, 1963.

Lemmo, Angelina. *La educación en Venezuela en 1870*. Caracas: Universidad Central de Venezuela, 1976.

Levit, Nancy. *The Gender Line: Men, Women and the Law*. New York: New York University Press, 1998.

Levy, Darline G., and Harriet B. Applewhite. "Women and Militant Citizenship in the French Revolution." In *Rebel Daughters: Women and the French Revolution*, ed. Sara E. Melzer and Leslie W. Rabine, 79–101. New York: Oxford University Press, 1992.

Lewin, Linda. "Natural and Spurious Children in Brazilian Inheritance Law from Colony to Empire: A Methodological Essay." *The Americas* 48, no. 3 (January 1992): 351–96.

Liddle, Mark A. "State, Masculinities, and Law: Some Comments on Gender and English State-Formation." *British Journal of Criminology* 36, no. 3 (1996): 361-80.

Lipsett-Rivera, Sonya. "A Slap in the Face of Honor: Social Transgression and Women in Late-Colonial Mexico." In Johnson and Lipsett-Rivera, eds., *Faces of Honor*, 179–200.

Lombardi, John V. *The Decline and Abolition of Negro Slavery in Venezuela, 1820–1854*. Westport CT: Greenwood, 1974.

———. *People and Places in Colonial Venezuela*. Bloomington: Indiana University Press, 1976.

———. *Venezuela: The Search for Order, the Dream of Progress*. New York: Oxford University Press, 1982.

López, Casto Fulgencio. *Juan Bautista Picornell y la conspiración de Gual y España: Narración documentada de la pre-revolución de independencia venezolana*. Caracas: Ediciones Nueva Cádiz, 1955.

López Bohórquez, Alí Enrique. *Los ministros de la Audiencia de Caracas (1786–1810): Caracterización de una elite burocrática del poder español en Venezuela*. Caracas: Academia Nacional de la Historia, 1984.

Lucena, Manuel. *Vísperas de la independencia americana: Caracas*. Madrid: Editorial Alhambra, 1986.

MacLaghlan, Colin. *Spanish Empire in the New World: The Role of Ideas in Institutional Change*. Berkeley: University of California Press, 1988.

Magallanes, Manuel Vicente. *Luchas e insurreciones en la Venezuela colonial*. Caracas: Academia Nacional de la Historia, 1982.

Mago de Chópite, Lila. *Caracas y su crecimiento urbano*. Caracas: Instituto Universitario Pedagógico de Caracas, 1986.

Martí, Mariano. *Obispo Mariano Martí: Documentos relativos a su visita pastoral de la Diócesis de Caracas, 1771–1784*. 7 vols. Caracas: Academia Nacional de la Historia, 1969.

Martínez-Alier, Verena. *Marriage, Class, and Colour in Nineteenth-Century Cuba: A Study of Racial Attitudes and Sexual Values in a Slave Society*. 2d ed. Ann Arbor: University of Michigan Press, 1989.

Matos Rodríguez, Félix V. "La mujer y el derecho en el siglo XIX en San Juan, Puerto Rico (1820–1862)," In *Género, familia y mentalidades en América Latina*, ed. Pilar Gonzalbo Aizpuru, 235–38. Río Piedras: Editorial de la Universidad de Puerto Rico, 1997.

Matthews, Robert P. "La turbulenta década de los Monagas, 1847–1858." In *Política y economía en Venezuela, 1810–1976*, ed. Fundación John Boulton, 93–127. Caracas: Italgráfica, 1976.

———. *Violencia rural en Venezuela*. Caracas: Monte Avila Editores, 1977.

McCaa, Robert. "Calidad, Clase, and Marriage in Colonial Mexico: The Case of Parral, 1788–90." *Hispanic American Historical Review* 64, no. 3 (1984): 477–501.

————. "Gustos de los padres, inclinaciones de los novios y reglas de una feria nupcial colonial: Parral, 1770–1814." *Historia Mexicana* 40, no. 4 (1991): 579–614.

————. "Marriageways in Mexico and Spain, 1500–1900." *Continuity and Change* 9, no. 1 (1994): 27-29.

McGee-Deutsch, Sandra. "Gender and Sociopolitical Change in Twentieth-Century Latin America." *Hispanic American Historical Review* 71, no. 2 (May 1991): 259–306.

McKinley, P. Michael. *Pre-revolutionary Caracas: Politics, Economy, and Society, 1777–1811.* Cambridge: Cambridge University Press, 1985.

Merryman, John Henry. *The Civil Law Tradition.* 2d ed. Stanford CA: Stanford University Press, 1985.

Miller, Gary M. "Bourbon Social Engineering: Women and Conditions of Marriage in Eighteenth-Century Venezuela." *The Americas* 46, no. 3 (January 1990): 261–90.

Mintz, Sydney W. *Caribbean Transformations.* Baltimore MD: John Hopkins Press, 1974.

Morón, Guillermo. *Historia de Venezuela.* 5 vols. Caracas: Italgráfica, 1971.

Morse, Kimberly Jane. "'Aún en la muerte separados': Class, Clergy, and Society in Aragua de Barcelona, Venezuela, 1820–1875." Ph.D. diss., University of Texas at Austin, 2000.

Múnera, Alfonso. *El fracaso de la nación: Región, clase y raza en el Caribe colombiano (1717–1821).* Bogotá: Ancora Editores, 1998.

Muñoz Oráa, Carlos Emilio. *Los comuneros de Venezuela: Una rebelión popular de pre-independencia.* Mérida, Venezuela: Universidad de los Andes, 1971.

Nader, Laura, and Duane Metzger. "Conflict Resolution in Two Mexican Communities." In *The Social Organization of Law,* ed. Donald Black and Maureen Mileski, 95–105. New York: Seminar, 1973.

Nava, Julián. "The Illustrious American: The Development of Nationalism in Venezuela under Guzmán Blanco." *Hispanic American Historical Review* 45, no. 4 (November 1965): 527–43.

Nazzari, Muriel. "Concubinage in Colonial Brazil: The Inequalities of Race, Class, and Gender." *Journal of Family History* 21, no. 2 (April 1996): 107–24.

————. *Disappearance of the Dowry: Women, Families, and Social Changes in São Paulo, Brazil, 1600–1900.* Stanford CA: Stanford University Press, 1991.

————. "Widows as Obstacles to Business: British Objections to Brazilian Marriage and Inheritance Laws." *Comparative Studies in History and Society* 37, no. 4 (October 1995): 781–802.

Nye, Robert A. *Masculinity and Male Codes of Honor in Modern France*. New York: Oxford University Press, 1993.

Ochoa, Francisco. *Estudios jurídicos*. Maracaibo: Imprenta Gutemberg, 1892.

Oficina de Compilación Clasificación y Publicación del Archivo del Libertador. *Toma de razón, 1810 a 1812: Registro de nombramientos y actos oficiales emanados de la primera Junta Patriótica y de la Primera República de Venezuela*. Caracas: Impresa Nacional, 1955.

Olívar, Norberto José, et al. *Ni monarquía ni república: Incapacidad de la élites frente al Proyecto Nacional*. Maracaibo, Venezuela: Dirección de la Cultura de LUZ, Centro Zuliano de Investigación Documental, 1996.

O'Malley, Ilene V. *The Myth of Revolution: Hero Cults and the Institutionalization of the Mexican State, 1920–1940*. Westport CT: Greenwood, 1986.

Ortega Noriega, Sergio. "El discurso teológico de Santo Tomás de Aquino sobre el matrimonio, la familia y los comportamientos sexuales." In *El placer de pecar y el afán de normar*, by Seminario de Historia de las Mentalidades y Religión en México Colonial and Instituto Naciónal de Antropología e Historia, 17–78.

———. *Historia del derecho español en América y del Derecho Indiano*. Madrid: Aguilar, 1967.

Pagden, Anthony. *Spanish Imperialism and the Political Imagination*. New Haven: Yale University Press, 1990.

Parra Pérez, Carracciolo. *Historia de la primera república de Venezuela*. 2 vols. Caracas: Tipografía Americana, 1939.

———. *Mariño y la independencia de Venezuela*. Madrid: Ediciones Cultura Hispánica, 1954.

Pateman, Carol. *The Sexual Contract*. Stanford CA: Stanford University Press, 1988.

Pellicer, Luis. *La vivencia del honor en la Provincia de Venezuela, 1774–1809: Estudios de casos*. Caracas: Fundación Polar, 1996.

Pensamiento político venezolano del siglo XIX. 15 vols. Caracas: Publicaciones de la Presidencia de la República, 1960–62.

Penyak, Lee Michael. "Criminal Sexuality in Central Mexico, 1750–1850." Ph.D. diss., University of Connecticut, 1993.

———. "Protecting and Punishing Deviant Women: The Casa de Depósito in México, 1750–1865." Paper presented at AHA/CLAH meeting, San Francisco, January 1994.

Perdomo Escalona, Carmen. *Heroínas y mártires venezolanas*. Caracas: Ediciones Librería Destino, 1994.

Pérez Perdomo, Rogelio. *Los abogados en Venezuela*. Caracas: Monte Avila, 1981.

———. "Teoría y práctica de la legislación en la temprana República (Venezuela, 1821–1870)," In *Modelli di legislatore e scienza della legislazione. Modelli storici e comparativi*, ed. A. Giuliani and N. Picardi, 313–74. Perugia: Ediziones Scientifiche Italiane, 1987.

Pérez Perdomo, Rogelio, and Miriam San Juan. "Iguales Ma Non Troppo . . . la condición jurídica de la mujer en Venezuela en el siglo XIX." In Troconis de Veracoechea, coord., *La mujer*, 258–82.

Pérez Vila, Manuel. "El gobierno deliberativo: Hacendados, comerciantes y artesanos frente a la crisis." In *Política y economía en Venezuela, 1810–1976*, ed. Fundación John Boulton, 35–89.

———. *Los libros en la colonia y en la Independencia*. Caracas: Imprenta Nacional, 1970.

Picón-Salas, Mariano, and Fundación Eugenio Mendoza. *Venezuela independiente, 1810–1960*. Caracas: Fundación Eugenio Mendoza, 1969.

Pietri, Alejandro. *El Código Civil de 1916*. Caracas: Litografía del Comercio, 1916.

Pino Iturrieta, Elías. *Contra lujuria, castidad: Historias de pecado en el siglo XVIII venezolano*. Caracas: Alfadil Ediciones, 1992.

———. *Fueros, civilización y cuidadanía: Estudios sobre el siglo XIX en Venezuela*. Caracas: Universidad Católica Andrés Bello, 2000.

———. *Las ideas de los primeros venezolanos*. Caracas: Fondo Editorial Tropykos, 1987.

———. *La mentalidad venezolana de la emancipación*. 2d ed. Caracas: Ediciones Eldorado, 1991.

———. *Ventaneras y castas, diabólicas y honestas*. Caracas: Editorial Planeta, 1993.

Pino Iturrieta, Elías, and Frédérique Lange, coords. *Quimeras de amor, honor y pecado en el siglo XVIII venezolano: Voces de la historia*. Caracas: Editorial Planeta Venezolana, 1994.

Pino Iturrieta, Elías, and Pedro Enrique Calzadilla, comps. *La mirada del otro: Viajeros extranjeros en la Venezuela del siglo XIX*. Caracas: Fundación Bigott, 1993.

Polanco Alcántara, Tomás. *Guzmán Blanco: Tragedia en seis partes y un epílogo*. 2d ed. Caracas: Editorial Texto, 1992.

Porter, Robert Ker. *Caracas Diary, 1825–1842*. Caracas: W. Dupouy, 1968.

Price, Richard. "An Absence of Ruins? Seeking Caribbean Historical Consciousness." *Caribbean Review* 14:3 (summer 1985): 24–29, 45.

Putnam, Lara Elizabeth. "Sex and Standing in the Streets of Port Límon, Costa Rica, 1890–1935." Paper presented at the Honor, Status, and Law in Modern Latin America Conference, University of Michigan, Ann Arbor, December 4–6, 1998.

Quintero Montiel, Inés, coord. *Antonio Guzmán Blanco y su época*. Caracas: Monte Avila Editores, 1994.

———. "Autoridades en conflicto: El cabildo y la audiencia de Caracas." *Anuario Colombiano de Historia Social y de la Cultura* 24 (1997): 269–81.

———. *Mirar tras la ventana, testimonios de viajeros y legionarios sobre mujeres del siglo XIX*. Caracas: AlterLibris Ediciones, Secretaría de la UCV, 1998.

Ramírez, Rafael L. *What It Means to Be a Man: Reflections on Puerto Rican Masculinity*. New Brunswick NJ: Rutgers University Press, 1999.

Rangel Lamus, Amenodoro. "El Código Civil de 1873 y sus antecedentes legales." In *Código Civil sancionado por el General Guzmán Blanco. Edición del Congreso de la República conmemorativa del Centenario del Código Civil de 1873*, v–xxix. Caracas: Imprenta del Congreso de la República, 1973.

Rodríguez, José Angel. *Babilonia de pecados: Norma y transgresión en Venezuela, siglo XVIII*. Caracas: Alfadil Ediciones: Universidad Central de Venezuela Facultad de Humanidades y Educación: Comisión de Estudios de Postgrado, 1998.

Rodríguez, Pablo. *Seducción, amancebamiento y abandono en la colonia*. Santa Fé de Bogotá: Fundación Simón y Lola Guberek, 1991.

Rodríguez Sáenz, Eugenia. *Hijas, novias y esposas: Familia, matrimonio y violencia doméstica en el Valle Central de Costa Rica (1750–1850)*. Heredia, Costa Rica: Editorial de la Universidad Nacional, 2000.

Rodulfo Cortés, Santos. "Las milicias de pardos de Venezuela durante el periodo hispánico." *Memoria del Tercer Congreso Venezolano de Historia* 3 (1979): 11–85.

———. *El régimen de las "Gracias al Sacar" en Venezuela durante el período hispánico*. 2 vols. Caracas: Academia Nacional de la Historia, 1978.

Rondón Márquez, R. A. *Guzmán Blanco: El autócrata civilizador*. 2d ed. 2 vols. Madrid: Impr. García Vicente, 1952.

Rout, Leslie B. *The African Experience in Spanish America: 1502 to the Present Day*. Cambridge: Cambridge University Press, 1976.

Ruggiero, Kristin. "Honor, Maternity, and the Disciplining of Women: Infanticide in Late Nineteenth-Century Buenos Aires." *Hispanic American Historical Review* 73, no. 3 (1992): 353–73.

Sabean, David W. *Power in the Blood: Popular Culture and Village Discourse in Early Modern Germany*. London: Cambridge University Press, 1984.

Salvatore, Ricardo D. "Death and Liberalism: Capital Punishment after the Fall of Rosas." In Salvatore, Aguirre, and Joseph, eds., *Crime and Punishment in Latin America*, 308–41.

Salvatore, Ricardo D., Carlos Aguirre, and Gilbert M. Joseph, eds. *Crime and Punishment in Latin America: Law and Society Since Late Colonial Times*. Durham NC: Duke University Press, 2001.

Sánchez-Albornoz, Nicolás. "The Population of Latin America, 1850–1930." In *The Cambridge History of Latin America*, ed. Leslie Bethell, 4:121–52. Cambridge: Cambridge University Press, 1986.

Sanojo, Luis. *Instituciones de derecho civil venezolano*. 4 vols. Caracas: Imprenta Nacional, 1873.

Sant'Anna, Affonso de Romano. *O canibalismo amoroso: O desejo e a interdição em nossa cultura através da poesía.* 2d ed. São Paulo: Brasiliense, 1985.

Schwarz, Philip J. *Twice Condemned: Slaves and the Criminal Laws of Virginia, 1705–1865.* Baton Rouge: Louisiana State University Press, 1988.

Scott, James C. *Domination and the Arts of Resistance: Hidden Transcripts.* New Haven CT: Yale University Press, 1990.

Scott, Joan Wallach. *Gender and the Politics of History.* New York: Columbia University Press, 1988.

———. *Only Paradoxes to Offer: French Feminists and the Rights of Man.* Cambridge: Harvard University Press, 1996.

Seed, Patricia. "American Law, Hispanic Traces: Some Contemporary Entanglements of Community Property." *William and Mary Quarterly,* 3d ser., 52, no. 1 (January 1995): 157–66.

———. *To Love, Honor, and Obey in Colonial Mexico: Conflicts over Marriage Choice, 1574–1821.* Stanford CA: Stanford University Press, 1988.

Seminario de Historia de las Mentalidades y Religión en el México Colonial, Instituto de Antropología e Historia. *El placer de pecar & el afán de normar.* México: Editorial Joaquín Mortiz, 1988.

Shammas, Carole. "Anglo-American Household Government in Comparative Perspective." *William and Mary Quarterly,* 3d Series, 52, no. 1 (January 1995): 104–44.

Skurski, Julie. "The 'Leader' and the 'People': Representing the Nation in Postcolonial Venezuela." Ph.D. diss., University of Chicago, 1993.

Sociedad Bolivariana de Venezuela. *Decretos del Libertador, 1828–1830.* 3 vols. Caracas: Imprenta Nacional, 1961.

Sociedad Económica de Amigos del País. *Anuario de la Provincia de Caracas de 1832 á 1833.* Caracas: Imprenta de A. Damirón, 1835.

Socolow, Susan M. "Women and Crime." In *The Problem of Order in Changing Societies,* ed. Lyman Johnson, 1–18. Albuquerque: University of New Mexico Press, 1990.

Soihet, Rachel. *Condição feminina e formas de violência: Mulheres pobres e ordem urbana, 1890–1920.* Rio de Janeiro: Forense Universitária, 1989.

Sosa, Arturo. *Ensayos sobre el pensamiento político positivista venezolano.* Caracas: Ediciones Centauro, 1985.

Stann, Eugene Jeffrey. "Caracas, Venezuela, 1891–1936: A Study of Urban Growth." Ph.D. diss., Vanderbilt University, 1975.

Stephens, Thomas M. *Dictionary of Latin American Racial and Ethnic Terminology.* Gainesville: University of Florida Press, 1989.

Stern, Steve J. *The Secret History of Gender: Women, Men, and Power in Late Colonial Mexico.* Chapel Hill: University of North Carolina Press, 1995.

Stevens, Donald F. "Passion and Patriarchy in Nineteenth-Century Argentina: María Luisa Bemberg's Camila." In *Based on a True Story: Latin American History at the Movies*, ed. Donald F. Stevens, 85–102. Wilmington DE: Scholarly Resources, 1998.

Stevens, Evelyn P. "Marianismo: The Other Face of Machismo in Latin America." In *Female and Male in Latin America: Essays*, ed. Ann Pescatello, 89–101. Pittsburgh: University of Pittsburgh Press, 1973.

Stolcke, Verena. "The 'Nature' of Nationality." In *Citizenship and Exclusion*, ed. Veit Bader, 61–80. New York: St. Martin Press, 1997.

Stone, Marilyn. *Marriage and Friendship in Medieval Spain*. New York: Peter Lang, 1990.

Sucre, Luis Alberto. *Gobernadores y Capitanes Generales de Venezuela*. Caracas: Lit y Tip de Comercio, 1928.

Tejada y Sainz, Juan de Dios. *Diccionario de comercio y derecho Inglés-Español*. Santa María del Rosario, Cuba: Editorial Var+I+Tec, 1945.

Texera Arnal, Yolanda. "Médicos y cirujanos pardos 'en condición de por ahora' en la Provincia de Venezuela, Siglo XVIII." *Colonial Latin American Historical Review* 8, no. 3 (summer 1999): 321–38.

Toro, Fermín. "Reflexiones sobre la Ley de 10 de abril." In *Pensamiento político venezolano del siglo XIX*, 1:107–25.

Torres Pantín, Carmen. "El acceso del esclavo a la justicia en causas civiles, siglo XVIII." In *Indice sobre esclavos y esclavitud (Sección Civiles-Esclavos)*. Serie Archivos y Catálogos. Caracas: Editorial Torino, 1997.

Troconis de Veracoechea, Ermila. *Gobernadoras, cimarronas, conspiradoras y barraganas*. Caracas: Alfadil Ediciones, 1998.

———. *Indias, esclavas, mantuanas y primeras damas*. Caracas: Alfadil Ediciones, 1990.

Troconis de Veracoechea, Ermila, coord. *La mujer en la historia de Venezuela*. Caracas: Arte, 1995.

Twinam, Ann. "Honor, Sexuality, and Illegitimacy in Colonial Spanish America." In Lavrin, ed., *Sexuality and Marriage*, 118–55.

———. "The Negotiation of Honor: Elites, Sexuality, and Illegitimacy in Eighteenth-Century Spanish America." In Johnson and Lipsett-Rivera, eds., *Faces of Honor*, 68–102.

———. *Public Lives, Private Secrets: Gender, Honor, Sexuality, and Illegitimacy in Colonial Spanish America*. Stanford CA: Stanford University Press, 1999.

Universidad Central de Venezuela, Consejo de Desarrollo Científico y Humanístico. *Materiales para el estudio de la cuestión agraria en Venezuela (1810–1865). Mano de obra: Legislación y administración*. Caracas: Universidad Central de Venezuela, 1979.

Uribe-Urán, Victor M. *Honorable Lives: Lawyers, Family, and Politics in Colombia, 1780–1850*. Pittsburgh PA: University of Pittsburgh Press, 2000.

Vallenilla Lanz, Laureano, and Nikita Harwich Vallenilla. *Cesarismo democrático y otros textos*. Caracas: Biblioteca Ayacucho, 1991.

Venezuela. *Recopilación de leyes y decretos de Venezuela*. Caracas: Imprenta Bolívar, 1874–.

Vannini, Maritza. *La influencia francesa en Venezuela*. Maracaibo: Universidad del Zulia, 1965.

Viqueira Albán, Juan Pedro. *Propriety and Permissiveness in Bourbon Mexico*, trans. Sonya Lipsett-Rivera and Sergio Rivera Ayala. Wilmington DE: Scholarly Resources, 1999.

Waldron, Kathleen. "A Social History of a Primate City: The Case of Caracas, 1750–1810." Ph.D. diss., Indiana University, 1977.

Waldron, Kathy. "The Sinners and the Bishop in Colonial Venezuela: The 'Visita' of Bishop Mariano Martí, 1771–1784." In Lavrin, ed., *Sexuality and Marriage*, 156–77.

Watson, Alan. *Slave Law in the Americas*. Athens: University of Georgia Press, 1989.

Watters, Mary. *A History of the Church in Venezuela, 1810–1930*. 1933. Reprint, New York: AMS Press, 1971.

Wise, George S. *Caudillo: A Portrait of Antonio Guzmán Blanco*. New York: Columbia University Press, 1951.

Wright, Winthrop R. *Café con Leche: Race, Class, and National Image in Venezuela*. Austin: University of Texas Press, 1990.

Zagarri, Rosemary. "The Rights of Man and Woman in Post-Revolutionary America." *William and Mary Quarterly* 55, no.2 (April 1998): 203–30.

Zawisza, Leszek. *Arquitectura y obras públicas en Venezuela*. 3 vols. Caracas: Ediciones de la Presidencia de la República, 1988.

Index

abduction, 70, 227, 228
abuse, 156, 231; physical, 77–78, 84–85, 165, 205, 231–33
Acereto, Juan Bautista, 206–7
Acosta, Angel María, 221–22, 224
adultery, 68–69, 76–77, 84–85, 153–54, 156–58, 205, 208, 236
age of majority, 196, 202
agriculture, 119–20, 134
Albelo, Josefa María, 155–57, 160
alcaldes ordinarios, 26–27, 37, 247n17; power of, 27, 47
alternativa law, 41–43
Angostura speech, 108–11
Aponte, Juana María, 90
Aquinas, Saint Thomas, 65–66
Aramburu, Dr. Gabriel Josef, 76
Arcaya, Pedro Manuel, 182, 237
Argentina, 122, 137, 184, 198
Arias, Francisco, 39
Arias Altamirano, Luis, 39
Aristeguieta, Miguel, 42, 99
aristocratic values, 23–36, 176. See also mantuanos
Arrom, Silvia M., 157
Ascanio, Nicolás, 55
Ascanio Rodríguez, A. B., 219–20, 230
Asteguieta, José Bernardo, 52
Aular, Antonio, 78

bail, 209–11
Barguilla, Pedro Ignacio, 82, 90
Basques, governors, 37, 252n84. See also Real Compañía Guipuzcoana
Belsinger, María Teresa, 206–7, 212, 213, 216, 226, 232, 233
bienes parafernales, 75, 152, 153, 262n64

blacks, 28–34, 56, 58, 132; and Bolívar, 108, 111; and the military, 79, 98, 101, 102
Blanco, Juan Félix, 39
Blanco, María del Carmen, 82, 90
Blanco de Ponte, Pedro, 39
Blanco Jerez de Aristeguieta, Carlota, 174
Blanco Uribe, Miguel, 39
Blanco y Herrera, Josefa María, 99
bodily harm, 147
Bolcán, Joseph Matías, 81, 92, 95
Bolívar, Juan Vicente, 40
Bolívar, María Antonia, 162–64
Bolívar, Simón, 3, 4, 57, 83, 108–16, 111–12, 117, 122, 134, 135, 136, 162, 173, 174, 178, 179, 180, 185; cult of, 110; and gendered ideas, 107
Bourbon monarchs, 37, 111; politics to reduce the authority of mantuanos, 42, 91
Bourbon reforms, 25, 43, 44, 45, 46, 252n84
bourgeois values, 176, 179–84, 190, 211–12, 214
Boyer, Richard, 161
breach of promise, 70, 79, 81, 82, 90, 92, 93, 95, 134, 146, 201, 203, 208, 217, 220, 221–24, 225, 226, 227
Brazil, 67
Briceño Méndez, Pedro, 119, 120
Buerta de Pompa, Juana, 217, 220
Burgos, María del Rosario, 78
Bushnell, David, 136
Butler, Judith, 245n33

cabildo, 26, 37, 39, 46; and audiencia, 46, 47; and gracias al sacar, 50, 51; and loss of power to audiencia, 47; and mantuano control of, 26, 41; members' conflicts with peninsulares, 42
cacao, 36, 37, 38, 43, 44
calidad, 62, 99, 101, 103

callejeras, 68, 95

Canary Islanders, 37, 40, 252n84

Canción Americana (song), 54

Canoso, Rosalía, 155, 159

Carmañola Americana (song), 54

carnival, 183

Carvalho, José Murilo de, 176

Castro, Juan Josef, 76

caución juratoria, 76, 77, 86, 263n70

caudillos, 118, 174, 175, 180, 184, 185

cédula de gracias al sacar, 34, 49–52, 55, 74

Chambers, Sarah C., 10, 136, 245n25

Cherpak, Evelyn, 9, 112

child custody, 78, 196–97

church, 41, 44; early republic, 119; ecclesiastical court rulings, 82, 84–86, 156, 160; and gender relations, 68–72, 115, 216; late nineteenth century, 180, 181, 183, 197–98, 216; legislation in colonial period, 68–72; synod (1687), 28–29, 33, 40, 66, 69, 80, 84

Churión, María Tomasa, 81, 92, 93, 95

citizenship, 5, 6, 7, 11, 12, 19, 108, 111, 116, 125, 132, 150, 155, 161, 168, 241, 169, 173, 238; and exclusion, 108; female claims of, 155, 157, 168, 169, 217, 241; and gender, 9, 12, 13, 14, 19, 133; passive and active 109, 133, 135, 242

civil codes, of 1873, 133, 186, 189, 195–209, 213; of 1916, 238; of 1922, 238

civil marriage, 197–201, 225, 236

civil rights, 11, 123, 133, 136, 239, 240

clergy, 123, 124

clothing, and honor, 23, 24, 31, 41; military uniforms, 41

Code of Civil Proceedings of 1916, 238

Code of Criminal Procedure of 1873, 210

Código Negro, 51

coffee, 43, 44

Colegio de Abogados de Caracas, 45

Compañía de Caracas, 43, 44. *See also* Real Compañía Guipuzcoana

Comte, August, 176, 187

concubinage. *See* consensual union

consensual union, 6, 40, 69, 90, 94, 147, 165–69, 198, 200–201, 229, 236, 241; stable 204, 229–30, 234

constitution, 155; of 1811, 3, 5, 7, 11, 19, 117, 132, 137, 150, 186, 240; of 1830, 119–23, 126, 133; of 1864, 239

contraband, 43; as result of imperial neglect, 3, 4, 27, 36; and revolutionary propaganda, 53

contumely, 136–37, 165

convents, 129, 148, 181

Coro's rebellion, 50, 112

corporatist society, 61, 68, 72, 92–93

Cortés, Santos Rodulfo, 50

Cortés Campomanes, Manuel, 53, 54, 55

Cortés de Madariaga, José, 57

Cortines, Francisco Ignacio, 52

costumbre (customs), 26, 46, 47

criminal offenses, 18, 70, 136, 147

Crónica Eclesiástica de Venezuela (journal), 115

cruel punishment, 120, 124

Cuba, 67, 72, 101

cult of national heroes, 179–80

culture of opposition, 93

death penalty, 18, 108, 120, 123, 124, 127–29, 135, 148, 149

Delpino y Lamas, Antonio, 184–85

democracy, 58, 109, 118

Depons, François, 97, 98, 102

depósito, 92, 154, 158, 213, 225, 228, 268n5

Díaz, Juana Francisca, 1, 2, 14, 20, 96

Diez Madroñero, Bishop Diego Antonio, 40

discursive strategies, 7, 15, 19, 20, 101, 130, 150, 161, 241

divorce, 198, 235–38; separation of bed and board, 75, 77, 78, 84–87, 90, 115, 139, 142, 145, 152, 156, 158, 205–8, 218

dowry, 75, 78

Earle, Rebecca, 112

education, 26, 109, 111, 141, 173–74, 176, 180, 181, 182, 184; and mothers, 124

El Constitucional (newspaper), 235

El Foro (journal), 124

Enlightenment, 3, 31, 52, 53

equality, 4, 53, 55, 108, 109, 111, 185; equality before the law, 7, 19, 123, 132, 150, 155, 168, 169, 186; equal protection of the law, 128; equal rights, 7, 20, 169, 213; expressions of among lower classes, 33, 150; rhetoric of, 4, 109, 113, 125, 134, 137; and wars of Independence, 7, 11; and women, 6, 123, 160, 168, 169

equidad, 60, 72–74, 76–78, 84, 86–91, 133

Ernst, Adolph, 173, 182

España, José María, 3, 53, 55

Espejo, Francisco, 46

Espinoza, Juan José, 145, 151

estupro, 70, 209–11, 227, 260n33

exchange of material and spiritual goods, 161–62, 163, 164

exclusion, 58, 109, 110, 113, 116, 125, 180, 238; logic of, 8, 13, 239–40; reactions to, 14, 116, 130; of women in politics, 113, 125, 238

Falcón, Juan Crisóstomo, 174, 177, 178
family: in church discourse, 66; in the early republic, 111; as image during wars of Independence, 5; in the late nineteenth century, 186–90, 197, 198; as a separate sphere, 6, 7, 122, 123, 152, 155, 197, 198
fatherland, heroes of, 178–79
fathers, 65, 68, 71, 258n6; and the church, 66; paternity, 71; power over children, 102. *See also* padres de familia; patria potestas
Federalists, 174, 175
Federal Wars, 174, 177
female-headed households, 73, 115, 123
feminist organizations, 241
Ferdinand VII (King of Spain), 56–59
Ferry, Robert, 27, 35, 73, 252n84
Figueroa, Pedro José, 113, 114
First Republic (1810–12), 56–57
Flores, Juan Fernando, 90
Founding Fathers, 6, 110, 113, 178, 179, 185
France: French Revolution and Venezuela, 4, 53, 54, 56, 59, 113, 115; French Revolution and women, 6, 112; influence on Venezuela, 19, 177, 180, 185. *See also* Rousseau, Jean-Jacques
Franco, Moreno, Manuel, 156, 157, 160
Friedman, Elisabeth J., 241

García, Mercedes, 213–14, 225, 233
García de Quintana, Francisco Antonio, 46
gender: and politics, 107, 112, 120; social construction, of, 18. *See* also citizenship
gender relations, 97, 241; in church and civil law, 68–72; different expectations according to gender, 167; as a domestic pact, 5–6, 160–61, 165, 166
Gil, Pedro Domingo, 76
Gil Fortoul, José, 173, 182, 235–39, 241
Gómez, Juan Vicente, 241
Gran Colombia, 9, 13, 107, 109, 116, 136, 150, 244n21
Grossberg, Michael, 197
Gual, Manuel, 3, 53, 55, 112
Gual and España conspiracy, 3, 52–55, 112
guardianship, 74, 196, 217–18
Guevara y Lira, Archbishop Silvestre, 181
Guillelmi, Juan, 76
Guzmán, Antonio Leocadio, 174

Guzmán Blanco, Antonio, 19, 174, 199, 212; image as a father, 179, 185; opposition, 184, 185; regime, 19, 110, 174–91

Haitian Revolution, 3, 30, 56
hegemony, 13–14
Hernández, Francisca Rosalía, 85, 92
Hernández, Ygnacio, 156, 159, 160
homosexuality, 16
honor, 17, 18, 20, 48, 99, 214, 219, 226, 227, 228, 231, 233; among mantuanos, 23, 24, 41, 48, 59, 84; among pardos, blacks, and zambos, 31, 103; defended by lower class, 103; and illegitimacy, 28; as a malleable concept, 24; masculine, 59, 91; as mechanism of social control, 24; and race, 28; and women, 95
Hospicio de la Caridad, 75, 84, 85, 89
Hünefeldt, Christine, 10, 160, 245n26
husbands, 68, 257n5, 258n6; and administration of women's property, 74, 76–77, 151–61; and adultery, 69, 76–77; and criticisms to court's protection of women, 159; and honor, 160. *See also* mantuanos; masculinity; padres de familia; patria potestas

Ibarra, Ana Teresa, 187, 199, 215
illegitimacy, 94, 198, 201
immigration, 183, 184, 198, 200, 237
Independence from Spain, 56–59, 139, 147, 150, 157
Indians, 29, 38, 54, 61, 66, 94, 108, 113, 132, 273n3
individuality, and ideas in the colonial period, 31, 33, 93
individual liberties/rights, 118, 121, 139, 151, 164–70; assertion of by nonwhites, 101, 103; protection of, 19
Intendencia de Ejército y Real Hacienda (Royal Intendancy), 44, 48–49

jail, 90. *See also* Hospicio de la Caridad
Jedler, Bárbara, 19, 169
Jerez de Aristequieta, Martín, 42, 75, 76, 77, 84, 88, 90, 99
Jocko, Isidoro, 223–24

laborers, 134–35, 198
Lander, Tomás, 123
Landes, Joan B., 112
landowners, 59, 107, 116, 119, 120, 175, 185
La Opinión Nacional (newspaper), 186–87, 197–98
Lardizábal, don Martín de, 37

Lavenda, Robert, 198–200, 219, 229

Lavrin, Asunción, 65, 245n34

laws, 109, 122, 135; of 10 April 1834, 119, 120; of azotes, 120, 136; hierarchy of, in the early republic, 132–33. *See also* civil codes; Code of Civil Proceedings of 1916; Code of Criminal Procedure of 1873; Penal Code of 1873; Recopilación de Castilla; Recopilación de los Reinos de Indias; Siete Partidas

lawyers, 45, 46, 59, 76, 116

legal profession, 45

legal reforms, 108

León, Juan Francisco de (Capt.), 38–39

León's Insurrection, 38, 39

Letter of Jamaica, 108, 111

Lezama, Ricardo, 202, 204

liberalism, 3, 7, 110, 118, 132, 150, 155, 181, 182, 186, 189; among plebeians, 33; contradiction in discourse and practice, 195–212, 213–15, 235, 240; and exclusion, 10; liberal ideas among lower class, 31; liberal press, 123; and patriarchy, 186, 189, 196–97, 238

liberals, 174, 197

liberty, 109, 113, 119, 121, 137, 160, 185; represented by women, 13, 112, 113

limpieza de sangre, 23, 24, 161, 163, 164; as defended by pardos and blacks, 101, 103; and gracias al sacar, 34; mantuano conflicts with peninsulars, 41, 42, 45, 59

Linares Alcántara, Francisco, 184

Lombardi, John V., 174

López, Luisa, 203, 204, 222

López Bohórquez, Alí, 42

López de Quintana, Antonio, 45

love, 151–53, 156, 161–65, 204, 220, 222, 229; letters, 202, 204, 223–24

Lovera, Josefa, 75, 76, 77, 84, 88

madres de familia, 123, 129, 148

mantuanos (creole aristocracy of Caracas), 17, 23–24, 47–48, 90, 162; as cabildo members, 26, 41, 42, 246n2; challenged by increased royal authority, 27–28, 37–38, 42, 44, 46; challenged by lower classes, 93; conflicts with peninsulars, 41, 42, 44, 45, 83; conjuración de los, 56, 57; criticized in early republic, 118; criticized by non-whites, 31; as defenders of the social order, 24, 31; defense of honor, 28, 29; fears of pardos, mulattos and blacks, 30, 31; and Gual and España conspiracy, 55, 57–58; and Independence from Spain, 56, 59; and intendentes, 49; moral behavior, 40, 41; participation in León's insurrection, 39; privi-

leges of, 23; radicalization of 39; and Real Audiencia, 46, 52

Manzo, Candelaria, 202, 204, 226

Marianismo, 188–89

Mariño, Santiago, 119

marriage, 6, 14, 78–83, 93–103, 134, 146, 151–61, 168, 169, 229, 233; in articulo mortis, 200; children's choices for, 83; clandestine, 100; as a contract, 97, 197, 198, 205, 208; difficulty of the legal ritual, 99–102, 236; disenchantment with this institution, 225–31, 234; interracial, 94; lack of, 115; laws in the early republic, 134; and love, 161, 204–5, 226; and men's political rights, 237, 238; as mutual pact, 6–7, 153, 160–61, 200, 217, 232, 233, 240; opposition to marriages, 81–83, 134, 146, 161; and procreation, 74; promise of, 95; as sacrament, 97; shotgun weddings, 201–5, 226; as slave regime, 96, 154–55, 157, 160, 168, 232. *See also* civil marriage; consensual unions

Martí, Bishop Mariano (1769–1792), 40, 41, 80, 92, 94

Martínez-Alier, Verena, 72, 101

masculinity, 8, 13, 25–26, 126, 179, 219–21; aristocratic, 35, 36, 45, 59, 174; and arms, 33; and bourgeois masculine values, 173–74; competition over, 25, 116–20, 125; erosion of hegemonic, 18, 108; and Guzmán Blanco, 179; and honor, 59, 60, 160; and law, 12; and mantuano honor, 24–25; and mistresses, 219–20, 230; and patriarchal powers, 33

Maucó, Ramón, 155, 156, 157, 158

McCaa, Robert, 94

McKinley, P. Michael, 45, 49

Mejías Bejarano, Diego, 51–52

Mejías Bejarano, Lorenzo, 52

memory, public, 178

men: argumentation of, according to women, 95–96; criticized by women, 169; and education, 108; and honor, 137, 155, 160; and ideas about marriage, 97; and impunity, 220; as less constrained by colonial laws, 68; of letters, 107, 110, 116; of military background, 19; moral and sexual conduct of, 81; not marrying their concubines, 100; not valuing hard work, 173; and promises of marriage, 95; running away, 95, 96, 220; strategies of, to discredit women, 95; and violence against women, 167; of virtue, 116. *See also* husbands; masculinity; padres de familia

merchants, 48, 59, 107, 175, 185, 199

México 9, 10, 11. *See also* New Spain

Mijares, Violante, 1, 2, 20, 226

Mijares y Tovar, Francisco Nicolás, 39
military, 110, 116–21, 126; and blacks, 98; Compañía de Fusileros del Batallón de Blancos, 41
military men, 12, 19, 59, 79, 107, 108, 110, 116, 119, 180; conflicts in the early republic, 118–20; criticized in the late nineteenth century, 173, 174
Miranda, Francisco de, 3, 41, 55, 56, 244n12
Miranda, Sebastián de, 41
Monagas, José Gregorio, 178
Montesinos Rico, Manuel, 54
Mora, Juan José, 99
moral economy, 94, 161
moral regeneration, 185, 186–89, 190
Mota, Mercedes, 221, 222
motherhood, 115, 123–24, 127–30, 226, 237; as generator of rights, 129, 152, 217–18, 240
mulatto/mulatta, 28, 31, 56, 81, 102, 108, 111, 132, 163
murder, 122, 147, 148

nation building, 239–40; in early republic, 107, 118; and independence, 59; and liberalism, 7; and masculinity, 13, 110
Nava, Julián, 219
New Spain, 36
nobility of Caracas. See mantuanos
Nos-Otras (journal), 241
notable citizens, 116–20, 125
Novísima Recopilación, 136, 142, 143, 148

Ochoa, Vicenta, 108, 119, 120–24, 131, 148
oligarchy, 107

padres de familia, 5, 6, 20, 72, 73, 78, 91, 102, 115, 123, 132, 134, 141, 160, 166, 208, 215, 218–20, 238, 257n5, 258n6; and cases of opposition to marriages, 81–83, 98–99, 102, 134; and challenges to elite in colonial period, 35, 36, 59, 83, 85, 86, 89–91, 102; and the church, 66; and control over women and family, 112, 142, 187; in early republic, 111, 134, 154; elite, 24; as jury members, 201; in late nineteenth century, 20, 187; legal rights of, 65, 68–72; and limits to their power, 150; mantuano, 24, 35; and paternal command of popular classes, 58, 111; rights of, not protected by judges, 76–77, 80, 83, 85–91, 145, 147; rights of, protected by judges, 144, 149, 196–212. See also patria potestas
Padrón, José Ignacio, 162–64
Páez, José Antonio, 116–20, 124–25, 135
pardas, 30, 92, 103, 112

pardos, 28, 29, 30, 81, 101, 132, 247n21; criticism of mantuanos, 31; defending their honor, 31; and gracias al sacar, 50–51; and Gual and España conspiracy, 53–54; and independence, 56, 58; militia battalion of, 30, 101–2; and Real Pragmática, 101–2
pasiones, 108, 111, 113, 125, 130, 131, 187
Pateman, Carol, 238, 243n7
paternalism, 112; and the state, 111, 135, 178, 182, 236–37
paternity, 71, 144–45, 196–97, 205; duties of, 206; investigation of, 236, 238
patria potestas, 5, 6; in the early republic, 138, 142–43, 150, 151, 153, 155, 157, 258n6; in the late colonial period, 65, 71, 74, 78, 83, 97; in the late nineteenth century, 195–97, 203, 218–19, 232, 237, 238. See also padres de familia
patriarchy, 13, 14, 20, 132, 237, 238; challenged by women, 132, 153, 158; and justice system, 60, 74, 78, 84, 91, 142–43, 195–212, 213, 235; and liberalism, 5–6; and property, 153; and the state, 5, 20, 65, 110–11, 132, 178, 179, 182, 188, 189, 211, 237, 239
Pedroza, Nepomuceno, 52
Pellicer, Luis, 24, 31
Penal code of 1873, 186, 209
peninsulars, 26; conflicts with mantuanos, 41, 42, 44, 57, 91; population of, 29
Peraza, Luis, 55
Pérez, María Antonia, 1, 2, 7, 14, 20, 155, 157, 158, 159, 168
Pérez, Vicente, 75, 84
Pérez Perdomo, Rogelio, 142
Perú, 10, 11
Picornell, Juan Bautista, 53–55, 243n3
Picton, Sir Thomas, 53
Pino Iturrieta, Elías, 52, 66–67, 243n3, 244n20
Ponte, Leonardo, 89
positivism, 19, 176, 180
positivists, 173, 186, 235
poverty, certificate of, 61, 142
premarital sex, 225. See also consensual union
press, 119–20
property: administration of women's, by men, 111, 115, 122, 125, 133, 142–44, 151; protection of, 107, 111, 118, 120, 132, 135, 136, 139, 152; and citizenship, 168–69, 238
pueblo, 4, 109, 110
Puerto Rico, 236–37
punishment, 69–72, 120, 124, 135–36, 147–49, 209–11

Quintero, Josef, 87

race, 16, 18
rape, 209–11
Ravelo y Alcántara, Micaela, 145, 151, 164, 168
Raynal, Guillaume-Thomas, 3, 53
Real Audiencia de Caracas, 44–47, 57, 79–80; and conflicts between peninsulars and creole elites, 44; as a court of first instance, 44, 52; rulings by, 76, 78
Real Compañía Guipuzcoana (royal commercial monopoly company), 30, 37–39, 43; reforms of, 39, 250n62. *See also* Compañía de Caracas
Real Consulado (merchant guild), 44, 48; conflicts with audiencia, 48; controlled by mantuanos, 48; jurisdictional problems, 48
Recopilación de Castilla, 122, 133
Recopilación de los Reinos de Indias, 32–33, 69, 133
resistance, 14, 20, 215, 245n37
revolts, 30, 32, 119, 248n35. *See also* Gual and España conspiracy; León's insurrection
Revolución de las Reformas, 119
Reyes, Juan Carlos, 88
Ribas, Francisco José, 57
Ricardos, Felipe, 38–40, 248n35, 252n84
Riera Aguinalde, Andrés Manuel, 187, 188, 208, 212
rights of man, 4, 54–55
robbery, 135, 162
Rodríguez del Toro, Francisco, 48, 90, 119
Roscio, Juan Germán, 3, 57, 58, 257n154
Rousseau, Jean-Jacques, 3, 53, 109, 115, 116
Roxas, María Manuela, 90
Royal Pragmatic on Marriages (1778), 52, 62, 79, 83, 97–99, 101; of 1803, 102; not supporting fathers' decisions, 98. *See also* padres de familia

Salvatore, Ricardo D., 122
sampling, 16–17
Sanojo, Luis, 142, 197
Sanz, José Miguel, 57–58
seduction, 82, 92, 93, 95, 227
Seed, Patricia, 70
sexuality, 95
sexual offenses/crimes, 68, 88–89; 209–11
Siete Partidas, 5, 6, 7, 65, 68–69, 74, 78–79, 111, 122, 132, 136, 145, 148, 151, 186, 239
Skurski, Julie, 110, 243n6
slavery, 28, 54, 55
slaves, 29, 37, 40, 43, 58, 64, 66, 86, 92, 93, 117, 120, 130, 143, 148, 159, 162, 165; juridical personality of, 61; litigating against owners, 86–88; marriages of, 80; 86–88; rebellion of, 112
social classes, 138, 192–93
social imagery, 176, 178, 179, 182
Sociedad Económica de Amigos del País, 118, 119
sociedad patriótica, 56
Soneto Americano (song), 54
Sosa, Félix, 57
Spain, 53, 124; and bias against Spaniards, 28, 41, 42, 44–52, 57, 134, 159; efforts to disassociate Venezuela from, 176; and family laws, 65–72, 97–98; and increased presence of authorities, 37, 45; Napoleonic invasion of, 56, 57, 59; and neglect over Venezuela, 3, 4, 26
state, and domestic affairs, 152, 155, 158, 197–98, 203, 208, 238
Stern, Steve J., 10, 34, 244n18, 245n24, 246n6, 247n7
Sucre, Juan Antonio, 203–4, 222, 224
support (alimentos), 74, 144–45, 156, 205, 207, 230, 232

tenientes de justicia mayor, 27, 38, 40, 47
theft, 135, 163
Toro y Istúriz, Francisco de Paula, 39
Tovar Ponte, Martín, 57
trade, 43, 44, 117–19. *See also* Compañía de Caracas; Real Compañía Guipuzcoana; Real Consulado; merchants
Trinidad, 52, 55
Troconis de Veracoechea, Ermila, 112
Truxillo, Juan, 85, 92
tutela y curatela, 74
Twinam, Ann, 24, 71, 247n8

United States, 3, 112, 198, 236–37; constitution of, 52
Universidad de Caracas, 51
Universidad Central de Venezuela, 173, 174, 181, 182
Urbaneja, Diego Bautista, 174

vagrancy laws, 134–35, 166, 167
Vallenilla Lanz, Laureano, 182, 237
Vargas, José María, 119, 120, 125, 126, 173
vecinos, 26
Venezuela Province, 44
Viana, Bishop Juan Antonio de la Vírgen María, 80

Villavicencio, Rafael, 173, 182
Villegas, Manuela, 223–24
Virgin Mary, 187, 188, 212

Waldron, Kathy, 73, 94
whitening, 174, 175, 183, 184
widows, 196
wives: and administration of property, 65, 68, 72–76, 139, 151, 236, 259n20; and identification with official ideals of womanhood, 216; juridical capacity of, 154; subversive, 152, 155, 159; and use of husband's last name, 215
women, 40, 111–16, 125, 127, 130, 150, 185; and adultery, 69, 76–77; and assertion of rights, 7, 94, 97, 129, 130, 161, 166–70, 231–33, 240; autonomy of, 93, 166–67, 225, 227, 228, 231–33; and avoiding confrontations with men, 208; and the colonial church, 66; and colonial law, 65–72; complaints about husbands by, 96; and criminal behavior, 149; and defense of individual liberties, 139, 168, 231–33, 240; and different application of the law, 68–70, 76–77, 207; and dignity, 226–27, 233; emanci-

pated, 228–29; and Eve, 66, 115; generational differences of, 228; and guardianship, 74, 196; as icons of liberty, 112–13; ideas about, in the colonial period, 65; juridical personality of, 61, 68, 138, 154, 225; and Marianismo, 188, 189; and lack of women's movement, 20, 234, 241; and the moral regeneration plan, 186–89, 195; and the "New Eve," 188; and participation in courts, 61, 62, 72–73, 90, 137, 190–95, 237; and participation in Independence movement and wars, 6, 9, 56, 112; privileged status of, 123, 128; reproductive capacities of, 71–72, 127, 130; responses to exclusion of, 8, 9, 125, 128; as seductors of men, 209; sexuality of, 68; as sexual property of men and society, 96–97, 127, 166, 240; strategies of, 125, 126, 128–30, 215, 218, 233–34, 240; suffrage of, 6, 188, 239, 241, 244n12; and virginity, 221–24, 227, 233; as the weak sex, 65, 68, 72, 123, 129; without padres de familia, 73

zambos, 29, 162
Zuloaga, Gabriel José de, 37, 38

In the Engendering Latin America series

Sex and Danger in Buenos Aires:
Prostitution, Family, and
Nation in Argentina
Donna J. Guy

Between Civilization and Barbarism:
Women, Nation, and Literary
Culture in Modern Argentina
Francine Masiello

Women, Feminism, and Social
Change in Argentina, Chile,
and Uruguay, 1890–1940
Asunción Lavrin

I'm Going to Have a Little House:
The Second Diary of Carolina
Maria de Jesus
Carolina Maria de Jesus
Translated by Melvin S. Arrington Jr.
and Robert M. Levine

White Slavery and Mothers Alive
and Dead: The Troubled Meeting
of Sex, Gender, Public Health, and
Progress in Latin America
Donna J. Guy

Class Mates: Male Student Culture
and the Making of a Political Class
in Nineteenth-Century Brazil
Andrew J. Kirkendall

Female Citizens, Patriarchs, and
the Law in Venezuela, 1786–1904
Arlene J. Díaz

False Mystics: Deviant Orthodoxy
in Colonial Mexico
Nora E. Jaffary

Mexican Karismata: The
Baroque Vocation of Francisca
de los Ángeles, 1674–1744
Ellen Gunnarsdóttir

The Case of the Ugly Suitor and
Other Histories of Love, Gender, and
Nation in Buenos Aires, 1776–1870
Jeffrey M. Shumway

A Culture of Everyday Credit:
Housekeeping, Pawnbroking, and
Governance in Mexico City, 1750–1920
Marie Eileen Francois

From Colony to Nation: Women
Activists and Gendering of
Politics in Belize, 1912–1982
Anne S. Macpherson

Domestic Economies: Family, Work,
and Welfare in Mexico City, 1884–1943
Ann S. Blum

To order or obtain more information on these or other University of Nebraska
Press titles, visit www.nebraskapress.unl.edu.

CPSIA information can be obtained
at www.ICGtesting.com
Printed in the USA
LVHW011711150821
695370LV00015B/1260